THEORIES OF
ORGANIZATION

THEORIES OF ORGANIZATION

HENRY L. TOSI
The University of Florida

Second Edition

John Wiley & Sons
New York · Chichester · Brisbane · Toronto · Singapore

Library of Congress Cataloging in Publication Data:

Main entry under title:

Theories of organization.
    Includes bibliographical references and index.
    1. Organization—Addresses, essays, lectures.
2. Industrial organization—Addresses, essays, lectures.
3. Industrial sociology—Addresses, essays, lectures.
I. Title.
HD31.T486 1984   302.3′5   83-3574
ISBN 0-471-87499-X

To Rosemary

PREFACE

A book like this is—of course—never complete, and I take full responsibility for omitting some works that others would certainly agree should be included. But that is a matter of taste, which is why some of us prefer Bordeaux to Burgundy or Picasso to Miro.

These summaries, extracts, and reviews have been gathered from a number of sources. I hope that they present the major variables and interrelationships of the various points of view about organizational theory. The elegance and logic of the originals may have been lost, but I hope not the substance.

The purpose of this collection is to expose the student quickly to a broad range of theories. It is not meant to be a substitute for the complete works themselves. Students have too much to learn by immersing themselves in the originals. I would have it no other way.

Henry L. Tosi

CONTENTS

ONE
THEORY AND ORGANIZATION THEORY

My own view of organizations is that they can be best understood as patterns of predictable relationships among the members. The level of predictability is caused by two factors: the formal organization structure and the unique differences among the individuals who are members of the organization.

The formal organization structure is the set of institutionalized norms and written rules, procedures, policies, job descriptions, and other factors which prescribe what a person is to do, how and when it should be done, and with whom it is to be done. For example, take the case of how a bank teller handles a transaction with a customer who wishes to withdraw a sum of money from her savings account. The bank employee has a procedure to follow. First, the balance in the account must be checked. Then the identity of the person making the withdrawal must be verified. It is only then that the teller may give the customer the money. This procedure is followed each time a depositor wishes to withdraw money. If an observer knows the formal procedure, each time a customer approaches the window for a withdrawal transaction, the observer can predict very accurately how the teller will behave. In fact, the observer can probably predict accurately the behavior of all the tellers in that bank and, quite probably, in most banks.

Yet there will be behavioral variations from these formal procedures. The observer may sometimes note that a teller does not verify the amount in an account or may fail to ask for some customer identification. This may be because the customer is familiar to the teller or the teller knows the account balance and does not need to check it. The formal system, the withdrawal procedure, has been altered by the individuals involved. Things such as this happen in every organization. But this does not mean that the ability to predict behavior patterns is diminished. It only takes longer to understand them because it is now necessary to learn them by observation of the interaction of humans in addition to knowing the rules or procedures. Eventually, the observer will learn which customers are known and by which tellers, when these customers usually come in, and what will transpire. When this occurs, the behavior pattern that is known as organization will be apparent.

One body of knowledge that deals with this phenomenon is organization theory. Broadly speaking, organization theory is concerned with the structure and process of organizations. In organization theory, the organization is the main focus of analysis, not the individuals and groups within it.

What Is Organization?

Every organizational theory has at least two possible aspects which tend to confuse (19)*. It either examines the process of subdividing work and work relationships into manageable units, or it may have a greater behavioral emphasis, concerned with the examination and analysis of relatively complex, structured behavior systems.

Conceptually, there are only slight differences in the way in which various theorists define organizations. Barnard (2) calls an organization a "system of consciously coordinated personal activities or forces," a "system of interrrelated activities." Davis (10) defines it as "group of people working together, under a leader, to accomplish an objective." Victor Thompson (44) characterizes bureaucracy as "a highly rationalized impersonal integration of a large number of specialists operating to achieve some objective, upon which is superimposed a highly elaborate structure of authority." Stogdill (41) defines the organization as a "structured" system of behavior, with the position and roles comprising it having the potential of being "prestructured," that is, designed and prescribed before the roles are filled by actors.

Yet, while the various definitions do not seem radically different from each other, the directions taken, the concepts used, and the relationships between them is varied. But the object of study is still the same—the large complex organization. The characteristics of these large complex organizations are presented in detail within the various theory discussions later, but some are briefly noted here to provide a frame of reference for those discussions.

Large size is an implicit characteristic. In general, organizations considered in theory are of such a size that within them it is extremely difficult, if not impossible, to maintain close interpersonal relationships with a large number of the members, relative to the total membership.

Formalization derives partially from the large size of the organization and the need for some kind of control structure. Guidelines become necessary to provide a basis for the different kinds and types of interactions required between members since the size of the organization makes it extremely difficult for members to work these out among themselves on any other basis. Formalization simply means that procedures and policies are written and stated in such a way that they become stable, quasi-permanent directions, ranging from very general to very specific, for interaction and decisions. Formalization generally refers to written, documented guides for action and behavior of members and is common to all bureaucracies. It provides a degree of stability to interaction patterns, regardless of the incumbent of the position in the organization. Thus, when an individual newly arrives in an organization, there

---

*Numbered references will be found in the references section at the end of this book.

are specified actions and interactions which facilitate his or her accommodation to the organization.

Rationality is another attribute sought by large organizations. The purpose of imposing a structure is to bring order to a system of activities intended to achieve a goal. The system should be ordered on the basis of "logic and science." The activities of the members should be directed toward the goal. If activities are goal-directed, then resources can be more effectively utilized. Rationality is partially achieved by "goal factoring." The organization has a general goal. This goal is factored, or broken down into subgoals. These are assigned to lower-level units. If these units achieve their purpose or goal, the general organization goal will be attained. Individuals in lower-level units essentially "assume" the goal of the unit when they accept a position. They have an obligation to achieve their goals. Their obligations may be viewed as responsibilities of the position. In addition to the obligation, an incumbent will have certain prerogatives to allocate organization resources to accomplish these subunit goals. These prerogatives are often called "authority."

Hierarchical structure is related to the nature of the factored goals. Hierarchy is the existence of different degrees of authority at the various levels of the organization. It is the chain of formal authority relationships from the top of the structure to its bottom, tying different levels of the organization together. The degree of authority at a particular level may be defined in terms of the range of discretion an individual has over resource allocation, both physical and human. In general, individuals in higher positions tend to have greater discretion and are accorded more status and deference than those at lower levels. It is through the authority structure that the various activities of the organization are tied together in order to achieve some degree of coordination in attaining goals.

Specialization is another dimension of the complex organization. Specialization refers to the particular grouping or configuration of activities performed *by an individual.* The range of activities assigned to a particular position, or individual, should be "rationally" grouped in such a way as to make sense in terms of effectiveness and efficiency.

Specialization may be one of two types. First, it may refer to the *division of labor.* The particular task is analyzed and broken down into subtasks, which are its primary components. An individual then is assigned to perform these subtasks, which are essentially simpler and more repetitive than the total task requirements required to achieve a result. The individual is able to learn the tasks quickly and also its concomitant skills. This leads to both increased "efficiency" and less reliance by the organization on the skills of a particular person. Hence, personnel replacement is facilitated and relatively simple.

The second type of specialization has been called *social specialization* by Victor Thompson (44). This is the case where the person, not the work, is specialized. It means that the individual possesses a type or range of skills that cannot be routinized, either because of their complexity and intensive development, or because they are not needed in the great quantity that other more routine tasks are.

The Content of This Book

This book presents a set of summaries of 14 theoretical formulations about organizations. Each summary includes the major variables of the theory and the relationships between them. Thus, the reader gets an abbreviated view of the whole theory, not just some part of it.

Without such a general theoretical overview, it is possible to misinterpret a particular theory and to use its concepts incorrectly. For example, it is quite common to contrast Barnard's (2) view of authority with the "classical" concept. Barnard's concept of authority is that it is accepted by the subordinates. The classical view is that authority is a right of a superior (10). There is, obviously, an important difference between these two positions, as stated above. Yet, when the "classical" theory is clearly understood and then compared to the Barnard formulation, the ostensible polarities tend to disappear.

The reader should also keep in mind that all of these theories are about the same phenomenon—organizations. What makes them different is that each theorist uses a different set of concepts to explain organization. Williamson and Ouchi (49) draw heavily from economics to explain why particular forms of organization structures exist. The literature of social psychology is the base for the set of concepts that is used by Stogdill (41). Thus, the reader should not expect that the concepts of one theory are similar to those of another. Theories are different because those who formulate them are interested in different things and seek to explain these things from their own perspective and with tools and concepts with which they are familiar. Here we will briefly note the theoretical content of each of the theoretical models associated with the writer which appear in this book.

Ralph C. Davis.   This is a statement of the standard, "classical," rational model of organization and management (10). Davis assumes that once organization goals are understood and/or defined, it is possible to design the organization structure to maximize returns. The focus of this model is on the formal organization.

Chester Barnard.   Barnard's work is important in the field of organization theory (2) because it represents an important departure from the "classical" notions about organization. Barnard stressed the significance of several important concepts such as *informal organization, authority,* and the role of *individual motivation.* Of particular importance is the effect which this work had on James March and Herbert Simon.

James March and Herbert Simon.   Their book *Organizations* (23) presented individual decision making as a conceptual framework for understanding complex organizations (23). This book is a source of much of the current thinking about organization processes.

Amitai Etzioni.   This is a set of useful concepts about organizations, organizational authority and individual compliance (13). Different types of authority are required in different organizations. The type of authority will affect individuals.

Victor Thompson.   Victor Thompson's work described the characteristics of the classic bureaucratic model, but brings into focus some of its particular weaknesses. (44) Thompson particularly shows some of the dysfunctional effects of organization on the members.

Philip Selznick.   His study, *TVA and The Grass Roots,* represents what many think is an important shift in thinking about organizations (39). It demonstrates *how* organizations adapt to environmental changes. This is the basic idea in *natural systems* views of organization, which differ sharply from rational systems approaches.

T. Burns and G. Stalker.   The authors present a distinction which has become classic in the study of organizations (5). Differences between *mechanistic* organizations and *organic* organizations are described and they show how these organizations exist in very different organizational environments.

Joan Woodward.   This study is grounded in ideas from classical management theory (50). Woodward and her colleagues studied 100 English firms to determine how organization design characteristics (such as span of control and departmental coordination) are related to organization effectiveness. This study shows the important role of technology in that Woodward found that the structure of an effective organization was related to the form of the organization's technology (i.e., for a given technology there was a way of organizing that is more effective than others).

James Thompson.   *Organizations in Action* is an important book because Thompson presents a theoretical framework which links different perspectives about organizations (43). Thompson's book is a theoretical synthesis, presenting a set of hypotheses about how organizations *qua* organizations behave.

Charles Perrow.   Perrow expands the discussion of technology and organization structure (30). He draws in some other critical elements of organization, notably ideas about group coordination, group interdependence, power, discretion and leadership.

Ralph Stogdill.   Stogdill's approach is unique for several reasons. He draws heavily from several different disciplines i.e., social psychology, psychology, and management (41). His concept of organization structure draws together ideas about formal and informal organization, ideas which are generally treated separately. Finally, he proposes the notion of multiple organization outcomes and speculates how these may be related to each other. There is no other organizational model which has such a set of concepts.

Henry Mintzberg. Mintzberg's model presents an analysis and description of five different organization types (26). Mintzberg proposes that these different types of organizations emerge both in response to different environmental circumstances and as a result of managerial decisions about the design of a particular structure.

Oliver Williamson. This selection outlines Williamson's view that organization structures are developed in order to respond to market conditions (48, 49). The reading is drawn heavily from economics and uses transaction costs as an explanatory variable.

Henry Tosi. Environmental volatility in markets and in the technological environment are basic forces which affect organization structure. Four forms of organization are described (46). A unique aspect of this approach is that it integrates concepts about organizations with concepts about individuals. The model is based on the premise that different types of organizations attract different types of individuals. This should logically lead to different managerial strategies.

THE ELEMENTS OF THEORY

A theory is a systematic abstract way to organize and describe reality. A theory, in the scientific sense, is "a systematically related set of statements, including some lawlike generalization that is empirically testable . . . [and] . . . the sort of systematic relatedness is deductive relatedness (27)." In this book, we present several approaches, or theories, to understand organizations and the behavior of people in organizations. These theories of organization are different attempts to present a systematic view of organizations or some important dimensions of organizations. Each theory does this by developing various concepts that describe some facet of an organization and then relates these concepts to each other.

Theoretic Systems

A theory is an abstract way to describe reality. It aids in understanding reality and in predicting what will occur under different conditions. For example, using economic theory one can predict what will happen to price when supply changes, when one firm takes monopolistic control of a market, or when there is a change in government spending. "Supply" and "price" are important concepts in economic theory and one must know what "supply" is and what "price" is, and how the two are related to each other to predict the effects.

A theory is a special case, or form of language. It is a way to communicate meaning about phenomena. As with any language, it is necessary to understand not only what specific terms, or words, mean but also to know how these terms are related to each other. Every language has a "vocabulary" and a "grammar." The vocabulary is a set of terms which have meaning. (In a theory these are called concepts.) The grammar is a set of rules which determine whether or not a particular combination of the terms is appropriate (27). There is more to a theoretical system, however, than simply a vocabulary and grammar. A theoretical system includes (1) concepts, (2) relational statements, (3) boundaries, (4) system states, (5) propositions, (6) empirical indicators, and (7) hypotheses (12).

Concept.   A concept, sometimes called a variable, is an "invention of the human mind to provide a means for organizing and understanding observations" (33). A concept is a way of attaching meaning to something. Usually a concept has a label which is then used in conveying the concept, the meaning, to others. For instance, a concept in organization theory is "the existence of different degrees of authority at the different levels of the organization." The label for this concept is "hierarchical structure."

These are two types of concepts that may be elements in theory: *primitive* and *derived.* The primitive concepts are the minimal set that constitute the theory. They are the basic concepts that exist. Derived concepts are those which can be construed, or defined, by using the primitive terms of a theory. Reynolds (32) gives the following example:

Primitive terms (shared agreement exists among users):

X	Individual	Goal oriented
Y	Interact	Social system
+ operation	Two or more	Formalized
performed	Regularly	Rules and procedures
with numerals		

Derived (nominal) terms (defined with primitive terms):

$Z = X + Y$	Group—two or more individuals that interact regularly	Formal organization— a goal-oriented social system with formalized rules and procedures

The concept "hierarchical structure" is a derived concept. Its primitive terms are authority and organizational level.

An important problem in organization theory, as well as other social sciences, is that there is often misunderstanding about concepts. This happens in at least two ways.

1.   The same label is often with different conceptual meanings. The term "authority" means one thing when used by Chester Barnard (2) and something else when used by Davis (10). Often proponents of one theoretical orientation argue that another theory is weak or insufficient because different concepts have the same label. The only way to ensure against such inappropriate criticism is to understand how each theorist defines a concept and to know what label is attached to it.

2. A second way that concepts are misconstrued is when "the members of the audience . . . add meaning to words that have been carefully defined by the originator, particularly if that word is used for other concepts" (32). This is particularly a problem because it adds meaning to the the theoretical structure other than that intended. It is particularly important to allow a theorist the privilege of defining concepts as he or she chooses. It is the responsibility of the reader, especially the critic, to understand what meaning the originator intends, not to impute more or less.

Relational Statements. Relational statements are statements about which concepts are related to other concepts and how they are related to each other. Reynolds (32) defines two types of relational statements associative and causal statements.

An associative statement states that concepts exist together in a particular way. Such a statement about organizations is "*personal specialization and social specialization occur in complex organizations.*" This statement simply tells us that these two types of specialization will be found in complex organizations. It is a correlational statement only. It implies no causal sequence among the concepts.

A causal statement, on the other hand, describes a causal sequence between or among the variables. An example of a causal theoretical statement is "*an increase in the level of formalization in an organization will result in higher productivity and lower member satisfaction.*" This statement is clear and unequivocal about what causes what.

Some statements have, or are assumed to have, lawlike properties with respect to the concepts in a theory. Such statements constitute "givens." They are attributed high truth value. These statements are either widely accepted among scientists because of convention or because the evidence is so compelling.

Other forms of statements (e.g., propositions and hypotheses) do not have such wide acceptance. They remain to be tested and are discussed below.

Boundaries. The boundaries define the scope of the theory, the "limited portions of the world" to which the theory is applicable and within which the theory is expected to hold (12). The scope of the theory is determined by the concepts with which it is constructed. In this book the scope of most of the theories is the complex organization. Yet, as will be apparent, there are some very basic differences among the theorists with respect to specific concepts and how they relate to each other. Thus, it is possible for theories to have similar scope but to be different in content. For example, Barnard (2) and Davis (10) are both concerned with organization structure and managerial processes. Davis uses concepts that describe formal organization phenomena while Barnard emphasizes the informal *and* the formal structure of organizations.

System States. To Dubin (12), system states are the values or the range of values that a variable (or characteristic) may take on. For example, the concept "organization structure" may range from the state of *organic* (relatively loose) to *mechanistic* (relatively rigid). The organic state exists when a large set of organizational variables occur at a particular level. According to Burns and Stalker (5) the organic organization exists when:

1. There is adjustment and continual redefinition of tasks through interaction.
2. There is a network structure of control, authority, and communication.
3. There is lateral, not vertical, communication.

A mechanistic organization state exists when:

1. There is precise definition of rights and objections and methods into the functional responsibilites of a position.
2. There is a hierarchical structure of control.
3. There are vertical communication patterns.

Propositions. Propositions are a type of relational statement. They are conclusions logically deduced from the theory. A proposition may be an idea or hunch that is presented in the form of a scientific statement.

Empirical Indicators. These are necessary in order to measure a concept. They are operational definitions of the variables in a theory. An operational definition is a way to "convey the meaning [of a concept] by specifying the operations required to test for the presence of the thing to which that term refers (35)." Empirical indicators are necessary to test both the lawlike statements which are the theoretical statements themselves and to test propositions derived from the theory.

For complex concepts such as organization structure, many empirical indicators may be used to assess it. There is always the question of whether a single indicator, or some set of several indicators, is a more appropriate measure. Organization strucutre has been assessed using indicators such as number of levels, number of different types of tasks, the degree of formalization and so forth.

Hypotheses. An hypothesis is the translation of concepts in a proposition into empirical indicators and then applying an analytical or statistical procedure to determine whether the hypothesis is to be rejected or to be retained as a theoretical deduction (12). It is, in the strictest sense, the hypotheses (which have been constructed with empirical indicators) which are subjected to empirical test or research—and not the concepts themselves.

When an hypothesis has been confirmed by research such that scientists accept it as a fundamental truth, it then becomes a "law." When there is "the same pattern of events found in a number of different studies" it is often called an empirical generalization (32).

Nontheoretic Formulations

These are formulations which do not meet the requirements of theory noted above. They fall into two groups, definitional system and analytical schema. A definitional system contains a set of statements which consist of a term and an attendant definition. An analytical schema, on the other hand,

> includes over and above its system of definitions a set of analytical, or logically true or truistic sentences. These are truistic not by reference to . . . empirical evidence, but by recourse to the systems definitions (35).

These nontheoretic systems are useful to the social scientist in that they may ultimately become part of a theory.

Rudner notes that it "would probably be fair to say that the vast preponderance of all formulations constituting the output of social scientists consist of such nontheoretic formulations as mentioned above." (35) If so, how does the term "organization theory" apply? Strictly speaking, it doesn't. But, there has been a general application of that label to formulations which deal with the organization phenomenon. This convention, then, is followed and the formulations presented here are, by our definition, called "organization theories."

The Bias of the Theorist

All social science theory is composed of both "systematic and doctrinal elements which are embedded in its language, logical tools, concepts, empirical relationships and normative considerations. . . . However, the systematic character of a theory is rarely explicit, since it is usually hidden in matters of substance. But in the systematic elements that circumscribe theories of the business firm reside some of the crucial factors that determine and pattern vision of the firm" (19). The concepts and variables which are the building blocks of theory contain implicit biases and assumptions which may escape those who use the theory.

The theorist builds a theoretical system by defining, with some degree of precision, the variables which are to be included. The values, beliefs, and background of the theorist tend to provide a limit of sorts on what these variables are. This is the "normative structure" of the theory (19). The theorist selects those variables which he or she believes, from general or empirical observation, are those which explain the system and/or are most amenable to control or change. This determines not only the variables and concepts which make up the theory, but also the manner in which they may be used to predict and explain. Whether or not a given phenomena may be studied in the laboratory, in a field experiment, or simply by observation is largely a function of the

extent to which the researcher is capable of, or perhaps willing to operation-
alize concepts from a theory and/or the degree to which one is willing to interpret results from a "controlled" experiment into generalized effects that would
occur in a "real world" environment.

The Use of Theory

To some, the term "theory" has a negative connotation. It implies that the
ideas have no practical use and that they are of interest only to professors and
researchers. This is especially the case, it seems, for some students who wish
to have more "know-how" as part of their education experience and for some
managers who want an answer to special problems. This is a naive view. What
is more likely is that those who do have this view are probably more interested
in other theories. For instance, a psychological theory of human motivation
may be of little interest to an economist though it may excite a social psychologist. Or, economic theory may seem useless to a manager but the same manager uses his or her own "theory" of cost/price relationships to make business
decisions. There is much truth to the statement that "there is nothing as useful
as a good theory." Theories are ways of organizing reality. They can be used
to explain and predict behavior, as a basis for the control of events and as a
guide research.

Explanation and Prediction.   "The logical structure of a scientific explanation is identical with that of scientific prediction (35)." In other words, if we
can explain an event, we can predict it. The differences between explanation
and prediction is simply one of temporal perspective or where one is located
in time with respect to the event.

   Three conditions are necessary for explanation or prediction. First there
must be a description of the event to be explained (E). Second there must be a
set of causal antecedents of the event ($C_1 \ldots C_n$) which describe the circumstances leading to E. Finally there must be a set of law-statements ($L_1 \ldots L_n$)
that specify how C and E are related (i.e., that when C occurs, then E will follow).

   A skeleton of scientific explanation looks like the following:

$$\frac{L_1 \ldots L_n}{C_1 \ldots C_n}$$
$$\overline{\ldots E}$$

. . . .In the case of explanation . . . E is a past event relative to the scientist's vantage
point [and] we seek L's and C's [to explain it]. In the case of prediction, we have our
L's and C's and seek instead an E (35).

Control.   There are many examples of theories, especially in the social sciences, which are used for control or attempted control of events. The theory of
operant conditioning "is used" to affect the behavior of school children, im-

prove worker performance, and train animals. Desired behaviors are re-warded and often undesirable behaviors are sanctioned to get intended re-sults. Economics is another discipline which provides theory that is used for control purposes. Competition is fostered (or monopoly is outlawed) because according to theory, this should lead to a more efficient allocation of re-sources. Government spending, tax policy and monetary policy are varied de-pending on what policy makers wish to happen to the level of stimulation of the ecomony. There are, likewise, control implications in organization theory which are of use to managers. Management theory is the set of ideas about how to manage and control an organization.

To be able to use a theory for control, it is still necessary to have casual antecedents $(C_1 \ldots C_n)$ for an event (E) and lawlike statements $(L_1 \ldots L_n)$ that specify how C's are related to E. But there is one more condition to con-sider: the C's must be subject to manipulation. In other words, we must be able to act on C in such a way that we can change its level or its state to achieve the intended event, E.

Consider the following example. The following statement is a simple ex-planatory or predictive statement.

An increase in the specificity of organizational goals will be followed by an increase in organization efficiency.

This theoretical statement has implications for control purposes if it is possi-ble to increase the specificity of goals. Therefore, if a manager can be more precise in defining objectives and communicating these to other organization members and if the statement is true, we can expect efficiency to increase.

Some critics argue that some theories, especially in the social sciences, are not well formulated enough to provide accurate prediction, therefore they should not be used for control. Economic theory, for example, is a conceptual framework which is often the subject of this criticism because the different economic policies such as increased government spending (C_s) or reduced taxes (C_{rt}) seem to have little consistent and predictable effect on the inflation rate (E_{ir}).

The second concern is that if a theory is powerful enough to be used for control, then it opens the possibility that the control of casual factors (the C's) will fall into the hands of an undesirable group. Thus, if some malevolent agents learn how to use theory to control the behavior of others in an undesira-ble way, considerable freedom is lost. Such a fear underlies much criticism of the power of the press and television—that by determining what the public hears and sees, those who control the media may exert inappropriate influ-ence over the population.

The third concern about the control issue is that a casual factor (C_1) or a set of factors $(C_1 \ldots C_n)$ may result in several outcomes $(E_1 \ldots E_n)$ and that there is a different preference ordering for different E's (i.e., that E_1 is preferred by some to E_3). This may lead to conflict over whether E_1 or E_3 should be the maximization criterion. For instance, suppose we modify our earlier predictive statement as follows.

An increase in the specificity of organizational goals will be followed by an increase in organization efficiency *and* an increase in individual tension.

One *E* (efficiency) may be of more concern to the managerial group but the other *E* (increased tension) is of concern to employees. Each group may wish to have its *E* receive the highest priority and may exert pressures to have it that way. Disagreement about preferred outcomes is a basis for conflict among individuals, groups and organizations.

Theory and Research.   Theory should also serve as the basis for research. The propositions and hypotheses which are explicit and implicit in theory provide guides and directions for empirical efforts toward verification or rejection of the theory itself, or its important hypothetical substructures. Rigby notes the use and importance of theory in research.

Theory, including principles and laws, does not provide information on the state of the world, but only on the nature of the world. The applied researcher is primarily interested in the state of the world. Theory, however, . . . will suggest . . . how he can proceed to study the state of the world . . . [It] provides . . . a set of concepts and information on the relationship between concepts.

Applied research based in theory is in strong contrast to problem-solving research based on nothing more than simple trial and error or uncritical imitation.

The role that theory can play in aiding applied research may seem obvious, but . . . is too frequently ignored in applied research (33).

Bits and pieces of theories, adequately investigated, will serve to sharpen the explanatory and predictive capacity of theory. Dill (11) emphasizes this point by stressing the importance of

the replication of studies which have found their way into some theoretical structures. In a few areas we have done replications with highly beneficial results. The early experiments on participative management . . . draw dramatic attention because of their apparently solid demonstration of the immediate practical benefits of participation. . . . Yet in each case . . . elaborations of the original experiment . . . have found that the simple relationships which they first hypothesized between participation, satisfaction, and productivity do not hold up . . . As a result . . . we are reopening many old questions to establish more clearly the conditions under which these methods will and will not work (11).

Organization Theory and Other Types

Organization theory is a set of interrelated constructs (concepts), definitions and propositions that present a systematic view of individuals, groups, and subgroups *interacting* in some relatively patterned sequences of activity, the intent of which is goal oriented. What differentiates organizations theory from other approaches to the study of behavior in organizations is the nature of the concepts. Organizational theories tend to focus on organization structure, organizational environments, formalization, technology, authority, groups, and departments, among other variables. The organization is the unit of analysis.

There are other theoretical formulations which focus on the same phenomena, but they do so from a different theoretical perspective and with a different set of concepts.

Organizational Behavior.   According to Cummings (8), organizational behavior is the study of individual and group behavior within organizations and the application of such knowledge. The concepts are drawn primarily from psychological disciplines. Attitudes, personality, motivation, and decision making are some of the more widely used concepts in organizational behavior.

One general distinction that Cummings draws between organizational behavior and organization theory is how the variable "organization structure" is empirically and theoretically positioned (8). Organization structure is typically conceived as an independent variable in organizational behavior, while dependent variables may be individual or group attitudes, job satisfaction, and performance. In organizational theory, structure is frequently the dependent variable, which is affected by the environment of the organization.

Management Theory and Organization Theory.   Stogdill (41) differentiates between organization theory and management theory. "A theory of organization is not necessarily a theory of management." While management theory must be based on organization theory, it contains *"philosophical assumptions and value orientations regarding the nature of human behavior that are not basic to a theory of organization."* Stogdill says that management theory is

> a theory of management of practice . . . interested in facts and sound principles. But theories of practice regarding human nature and human relations almost always involve schools of thought that differ in their philosophical orientations. The disputes between social scientists and classical theories are concerned with differences in recommended practice. . . . [While] these differences are significant for the practice of management, they do not affect any of the realities regarding the dimensions of organization. It is argued that organization theory is an instrument not for conducting ideological dispute but the acquiring verifiable knowledge (41).

Organization theory is descriptive and/or predictive. It is concerned with what an organization *is* and what will occur under certain kinds of structural or structural-interpersonal arrangements. It tells us what is and/or what will be. *It does not tell us what to do.* Organization theory, then, may be described as a set of related propositions, statements, and hypotheses about (1) a set of variables which describe the parameters of organization, and perhaps organization behavior, and/or (2) a series of "if . . . then" statements which *predict* the effect of certain structural arrangements on performance and behavior.

Once the theorist reaches this point, of course, he or she must indeed find it easy to enter into the domain of management theory. Management theory is a "theory of practice." It must *prescribe* what to do to achieve a *particular* outcome, or to prevent a condition from developing which might be considered as undesirable. These prescriptions have manipulation or change as their intent. When these results are intended it is easy to provoke controversy and argument, since personal values come into consideration. *Management theory is best conceived of as a series of "if . . . then" statements to which are added "therefore, do . . . "* This argues, then, that approaches to organizational issues such as those of Taylor, Likert, Argyris, and McGregor which suggest a "better" way to organize or which describe how to manage "more effectively" should be characterized as management theories since they tend to be largely prescriptive in nature.

Management theory, sometimes called design theory, is a set of normative prescriptions about what conditions and relations *should* exist in organizations. How should work be organized? How should authority and responsibility be assigned? What are the "principles" that should be complied with? Design theory has value in development and prescription of organizational relationships prior to the entrance of an individual into the system. It can throw up a "red flag," suggesting that when prescriptions are violated, problems *may* develop.

Design theory, then, has a sort of predictive aspect to it. For instance, the "traditional" concept of unity of command would lead to a general prediction of role conflict if violated. Obviously, however, there are conditions where role conflict may be less likely to occur. Theories which specify these conditions may have a greater explanatory capability, but may be less effective in the design of an organization since consideration of *all* the variables would result in a complex construction extremely difficult to deal with.

Organization Theory and the "Theory of the Firm." McGuire (25) describes the major components of economic theory, or the "Theory of the Firm," as follows.

1. The firm has a goal (or goals) toward which it drives.
2. It moves toward [them] in a "rational" manner.
3. The firm's function is to transform economic inputs to outputs.
4. The environment within which the firm operates is given.
5. The theory concentrates particularly upon changes in the price and quantities of inputs and outputs.

With the exception of the last point, the list is similar to attributes of organization generally implied, or made explicit, in most theories of organization. For instance, in our earlier survey of definitions of organization we found that most included some sort of "goal orientation."

What, then, is the difference? First, the external environment with which the firm is concerned in economic theory is the "market." In some organization theories the treatment of the environment includes external interest and pressure groups which are not "customers." Selznick (38) treats the "community" in *TVA and the Grass Roots.* March and Simon point out that while they structure their theoretical formulation around decisions made by those normally viewed as organization members, one may well use the same kind of analysis for other groups, such as "customers" (23). Second, the focal point in economic theory tends to be factor prices and quantities—or supply and demand. The following states nicely that the distinction between organization theory and economic theory intended here.

> Formal economic analysis simplifies the empirical properties in the firm and molds it into a body of theory . . . Organization theory looks at the internal characteristics of the firm (19).

> [Organization] theory focuses on a set of problems that are different from those of the economic theory of the firm. Its problems are not specifically economic; virtually nothing is said about how output levels are set, advertising expenditures determined and so forth . . . . Unlike the theory of the firm, there is not consideration of "aggregation." Indeed, there is nothing to aggregate (9).

In fact, then, one of the concepts or variables in economic theory is the firm, or organization. Actions in the market place taken by different firms explain or predict factor prices. In organization theory, the firm (or the organization) is dissected into variables and an attempt is made to explain or predict the behavior of the organization or its members. In short, economic theory tends to look from the firm's boundaries outward, while organization theory looks from the boundaries inward.

SUMMARY

> At present [those interested in organizations are] confronted with a situation in which numerous fragments of theories are presented as complete theories . . . . The systems developed [by the various schools of thought] are likely to consist of widely different variables that are really important to an organization (41).

A cursory reading of several organizational theory tests will lead most of us to a conclusion consistent with Stogdill's, as given above. The intent of this book is to present a selection of the different theories, and attempt to delineate their skeletal structure, in the hope that thereby points of similarity and distinction may emerge and that thus other theoretical efforts can be devoted to refining those points. The theories presented in this book were selected because they are representative of certain approaches, have been widely used as point of reference, attack and/or present a formulation of an aspect of organization of particular interest to the author.

The approaches have been condensed or summarized, or presented in some other brief form to show how the various elements within each theory are related to other elements. The selections are abstracts and represent what someone, generally other than the theorists, believes to be the main set of ideas and concepts in the particular theory. In the original work, the theorist usually marshals support for the concepts and ideas either by extensive reference to empirical research literature as Stogdill (42) does, or from personal observations, as does Barnard (2). It is the responsibility of the serious student of organization theory to examine all theories in detail, so that he or she becomes aware of the bases for relationships as developed by the theorist.

The formulations presented here by no means exhaust the approaches to the study of organization. Stogdill, for example, has categorized no less than 18 orientations which have been used in the analysis of organizations. Among these are viewing an organization as a cultural product, or as an exchange agent with environment, or as an independent agency, or as a system of structures and functions, or as a structure in action over time, or as a system of dynamic functions, or as a processing system, or as an input-output system, or as a structure of subgroups.

Additionally, some theories of organized behavior focus on groups. They may emphasize groups as biological social necessities, or as cultural products, or as independent entities, or as an interaction in systems, or as interaction-expectation systems, or as a collection of individual members, or as a summation of member characteristics.

Finally, subgroups may be the central analytical unit, with the focus on subgroups in interaction with the organizations, or as in interaction with each other.

Each of these orientations represents a legitimate point of departure for inquiry, each has a different set of biases and value judgments which affect the manner in which the theory is developed, yet each focuses on organized behavior.

TWO
AN OVERVIEW OF THE FIELD

In a much-cited article treating the general subject of organization theory, William Scott defines three major approaches to the theory of organization and outlines the major underpinnings of each. The classical school is described as placing primary emphasis on division of labor, scalar and functional processes, structure, and span of control. The neoclassical school superimposes on these "pillars of classical doctrine . . . modifications resulting from individual behavior, and the influence of the informal group." Modern organizational theory, relying on empirical research goes beyond both classical and neoclassical. It directs itself toward a system perspective.

In the following section, Scott deals in detail with these various approaches to conceptualizing organizations, and he presents some interesting and important insights into where organization theory is heading.—H.L.T.

"ORGANIZATION THEORY"*

WILLIAM G. SCOTT

Man is intent on drawing himself into a web of collectivized patterns. "Modern man has learned to accommodate himself to a world increasingly organized. The trend toward every more explicit and consciously drawn relationships is profound and sweeping; it is marked by depth no less than by extension."[1] This comment by Seidenberg nicely summarizes the pervasive influence of organization in many forms of human activity.

Some of the reasons for intense organizational activity are found in the fundamental transitions which revolutionize our society, changing it from a rural culture, to a culture based on technology, industry, and the city. From these changes, a way of life emerged characterized by the *proximity* and *dependency* of people on each other. Proximity and dependency, as conditions of social life, harbor the threat of human conflict, capricious antisocial behavior, instability of human relationships, and uncertainty about the nature of the social structure with its concomitant roles.

*Reprinted by permission of the author and the publisher from the *Journal of the Academy of Management,* Vol. 4, No. 1, (April, 1961) pp. 7–26.

Of course, these threats to social integrity are present to some degree in all societies, ranging from the primitive to the modern. But, these threats become dangerous when the harmonious functioning of a society rests on the maintenance of a highly intricate, delicately balanced form of human collaboration. The civilization we have created depends on the preservation of a precarious balance. Hence, disrupting forces impinging on this shaky form of a collaboration must be eliminated or minimized.

Traditionally, organization is viewed as a vehicle for accomplishing goals and objectives. While this approach is useful, it tends to obscure the inner workings and internal purposes of organization itself. Another fruitful way of treating organization is a mechanism having the ultimate purpose of offsetting those forces which undermine human collaboration. In this sense, organization tends to minimize conflict and to lessen the significance of individual behavior which deviates from values that the organization has established as worthwhile. Further, organization increases stability in human relationships by reducing uncertainty regarding the nature of the system's structure and the human roles which are inherent to it. Corollary to this point, organization enhances the predictability of human action, because it limits the number of behavioral alternatives available to an individual. As Presthus points out:

> Organization is defined as a system of structural interpersonal relations . . . individuals are differentiated in terms of authority, status, and role with the results that personal interaction is prescribed . . .
> Anticipated reactions tend to occur, while ambiguity and spontaneity are decreased.[2]

In addition to all of this, organization has built-in safeguards. Besides prescribing acceptable forms of behavior for those who elect to submit to it, organization is also able to counterbalance the influence of human action which transcends its established patterns.[3]

Few segments of society have engaged in organizing more intensively than business.[4] The reason is clear. Business depends on what organization offers. Business needs a system of relationships among functions; it needs stability, continuity, and predictability in its internal activities and external contacts. Business also appears to need harmonious relationships among the people and processes which make it up. Put another way, a business organization has to be free, relatively, from destructive tendencies which may be caused by divergent interests.

As a foundation for meeting these needs rests administrative science. A major element of this science is organization theory, which provides the grounds for management activities in a number of significant areas of business endeavor. Organization theory, however, is not a homogeneous science based on generally accepted principles. Various theories of organization have been, and are being evolved. For example, something called "modern organization theory" has recently emerged, raising the wrath of some traditionalists, but also capturing the imagination of a rather elite *avant-garde.*

The thesis of this paper is that modern organization theory, when stripped of its irrelevancies, redundancies, and "speech defects," is a logical and vital evolution in management thought. In order for this thesis to be supported, the reader must endure a review and appraisal of more traditional forms of organization theory which may seem elementary to him.

In any event, three theories of organization are having considerable influence on management thought and practice. They are arbitrarily labeled in this paper as the classical, the neoclassical, and the modern. Each of these is fairly distinct; but they are not unrelated. Also, these theories are ongoing, being actively supported by several schools of management thought.

THE CLASSICAL DOCTRINE

For lack of a better method of identification, it will be said that the classical doctrine deals almost exclusively with the *anatomy of formal organization.* This doctrine can be traced back to Frederick W. Taylor's interest in functional foremanship and planning staffs. But most students of management thought would agree that in the United States, the first systematic approach to organization, and the first comprehensive attempt to find organizational universals, is dated 1931 when Mooney and Reiley published *Onward Industry.*[5] Subsequently, numerous books, following the classical vein, have appeared. Two of the more recent are Brech's *Organization*[6] and Allen's *Management and Organization.*[7]

Classical organization theory is built around four key pillars. They are the division of labor, the scalar and functional processes, structure, and span of control. Given these major elements just about all of classical organization theory can be derived.

1. *The division of labor* is without doubt the cornerstone among the four elements.[8] From it the other elements flow as corollaries. For example, *scalar* and *functional* growth requires specialization and departmentalization of functions. Organization *structure* is naturally dependent upon the direction which specialization of activities travels in company development. Finally, *span of control* problems result from the number of specialized functions under the jurisdiction of a manager.

2. *The scalar and functional processes* deal with the vertical and horizontal growth of the organization, respectively.[9] The scalar process refers to the growth of the chain of command, the delegation of authority and responsibility, unity of command, and the obligation to report.

    The division of the organization into specialized parts and the regrouping of the parts into compatible units are matters pertaining to the functional process. This process focuses on the horizontal evolution of the line and staff in a formal organization.

3. *Structure* is the logical relationships of functions in an organization, arranged to accomplish the objectives of the company efficiently. Structure implies system and pattern. Classical organization theory usually

works with two basic structures, the line and the staff. However, such activities as committee and liaison functions fall quite readily into the purview of structural considerations. Again, structure is the vehicle for introducing logical and consistent relationships among the diverse functions which comprise the organization.[10]

4. *The span of control* concept relates to the number of subordinates a manager can effectively supervise. Graicunas has been credited with first elaborating the point that there are numerical limitations to the subordinates one man can control.[11] In a . . . statement on the subject, Brech points out, "span" refers to" . . . the number of persons, themselves carrying managerial and supervisory responsibilities, for whom the senior manager retains his overembracing responsibility of direction and planning coordination, motivation, and control."[12] Regardless of interpretation, span of control has significance, in part, for the shape of the organization which evolves through growth. Wide span yields a flat structure; short span results in a tall structure. Further, the span concept directs attention to the complexity of human and functional interrelationships in an organization.

It would not be fair to say that the classical school is unaware of the day-to-day administrative problems of the organization. Paramount among these problems are those stemming from human interactions. But the interplay of individual personality, informal groups, interorganizational conflict, and the decision-making processes in the formal structure appears largely to be neglected by classical organization theory. Additionally, the classical theory overlooks the contributions of the behavioral sciences by failing to incorporate them in its doctrine in any systematic way. In summary, classical organization theory has relevant insights into the nature of organization, but the value of this theory is limited by its narrow concentration on the formal anatomy of organization.

NEOCLASSICAL THEORY OF ORGANIZATION

The neoclassical theory of organization embarked on the task of compensating for some of the deficiencies in classical doctrine. The neoclassical school is commonly identified with the human relations movement. Generally, the neoclassical approach takes the postulates of the classical school, regarding the pillars of organization as givens. But these postulates are regarded as modified by people, acting independently or within the context of the informal organization.

One of the main contributions of the neoclassical school is the introduction of behavioral sciences in an integrated fashion into the theory of organization. Through the use of these sciences, the human relationists demonstrate how the pillars of the classical doctrine are affected by the impact of human actions. Further, the neoclassical approach includes a systematic treatment of the informal organization, showing its influence on the formal structure.

Thus, the neoclassical approach to organization theory gives evidence of accepting classical doctrine, but superimposing on it modifications resulting from individual behavior, and the influence of the informal groups. The inspiration of the neoclassical school were the Hawthorne studies.[13] Current examples of the neoclassical approach are found in human relations books like Gardner and Moore, *Human Relations in Industry*,[14] and Davis, *Human Relations in Business*.[15] To a more limited extent, work in industrial sociology also reflects a neoclassical point of view.[16]

It would be useful to look briefly at some of the contributions made to organization theory by the neoclassicists. First to be considered are modifications of the pillars of classical doctrine; second is the informal organization.

Examples of the Neoclassical Approach to the Pillars of Formal Organization Theory

1. The *division of labor* has been a long standing subject of comment in the field of human relations. Very early in the history of industrial psychology study was made of industrial fatigue and monotony caused by the specialization of the work.[17] Later, attention shifted to the isolation of the worker, and his feeling of anonymity resulting from insignificant jobs which contributed negligibly to the final product.[18]

   Also, specialization influences the work of management. As an organization expands, the need concomitantly arises for managerial motivation and coordination of the activities of others. Both motivation and coordination in turn relate to executive leadership. Thus, in part, stemming from the growth of industrial specialization, the neoclassical school has developed a large body of theory relating to motivation, coordination, and leadership. Much of this theory is derived from the social sciences.

2. Two aspects of the *scaler and functional* processes which have been treated with some degree of intensity by the neoclassical school are the delegation of authority and responsibility, and gaps in or overlapping of functional jurisdictions. The classical theory assumes something of perfection in the delegation and functionalization processes. The neoclassical school points out that human problems are caused by imperfections in the way these processes are handled.

   For example, too much or insufficient delelgation may render an executive incapable of action. The failure to delegate authority and responsibility equally may result in frustration for the delegatee. Overlapping of authorities often causes clashes in personality. Gaps in authority cause failures in getting jobs done, with one party blaming the other for shortcomings in performance.[19]

The neoclassical school says that the scalar and functional processes are theoretically valid, but tend to deteriorate in practice. The ways in which they break down are described, and some of the human causes are pointed out. In addition the neoclassicists make recommendations, suggesting various "human tools" which will facilitate the operation of these processes.

3. *Structure* provides endless avenues of analysis for the neoclassical theory of organization. The theme is that human behavior disrupts the best laid organizational plans, and thwarts the cleanness of the logical relationships founded in the structure. The neoclassical critique of structure centers on frictions which appear internally among people performing different functions.

Line and staff relations is a problem area, much discussed, in this respect. Many companies seem to have difficulty keeping the line and staff working together harmoniously. Both Dalton[20] and Juran[21] have engaged in research to discover the causes of friction, and to suggest remedies.

Of course, line-staff represent only one of the many problems of structural frictions described by the neoclassicists. As often as not, the neoclassicists will offer prescriptions for the elimination of conflict in structure. Among the more important harmony-rendering formulae are participation, junior boards, bottom-up management, joint committees, recognition of human dignity, and "better" communication.

4. An executive's *span of control* is a function of human determinants, and the reduction of span to a precise, universally applicable ratio is silly, according to the neoclassicists. Some of the determinants of span are individual differences in managerial abilities, the type of people and functions supervised, and the extent of communication effectiveness.

Coupled with the span of control question are the human implications of the type of structure which emerges. That is, is a tall structure with a short span or a flat structure with a wide span more conducive to good human relations than high morale? The answer is situational. Short span results in tight supervision; wide span requires a good deal of delegation with looser controls. Because of the individual and organizational differences, sometimes one is better than the other. There is a tendency to favor the looser form of organization, however, for the reason that tall structures breed autocratic leadership, which is often poined out as a cause of low morale.[22]

The Neoclassical View of the Informal Organization

Nothing more than the barest mention of the informal organization is given even in the most recent classical treatises on organization theory.[23] Systematic discussion of this form of organization has been left to the neoclassicists.

The informal organization refers to people in group associations at work, but these associations are not specified in the "blueprint" of the formal organization. The informal organization means natural groupings of people in the work situation.

In a general way, the informal organization appears in response to the social need—the need of people to associate with others. However, for analytical purposes, this explanation is not particularly satisfying. Research has produced the following, more specific determinants underlying the appearance of informal organizations.

1.   The *location* determinant simply states that in order to form into groups of any lasting nature, people have to have frequent face-to-face contact. Thus, the geography of physical location in a plant or office is an important factor in predicting who will be in what group.[24]
2.   *Occupation* is a key factor determining the rise and composition of informal groups. There is a tendency for people performing similar jobs to group together.[25]
3.   *Interests* are another determinant for informal group formation. Even though people might be in the same location, performing similar jobs, differences of interest among them explain why several small, instead of one large, informal organizations emerge.
4.   *Special issues* often result in the formation of informal groups, but this determinant is set apart from the three previously mentioned. In this case, people who do not necessarily have similar interests, occupations, or locations may join together for a common cause. Once the issue is resolved, then the tendency is to revert to the more "natural" group forms.[26] Thus, special issues give rise to a rather impermanent informal association; groups based on the other three determinants tend to be more lasting.

When informal organizations come into being they assume certain characteristics. Since understanding these characteristics is important for management practice, they are noted below.

1.   Informal organizations act as agencies of *social control.* They generate a culture based on certain norms of conduct which, in turn, demands conformity from group members. These standards may be at odds with the values set by the formal organization. So an individual may very well find himself in a situation of conflicting demands.
2.   The form of human interrelationships to the formal organization requires *techniques of analysis* different from those used to plot the relationships of people in a formal organization. The method used for determining the structure of the informal group is called sociometric analysis. Sociometry reveals the complex structure of interpersonal relations which is based on premises fundamentally unlike the logic of the formal organization.

3. Informal organizations have *status and communication* systems peculiar to themselves, not necessarily derived from the formal systems. For example, the grapevine is the subject of much neoclassical study.
4. Survival of the informal organization requires stable continuing relationships among the people in them. Thus, it has been observed that the informal organization *resists change.*[27] Considerable attention is given by the neoclassicists to overcoming informal resistance to change.
5. The last aspect of analysis which appears to be central to the neoclassical view of the informal organization is the study of the *informal leader.* Discussion revolves around who the informal leader is, how he assumes this role, what characteristics are peculiar to him, and how he can help the manager accomplish his objectives in the formal organization.[28]

This brief sketch of some of the major facets of informal organization theory has neglected, so far, one important topic treated by the neoclassical school. It is the way in which the formal and informal organizations interact.

A conventional way of looking at the interaction of the two is the "live and let live" point of view. Management should recognize that the informal organization exists, nothing can destroy it, and so the executive might just as well work with it. Working with the informal organization involves not threatening its existence unnecessarily, listening to opinions expressed for the group by the leader, allowing group participation in decision-making situations, and controlling the grapevine by prompt release of accurate information.[29]

While this approach is management centered, it is not unreasonable to expect that informal group standards and norms could make themselves felt on formal organizational policy. An honestly conceived effort by managers to establish a working relationship with the informal organization could result in an association where both formal and informal views would be reciprocally modified. The danger which at all costs should be avoided is that "working with the informal organization" does not degenerate into a shallow disguise for human manipulation.

Some neoclassical writing in organization theory, especially that coming from the management-oriented segment of this school, gives the impression that the formal and informal organizations are distinct, and at times, quite irreconcilable factors in a company. The interaction which takes place between the two is something akin to the interaction between the company and a labor union, or a government agency, or another company.

The concept of the social system is another approach to the interactional climate. While this concept can be properly classified as neoclassical, it borders on the modern theories of organization. The phrase "social system" means that an organization is a complex of mutually interdependent, but variable, factors.

These factors include individuals and their attitudes and motives, jobs, the physical work setting, the formal organization, and the informal organizations. These factors, and many others, are woven into an overall pattern of interdependency. From this point of view, the formal and informal organizations lose their distinctiveness, but find real meaning, in terms of human behavior, in the operation of the system as a whole. Thus, the study of organization turns away from descriptions of its component parts, and is refocused on the system of interrelationships among the parts.

One of the major contributions of the Hawthorne studies was the integration of Pareto's idea of the social system into a meaningful method of analysis for the study of behavior in human organizations.[30] This concept is still vitally important. But unfortunately some work in the field of human relations undertaken by the neoclassicists has overlooked, or perhaps discounted the significance of this consideration.[31]

The fundamental insight regarding the social system, developed and applied to the industrial scene by the Hawthorne researchers, did not find much extension in subsequent work in the neoclassical vein. Indeed, the neoclassical school after the Hawthorne studies generally seemed content to engage in descriptive generalizations, or particularized empirical research studies which did not have much meaning outside their own context.

The neoclassical school of organization theory has been called bankrupt. Criticisms range from, "human relations is a tool for cynical puppeteering of people," to "human relations is nothing more than a trifling body of empirical and descriptive information." There is a good deal of truth in both criticisms, but another appraisal of the neoclassical school of organization theory is offered here. The neoclassical approach has provided valuable contributions to lore of organization. But, like the classical theory, the neoclassical doctrine suffers from incompleteness, a shortsighted perspective, and lack of integration among the many facets of human behavior studied by it. Modern organization theory has made a move to cover the shortcomings of the current body of theoretical knowledge.

MODERN ORGANIZATION THEORY

The distinctive qualities of modern organization are its conceptual-analytical base, its reliance on empirical research data and, above all, its integrating nature. These qualities are framed in a philosophy which accepts the premise that the only meaningful way to study organization is to study it as a system. As Henderson put it, the study of a system must rely on a method of analysis," . . . involving the simultaneous variations of mutually dependent variables."[32] Human systems, of course, contain a huge number of dependent variables which defy the most complex simultaneous equations to solve.

Nevertheless, system analysis has its own peculiar point of view which aims to study organization in the way Henderson suggests. It treats organization as a system of mutually dependent variables. As a result, modern organization theory, which accepts system analysis, shifts the conceptual level of organization study above the classical and neoclassical theories. Modern organization theory asks a range of interrelated questions which are not seriously considered by the two other theories.

Key among these questions are: (1) What are the strategic parts of the system? (2) What is the nature of their mutual dependency? (3) What are the main processes in the system which link the parts together, and facilitate their adjustments to each other? (4) What are the goals sought by systems?[33]

Modern organization theory is in no way a unified body of thought. Each writer and researcher has his special emphasis when he considers the system. Perhaps the most evident unifying thread in the study of systems is the effort to look at the organization in its totality. Representative books in this field are March and Simon. *Organizations*,[34] and Haire's anthology, *Modern Organization Theory.*[35]

Instead of attempting a review of different writers' contributions to modern organization theory, it will be more useful to discuss the various ingredients involved in system analysis. They are the parts, the interactions, the processes, and the goals of systems.

The Parts of the System and Their Interdependency

The first basic part of the system is the *individual,* and the personality structure he brings to the organization. Elementary to an individual's personality are motives and attitudes which condition the range of expectancies he hopes to satisfy by participating in the system.

The second part of the system is the formal arrangement of functions, usually called the *formal organization.* The formal organization is the interrelated pattern of jobs which make up the structure of a system. Certain writers, like Argyris, see a fundamental conflict resulting from the demands made by the system, and the structure of the mature, normal personality. In any event, the individual has expectancies regarding the job he is to perform; and conversely, the job makes demands on, or has expectancies relating to, the performance of the individual. Considerable attention has been given by writers in modern organization theory to incongruencies resulting from the interaction of organizational and individual demands.[36]

The third part in the organization system is the *informal organization.* Enough has been said already about the nature of this organization. But it must be noted that an interactional pattern exists between the individual and the informal group. This interactional arrangement can be conveniently discussed as the mutual modification of expectancies. The informal organizations had demands which it makes on members in terms of anticipated forms of behavior and the individual has expectancies of satisfaction he hopes to derive from association with people on the job. Both these sets of expectancies interact, resulting in the individual modifying his behavior to accord with the demands of the group, and the group, perhaps, modifying what it expects from an individual because of the impact of his personality on group norms.[37]

Much of what has been said about the various expectancy systems in an organization can also be treated using status and role concepts. Part of modern organization theory rests on research findings in social-psychology relative to reciprocal patterns of behavior stemming from role demands generated by both the formal and informal organizations, and role perceptions peculiar to the individual. Bakke's *fusion process* is largely concerned with the modification of role expectancies. The fusion process is a force, according to Bakke, which acts to weld divergent elements together for the preservation of organizational integrity.[38]

The fifth part of system analysis is the *physical setting* in which the job is performed. Although this element of the system may be implicit in what has been said already about the formal organization and its functions, it is well to separate it. In the physical surroundings of work, interactions are present in complex man-machine systems. The human "engineer" cannot approach the problems posed by such interrelationships in a purely technical, engineering fashion. As Haire says, these problems lie in the domain of the social theorist.[39] Attention must be centered on responses demanded from a logically ordered production function, often with the view of minimizing the error in the system. From this standpoint, work cannot be effectively organized unless the psychological, social, and physiological characteristics of people participating in the work environment are considered. Machines and processes should be designed to fit certain generally observed psychological and physiological properties of men, rather than hiring men to fit machines.

In summary, the parts of the system which appear to be of strategic importance are the individual, the formal structure, the informal organization, status and role patterns, and the physical environment of work. Again, these parts are woven into a configuration called the organizational system. The processes which link the parts are taken up next.

The Linking Process

One can say, with a good deal of glibness, that all the parts mentioned above are interrelated. Although this observation is quite correct, it does not mean too much in terms of system theory unless some attempt is made to analyze the processes by which the interaction is achieved. Role theory is devoted to certain types of interactional processes. In addition, modern organization theorists point to three other linking activities which appear to be universal to human systems of organized behavior. These processes are communication, balance, and decision making.

1. Communication is mentioned often in neoclassical theory, but the emphasis is on description of forms of communication activity (i.e., formal-informal, vertical-horizontal, line staff). Communication, as a mechanism which links the segments of the system together, is overlooked by way of much considered analysis.

One aspect of modern organization theory is study of the communication network in the system. Communication is viewed as the method by which action is evoked from the parts of the system. Communication acts not only as stimuli resulting in action, but also as a control and coordination mechanism linking the decision centers in the system into a synchronized pattern. Deutsch points out that organizations are composed of parts which communicate with each other, receive messages from the outside world, and store information. Taken together, these communication functions of the parts comprise a configuration representing the total system.[40] More is to be said about communication late in the discussion of the cybernetic model.

2. The concept of *balance* as a linking process involves a series of some rather complex ideas. Balance refers to an equilibrating mechanism whereby the various parts of the system are maintained in a harmoniously structured relationship to each other.

The necessity for the balance concept logically flows from the nature of systems themselves. It is impossible to conceive of an ordered relationship among the parts of a system without also introducing the idea of a stabilizing or an adapting mechanism.

Balance appears in two varieties—quasi-automatic and innovative. Both forms of balance act to insure system integrity in face of changing conditions either internal or external to the system. The first form of balance, quasi-automatic, refers to what some think are "homeostatic" properties of systems. That is, systems seem to exhibit built-in propensities to maintain steady states.

If human organizations are open, self-maintaining systems, then control and regulatory processes are necessary. The issue hinges on the degree to which stabilizing processes in systems, when adapting to change, are automatic. March and Simon have an interesting answer to this problem, which in part is based on the type of change and the adjustment necessary to adapt to the change. Systems have programs of action which are put into effect when a change is perceived. If the change is relatively minor, and if the change comes within the purview of established programs of action, then it might be fairly confidently predicted that the adaptation made by the system will be quasi-automatic.[41]

The role of innovative, creative balancing efforts now needs to be examined. The need for innovation arises when adaptation to a change is outside the scope of existing programs designed for the purpose of keeping the system in balance. New programs have to be evolved in order for the system to maintain internal harmony.

New programs are created by trial and error search for feasible action alternatives to cope with a given change. But innovation is subject to the limitations and possibilities inherent in the quantity and variety of information present in a system at a particular time. New combinations of alternatives for innovative purposes depend on:

1. The possible range of output of the system, or the capacity of the system to supply information.
2. The range of available information in the memory of the system.

3. The operating rules (program) governing the analysis and flow of information within the system.
4. The ability of the system to "forget" previously learned solutions to change problems.[42] A system with too good a memory might narrow its behavioral choices to such an extent as to stifle innovation. In simpler language, old learning programs might be used to adapt to the change, when newly innovated programs are necessary.[43]

Much of what has been said about communication and balance brings to mind a cybernetic model in which both these processes have vital roles. Cybernetics has to do with feedback and control of all kinds of systems. Its purpose is to maintain system stability in the face of change. Cybernetics cannot be studied without considering communication networks, information flow, and some kind of balancing process aimed at preserving the integrity of the system.

Cybernetics direct attention to key questions regarding the system. These questions are: How are communication centers connected, and how are they maintained? Corollary to this question: What is the structure of the feedback system? Next, what information is stored in the organization, and at what points? And as a corollary: How accessible is this information to decision-making centers? Third, how conscious is the organization of the operation of its own parts? That is, to what extent do the policy centers receive control information with sufficient frequency and relevancy to create a real awareness of the operation of the segments of the system? Finally, what are the learning (innovating) capabilities of the system?[44]

Answers to the questions posed by cybernetics are crucial to understanding both the balancing and communication processes in systems.[45] Although cybernetics has been applied largely to technical engineering problems of automation, the model of feedback, control, and regulation in all systems has a good deal of generality. Cybernetics is a fruitful area which can be used to synthesize the processes of communication and balance.

3. A wide spectrum of topics dealing with types of decisions in human systems makes up the core of analysis of another important process in organizations. Decision analysis is one of the major contributions of March and Simon in their book *Organizations*. The two major classes of decisions they discuss are decisions to produce and decisions to participate in the system.[46]

Decisions to produce are largely a result of an interaction between individual attitudes and the demands of organization. Motivation analysis becomes central to studying the nature and results of the interaction. Individual decisions to participate in the organization reflect on such issues as the relationship between organizational rewards versus the demands made by the organization. Participation decisions also focus attention on the reasons why individuals remain in or leave organizations.

March and Simon treat decisions as internal variables in an organization which depend on jobs, individual expectations and motivations, and organizational structure. Marschak[47] looks on the decision process as an independent variable upon which the survival of the organization is based. In this case, the organization is viewed as having, inherent in its structure, the ability to maximize survival requisites through its established decision process.

The Goals of Organization

Organization has three goals which may be either intermeshed or independent ends in themselves. They are growth, stability, and interaction. The last goal refers to organizations which exist primarily to provide a medium for association of its members with others. Interestingly enough these goals seem to apply to different forms of organization at varying levels of complexity, ranging from simple clockwork mechanisms to social systems.

These similarities in organizational purposes have been observed by a number of people, and a field of thought and research called system theory has developed, dedicated to the task of discovering organizational universals. The dream of general system theory is to create a science of organizational universals, or if you will, a universal science using common organizational elements found in all systems as a starting point.

Modern organization theory is on the periphery of general system theory. Both general system theory and modern organization theory studies:

1. The parts (individuals) in aggregates, and the movement of individuals into and out of the system.
2. The interaction of individuals with the environment found in the system.
3. The interactions among individuals in the system.
4. General growth and stability problems of systems.[48]

Modern organization theory and general system theory are similar in that they look at organization as an integrated whole. They differ, however, in terms of their generality. General system theory is concerned with every level of system, whereas modern organizational theory focuses primarily on human organization.

The question might be asked, what can the science of administration gain by the study of system levels other than human? Before attempting an answer, note should be made of what these other levels are. Boulding presents a convenient method of classification:

1. The static structure—a level of framework, the anatomy of a system; for example, the structure of the universe.
2. The simple dynamics system—the level of clockworks, predetermined necessary motions.
3. The cybernetic system—the level of the thermostat, the system moves to maintain a given equilibrium through a process of self-regulation.
4. The open system—level of self-maintaining systems, moves toward and includes living organisms.
5. The genetic-societal system—level of cell society, characterized by a division of labor among cells.

6. Animal systems—level of mobility, evidence of goal-directed behavior.
7. Human systems—level of symbol interpretation and idea communication.
8. Social system—level of human organization.
9. Transcendental systems—level of ultimates and absolutes which exhibit systematic structure but are unknowable in essence.[49]

This approach to the study of systems of finding universals common at all levels of organization offers intriguing possibilities for administrative organization theory. A good deal of light could be thrown on social systems if structurally analogous elements could be found in the simpler types of systems. For example, cybernetic systems have characteristics which seem to be similar to feedback, regulation, and control phenomena in human organizations. Thus, certain facets of cybernetic models could be generalized to human organization. Considerable danger, however, lies in poorly founded analogies. Superficial similarities between simpler system forms and social systems are apparent everywhere. Instinctually based ant societies, for example, do not yield particularly instructive lessons for understanding rationally conceived human organizations. Thus, care should be taken that analogies used to bridge system levels are not mere devices for literary enrichment. For analogies to have usefulness and validity, they must exhibit inherent structural similarities or implicity identical operational principles.[50]

Modern organization theory leads, as it has been shown, almost inevitably into a discussion of general system theory. A science of organizational universals has some strong advocates, particularly among biologists.[51] Organization theorists in administrative science cannot afford to overlook the contributions of general system theory. Indeed, modern organization concepts could offer a great deal to those working with general system theory. But the ideas dealt with in the general theory are exceedingly elusive.

Speaking of the concept of equilibrium as a unifying element in all systems, Easton says, "It (equilibrium) leaves the impression that we have a useful general theory when in fact, lacking measurability, it is a mere pretense for knowledge."[52] The inability to quantify and measure universal organization elements undermines the success of pragmatic tests to which general system theory might be put.

Organization Theory: Quo Vadis?. . . .

Footnotes

[1]Roderick Seidenburg, *Post Historic Man* (Boston: Beacon Press, 1951), p. 1.
[2]Robert V. Presthus, "Toward a Theory of Organizational Behavior," *Administrative Science Quarterly* (June, 1958), p. 50.
[3]Regulation and predictability of human behavior are matters of degree varying with different organizations on something of a continuum. At one extreme are bureaucratic type organizations with tight bonds of regulation. At the other extreme are voluntary associations, and informal organizations with relatively loose bonds of regulation.

This point has an interesting sidelight. A bureaucracy with tight controls and a high degree of predictability of human action appears to be unable to distinguish between destructive and creative deviations from established values. Thus the only thing which is safeguarded is the *status quo*.

[4]The monolithic institutions of the military and government are other cases of organizational preoccupation.

[5]James D. Mooney and Alan C. Reiley, *Onward Industry* (New York: Harper and Brothers, 1931). Later published by James D. Mooney under the title *Principles of Organization*.

[6]E. F. L. Brech, *Organization* (London: Longmans, Green and Company, 1957).

[7]Louis A. Allen, *Management and Organization* (New York: McGraw-Hill Book Company, 1958).

[8]Usually the division of labor is treated under a topical heading of departmentation, see for example: Harold Koontz and Cyril O'Donnell, *Principles of Management* (New York: McGraw-Hill Book Company, 1959), chapter 7.

[9]These processes are discussed at length in Ralph Currier Davis, *The Fundamentals of Top Management* (New York: Harper Brothers, 1951), chapter 7.

[10]For a discussion of structure, see William H. Newman, *Administrative Action* (Englewood Cliffs, New Jersey: Prentice-Hall, Incorporated, 1951), chapter 16.

[11]V. A. Graicunas, "Relationships in Organization," *Papers on the Science of Administration* (New York: Columbia University, 1937).

[12]Brech, *op. cit.,* p. 78.

[13]See F. J. Roethlisberger and William J. Dickson, *Management and the Worker* (Cambridge: Harvard University Press, 1939).

[14]Burleigh B. Gardner and David G. Moore, *Human Relations in Industry* (Homewood, Illinois: Richard D. Irwin, 1955).

[15]Keith Davis, *Human Relations in Business* (New York: McGraw-Hill Book Company, 1957).

[16]For example, see Delbert C. Miller and William H. Form, *Industrial Sociology* (New York: Harper and Brothers, 1951).

[17]See Hugo Munsterberg, *Psychology and Industrial Efficiency* (Boston: Houghton Mifflin Company, 1913).

[18]Probably the classic work is Elton Mayo, *The Human Problems of an Industrial Civilization* (Cambridge: Harvard University, 1946, first printed 1933).

[19]For further discussion of the human relations implications of the scalar and functional processes, see Keith Davis, *op. cit.,* pp. 60–66.

[20]Melville Dalton, "Conflicts Between Staff and Line Managerial Officers," *American Sociological Review* (June, 1950), pp. 342–351.

[21]J. M. Juran, "Improving the Relationships Between Staff and Line," *Personnel* (May, 1956), pp. 515–524.

[22]Gardner and Moore, *op. cit.,* pp. 237–243.

[23]For example, Brech, *op. cit.,* pp. 27–29, and Allen, *op. cit.,* pp. 61–62.

[24]See Leon Festinger, Stanley Schachter, and Kurt Back, *Social Pressures in Informal Groups* (New York: Harper and Brothers, 1950), pp. 153–163.

[25]For example, see W. Fred Cottrell, *The Railroader* (Palo Alto: The Stanford University Press, 1940), chapter 3.

[26]Except in cases where the existence of an organization is necessary for the continued maintenance of employee interest. Under these conditions the previously informal association may emerge as a formal group, such as a union.

[27]Probably the classic study of resistance to change is Lester Coch and John R. P. French, Jr., "Overcoming Resistance to Change," in Schuyler Dean Hoslett (editor) *Human Factors in Management* (New York: Harper and Brothers, 1951), pp. 242–268.

[28]For example, see Robert Saltonstall, *Human Relations in Administration* (New York: McGraw-Hill Book Company, 1959), pp. 330–331; and Keith Davis,i op. cit., pp. 99–101.

[29]For an example of this approach, see John T. Doutt, "Management Must Manage the Informal Group, Too," *Advanced Management* (May, 1959), pp. 26–28.

[30]See Roethlisberger and Dickson, *op. cit.,* chapter 24.

[31]A check of management human relations texts, the organization and human relations chapters of principles of management texts, and texts on conventional organization theory for management courses reveals little or not treatment of the concept of the social system.

[32]Lawrence J. Henderson, *Pareto's General Sociology* (Cambridge: Harvard University Press, 1935), p. 13.

[33]There is another question which cannot be treated in the scope of this paper. It asks, what research tools should be used for the study of the system?

[34]James G. March and Herbert A. Simon, *Organizations* (New York: John Wiley and Sons, 1958).

[35]Mason Haire (editor), *Modern Organization Theory* (New York: John Wiley and Sons, 1959).

[36]See Chris Argyris, *Personality and Organization* (New York: Harper and Brothers, 1957), esp. chapters 2, 3, 7.

[37]For a larger treatment of this subject, see George C. Homans, *The Human Group* (New York: Harcourt, Brace and Company, 1950), chapter 5.

[38]E. Wight Bakke, "Concept of the Social Organization," in *Modern Organization Theory,* Mason Haire (editor) New York: John Wiley and Sons, 1959), pp. 60–61.

[39]Mason Haire, "Psychology and the Study of Business: Joint Behavioral Sciences," in *Social Science Research on Business: Product and Potential* (New York: Columbia University Press, 1959), pp. 53–59.

[40]Karl W. Deutsch "On communication Models in the Social Sciences," *Public Opinion Quarterly,* 16 (1952), pp. 356–380.

[41]March and Simon, *op. cit.,* pp. 139–140.

[42]Mervyn L. Cadwallader "The Cybernetic Analysis of Change in Complex Social Organization," *The American Journal of Sociology* (September, 1959), p. 156.

[43]It is conceivable for innovative behavior to be programmed into the system.

[44]These are questions adapted from Deutsch, *op. cit.,* pp. 365–370.

[45]Answers to these questions would require a comprehensive volume. One of the best approaches currently available is Stafford Beer, *Cybernetics and Management* (New York: John Wiley and Sons, 1959).

[46]March and Simon, *op. cit.,* chapters 3 and 4.

[47]Jacob Marschak, "Efficient and Viable Organizational Forms" in *Modern Organization Theory,* Mason Haire (editor) (New York: John Wiley and Sons, 1959), pp. 307–320.

[48]Kenneth E. Boulding, "General System Theory—The Skeleton of Science," *Management Science* (April, 1956), pp. 200–202.

[49]*Ibid.,* pp. 202–205.

⁵⁰Seidenberg, *op. cit.,* p. 136. The fruitful use of the type of analogies spoken of by Seidenberg is evident in the application of thermodynamic principles, particularly the entrophy concept, to communication theory. See Claude E. Shannon and Warren Weaver. *The Mathematical Theory of Communication* (Urbana: The University of Illinois Press, 1949). Further, the existence of a complete analogy between the operational behavior of thermodynamic systems, electrical communication systems, and biological systems has been noted by Y. S. Touloukian, *The Concept of Entropy in Communication, Living Organisms, and Thermodynamics,* Research Bulletin 130, Purdue Engineering Experiment Station.

⁵¹For example, see Ludwig von Bertalanffy, *Problem of Life* (London: Watts and Company, 1952).

⁵²David Easton, "Limits of the Equilibrium Model in Social Research," in *Profits and Problems of Homeostatic Models in the Behavioral Sciences,* Publication 1, Chicago Behavioral Sciences (1953), p. 39.

EPILOGUE TO SCOTT: AN OVERVIEW SINCE 1960

HENRY TOSI

Since Scott's classic paper appeared in 1961, it is possible to respond to the question, "Organization theory: quo vadis?" For the study of organizations, the 1960s were vigorous years. There were different ways of looking at organizations, their members, and their management. Perhaps the most dominant theme is a point of view which has come to be called "contingency theory."

Contingency theory is an approach to organizations which posits that the appropriate form of organization and the best way to manage it is dependent (contingent) on the nature of the organization's environment. The classic bureaucracy, the presumed bedrock of classic approaches, was not an adequate way to represent organizations in the real world. There were some highly rigid organizations and there were some that were not so rigid. To accommodate reality in organization theory it was necessary to add concepts which captured the essence of these alternate forms of organization. This is what contingency approach accomplished.

Contingency theory formulations are based on the compelling logic grounded in the criticisms of classical management and organization theory. These criticisms were developed in two different forms. One set was advanced by the neohumanists (1, 24).* These writers argued with great conviction that the bureaucratic models attributed to the scientific management school, the administrative school, and Weber's bureaucratic model were op-

*Numbered references found in the references at the end of the book.

pressive and nonmotivating to the human condition. Individuals, these writers argued, could not operate effectively under bureaucratic constraints.

March and Simon (1958) best articulated the second criticism. There was not, they said, one best way to manage as the classical writers had implied. There was a need for more logical and theoretical formulations to replace the "proverbs of administration."

Contingency theories proposed alternative forms of organization structure and they were attractive approaches for those who criticized classical management theory. In contingency theories, the neohumanists found an alternative in the stifling bureacracy, the "organic" organization. This is a more humanistic work environment, one in which a more diverse set of human needs could be met. These advocates generally ignored the fact that the organic organization was but one of the two appropriate forms proposed by Burns and Stalker (5). The mechanistic (bureaucratic) organization was equally effective under the appropriate circumstances of environmental placidity.

For those critics of scientific management's advocacy of the "one best way," contingency approaches provided alternative "ways." The classical approaches were, prescriptively, too narrow. The structures and strategies proposed in contingency theories could be cut to fit the problem. Perhaps there was one best way, but it was dependent upon the circumstances. Contingency theories were models which specified the circumstances on which the one best way depended.

The roots of contingency theories are embedded in "natural systems" sociology, a view of organizations which acquired a good deal of currency in the late 1960s. "Natural" models were posed, particularly, as alternatives to the positions advocated by rational organization theorists.

Rational models of organization are based on the premise that an organization's goals could be defined by an elite group (i.e., top management, elected officials, etc.) and then an organization structure could be designed to achieve those objectives. From such a rational position rules, principles, guides, or similar directions could be formulated to design a structure and to manage such an entity. This logic provided the theoretical assumptions which underlie the "principles" school of administration and management.

Natural systems advocates found this "rational" view lacking. They argued, rather convincingly, that such a view of organizations was not only too narrow, but also wrong. Organizations could not be rationally designed because to do so required that goals be defined by organization elites. The natural systems view held that goals could not be defined because the organization must adapt to the external environment to survive. It is, therefore, the environment which determines goals, not the organization's elite. The "natural" systems advocates see organizations as malleable human interaction systems susceptible to external pressures and molded by these pressures.

The natural systems view is further developed in the work of Burns and Stalker (5). In what is perhaps the most elaborate and articulate statement of the differences in organization structure, Burns and Stalker constructed some important concepts for the budding contingency theory of organization. In their studies of several firms in the United Kingdom, they found no consistent patterns of organizational relationships among the successful firms. Some had organization and management systems consistent with traditional management principles while others did not. Burns and Stalker did conclude, however, that there were differences in organizational structures between firms that operated in different types of environments.

In the more placid environment firms were *mechanistic,* a term which has come to connote an organization structure approximating the classic bureaucratic form. The *organic* organization, operating in rapidly changing environments, is a more loosely structured organization with flexible rules and policies. The appropriate organization structure, concluded Burns and Stalker, is dependent upon the rate and the degree of change in both the firm's market and the technology which it uses.

Joan Woodward (50) added to the contingency literature with a study in 100 firms to test the validity of "classical management theory." She found little information when she first examined the data. When she regrouped the firms on the basis of technology, she found that firms with similar production systems had similar structural characteristics (i.e., chains of command, span of control, and so forth). She also found that the importance of a particular subunit in an organization varied, depending on the production technology and the subunit's role in coordination of activities. In small batch technologies, for instance, the development subunit is most important, then production units and then marketing units. In process production systems, the development function still has primary importance, then marketing and finally production.

Lawrence and Lorsch (20) studied firms in the plastics industry, food manufacturers, and container firms. These firms were selected, *a priori,* because they were in settings with different degrees of environmental uncertainty. Lawrence and Lorsch found, generally, that there is a different level of differentiation and integration required for each environment, depending on the degree of uncertainty. The more dynamic the environment, the greater the degree of differentiation and the more important the role of integrating units.

Thompson's *Organizations in Action* was essentially an argument that rational models and natural systems models were not at counterpoint, as was suggested earlier (43).

> Technical rationality is a necessary component but never enough to provide *organizational rationality* which involves acquiring the inputs which are taken for granted by the technology and dispensing inputs which are again outside the scope of the core technology.
>
> Technical and organizational rationality must occur within the constraints, or contingencies, of the environment.

Organizations in Action was perhaps the most elaborate contingency theory to that point in time. Unlike other theoretical formulations up to that date which resulted from a research program [e.g., Burns and Stalker, (5); Woodward,

(20); Lawrence and Lorsch, (50)] Thompson (43) developed a systematic set of related propositions about how the rational organization would act toward and react to its "domains" in order to operate its technical core.

Another important, though neglected aspect of Thompson's work, is his effort to bring into contingency theory "the variable human." This is an important point in that it is necesary to integrate concepts about human behavior such as motivation, leadership, groups and group processes into the fabric of organization theory.

SUMMARY

Contingency theories have been a prominent part of the literature of organization theory, organizational behavior and management since the early 1960s. By the late 1960s and early 1970s, these approaches were thought to hold strong potential as models for new, more powerful theories of how organizatons develop, how people in them behave, and how these human systems could be effectively managed.

This would have been a welcome and an important development. It would provide the discipline—organization science—with a dominant theoretical theme which could serve as a basis for future theory development and research. Organization science currently lacks such a paradigm, without which it is unlikely to find wide acceptance outside its own boundaries as a scholarly pursuit. Other branches of administrative studies such as finance, accounting, and marketing are firmly grounded in economics, statistics, and mathematics.

Organization science draws, in a piecemeal fashion, from industrial and social psychology, sociology, cultural anthropology and political science. The fragments from these diverse social sciences have yet to be drawn together into any sort of logical, theoretical, and widely accepted model. The current state of the field, at best, consists of a set of relatively tight but narrow theoretical formulations in organization behavior such as reinforcement theory, attribution theory, and so forth. At worst, the field is given meaning by metaphors such as seesaws (6) and garbage cans (16). Like projective tests, the loose configuring of concepts can be construed as the observer chooses.

It is disappointing that, to this point, theoretical development in organization science has not progressed to any significant degree beyond the level in the late 1960s. To be sure, there is an extensive and increasingly rigorous body of empirical research on human problems in organization though this has led to little, if any, theoretical enhancement.

THREE
THE CLASSICAL APPROACH

Skim this one

The classical theorists, as described by Scott, deal extensively with the anatomy of formal organization. The work of Ralph C. Davis is representative of this approach. In it he deals with most of the variables typically associated with this school of thought.

Davis' work falls into the group that James Thompson(43) calls "administrative management," part of the closed system strategy for studying organization. This is a "rational" approach to organization. Once goals of the organization have been determined, or specified, then the development of structure, the flow of authority, and the other relationships clearly follow in a logical fashion. It is, however, important to note that such a strategy does not preclude other important considerations.

Before we delve more deeply into the structure of the theory, let us comment on two of its major aspects, the nature of objectives and the authority/responsibility question.

Davis has as a point of departure the notion that the primary objective of a business organization is an economic service. This is based on the simple question of survival. There is no justification for an economic organization that is not providing economic values. Therefore, to survive, the firm must produce some salable values. These values are created by work and they are the beginning point of the logical development of structure; that is, organization structure needs to be developed in a way that will facilitate providing these values to the consuming public of the organization. Translation of these objectives into products, or services, leads to the determination of activities necessary to create them. These activities are grouped together in such a way as to form the structure of the organization. It does not seem unreasonable to conclude in terms of hierarchy and distribution of authority that the structure of the organization, since it is contingent upon the objectives, depends upon what the objective is.

The second aspect for comment is authority. The notion of authority parallels that of other classical organization theorists. Authority is viewed as a function of, or contingent upon, the position to which one is assigned in the organization and it derives from the duties and obligations attendant to the particular job or assignment.

To achieve the goals of the organization—that is, to provide the values expected by the consumers—certain activities must be performed. Carrying out these activities is the responsibility of the individual in the position. Thus, responsibility is the obligation to perform an assignment which one accepts when he or she takes a position with an organization. In order to carry out these obligations, the individual must be able to utilize, direct, and allocate both physical and human resources. When these are at the person's disposal, and this is formally specified, then his or her "right" to utilize them has been determined. In this situation the person is said to have "authority."

The notion of formal authority, as used in the classical approach, is not an active, or an action, concept. It does not imply that members will take some action that is prescribed for them or that the holder of these rights to utilize resources will exercise them. It refers only to the organizational right of the incumbent. Another concept is required to activate compliance. Power is the "force which maintains the right." When power is exerted, some action will be taken by the subordinates. This power may be physical, or it may be moral, but it is power, not rights, which activates compliance.

What makes this authority legitimate? Because it has been treated so often in the literature of organization theory, this seems an important question. The basis for the legitimation of authority in the Davis formulation, as well as in those by other classical writers, rests on how it is related to the right of private property. Individuals have rights to utilize their property, within some constraints, as they see fit. The right of the private business organization to use resources depends upon the delegation, to the owners of the business, of the property rights by organized society through its representatives. The right of an executive to plan, organize, and control the use by the business organization is a right delegated by ownership.

Within the organization, of course, the amount of authority and responsibility in any one position is a function largely of the manner and the degree in which the general objectives have been factored into activities and responsibilities for that position. Therefore, the right of a manager (or his authority), at any level in the organization, can be traced back to the property rights of individuals in the society in general.

The concept of authority in the classical theory deals with formal, documented rights. It does not include reasons why individuals comply. Since there is generally only limited treatment of reasons why people comply with demands from authority in the classical theory, a number of criticisms of the theory have emerged. This has led to points of view about authority that are expressed in other theories presented in this book—H.L.T.

"FUNDAMENTALS OF TOP MANAGEMENT"*

RALPH C. DAVIS

Management is the function of executive leadership. Its organic subfunctions are the creative planning, organizing, and controlling of the organizational activities for which the executive is responsible. They have to do with the accomplishment of the group and project objectives of the organization.

Creative planning provides the answers to such questions as what should be done, how and where it should be done, who should do it, what physical and human resources are necessary for the accomplishment of the particular mission, and other questions of a similar nature. Its purpose is to determine an effective, economical basis for the accomplishment of designated objectives.

Organizing sets up the common basic conditions that underlie effective, economical execution by a particular group over a period of time. They must be created before work starts on the kinds of activities for which they are a prerequisite. These general conditions are specified in the plan, or derived from it.

Controlling constrains and regulates action in accordance with the requirements of the plan. Business standards are criteria that enable us to measure, proportion, and maintain business factors, forces, and effects in proper condition and relation to one another. They are necessary for the satisfactory performance of all management functions. Effective economical execution requires these conditions and relationships to be adequately standardized.

There must be and is a body of related knowledge that concerns the solution of management problems. The pioneers in the field recognized this fact clearly at the turn of the century. They saw the need for a science of management. The term science seems to perturb some people unnecessarily. It may refer to any classified body of fundamental facts, principles, and techniques that explains certain basic phenomena. It supplies a basis for the solution of problems associated with these phenomena.

Scientific management attempts to apply the logic of effective thinking to the solution of business problems. It depends on and leads to a further development of a philosophy of management. The latter is any system of thought that explains basic business problems. It is based on logical relationships between business factors, forces, effects, and principles. It must supply the basis for an intelligent approach to the solution of these problems. The principal problems have to do with business objectives, standards of business conduct, executive leadership, business policy, business functions, personnel, physical performance factors, organization structure, business procedure, and organization morale.

The consuming public does not exist to serve the owners and employees of business organizations. Business exists to serve the public. The sanctions that enable the owners of business establishments to engage in private enterprise rest on the individual's right of private property in his capital. This right is the basis of free enterprise. The sanctions that enable either executive or operative employees to engage in individual or collective bargaining are based on the individual's right of private property in his services. The right is the basis of free labor. The right of private property is delegated by the body politic through its elected representatives. It can be modified if it is abused by either labor or capital. It has been so abused in the past. Such modifications move in the direction of state capitalism and socialism, even though they may be necessary.

There are certain obligations that are a condition of the granting of the right of private property for the performance of economic functions. They have to do basically with the obligation to provide the public with the goods and services it requires in the quantities and qualities it desires, when and where it wants them and at a competitive price. They require the maintenance of free competition and free markets for both capital and labor, subject to such a minimum of government regulation as may be necessary in the public interest. They require the maintenance of the customer's right of freedom of choice in the market to the maximum degree that is practicable.

An objective is any value or values that are needed or desired by an individual or group, provided that the person or group is willing to make some sacrifice or effort to obtain them. An economic value is any satisfaction of need or a desire for which an individual or group is willing to exchange other values. These values may or may not be tangible. The primary objective of the business organization is necessarily its service objectives. They are customer satisfactions, in terms of business' basic obligation to supply goods and services as required. The desire or need of owners for a profit and of employees for a wage are collateral objectives. They are earned to the extent that the public is well served. The business organization also has certain secondary objectives. They have to do with economy and effectiveness in the performance of business functions. They are set up by the obligation to serve the public at a competitive price.

The general relations between business objectives may be summarized as follows: The primary objective of the business organization is an economic service. A profit is a personal objective of owners. Wages, salaries, bonuses, and related benefits are the personal objectives of executive and operative employees. Any personal objectives are necessarily collateral business objectives. There are many subclasses of these objectives. The accomplishment of any objectives must conform to accepted standards of business conduct.

Values must be created by work. Business objectives condition accordingly the work of the organization. They are the starting points of business thought and action. The determination and analysis of objectives involve forecasting. Many techniques for estimating and specifying the objective have been developed. Their importance suggests that further development of them may be expected.

An organization basically is any group of individuals who are cooperating to a common end under the guidance of leadership. A particular organization may be good, bad, or indifferent from the standpoint of objectives, policies, or any other criterion. A leader is anyone who accepts responsibility for the accomplishment of group objectives. He must usually discharge this responsibility to the satisfaction of the group. Otherwise, there may be a loss of morale and organizational effectiveness that may cost him his position. He is expected to motivate, coordinate, and direct the organization, or some element of it, in the achievement of its objectives.

Satisfactory accomplishment implies an effective, economical performance of both managerial and operative functions. The requirements and conditions of such accomplishment change as our society develops and our economy changes accordingly. There have been and are various kinds, grades, and conditions of executive leadership in business organizations. A great business leader who was successful in one era might not be successful in the next. The conditions of executive leadership under a war economy are different from those in peacetime. The founder of a business often lacks the executive ability to lead it successfully from its pioneer stage through the stage of exploitation to the stage of relative stabilization. Leadership that is successful during a period of inflation may be unable to lead the organization successfully through a period of depression. Positive leadership is usually more effective than negative leadership in the long run. There are times, however, when negative leadership is necessary for the successful handling of disciplinary cases or emergency situations. The leadership responsibilities of the administrative executive are related to but different from those of the operative executive. It is evident that any formula for continuing executive success must be open to question. There are principles of effective executive leadership. They are the principles of good management.

Administrative management is chiefly group management. Operative management is chiefly project management. The former is concerned largely with long-time projections of the activities of organizational groups. Operative management is concerned largely with short-time action in the execution of specific projects. Usually they must be accomplished with reference to time objectives in the immediate future. Other fundamental distinctions between administrative and operative management . . . account partly for the fact that many capable operative executives are unable to rise to top business leadership.

The big financial rewards are found in the echelon of top administrative management. They supply much of the incentives that induce bright, ambitious young men to strive for advancement in an organization. There is no easy road to success, however. These rewards are usually paid for inspiration rather than for perspiration. There is a high rate of obsolescence among executives who are too "practical" to keep abreast of the developing science of management.

Policy is a basic factor in business organization. A business policy is essentially a principle or group of related principles, and their consequent rules of action. They condition and govern the successful achievement of certain business objectives toward which they are directed. A principle is an expression of the relationships between cause and effect in a particular problem. It is a statement of these relationships that is accepted as a significant truth. A good statement of sound policy supplies, therefore, a cogent relationship between business objectives and ideals on the one hand, and organizational functions, physical factors, and personnel on the other. Sound policy is obviously a requisite for sound planning. A statement of policy, express or implied, is often found in the statement of a plan. Nevertheless, a policy is not a plan.

The policy-making function breaks down into certain definite phases. They are policy formulation, promulgation, education, acceptance, application, interpretation, and control. They are part of any executive job in some degree. Much of the top executive's time is spent on problems of general administrative policy. Such policies enter into long-range planning and the subsequent work of organizing. Rules, on the other hand, are restrictive. They enter into control. Even a minor operative executive occasionally makes rules for the guidance of operatives under his supervision. If not, he must interpret rules that have been made by his superior. These rules must be made within the framework of the broader policies that are originated on higher levels.

The intelligence with which policies are made and applied can stimulate or depress the morale of the organization. Unity of action depends on unity of thought. Effective accomplishment depends on unity of action. A common body of principle is an important factor in the development of unity of thought. There appears, in consequence, to be a growing tendency to commit important policies to writing in the form of policy manuals and rule books. There is also a tendency to link management's policy-making responsibilities more closely with the lower echelons of the business organization in which they are applied. Executives on operative levels are included in the work of policy formulation to a greater degree, through application of the Principle of Participation. Policy control in large organizations tends to be decentralized.

Business functions are the work of accomplishing the various objectives of the business organization. The nature and amount of this work depend on the characteristics and requirements of these objectives. Business is an economic institution. Its objectives are primarily economic. The mission of the business organization is to supply the portion of the public which it serves with certain goods and services. Structural and procedural planning for an organization rests necessarily on some theory of functionalization. Any such theory in business organization must rest on the concept of economic utility. Such utility may be defined as the ability of an economic good or service to supply the customer with the satisfactions of his needs or desires for which he spends his money. He may transfer his patronage to a competitor if he does not get these satisfactions in satisfactory amounts. The customer still has the right of freedom of choice in the market place. The attributes of the product or service that give it the required utilities are its quality attributes. They are so recognized in industry by marketing experts, engineering executives, and quality managers.

The organic functions of a business establishment are, therefore, the creation of economic utilities, the distribution of these utilities, and the provision of the capital that is necessary for the performance of the first two functions. They are the functions of production, distribution, and finance in a manufacturing establishment. They are different in other basic types of economic institutions, except for the common function of finance.

All chains of command within a business organization stem originally from one of its organic functions. They develop, by the processes of functional differentiation, with increasing business volume and consequent organizational growth. The devolution of a line organization leads directly downward to a division of operative work and specialization in the creation of primary service values. Finance is an exception to this statement . . .A staff organization evolves from a line organization. It makes possible a division of managerial work and specialization in the creation of collateral or secondary service values. It may be appended to a line organization at any level where such managerial service is needed. It cannot be part of the line organization however. Both line and staff functions have their executive and operative phases. There are no distinctions between them in this respect. There are various distinguishing characteristics, of course. One simple test of a staff function is this: Does its devolution lead directly to specialization in the creation or distribution of salable values? If it does not, it is probably staff.

Functions must be grouped on a logical basis as they are differentiated from one another. This basis should permit the development of good cooperation, coordination, and leadership. There are various principles of functionalization that underlie structural and procedural planning. They have these objectives in view. Some functions are similar to one another. They have similar objectives, factors, and difficulties. They require for their performance personnel having similar background, training, experience, personality, and other attributes. We may group functions in accordance with these similarities. We may relate these groups by lines of responsibility and authority. The result is some form of organization structure. Some functions are complementary to one another. They produce values that are a prerequisite for other values that must be produced subsequently in accomplishing the mission. These functions may be grouped in steps in its accomplishment. They may be related to one another on the basis of their complementary nature, but with due regard for organizational lines. The result is some form of business procedure. All business functions have complementary and similar characteristics with respect to other related functions.

The complexity of functionalization necessarily increases as the volume of business grows. There is some evidence that this complexity tends to increase in geometric progression. Much of it is a result of staff organization growth. Staff contributes necessary collateral and secondary values. Otherwise the staff personnel would not be retained on the payroll. It is overhead expense, nevertheless. This suggests that there is an optimum size for a business establishment. Yet a rising standard of living requires increasing aggregations of capital and labor in some industries. "Bigness" in business organizations is not bad *per se*. If it were, the difficulty could not be cured by bigger state trusts that are run by governmental functionaries. The answer in business organization is usually some form and degree of economic integration and decentralization. It is not necessarily dissolution.

The problems of business functionalization are not simple. The design of organization structure and procedure has become, in consequence, an increasingly important part of the work of administrative planning in large organizations. Some good techniques for functional investigation and analysis have been developed. Some sound principles of functionalization have been established. Nevertheless, the subject can benefit from more research.

Effective performance, in any organized activity, requires a delegation of responsibility and authority. This is true for both executive and operative performance. Responsibility is an individual rather than a group phenomenon. It is the obligation that an individual acquires in any organization when he accepts an assignment of certain objectives, functions, and duties. An executive responsibility is an obligation to perform leadership functions under certain conditions. It necessarily involves the direction and supervision of others. An operative responsibility is an obligation to perform, to the best of one's ability, certain assigned duties, under executive direction, in the accomplishment of a particular project. An operative responsibility does not involve direction and supervision of the work of others. Authority is the term for the rights that are necessary for the satisfactory discharge of one's organizational obligations. Executive authority includes, therefore, the rights of decision and command with respect to the organizational activities of one's subordinates. Operative authority includes such rights of decision as are necessary for the proper performance of assigned operative duties.

Accountability is a condition of membership in an organization. It requires that each member must render a report of his discharge of responsibilities, and be judged fairly on the basis of his record of accomplishment. Such judgments rest on qualitative and quantitative evaluations of individual and group performance. These evaluations result chiefly from the performance of the control functions of supervision and comparison. They determine the extent to which the individual has accomplished the assigned objectives. The operative employee is accountable for the accomplishment of operative objectives that have been assigned to him. The executive employee is accountable for the results accomplished by the individuals and groups who are working under his direction. The principal phases of the problem are: (1) analysis of objectives, (2) functional analysis with respect to the requirements for the accomplishment of these objectives, (3) functional grouping and the division of responsibility as a basis for structural and procedural design, (4) determination of the authority required for each allocation of functions and responsibility, (5) the delegation of responsibility and authority, (6) the establishment of control, and (7) the development of accountability. Many problems are involved. The economy and effectiveness with which the organization accomplishes its mission depend on how well they are solved.

The division, allocation, and delegation of responsibility rest on whatever groupings of functions have been made. They may be line or staff. The ultimate unit function, in any case, is a single, simple act of operative performance, either mental or physical. It must have definite points of starting and stopping. This concept enters directly into the techniques of motion and time study. The motion principles associated with it enter directly into the desgin of organization structure, however. The ultimate unit of operative responsibility is the obligation of an operative employee to perform assigned duties within his job classification. It is based on the general work assignment that is set up in his job specification. The ultimate unit of executive responsibility is the unit of operative supervision. It is the number of units of operative responsibility that is suitable for direction and the exercise of face-to-face leadership by a first-level supervisory executive. Experience indicates that the size of this supervisory unit tends to range from ten to thirty operatives. The reasons have to do with the economy and effectiveness of supervisory leadership. There is also an effective, economical unit of executive supervision. Experience indicates that its size tends to range from three to eight or nine subordinate executives. The relations in organization structure between these units of operative and executive supervision have an important influence on the success of the organization.

The value of the contribution that an individual is required to make increases with the service level on which he works. There is some good evidence that it tends to increase in geometric progression. A given job is and should be worth more in a big concern than in a small one. The importance of the individual in organization success tends to vary inversely with organization size, nevertheless. The "indispensable men" are more likely to be found in small concerns than in large ones. The division and allocation of responsibility may be made in the former with respect to the individual ability and know-how of the present executive personnel. The supply of leadership material may be quite limited in the small organization. In the big concern, it may be made largely with respect to the requirements of functions for proper performance. Any modifications of sound organizational relationships to suit the inadequacies of present personnel are likely to be temporary. The large organization tends to have greater stability and permanence for these and other reasons.

A delegate is a person who is appointed to represent and act for another. Any subordinate, whether executive or operative, is in a sense a delegate of the superior executive to whom he reports directly. The process of delegation is one whereby certain of the executive's functions, responsibilities, and authorities are released and committed to designated subordinate positions. Responsibility and authority are attributues of the job. Delegation enables an executive to extend his abilities beyond the limits of his personal powers. It makes possible a division of labor and the development of specialization, whether executive or operative. It may stimulate or depress organization morale, depending on how well it is done. It has other effects on the organization. It is, accordingly, an important managerial problem. There are various principles of delegation. An understanding of them is an important part of an executive's know-how.

Decentralization takes place when a higher central source of responsibility and authority assigns certain functions to subordinate individuals and groups. These functions may be managerial or operative, line or staff. Their decentralization is accomplished through delegation. Any assignment of functions to subordinates should be accompained by adequate delegation of responsibility and authority. Otherwise the individual cannot justly be held accountable for results. There are various advantages and disadvantages of decentralization. There are various principles and conditions that govern the extent to which it is practicable. This extent tends to vary directly with the size of the organization. There are some obvious limitations, however. Delegation cannot result in the abdication of one's responsibilities and authorities. There is no direct relation between processes of delegation and the democratic process. The latter is a political concept. The business organization is an economic institution, under a condition of free enterprise and the right of private property.

Organization structure is the structure of relationships between groups of similar functions, physical factors, and personnel. These relationships have to do largely with responsibility, authority, and accountability. They affect organizational morale. It is possible, therefore, to have a good organization structure, a beautiful organization chart, and a poor organization. An effective, economical accomplishment of assigned objectives is not characteristic of poor organizations.

There are only two basic forms of organization structure: line and staff. All other forms are variants of them. The "line" is the primary form. It is the backbone of the organization. A primary hierarchy of functions leads directly from an organic business function to a division of primary operative labor. It is an effect of functional differentiation. It results directly in specialization in the creation and distribution of salable values. A primary chain of command is the hierarchy of responsibility, authority, and accountability that is related directly to the primary functional hierarchy. A primary line organization is the present hierarchy of individuals, both managerial and operative, who perform line functions. The necessary responsibility and authority for such performance should be delegated to their job assignments. All staff groups exist to serve the line organizations, or other staff groups, for this reason. The tendency in most business concerns has been to resist the transfer of line authority to staff groups. Such transfer tends to break down the line organization. It leads to the defeat of the enterprise in the battle of competition, as it approaches a condition of complete functionalization.

The growth and devolution of the line organization begins, theoretically, with the owner-manager. Some concerns have actually started from this point. It results increasingly in the grouping of primary operative functions on one or more of the following bases: (1) product, commodity, or service, (2) process or method, (3) equipment or other dominant physical factors, and (4) the physical dispersion of business activities on a geographical basis.

These functions must be grouped in units of operative and executive supervision. The relationships that should exist between these units are primary determinants of line organization form. The basic relationships between them can be expressed mathematically. Such relationships assist in the provisional determination of the number of major service levels or echelons that are needed by an organization. They help in determining general criteria of the number of line executives required by the organization at various levels. They underlie the solution of other organizational problems. An application of these relationships results in some interesting conclusions. Very few major echelons are required to command a very large organization. The percentage of line executives to primary operatives should increase very little with organization growth. Top executive payroll is and should be insignificant, relative to the total payroll of the organization and the contributions of effective top leadership. Other significant conclusions may be drawn. It should of course be remembered that there is no mathematical substitute for executive judgment. A concern does not manage by formulas.

The structural form of the small organization is predominately line. The characteristics of line organization make its use particularly advantageous in the small business. Its advantages may be lost with organizational growth. This will take place unless the line is supplemented increasingly with staff organization. Management must be decentralized increasingly without loss of control of the organization's activities. Lack of organizational know-how may limit the growth of the small business much as the competition of big business, and possibly more.

Staff organization structure is an evolution from a primary functional hierarchy. It is made necessary chiefly by increases in the load of managerial work and increasing requirements for specialized background, training, experience, and ability. Hence it has to do with a division and specialization of managerial labor. It takes place necessarily above the level of operative performance. A staff organization, accordingly, assists the line and other staff organizations in the performance of some phase of an organic managerial function. It usually performs some facilitative services in addition. The nature, extent, and degree of staff performance are determined and limited by delegation.

The basic classification of staff functions must rest, therefore, on the classification of organic managerial functions. These functions are the creative planning, organizing, and controlling of the activities of organizational members in the accomplishment of a common objective. Technical staff functions assist the organization in planning. They may assist it by performing certain specialized functions that are purely facilitative. They may do both. They require a certain specialized background, training, and experience for their performance. They may or may not be professional, however. Coordinative staff functions assist the organization in control. They too may perform certain facilitative functions. Successful performance of staff control functions usually requires breadth of background, training, and experience, rather than intensity. There are no staff groups that specialize solely in organizing.

All managerial functions, whether line or staff, have their operative phases. This is evident, since all functional devolution leads to operative specialization, either primary or secondary. Staff objectives are principally secondary. Staff organizations supply values that the line organization must have for the accomplishment or primary objectives. The latter are certain utilities in goods or services. They enable the customer to enjoy the values for which he pays his money. It is evident that staff objectives and functions are necessarily secondary in incidence of service to the public. They are not necessarily secondary in the importance and value of their contributions, however.

Organizational growth, whether line or staff, tends to follow a typical structural pattern. It is helpful in analyzing structural problems, if it does not result in a formulistic approach to organizational planning. Any general pattern must be modified and adjusted to fit the realities of the particular situation. We saw, during the the discussion of organization structure, that the assigned mission of a staff group, and the conditions under which it must be accomplished, govern the detailed form that this pattern tends to take. It is evident that the devolution of a technical staff function must lead to professional or other operative specialization in planning, when the principal objective of the staff group is certain types of plans. The engineering department is a classic example. The devolution of a technical staff function must lead to professional or other operative specialization in facilitation, when the principal objective of the staff group is facilitative assistance. The devolution of a coordinative staff function must lead to operative specialization in control. Such specialization must be based on the organic staff phases of control. Any supporting planning services or associated services of facilitation for any staff organization must be placed in a secondary technical staff function in business organization, regardless of how vitally important it may be and how great its development is in the particular concern. Any supporting control services also must be placed in a secondary coordinative staff position. Such a position means that the particular function is attached directly to a secondary chain of command in a staff relationship.

Any staff organization is overhead. There is nothing scientific about an elaborate, complicated, and expensive staff organization that is not needed. It is not good business on the other hand to refuse to spend money for staff organization that is needed.

The development and growth of staff organization results from the growth in the demand for the company's services. It is both a cause and an effect of business success. The development of staff services has to do largely with the development and expansion of the basic staff duties. These duties are (1) investigation, including research, (2) analysis of facts and information, (3) interpretation, including services of information, (4) recommendation, including the formulation of plans, (5) coordination, including assistance in control, and (6) facilitation, including assistance in organizing and executing plans. Such development often requires continuing staff evolution with business growth. The principal stages of staff evolution are (1) line integration, (2) distinct staff differentiation, (3) complete staff differentiation. (4) staff integration, (5) staff elevation, (6) staff decentralization, and (7) complete staff separation. It is not necessary that all staff development begin with the first stage. It is not necessary either that the development of all staff functions be carried through to the final stage. It is helpful in diagnosing present staff difficulties to be able to recognize the stage of development of the particular staff organization. One must of course know the basic requirements for staff economy and effectiveness that are associated with this stage. It is helpful in organizational planning for staff growth to know the subsequent stages and their requirements. Such knowledge should be part of the professional background of the modern executive. In too many cases, it is not.

There has been increasing interest, in recent years, in top administrative management. The importance of top leadership in rapidly changing situations is apparent. The desirability of relieving top executives of some of the burden of administrative management has been realized. Some interesting developments in the field of top administrative staff organization have taken place as a result.

A staff organization that assists the chief executive in administrative planning is concerned with interdivisional coordination of thought. It is concerned, therefore, with problems of top administrative organization structure, procedure, general policies and objectives, and the general condition of organizational morale. It has close relations necessarily with financial planning. It does not do the work of any major technical staff division. Such divisions are still responsible for the development of plans and policies for activities within their fields of specialization. A vice-president in charge of personnel and industrial relations, for example, is still responsible for developing and recommending personnel plans and policies. A staff executive for administrative planning merely achieves a meeting of minds between the immediate line and staff subordinates of the chief executive. Any resulting plans are subject to the latter's approval.

A staff organization that assists the chief executive in adminsitrative control is concerned largely with the interdivisional coordination. Much of the work at this level has to do with long-range planning. Accordingly, it is concerend with progress in the accomplishment of planning projects. It is concerned subsequently with the progress of the major divisions of the business in organizing for the execution of plans. It must evaluate divisional performance in the accomplishment of assigned objectives. Administrative control deals with the constraint and regulation of group action in the completion of administrative projects. These projects may extend over considerable time periods—a month, a quarter, a year, or longer. It is not concerned directly with the current execution of operative projects and their schedules. General administrative control performs its functions at the top administrative level of the organization.

There are a great many structural problems, such as the difficulties associated with functional emergence; the location of dissimilar staff functions; the duties, responsibilities, and authority of headquarters staff executives; the development of staff parallelism; the use and limitations of committees; and many others. They greatly affect the development of top administrative organization. Much more information concerning their characteristics and requirements would be helpful. The literature of business management deals largely with the discussion of technical and coordinative staff problems at the various levels of operative management. It is only in comparatively recent years that we have been getting some worth-while contributions from executives with practical experience in top administrative management. It is probable that the next great advance in managerial science will take place in this area.

The United States is committed to the policy that the standard of living of its people must increase continuously. An ultimate objective is the maximum average living standard that is practicable at any point in time. Progress has been uneven, with many temporary setbacks, for a number of reasons. They have to do with the errors of omission and commission of our economic and political leadership, the weaknesses of an industrial democracy that must be based on the right of private property, and many other factors that are well known. The result has been, nevertheless, a strong, upward growth trend in a dynamic, industrial economy. These objectives and policies place certain responsibilities on business for the maintenance of a corresponding growth in the number and size of the business establishments that serve our people. Such business growth inevitably creates many major organizational problems within the business establishment. These responsibilities require executives to understand the attributes of business organization that are required for growth. They are, in general, the attributes of good organization anywhere. The principal ones are (1) effective executive leadership, (2) sound business objectives and policies, (3) sound functional relationships as determined by objectives, (4) adequate physical implementation that will make possible an economical, effective accomplishment of objectives, (5) a complement of abilities, both executive and operative, to handle present business problems economically and effectively, (6) organizational stability, (7) organizational flexibility, (8) organizational capacity for growth, (9) organizational balance, and (10) good organizational morale.

The first five of these attributes were discussed earlier in this chapter. The remaining five require further comment. Organizational stability is the quality that enables an organization to adjust itself promptly to personnel losses without serious losses of economy or effectiveness. Organizational flexibility is the quality that enables it to adjust itself to temporary changes in business volume and conditions without serious losses of economy or effectiveness. Many concerns have done a good job of developing these organizational attributes. Most concerns appear to have done a poor job of developing capacity for growth. The exceptions are found usually among large, successful corporations. This attribute may be defined as the ability of an organization to adjust its personnel and structure to permanent changes in business volume, without serious losses of economy or effectiveness. It is concerned usually with the permanent expansion and development of the organization. This is likely to be a continuing problem, as long as our economy is expanding. Growth is a requirement, in some industries, for the maintenance of competitive effectiveness. Many concerns do not conform to the requirements of this definition, because they handle growth problems on the basis of short-range planning, trial and error, and expediency. Their weaknesses show up quickly when they are forced to expand to a large size quickly during a war emergency.

Some of the greatest failures of executive leadership have been in the field of morale. It has appeared, at times, as though anyone could take away from the executive the leadership of his employees by the simple expedient of offering something for nothing. It is possible that this has been another effect of too many business mechanics and too few professional executives who are capable of exercising economic statesmanship.

Morale is a mental condition of individuals and organizations. It determines their attitudes. As a result, it conditions the degree of acceptance of executive leadership by organization members. It governs the quality of their cooperation in the accomplishment of organizational objectives. Good organizational morale is a condition in which individuals and groups voluntarily make a reasonable subordination of their personal objectives to the service objectives of their organization. An industrial society can be overthrown by the destruction of the morale of its industrial organizations. There is an organizational Principle of the Primacy of the Service Objective. It says that an organization may fail when any important individuals or groups in it succeed in placing their personal interests ahead of its interests for any considerable period of time.

The morale-building process is, accordingly, a process of integrating interests. It is any process that develops and maintains identities and interdependencies between the organization's service objectives and the personal objectives of its members. The interests of individuals are most acute with respect to the values they desire for themselves and for those immediately dependent on them. The process has to do, therefore, with creating the conditions that will assure an adequate satisfaction of personal objectives. It must do this in a manner that is compatible with competitive effectiveness.

Confidence in the integrity and ability of executive leadership is an important condition for the successful operation of the morale-building process. There must exist some belief that the present subordination of personal interests to organizational interests will result in worthwhile future benefits for the individual or group. The desired benefits may be tangible or intangible, or both. Surveys of employee interests have indicated, for example, that wages, hours and working conditions are not always the principal considerations of operatives. This may happen when employees in a particular organization generally regard the benefits associated with such considerations to be fair and adequate. Such surveys suggest that a feeling of worthwhileness, a feeling of belonging to an organization in which one can take pride, a feeling of security, or some other intangible value may be the thing that is desired.

The morale problem, like any other, must be broken down into its principal elements before a general method of approach to its solution can be devised. The following are the principal functions in the morale-building process: (1) analyses of individual and group interests and objectives and of their relation to organizational service objectives, (2) establishment of common concepts and yardsticks of value, (3) provision of values that are desired by individuals and groups in the organization in adequate and proper amounts, (4) prompt, equitable adjustments of conflicts between personal and organizational interests as they develop, (5) morale maintenance, including continuous identification of organizational and personal objectives.

No problems can be solved without adequate facts that are reasonably accurate. Various techniques for getting morale facts have been devised. They involve some form of intermittent or continous morale surveys. The former are usually a statistical approach, based on the use of questionnaires. The latter are usually a qualitative approach, based on the use of trained observers. The most effective observers should be line supervisors, provided that they have been trained to do the job and have the ability. The most effective method for getting morale facts is likely to involve a combination of statistical and qualitative techniques.

A distinction between morale factors and morale effects should be made in applying any survey method. The attitudes of individuals and groups toward the organization and its leaders are obviously effects of their state of mind. They directly affect the economy and effectiveness with which the organization accomplishes its mission. Some of the more important effects of good morale are willing cooperation, loyalty to the organization and its leadership, good discipline, and organizational initiative. There are others. A morale index is a relative measure of the attitudes that indicate morale effects.

A morale factor is anything within or outside the organization that affects the personal interests of its members in relation to its own. We saw above that these interests include more than money. A morale stimulant is any factor that tends to produce favorable attitudes toward the organization and its leadership. A morale depresssant is a factor that tends to produce unfavorable attitudes. It is possible for a particular morale factor to be a stimulant and a depressant at different times and under different circumstances. Some of the more common factors in good morale are worthwhile organizational and personal objectives, good leadership based on a sound philosophy of management, homogeneity of group characteristics and interests, decentralization, indoctrination, satisfactory physical work environment, and many others. They should be determined and specified clearly, concisely, and in as much detail as is practicable.

The scale of values that individuals and groups in an organization apply to their interests is obviously an important factor in morale development and maintenance. It is an effect of their philosophy. It affects morale directly, insofar as it bears on the activities of the organization and its leadership. An outside agency has an opportunity to substitute a scale that suits its purposes when the organization's members have no philosophy of their own.

A philosophy is a body of doctrine. The latter term refers to any formal statement, either express or implied, of objectives, ideals, principles, points of view, and general modes of procedure. A doctrine is laid down for the guidance of others, either with or without the authority to compel its acceptance. It can relate to physical or psychical phenomena, or both. The purpose of a managerial philosophy is to make clear the significance of business concepts. It underlies the mission of rendering an economic service for producers and consumers. Proper indoctrination of its members is a leadership responsibility in any type of organization. Business organization is no exception. Complete indoctrination in a business organization is not proper, of course. It is practically impossible, so long as we retain the rights underlying freedom of press, freedom of speech, and freedom of assembly. It is not in the long-term interests of business executives in a competitive society. The process in the business organization is one of self-indoctrination. It is a process of education. . . .

Poor morale cannot be blamed successfully on professional labor leaders. Organizational morale is a responsibility of the organization's leadership. This is not an argument against collective bargaining. Free enterprise, collective bargaining, and individual liberty rest squarely on the right of private property. The destruction of any one of them tends to destroy the right of private property. The destruction of the right of private property tends to destroy them all.

Voluntary cooperation, an intelligent exercise of initiative, self-coordination, and similar values are effects of good morale. They reduce the degree and extent of control that is necessary. Good morale cannot be a substitute for good control, however, even in small organizations. Self-control breaks down quickly with increasing organization size. Increasing executive control must be developed with organizational growth. Otherwise, paradoxically, an organization may fail in accomplishing its mission as a result of its success.

It was noted earlier that the organic functions of management are the creative planning, organizing, and controlling of the activities of the organization's members in the execution of their assigned tasks. They are the functions of executive leadership. The function of control is the work of constraining and regulating such actions in accordance with plans for the accomplishment of specified objectives. The economy and effectiveness of execution and control depend directly on creative planning and organizing. The ultimate objectives of control are, of course, the ultimate service objectives of business. They are, therefore, better customer values. Control coordinates and correlates action in accordance with a plan for the accomplishment of such objectives. The immediate objectives of control are derived from the objectives of the particular plan. They are, in general, (1) assurance of correct performance as specified by the plan, (2) a well-coordinated condition of action, and (3) a minimum of losses due to interferences with the proper execution of the plan.

The two grand divisions of the work of executive leadership are administrative management and operative management. Each division has its line and staff phases. They may be completely differentiated and highly developed in large organizations. Staff functions may exist only potentially in the very small organization. A distinction must be made accordingly between operative control and administrative control. Operative control is chiefly project control. Administrative control is chiefly group control. It is the function of constraining and regulating group action in the completion of assigned programs. The latter summarize the results that are anticipated from the completion of assigned projects during a designated period of time. The cumulation of values resulting from the completion of these projects during this period provides a measure of the degree of accomplishment of organizational objectives. The latter were set up when the program was planned. The facts that are necessary for the operation of a system of administrative control come, then, from the reports originated by the system of operative control on the lower echelons.

Control on any echelon tends to break down into eight basic subfunctions. They are the organic phases of control. They are (1) routine planning, (2) scheduling, (3) preparation, (4) dispatching, (5) direction, (6) supervision, (7) comparison, and (8) corrective action. . . . [The] eight control functions tend to be performed in the order indicated. This temporal order is not mandatory, of course. However, it provides a useful basis for the analysis of control procedure. The line phases of control are direction, supervision, and corrective action. They cannot be differentiated from the line organization and assigned to staff groups, except to a very limited degree with respect to their most routine aspects. The reasons are found in their direct relations to line leadership responsibilities. The remaining five control functions may be assigned to staff control groups in a very high degree.

The extent to which control is exercised by subordinates is governed by the extent to which control responsibilities have been delegated and decentralized. Supervisory executives are responsible only for the line phases of control when the staff phases are highly centralized. They have certain responsibilities for morale maintenance that are inherent in the relation of face-to-face leadership. They have no control responsibilities if they have no obligations and rights with respect to direction, supervision, and corrective action. Their leadership position is undermined. They are not likely to discharge their morale responsibilities satisfactorily in such case. A centralized staff control sets up a completely functionalized relationship. It tends to concentrate responsibility and authority in the hands of higher line executives.

Differing degrees of centralized control may exist within one organization for the same function. The administrative control of production is highly decentralized down to the plant level in large concerns engaged in continuous manufacturing. It is highly centralized within the plant, down to and including plant stores and the production lines. The reasons are found in the principles of decentralization that have been discussed.

Just as morale conditions the quality of control, so control conditions the quality of morale. Disciplinary action, for example, is a phase of corrective action. Good discipline is an effect of good morale. It is a condition of voluntary conformity with policies, rules and regulations. The latter are necessary for coordinated and cooperative action in the accomplishment of group objectives. Good discipline is related to other morale effects such as willing acceptance of executive decisions, voluntary cooperation, and organizational pride. Disciplinary action is a managerial process for conditioning individual and group behavior. Its objectives are the inhibition of improper behavior, the integration of personal and organizational interests, and the assurance of correct action in the future. It accomplishes these objectives by means of penalities or rewards. Disciplinary action has to do, therefore, with the addition or subtraction of certain values in the situation of an individual or a small group. It may be taken with respect to a person, but it should not be personal. The intent is usually to condition the quality of future action by the group of which the individual is a part.

Control may have other important effects. Their implications may go far beyond the limits of the particular undertaking that is being controlled. An understanding of the basic principles and significances of control is an important part of the background of the professional executive.

Business procedure is a basic factor in the performance of organizational functions. It is a relationship of complementary functions that is set up as a basis for the execution of a project. The latter may be managerial or operative. It may be line or staff. It must be planned, in any event, with regard for the requirements for the successful accomplishment of project objectives. It must consider the requirements for human and physical factors in performance, and the limitations of their use that must be observed. The specified procedure is an important part of a project plan, since it supplies a basis of action. The installation of standard procedures is often an important part of the work of organizing.

A procedure specifies, among other things, the order in which the various steps in the accomplishment of the project must be performed. It states the quantitative time requirements for the performance of each step, or indicates where such information may be obtained. A procedure necessarily cuts across organizational lines, because of the complementary nature of its functions. Coordination of action is a control responsibility. It has to do largely with the time and order in which the steps or phases of an undertaking are performed. Business procedure is therefore a basic factor in control.

The economy and effectiveness with which project and organizational objectives are accomplished depend greatly on the quality of procedural planning. The executive head of each group is responsible for developing and using the best methods for the accomplishment of his objectives. A mark of a good executive is ability to make effective use of staff, whether his own or others'. No one usually cares, within reason, how he develops the best methods, provided that he uses them. This concept brings up some interesting problems in line and staff relationships as the organization grows. They must be solved, if the organization is to enjoy continued success.

The objectives of procedural development are secondary values. The principal values are (1) orderliness in the execution of business undertakings, (2) consequent uniformity of results, (3) facilitation of specialization, (4) a more effective and economical utilization of personnel, (5) conservation of executive ability, time, and health, (6) facilitation of executive and self-coordination, and (7) economy and effectiveness in the performance of managerial and operative functions. Responsibility for developing a particular type of business procedure is often delegated to the staff group in whose special field the problem falls. It would be impractical for top line executives, for example, to concern themselves personally with the details of planning a top administrative procedure. This is too important, on the other hand, to be delegated to people with limited ability and then forgotten. The result of such action may be ineffectiveness, high cost, and red tape. A top staff executive for administrative planning can be given staff responsibility for coordinating thought concerning structural planning, procedural planning, and other problems of administrative planning. The scope of his responsibility must be limited to the top administrative echelons. He should be available for consultation when executives on lower echelons are unable to achieve a meeting of minds on their procedural problems. This may be an intelligent compromise. There is some evidence of a trend in this direction.

A profit is a legitimate reward of capital for the successful acceptance of business risk in rendering an economic service. It is necessary for the formation of private capital and the continuation of the free enterprise system. It is necessary for the maintenance of the right of private property, and in consequence the freedom of the individual. Ability to operate a business at a profit should not be the sole criterion of managerial excellence, however. A profit may be a legitimate objective of businessmen. It should not be the primary objective of a business organization. The objective of the latter is an economic service. There are collateral business objectives. Business operations vitally affect the public interest. The sum total of all goods and services produced and distributed by all business enterprises everywhere, great and small, approximates the total national income. It represents the material benefits that support a high standard of living in an industrial economy.

Management is a principal form of economic leadership. Accordingly, the executive in private business has a great public responsibility. This has been recognized increasingly by organized business. One effect has been the development of more professional executives. Their numbers are still too few, however. Their development has been limited by the evolution of a sound philosophy of management. This evolution has been taking place, of course. Such a philosophy will be needed badly if it becomes necessary to expand our industrial organizations quickly for war purposes. It will be needed for the preservation of our democratic institutions when the subsequent contraction of business activities takes place. It will be necessary for a further, sound development of our economy. . . .

FOUR
DECISION-MAKING ORIENTATIONS

The two theories in this chapter—those of Chester Barnard and of James March and Herbert Simon—are together because they are related. The work of March and Simon draws heavily from that of Barnard and there is a substantial degree of conceptual overlap.

There are, however, different points within each theory that have been the focus of those interested in organizational theory. For instance, Barnard's work is most often associated with the "acceptance theory" of authority, while March and Simon's work has often been referred to as a "decision approach" to organizations.

One of the primary thrusts in the attack on the classical theory is toward its treatment of authority, and many have used Barnard's treatment as the main weapon in their arsenal. Barnard has defined authority differently than the classical theorists. To Barnard, authority is not a right but rather the "character of a communication . . . by virtue of which it is accepted by a . . . member." The "acceptance approach" revolves around the necessity of assent of the individual, which will occur when

1. The order is understood.
2. It is in the individual's best interest to comply.
3. The individual perceives it as consistent with the purpose of the organization.
4. The individual is mentally and physically able to comply.

These conditions will prevail if the order is within the individual's "zone of indifference." If all orders were ranked in their order of acceptability, some would be unacceptable, and would therefore not be obeyed. Other orders would be neutral. The remainder the individual would comply with. It is this last group of orders which fall in the zone of indifference. March and Simon have called this same concept the "acceptance zone."

There is no question about compliance, or the acceptability of an order, when it falls within this zone. The individual may act out of habit or may decide to comply because he or she fears the consequences of noncompliance or because he or she desires to satisfy a superior in order to obtain rewards of the system.

The width of the zone of indifference, according to Barnard, depends upon the subordinate's evaluation of the inducements/contribution balance. That is, the greater the individual perceives the surplus of inducements over contributions required, the wider the zone of indifference—and the boundaries of this zone may shift.

But Barnard is describing the "action" side of authority, or the case where one does, in fact, respond. Some have interpreted Barnard's position to mean that authority is "accepted." Actually, the lower participant is one link in an influence process that may be initiated at higher levels. Individuals acquiesce to these influence attempts because they fall within his zone. But what are the reasons for this, beyond the previously mentioned inducements/contributions assessments? Subordinates may respond when a superior acts in an official capacity. Officialness results from the position of the superior. Thus a position may impute a degree of legitimation to the communication. Barnard calls this the "authority of position," yet this is not a great deal different from the concept of authority described in the classical literature. Barnard's concept of authority is different, however, because he is defining it in terms of the response of the subordinate, not in terms of bases of power. Classical theory tends to emphasize primarily one basis, positional power.

March and Simon, in dealing with the "decision to produce," seem to follow closely Barnard's notion of acceptance theory. The individual's motivation to produce is a function of

1. The character and consequences of the evoked set of alternatives.
2. The values the individual compares these to.
3. Group norms.
4. Formal policies and incentive practices.

March and Simon have refined, extended, and supported the hypothetical observations of Barnard by an examination of the empirical research evidence which supports the various propositions.

There are those who have argued that the acceptance theory of authority assumes free will on the part of the individual who is the object of the influence attempt. Krupp (19), for instance, argues that it implies "consent" and that the choice is "free." His use of "consent" and "free," we believe, sets an emotional tone to his argument which is unnecessary. Others, who have criticized the classical theory and subscribed to the acceptance approach, couch their arguments in terms of a democratic bias. Does the zone of indifference or acceptance mean that an individual responds because she or he wishes to? No, we may "accept," though grudgingly, directives that carry negative sanctions. One may not be happy, and may wish to leave the organization, but under these conditions acceptance must mean carrying out the request.

Let us turn briefly to the March and Simon formulation. This has been called a "decision approach" to organizations, but why is this so? March and Simon, and Barnard, devote a great deal of time to a discussion of the individual in an organization, as distinct from looking at the organization as the classicists did. They, and Barnard, posit that an individual in an organization is faced with two major decisions, the decision to participate and the decision to produce. These two decisions are affected by two different sets of factors. The decision to participate is based upon the concept of organizational equilibrium, or the inducements/contributions balance. The decision to produce is based on such factors as the individual's goals and values, his group affiliations, and the cues the individual receives from the internal and external environment.

The theories presented in this chapter are rich in hypotheses and ideas for those studying organizations. Many of Barnard's thoughts for instance, have found expression in other theories. Examine his discussion of the composition of formal organizations, for example. Organizations are made up of smaller organizations called "organization cells." The number of these cells increases because a leader is limited regarding the number of people with whom he or she can communicate. This notion is strangely reminiscent of "span of control." When an individual cannot communicate with a large number of people, organizational growth can occur only by grouping two or more of these unit organizations. This grouping needs a superior. Thus, as the number of unit organizations increase, there is a corresponding need for more superiors. Then groups of groups are combined, and so on. The leader of a group, or unit organization is a member of two groups; his or her own working unit in which the leader is a superior, and his or her own superior group which he or she is a subordinate. This is not unlike the "linking-pin" concept generally attributed to Likert (21).

But these notions are expressed within the extracts and the summary/review that follow. In these, an effort is made to link these concepts with other major elements of the theories—H.L.T.

"THE FUNCTIONS OF THE EXECUTIVE"*

CHESTER BARNARD

The individual possesses certain properties which are comprehended in the word "person." Usually it will be most convenient if we use the noun "individual" to mean "*one* person" and reserve the adjectival form "personal" to indicate the emphasis on the properties. These are (a) activities or behavior,

---

*The materials in this section generally are drawn from opening statements of passages which are carefully developed and explained in the original work. The purpose of the excerpt is to highlight main themes. The development of these themes can be found in the original work. Excerpted by permission of the publishers from Chester I. Barnard, *The Functions of the Executive,* Cambridge, Mass.: Harvard University Press, copyright 1938, 1968 by the President and Fellows of Harvard College; 1966 by Grace F. Noera Barnard.

arising from (*b*) psychological factors, to which are added (*c*) the limited power of choice, which results in (*d*) purpose.

(*a*) An important characteristic of individuals is activity; and this in its gross and readily observed aspects is called behavior. Without it there is no individual person.

(*b*) The behavior of individuals we shall say are the result of psychological factors. The phrase "psychological factors" means the combination, resultants, or residues of the physical, biological, and social factors which have determined the history and the present state of the individual in relation to his present environment.

(*c*) Almost universally in practical affairs, and also for most scientific purposes, we grant to persons the power of choice, the capacity of determination, the possession of free will. By our ordinary behavior it is evident that nearly all of us believe in the power of choice as necessary to normal, sane conduct. Hence the idea of free will is inculcated in doctrines of personal responsibility, of moral responsibility, and of legal responsibility. This seems necessary to preserve a sense of personal integrity. It is an induction from experience that the destruction of the sense of personal integrity is the destruction of the power of adaptation, especially to the social aspects of living. We observe that persons who have no sense of ego, who are lacking in self-respect, who believe that what they do or think is unimportant, who have no initiative whatever, are problems, pathological cases, insane, not of this world, *unfitted for cooperation.*

This power of choice, however, is limited. This is necessarily true if what has already been stated is true, namely, that the individual is a region of activities which are the combined effect of physical, biological, and social factors. Free will is limited also, it appears, because the power of choice is paralyzed in human beings if the number of equal opportunities is large. This is an induction from experience. For example, a man set adrift while sleeping in a boat, awaking in a fog in the open sea, free to go in any direction, would be unable at once to choose a direction. Limitation of possibilities is necessary to choice. Finding a reason why something should *not* be done is a common method of deciding what should be done. The processes of decision as we shall see are largely techniques for narrowing choice.

(*d*) The attempt to limit the conditions of choice, so that it is practicable to exercise the capacity of will, is called making or arriving at a "purpose." It is implied usually in the verbs "to try," "to attempt." . . . We are greatly concerned with purposes in relation to organized activities.

It is necessary to impress upon the reader the importance of this statement of the properties of persons. ˙. . . It will be evident as we proceed, I think, that no construction of the theory of cooperative systems or of organizations, nor any significant interpretation of the behavior of organizations, executives, or others whose efforts are organized, can be made that is not based on *some* position as to the psychological forces of human behavior. . . (pp. 13–14). . . .

1. The individual human being possesses a limited power of choice. At the same time he is a resultant of, and is narrowly limited by, the factors of the total situation. He has motives, arrives at purposes, and wills to accomplish them. His method is to select a particular factor or set of factors in the total situation and to change the situation by operations on these factors. These are, from the viewpoint of purpose, the limiting factors; and are the strategic points of attack.

2. Among the most important limiting factors in the situation of each individual are his own biological limitations. The most effective method of overcoming these limitations has been that of cooperation. This requires the adoption of a group, or nonpersonal, purpose. The situation with reference to such a purpose is composed of innumerable factors, which must be discriminated as limiting or nonlimiting factors.

3. Cooperation is a social aspect of the total situation and social factors arise from it. These factors may be in turn the limiting factors of any situation. This arises from two considerations: (*a*) the processes of interaction must be discovered or invented, just as a physical operation must be discovered or invented; (*b*) the interaction changes the motives and interest of those participating in the cooperation.

4. The persistence of cooperation depends upon two conditions: (*a*) its effectiveness; and (*b*) its efficiency. Effectiveness relates to the accomplishment of the cooperative purpose, which is social and non-personal in character. Efficiency relates to the satisfaction of individual motives, and is personal in character. The test of effectiveness is the accomplishment of a common purpose or purposes; effectiveness can be measured. The test of efficiency is the eliciting of sufficient individual wills to cooperate.

5. The survival of cooperation, therefore, depends upon two interrelated and interdependent classes of processes: (*a*) those which relate to the system of cooperation as a whole in relation to the environment; and (*b*) those which relate to the creation or distribution of satisfactions among individuals.

6. The instability and failures of cooperation arise from defects in each of these classes of processes separately, and from defects in their combination. The functions of the executive are those of securing the effective adaptation of these processes (pp. 60–61). . . .

It is [a] central hypothesis . . . that the most useful concept for the analysis of experience of cooperative systems is embodied in the definition of a formal organization as a *system of consciously coordinated activities or forces of two or more persons* (p. 73). . . .

The system, then, to which we give the name "organization" is a system composed of the activities of human beings. What makes these activities a system is that the efforts of different persons are here coordinated (p. 77). . . .

[a] If organizations are systems, it follows that the general characteristics of systems are also those of organizations. For our purposes we may say that a system is something which must be treated as a whole because each part is

related to every other part included in it in a significant way. What is significant is determined by order as defined for a particular purpose, or from a particular point of view, such that if there is a change in the relationship of one part to any or all of the others, there is a change in the system. It then either becomes a new system or a new state of the same system.

Usually, if the parts are numerous, they group themselves into subsidiary or partial systems. Where this is the case, each partial system consists of relationships between its own parts which can change, creating a new state of the partial system, without altering the system as a whole in significant degree. But this is true only when the system is viewed from a single or special point of view and the changes of the subsidiary system are within limits. When this is the case we may disregard the larger systems, treating them as constants or the subsidiary system as if it were isolated. Thus the whole physical universe is the single and fundamental system, consisting of parts—which, let us say, are electrons, neutrons, and protons—and relationship between them; but in practice, if our interest is narrow enough, we can deal with the solar system, or the sun, or the earth, or a piece of iron, or a molecule, or an atom, as if each were a complete and final system. This we can do if we do not exceed certain limits. These are determined by whether or not exceeding these limits involves important changes in, or important reactions from, the larger system.

This is similarly true of the systems called organizations. First of all each organization is a component of a larger system which we have called a "cooperative system," the other components of which are physical systems, social systems, biological systems, persons, etc. Moreover, most formal organizations are partial systems included within larger organization systems. The most comprehensive formal organizations are included in an informal, indefinite, nebulous, and undirected system usually named a "society." . . .

[b] But we must now refer to one question about systems in general, and about organization systems in particular, the answer to which is of fundamental importance. I refer to the question as to whether the whole is more than the sum of the parts; whether a system should be considered as merely an aggregate of its components; whether a system of cooperative efforts, that is, an organization, is something more or less than or different from its constituent efforts; whether there emerge from the system properties which are not inherent in the parts.

The opinion that governs [here] is that when, for example, the efforts of five men become coordinated in a system, that is, an organization, there is created something new in the world that is more or less than or different in quantity and quality from anything present in the sum of the efforts of the five men (pp. 77–79). . . .

[c] It remains to present a few remarks on the dimensional characteristics of the system of cooperative interactions which we define as organizations. It perhaps has impressed many executives how indefinitely organizations are located in space. The sense of being 'nowhere" is commonly felt. With the great extension of the means of electrical communication this vagueness has

increased. To be sure, since the material of organizations is acts of persons, and since they relate in some degree to physical objects or are fixed in some physical environment, they have some degree of physical location. This is especially true of organizations in factories, or connected with railroad or communication systems. But even in these cases location is indirect, by attachment to a system of physical things; and in the case of political and religious organizations even mere location is only feebly conceivable. The notion of spatial dimensions of these systems is hardly applicable.

On the other hand, the dimension of time is of prime importance. Temporal relationship and continuity are primary aspects of organizations. When and how long are the first items of description. . . . The persons whose acts are the components of these systems are continually changing, yet the organization persists (p. 80).

THE THEORY OF FORMAL ORGANIZATION

An organization comes into being when (1) there are persons able to communicate with each other (2) who are willing to contribute action (3) to accomplish a common purpose. The elements of an organization are therefore (1) communication; (2) willingness to serve; and (3) common purpose. These elements are necessary and sufficient conditions initially, and they are found in all such organizations. The third element, purpose is implicit in the definition. Willingness to serve, and communication, and the interdependence of the three elements in general, and their mutual dependence in specific cooperative systems, are matters of experience and observation.

For the continued existence of an organization either *effectiveness* or *efficiency* is necessary; and the longer the life, the more necessary both are. The vitality of organizations lies in the willingness of individuals to contribute forces to the cooperative system. This willingness requires the belief that the purpose can be carried out, a faith that diminishes to the vanishing point as it appears that it is not in fact in process of being attained. Hence, when effectiveness ceases, willingness to contribute disappears. The continuance of willingness also depends upon the satisfactions that are secured by individual contributors in the process of carrying out the purpose. If the satisfactions do not exceed the sacrifices required, willingness disappears, and the condition is one of organization inefficiency. If the satisfactions exceed the sacrifices, willingness persists, and the condition is one of efficiency of organization.

In summary, then, the initial existence of an organization depends upon a combination of these elements appropriate to the external conditions at the moment. Its survival depends upon the maintenance of an equilibrium of the system. This equilibrium is primarily internal, a matter of proportions between the elements, but it is ultimately and basically an equilibrium between the system and the total situation external to it. This external equilibrium has two terms in it: first, the effectiveness of the organization, which comprises the relevance of its purpose to the environmental situation; and, second, its efficiency, which comprises the interchange between the organization and individuals. Thus the elements stated will each vary with external factors, and they are at the same time interdependent; when one is varied compensating variations must occur in the other if the system of which they are components is to remain in equilibrium, that is, is to persist or survive (p. 83).

Willingness to cooperate, positive or negative, is the expression of the net satisfactions or dissatisfactions experienced or anticipated by each individual in comparison with those experienced or anticipated through alternative opportunities. These alternative opportunities may be either personal and individualistic or those afforded by other organizations. That is, willingness to cooperate is the net effect, first, of the inducements to do so in conjunction with the sacrifices involved, and then in comparison with the practically available net satisfactions afforded by alternatives. The questions to be determined, if they were matters of logical reasoning, would be, first, whether the opportunity to cooperate grants any advantage to the individual as compared with independent action; and then, if so, whether that advantage is more or less than the advantage obtainable from some other cooperative opportunity (p. 85). . . .

Willingness to cooperate, except as a vague feeling or desire for association with others, cannot develop without an objective of cooperation. Unless there is such an objective it cannot be known or anticipated what specific efforts will be required of individuals, nor in many cases what satisfactions to them can be in prospect. Such an objective we denominate the "purpose" of an organization. The necessity of having a purpose is axiomatic, implicit in the words "system," "coordination," "cooperation." It is something that is clearly evident in many observed systems of cooperation, although it is often not formulated in words, and sometimes cannot be so formulated. In such cases what is observed is the direction or effect of the activities, from which purpose may be inferred.

A purpose does not incite cooperative activity unless it is accepted by those whose efforts will constitute the organization. Hence there is initially something like simultaneity in the acceptance of a purpose and willingness to cooperate. (p. 86). . . .

In other words we have clearly to distinguish between organization purpose and individual motive. It is frequently assumed in reasoning about organizations that common purpose and individual motive are or should be identical. With the exception noted below, this is never the case; and under modern conditions it rarely ever appears to be the case. Individual motive is necessarily an internal, personal, subjective thing; common purpose is necessarily an external, impersonal, objective thing even though the individual interpretation of it is subjective. The one exception to this general rule, an important one, is that the accomplishment of an organization purpose becomes itself a source of personal satisfaction and a motive for many individuals in many organizations. It is rare, however, if ever and then I think only in connection with family, patriotic, and religious organizations under special conditions, that organization purpose becomes or can become the *only* or even the major individual motive (pp. 88–89). . . .

The possibility of accomplishing a common purpose and the existence of persons whose desires might constitute motives for contributing toward such a common purpose are the opposite poles of the system of cooperative effort. The process by which these potentialities become dynamic is that of communication. Obviously a common purpose must be commonly known, and to be known must be in some way communicated. With some exceptions, verbal communication between men is the method by which this is accomplished. Similarly, though under crude and obvious conditions not to the same extent, inducements to persons depend upon communication to them (p. 89). . . .

The size of a unit organization being usually restricted very narrowly by the necessities of communication, it follows that growth of organization beyond the limits so imposed can only be accomplished by the creation of new unit organizations, or by grouping together two or more unit organizations already existing. When an organization grows by the addition of the services of more persons it is compelled, if it reaches the limit of size, to establish a second unit; and henceforward it is a complex of two unit organizations. All organizations except unit organizations are a group of two or more unit organizations. Hence a large organization of complex character consists not of the services of individuals directly but of those of subsidiary unit organizations. Nowhere in the world, I think can there be found a large organization that is not composed of small units. We think of them as having descended from the mass, whereas the mass can only be created from the units.

Usually when two and always when several unit organizations are combined in one complex organization, the necessities of communication impose a superleader, who becomes, usually with assistants, an "overhead" unit of organization. Similarly, groups of groups are combined into larger wholes. The most obvious case of complex structures of this type is an army. The fact that these large organizations are built up of small unit organizations is neglected in the spectacular size that ensues, and we often pass from the whole or major divisions to "men." The resulting dismissal from the mind of the inescapable practice of unit organization often leads to utterly unrealistic attitudes regarding organization problems (pp. 110–111).

In summary, we may say that historically and functionally all complex organizations are built up from units of organization, and consist of many units of "working" or "basic" organizations, overlaid with units of executive organizations; and that the essential structural characteristics of complex organizations are determined by the effect of the necessity for communication upon the size of a unit organization (p. 113).

INFORMAL ORGANIZATIONS AND THEIR
RELATION TO FORMAL ORGANIZATIONS

The purpose [here] has been to show (1) that those interactions between persons which are based on personal rather than on joint or common purposes, because of their repetitive character become systematic and organized through their effect upon habits of action and thought and through their promotion of uniform states of mind; (2) that although the number of persons with whom any individual may have interactive experience is limited, nevertheless the endless-chain relationship between persons in a society results in the development, in many respects, over wide areas and among many persons, of uniform states of mind which crystallize into what we call mores, customs, institutions; (3) that informal organization gives rise to formal organizations and that formal organizations are necessary to any large informal or societal organization; (4) that formal organizations also make explicit many of the attitudes, states of mind, and institutions which develop directly through informal organizations, with tendencies to divergence, resulting in interdependence and mutual correction of these results in a general and only approximate way; (5) that formal organizations, once established, in their turn also create informal organizations; and (6) that informal organizations are necessary to the operation of formal organizations as a means of communication, of cohesion, and of protecting the integrity of the individual (pp. 122–123). . . .

[Earlier] it was shown that the primary aspect of cooperative systems was the effect of coordination of the activities of two or more persons on the overcoming of the limitations involved in the relations between the biological capacities of individuals and the natural environment. The coordination may proceed on one of two principles: on the principle of simultaneity of effort, or on that of efforts in series (p. 132) . . .

Thus, in an important aspect, "organization" and "specialization" are synonyms. The ends of cooperation cannot be accomplished without specialization. The coordination implied is a functional aspect of organization. This function is to correlate the efforts of individuals in such a way with the conditions of the cooperative situation as a whole that purpose may be accomplished.

The way in which this correlation is accomplished is to analyze purpose into parts or detailed purposes or ends, the accomplishment of which in proper order will permit the attainment of the final objective; and to analyze the situation as a whole into parts which may be specifically coordinated by organization activity with detailed ends. These when accomplished become means toward the final attainment. The nature of this process and the function of specialization are of critical importance in the understanding of executive work.

A final observation may now be made. Since every unit organization in a complex organization is a specialization, the general purpose of the complex must be broken into specific purposes for each unit of organization. Since purpose is the unifying element of formal organization, it is this detailed purpose at the unit level that is effective in maintaining the unit. It is this purpose which must be accepted first of all in each unit in order that there may be units of which a complex may be composed. If this local or detailed purpose is not understood or accepted, disintegration of the unit organization follows. This is not more than an induction from my personal experience and observation, as is what now follows: and it is obvious in any event that much qualification for time elements and degrees of disintegration would be required for a complete statement.

Understanding or acceptance of the *general* purpose of the complex is not, however, essential. It may be, and usually but not always is, desirable as explaining or making acceptable a detailed purpose; and if this is possible it no doubt in most cases strengthens the unit organization. But in general complex organizations are characterized by obvious lack of complete understanding and acceptance of *general* purposes or aims. Thus it is not essential and usually impossible that the company should know the specific objectives of the army as a whole; but it is essential that it know and accept *an* objective of its own, or it cannot function. If it feels that the whole depends upon the achievement of this objective, which it is more likely to do if it understands what the whole objective is, the intensity of its action will ordinarily be increased. It is belief in the cause rather than intellectual understanding of the objective which is of chief importance. "Understanding" by itself is rather a paralyzing and divisive element (pp. 136–138). . . .

. . . The individual is always the basic strategic factor in organization. Regardless of his history or his obligations he must be induced to cooperate, or there can be no cooperation (p. 139). . . .

The net satisfactions which induce a man to contribute his efforts to an organization result from the positive advantages as against the disadvantages which are entailed. It follows that a new advantage may be increased or a negative advantage made positive either by increasing the number or the strength of the positive inducements or by reducing the number or the strength of the disadvantages (p. 140). . . .

It will be evident, perhaps, without more elaborate illustration, that in every type of organization, for whatever purpose, several incentives are necessary, and some degree of persuasion likewise, in order to secure and maintain the contributions to organization that are required. It will also be clear that, excepting in rare instances, the difficulties of securing the means of offering incentives, of avoiding conflict of incentives, and of making effective persuasive efforts, are inherently great; and that the determination of the precise combination of incentives and of persuasion that will be both effective and feasible is a matter of great delicacy. Indeed, it is so delicate and complex that rarely, if ever, is the scheme of incentives determinable in advance of application. It can only evolve; and the questions relating to it become chiefly those of strategic factors from time to time in the course of the life of the organization. It is also true, of course, that the scheme of incentives is probably the most unstable of the elements of the cooperative system (p. 158). . . .

. . . Authority is the character of a communication (order) in a formal organization by virtue of which it is accepted by a contributor to or "member" of the organization as governing the action he contributes; that is, as governing or determining what he does or is not to do so far as the organization is concerned. According to this definition, authority involves two aspects: first, the subjective, the personal, the *accepting* of a communication as authoritative . . . , and, second, the objective aspect—the character in the communication by virtue of which it is accepted (p. 163). . . .

The necessity of the assent of the individual to establish authority *for him* is inescapable. A person can and will accept a communication as authoritative only when four conditions simultaneously obtain: (*a*) he can and does understand the communication; (*b*) *at the time of his decision* he believes that it is not inconsistent with the purpose of the organization; (*c*) *at the time of his decision,* he believes it to be compatible with his personal interest as a whole; and (*d*) he is able mentally and physically to comply with it (p. 165). . . .

Naturally the reader will ask: How is it possible to secure such important and enduring cooperation as we observe if in principle and in fact the determination of authority lies with the subordinate individual? It is possible because the decisions of individuals occur under the following conditions (p. 167): . . .

(*a*) There is no principle of executive conduct better established in good organizations than that orders will not be issued that cannot or will not be obeyed (p. 167). . . .

(*b*) The phrase "zone of indifference" may be explained as follows: If all the orders for actions reasonably practicable be arranged in the order of their acceptability to the person affected, it may be conceived that there are a number which are clearly unacceptable, that is, which certainly will not be obeyed; there is another group somewhat more or less on the neutral line, that is, either barely acceptable or barely unacceptable; and a third group unquestionably acceptable. This last group lies within the "zone of indifference." The person affected will accept orders lying within this zone and is relatively indifferent as to what the order is so far as the question of authority is concerned. Such an order lies within the range that in a general way was anticipated at time of undertaking the connection with the organization (pp. 168–169). . . .

The zone of indifference will be wider or narrower depending upon the degree to which the inducements exceed the burdens and sacrifices which determine the individual's adhesion to the organization. It follows that the range or orders that will be accepted will be very limited among those who are barely induced to contribute to the system (p. 169). . . .

Authority has been defined in part as a "character of a communication in a formal organization." A "superior" is not in our view an authority nor does he have authority strictly speaking; nor is a communication authoritative except when it is an effort or action or organization. This is what we mean when we say that individuals are able to exercise authority only when they are acting "officially," a principle well established in law, and generally in secular and religious practice. Hence the importance ascribed to time, place, dress, ceremony, and authentication of a communication to establish its official character. These practices confirm the statement that authority relates to a communication "in a formal organization." There often occur occasions of compulsive power of individuals and of hostile groups; but authority is always concerned with something *within* a definitely organized system. Current usage conforms to the definition in this respect. The word "authority" is seldom employed except where formal organization connection is stated or implied (unless, of course, the reference is obviously figurative) (pp. 172–173). . . .

Thus men impute authority to communications from superior positions, provided they are reasonably consistent with advantages of scope and perspective that are credited to those positions. This authority is to a considerable extent independent of the personal abililty of the incumbent of the position. It is often recognized that though the incumbent may be of limited personal abililty his advice may be superior solely by reason of the advantage of position. This is the *authority of position*.

But it is obvious that some men have superior ability. Their knowledge and understanding regardless of position command respect. Men impute authority to what they say in an organization for this reason only. This is the *authority of leadership* (p. 173). . . .

THE FUNCTIONS OF THE EXECUTIVE

. . . Functions of executives relate to all the work essential to the vitality and endurance of an organization, so far, at least, as it must be accomplished though formal coordination (p. 255). . . .

Executive work is not that *of* the organization, but the specialized work of *maintaining* the organization in operation (p. 215). . . .

. . . The problem of the establishment and maintenance of the system of communication, that is, the primary task of the executive organization, is perpetually that of obtaining the coalescence of the two phases, executive personnel and executive positions (p. 218). . . .

The second function of the executive organization is to promote the securing of the personal services that constitute the material of organizations.

The work divides into two main divisions: (1) the bringing of persons into cooperative relationship with the organization; (2) the eliciting of the services after such persons have been brought into the relationship (p. 227). . . .

The third executive function is to formulate and define the purposes, objectives, ends, of the organization. It has already been made clear that, strictly speaking, purpose is defined more nearly by the aggregate of action taken than by any formulation in words; but that the aggregate of action is a residuum of the decisions relative to purpose and the environment, resulting in closer and closer approximations to the concrete acts. It has also been emphasized that purpose is something that must be accepted by all the contributors to the system of efforts. Again, it has been stated that purpose must be broken into fragments, specific objectives, not only ordered in time so that detailed purpose and detailed action follow in the series of progressive cooperation, but also ordered contemporaneously into the specializations— geographical, social, and functional—that each unit organization implies. It is more apparent here than with other executive functions that it is an entire executive organization that formulates, redefines, breaks into details, and decides on the innumerable simultaneous and progressive actions that are the stream of syntheses constituting purpose or action. No single executive can under any conditions accomplish this function alone, but only that part of it which relates to his position in the executive organization. (p. 231)

"ORGANIZATIONS" AS VIEWED BY JAMES MARCH AND HERBERT SIMON*

HENRY L. TOSI

The literature about organizations is basically the result of the experience of executives, the scientific management movement, sociologists, social psychologists, political scientists, and economists, little of which has been well substantiated empirically. Much organization theory was developed by the "classical" school, and this has been directed largely into two areas. The first is "scientific management." Theorists such as Taylor and Gilbreth brought a great deal of precision into the analysis, management, and reorganization of routine tasks. They attempted to develop a prescribed set of operating procedures to be used in analyzing and setting forth guidelines for effectiveness in organization.

The second category might be termed the "administrative management school." These writers were generally concerned with the most effective way to group tasks in order to achieve organizational purpose, dealing with problems such as how to group tasks into jobs, jobs into larger administrative units, these administrative units into larger units, and so on so as to minimize the cost of performing these activities. In general, these theorists attempt to develop principles of organization to be applied across organization types.

These theories were untested. The motivational assumptions they make about men and work tend to be inaccurate. There is little appreciation of

*The material analyzed here is drawn from James G. March and Herbert Simon, *Organizations* (New York: John Wiley, 1958). I assume full responsibility for the interpretation herein.

intraorganizational conflict. By and large they may be criticized for their lack of consideration of the human factor. They give little attention to the role of cognition in task identificaiton, nor does the concept of program elaboration receive much attention. It is with these limitations regarding classical organization theory that March and Simon begin their work.

SOME ASSUMPTIONS

An organization is a system of interrelated social behaviors of a number of participants. While the definitions generally used by the classical school fall within this construct, March and Simon derive their conclusions from the model of influence processes in organizations.

Behavior results from a stimulus. Stimuli are perceived by the individual. They act upon memory. Memory is composed of values, perceptions, beliefs, experiences, programs, alternatives, and other knowledge stored in the psychological bank of the individual. As a result of perceiving an external change in the environment, or stimuli, the individual evokes, or calls, for certain of these stored values or perceptions which he believes particularly pertinent to the situation. This "evoked set" contains some behavior program which the individual will enact. The "evoked set" is that part of the memory which influences the behavior of the individual. Memory content may move from an unevoked state, and so on.

Behavior can be changed, or influenced, in at least two ways. First, behavior may be changed by learning, or changing the memory set of the individual. Then, in reacting to stimuli, the individual may evoke part of the new memory content. This, then should impact his behavior. Second, change in the stimuli may change behavior. Different stimuli may evoke different sets, which include different behavior programs, resulting in different behaviors.

There are several alternative outcomes that may occur using this influence model. First, the stimuli may act upon the memory and may obtain the desired behavior. Another possibility is that the stimuli is misunderstood by the individual and may evoke a different set than originally intended. The resulting behavior may be undesired. For example, a person may perceive an unintended stimulus; that is, changes in the environment which were not planned by one who might have some control over it. This perceived stimuli may then evoke a certain set and perhaps trigger responses other than those intended.

In classical theory, most of these possibilities were overlooked, or not dealt with. The classical theorists did not consider in detail the fact that stimuli may generate unanticipated consequences because they may evoke a larger, or a different, memory set than expected. They believed that the environment contained well-defined stimuli which evoked a predictable memory set. This included a program for generating the appropriate, or desirable, response. For instance, use of the concept of economic man may result in offering increases in economic well-being to the employee, or organization member, as a stimulus. This presumably would evoke a set which contained values oriented toward improving one's economic status, a belief that such improvement is desirable, and a behavior program which includes the "appropriate" response of engaging in the activity desired by the management.

ORGANIZATION EQUILIBRIUM: THE DECISION TO PARTICIPATE

The individual in an organization is essentially faced with two different decisions. The first is the decision to participate, and the second is the decision to produce. These reflect different considerations by the individual. The *decision to participate* is based on the concept of organization equilibrium which refers to the balance of payments to members for their continued participation and contribution to the organization. The underlying concepts of organization equilibrium state that:

1. The organization is a system of interrelated social behavior of participants.
2. Each participant and group receives inducements from the organization for their contribution.
3. The individual continues to participate so long as the inducements he receives are greater than his contribution. This evaluation, incidentally, may be measured by the individual in terms of his own values, which may reflect or include those other than economic.
4. The contributions of various groups are sources from which the organization manufactures inducements to pay the others.
5. Equilibrium (or solvency) occurs when the organization can continue to provide inducement to members to obtain their contributions.

The individual and subgroups may be any groups or individuals which make some sort of contribution to the existence of the organization. In short, anyone providing input needed by the organization for its continued existence and survival must be viewed as an integral part of the system. Should one group leave, or change basically in nature, then the organization's equilibrium is disturbed, and a new level must be sought and achieved. This may require a redistribution of inducements to others in order to obtain their participation. The general scope of the concept of organization equilibrium considers managers, employees, customers, suppliers, investors, the communities, and lenders. The March-Simon structure could be slightly modified to apply to each of them. It has been common practice, however, to deal with the questions of membership in terms of employees and managers of organizations. March and Simon stay within this tradition.

The basic notion of organization equilibrium may be stated as follows: Increases in the balance of inducement utilities over contribution utilities decrease the propensity of the individual to move; decreases in the balance of inducement utilities over contribution utilities conversely increase the propensity to move. Inducement utilities received by an individual or group represent more than economic consideration such as wages. Satisfaction with the organization, identification with group members, and other noneconomic values all contribute to the inducement-contribution balance.

This balance is affected by two major considerations. These are (1) the perceived desirability of leaving the job, and (2) the perceived ease of movement from the organization. The perceived desirability of leaving is a function of the individual's satisfaction with his job and the possibility of intraorganizational transfer. When individual job satisfaction is high, it may be less desirable for one to move. There are a host of factors which affect job satisfaction (such as compatibility of work requirements with other roles, conformity of the work roles with the individual's self-characterization, and the predictability of instrumental relationships on the job), and when the individual is not satisfied with his job, he may consider the possibility of an intraorganizational transfer. If this possibility is high, then there is less likelihood of leaving the organization. Intraorganizational transfer possibilities may be related to the organizational size; that is, in large organizations there is a greater possibility of internal transfer than in small.

The second factor involved in the inducement-contribution balance is the individual's perceived ease of movement, or the number of alternatives he feels to be available to him. The more job offers he believes he has, the greater he perceives his ease of movement to be. Personal characteristics, such as sex, age, and social status may affect the degree to which he perceives external alternatives to be available. His skill and his increased length of service in an organization reduce, perhaps, the external alternatives he perceives available.

Thus, the likelihood of the individual leaving must be regarded as a function of his desire to leave and his perceived ease of movement. If he has no desire to leave, then perceived ease of movement is not important. If he is highly dissatisfied with the organization and does wish to leave, but he has few perceived external alternatives available, then it is highly likely that he will decide to remain in the organization—or participate.

THE DECISION TO PRODUCE

The decision to participate is based upon a set of different factors than those for the *decision to produce.* The motivation to produce is a function of the character of, and the perceived consequences of, the evoked set of alternatives. These are weighed against the individual's goals and values. The evoked set of alternatives evolves from the cues the individual perceives within the environment, both internal and external to the organization.

One factor which affects the decision of an individual regarding his organizational activities may be the perceived external alternatives. It may be more desirable to leave the organization than to comply with the production requirements or group norms. The factors involved in the individual's evaluation of these external alternatives have been discussed earlier. A second factor, the work group and its norms, also affect the individual's evaluation of alternatives. One evaluates alternatives in terms of group norms, or those behaviors which the group may define acceptable. Thus, behavior of those in close social and physical proximity affect alternatives one may consider.

Formal organization practices, appraisal systems, compensation systems and management policies may elicit types of behavior which may, in fact, be considered organizationally undesirable. For instance, some managers may forego required short-run maintenance expenditures in a department in order to produce short-run results. The behavior elicited, and the evoked set of which it is a part, represent organizational problems that must be solved.

By and large, these alternatives represent action that an individual considers to be possible behavior. They do not emerge in a vacuum. We simultaneously consider behavior possibilities and evaluate, or assess, the perceived consequences of the evoked set. Conformity to organizational requirements will be less important when the individual perceives that he has other alternatives to participation in the organization, which may be largely determined by his perception of the job market or general labor market conditions. It is also a function of his perceived ease of movement to other organizations. When the individual feels that it would be difficult for him to move, that few jobs are available, he may view organizational conformity as important. He may also perceive only limited alternatives to participation and thus conform.

The degree to which the desired alternatives violate organizational requirements is another important individual consideration in the evaluation of alternatives. Effective compliance with organizational requirements is intended to result in the attainment and acquisition of organizational rewards. The reward-sanction system in an organization will have an effect on activity of members. Obtaining organizationally-based values is largely a function of an individual's ability to meet the performance requirements of the organization.

It is difficult to determine organizational performance criteria. These criteria may be a function of work group size; that is, the larger the work group, the more difficult it is to develop performance criteria and apply incentive systems. Second, the degree to which activities have been routinized and measured are an important dimension in criteria development. Organizational level is relevant here. Activities at the lowest level of the organization are more routine and programmed than higher-level activities. Operational criteria are generally more difficult to determine for higher-level officials. It may be extremely difficult to tie organizational rewards to current performance at high levels. For example, the success of an organization today may be a result of decisions made three, five, or ten years ago by some other chief executive, yet it is the incumbent chief executive who receives praise.

Identification with internal or external groups affects one's evaluations of the consequences. Group pressures will largely be a function of the degree to which the individual identifies with the group. The stronger the group identification, the greater the potential group pressures.

Group pressures are significant for other reasons, also. Group consensus, or opinion uniformity, and the extent to which the group controls the environment, represent pressures that may have an impact on the individual even though he may not identify with the group. If the group is able to influence organizational activity, or control the reward-sanction system, the individual may be forced to respond to group pressures even though he does not identify with the group.

When an individual perceives a stimulus to engage in behavior, a set is evoked which includes alternative actions. Each of these alternatives is evaluated in terms of its perceived consequences. They are compared to some values, or standards, which are a function of the individual's goals. These do not develop in a sterile environment. Humans, in general, evaluate their own positions in relation to the values of others and may accept other's goals as their own. Individual goals emerge from the process of identification with others. Here the concern is with the degree to which groups of one sort or the other affect and condition the goals of the individual.

An individual may identify with any or all, at different points in time, of the following types of groups. First he may identify with professional associations, family, or other types of extraorganizational groups. Second, he may identify with friendship groups and other social-emotional subgroups within the organization environment. Third, he may identify with the organization itself. Finally, task groups in the organization involved in the performance of specific organizational assignment, similar perhaps to departments, may be the identification focus. Obviously, the stronger the group identification, the more likely it is that individual's goals will conform to those prescribed by group norms. These, then, are the factors related to group identification:

1. The greater the perceived prestige of the group, the stronger the propensity of the individual to identify with it. Prestige may be a function of success, status, or the individual's perception.
2. The greater the extent to which perceived goals are shared by members, the greater the identification with the group.
3. The more the perceived goals are shared by group members, the greater interaction of members.
4. The more frequent the interaction among members, the greater the propensity to identify with the group.
5. The greater the number of needs satisfied in the group, the greater the propensity of any individual to identify with the group.
6. The amount of competition between the individual and the group is negatively related to the degree of individual identification with the group.

GROUP CONFLICT

March and Simon separate the decision to produce from the decision to participate. Simply because one elects to remain in an organization and operate at a given activity level, internal conflict and bargaining among members and member units are not precluded. The inducements/contributions balance is flexible and the level of productive activity is elastic. This permits the degree of latitude within which organization conflict and bargaining can occur. The decision to produce and to participate may be within the range of "semi-conscious" motivational factors but conflict is more a "conscious and deliberate power phenomenon."

Conflict among organizational units arises from the following factors: the existence of a "felt need for joint decision making," differences in goals, and differences in perceptions of reality. Individuals may feel that certain decision-making situations call for representatives from several units. There may be a high degree of instrumental interdependence among units. Unit A may perform an operation on a product which may limit or condition the degree of success of Unit B. For instance, if Unit A is a metal-finishing department and Unit B is a paint shop, then the metal finish may significantly affect the quality of the paint job. Mutual dependence upon limited resources may increase the need for joint decision-making. Where several units rely on a limited budget for support, it is likely that members desire to jointly determine budget allocations.

Differences in perceived goals may be a condition that precedes conflict. Different organizaitonal units may perceive different ends as justified. Organizational units may view their function as being more significant than other units, justifiably believing they should have a larger share of resources. Differences in goals may be a function of the size of the unit, particularly when it is reflected in the existence of a greater number of departments, which results in a larger number of differentiated goals.

Individual perceptions of reality may foster intergroup conflict. There may be great variance among the goals of individual members. The departmental affiliation of a member may alter his perception of problems. The kind of information and the communication channels through which it flows affects the perceptions of the reality of the problem. As the number of communications channels increases, the possibility for increased differentiation of perception within the organization occurs. When the same information passes through many different channels, each may distort, filter, and edit it to suit its own needs.

These factors lead to intergroup conflict. When conflict exists, it must be resolved to obtain equilibrium. Organization conflict may be resolved by analytic or bargaining processes. Analytic processes are those methods where public and private agreement among the conflicting groups is sought. Problem-solving and resolution of conflict by higher level officials are *analytic* processes. These tend to be used when the conflict situation is more a function of individuals than intergroup differences. The general characteristic of these processes is increased information of alternatives and evaluation of the consequences of them.

Bargaining processes are attempts to resolve conflicts through the use of "politics" or "gamesmanship." These techniques are predominant when the nature of the differences is between groups rather than individuals. Bargaining processes, however, require the use of power and status. This may have a negative impact on members. Power and status differences may be strengthened or weakened in the process. In either event, one group may suffer. Hence, there will be a tendency to treat conflict as "individual" and resolve it using an analytical method.

THE COGNITIVE LIMITS OF RATIONALITY

The classical concept of the "rational" decision-making situation is somewhat limited in practice. Rational, or optimum, decisions require that all alternatives to a problem are perceived by the problem-solver. Criteria must be available which permit these to be evaluated and compared. The alternative finally selected should be that preferred above all others.

This is hardly the case in organizational life, where it is unlikely that all alternatives are known. It is even less likely that criteria exist for adequate comparison of all alternatives. Thus, decision making can only be rational within certain limits. The known alternatives, then, represent the boundaries, or parameters, of decision rationality.

Rather than "optimizing" as an organizational decision-making methodology, decision makers "satisfice." An alternative is considered satisfactory if (1) a set of criteria exists that describe minimally satisfactory alternatives, and (2) the alternative in question meets or exceeds all these criteria. Most human decision making, whether individual or organizational, is concerned with the discovery and selection of satisfactory alternatives. Only in exceptional cases is it concerned with the discovery and selection of optimal alternatives.

Decision making may be of many types, ranging from a case in which an individual searches for various alternative behavior to one where an environmental stimuli invokes a highly complex and organized set of responses. These highly complex sets of responses are called "programs." The existence of programs accounts, in large part, for the predictability of individual performance and behavior. Programs may be viewed as a part of of the organizational control system. Individuals in the organization accept programs based on the factors discussed previously under the "decision to produce."

Programs exist as a function of the ability to group activities and a need for coordination. When it is relatively easy to observe and relate job output and activities, then it is possible to develop programs. As the difficulty of observing this relationship increases, the difficulty of devising organizational programs increases. Programs may also exist, or be developed, when there is a need for coordination of either activity or output. Where there is a need for a great deal of coordination, then some method will be developed to insure that it occurs.

Programs are not meant to be extremely rigid behavioral specifications in all cases, but they may be. For instance, a program which prescribes behavior for an emergency breakdown of a production line may be highly specific. On the other hand, a program dealing with price determination of special job-lot produced equipment may be relatively flexible. Individual discretion in the use of programs is determined by whether it specifies outcome, or ends, to a greater degree than it specifies the means of achieving these ends. Programs which describe how to do something allow less discretion than programs which simply state the results desired. The hierarchical structure of programs within the organization is related to the concept of organizational levels. Higher-level officials in an organization modify programs implemented by lower-level personnel.

The organization's structure may be viewed as a function of the problem-solving process. The existence of structure, or programs, provides boundaries or parameters of rationalities for the decision-making process. Its existence provides some degree of stability and permanency to behavior within an organization, and this is a necessary characteristic of an organization's behavior.

Rational behavior rests upon the concept of "goal." The individual defines his behavior in terms of goal attainment. Selection of alternative which enhance the probability of obtaining goals may be viewed as rational behavior. Thus, the goals of the individual condition whether his behavior is "rational" or "irrational." The behavior of one unit may be viewed by another as being nonrational behavior because of discrepant goal perception. This may be due to factoring organizational views into subgoals for lower-level units.

Goal factoring may be viewed as a type of means-end analysis. if the overall organizational goal is viewed as the end, then those units at the highest level engage in the means of achieving that end. When one of these units is subdivided into small organization components, the means of the larger unit become the objective (or the end) of the smaller unit. This continues until such a condition exists that the overall organizational goal has been factored into small behavior components. The factoring of overall organizational goals may result in units directing attention to its own goals. The degree of goal differentiation is important, since members of units often see goals in some particular frame of reference. Thus the number of departmental units, and the one with which an individual is affiliated, affects his goal perception.

As the goal becomes factored at lower and lower organizational levels, specialization of function and labor occur. Specialization of labor allows the organization to take advantage of repetitive programs. The type of specialization of labor, or the manner in which the goals have been factored, will affect the interdependence relationships among various departments. For instance, the greater the process specialization, the greater the interdependencies among departments.

The interdependencies and complexities that can occur within an organization are limited by the effectiveness of the communication processes and channels. the communication channels, or systems, in an organization are both planned and spontaneous. Certain methods for transmission of specific types of information must be provided to satisfy formal organization requirements. Additionally, there may be a need for information that is not specifically sanctioned formally. Where this information gap exists, a channel will develop to provide it. The greater the efficiency in communications, the greater the tolerance among members for departmental interdependence.

THE INNOVATION AND ELABORATION OF PROGRAMS

When the structure of active programs does not contain any which are adequate to meet organizational criteria, then they will be initiated to solve the problem. Programmed activity involves routine problem-solving. The details of behavior are relatively well-defined. Changing old programs, or devising new ones, requires a process of innovation and initiation. New program possibilities must be generated and their consequences examined. This innovating process is closely related to "problem-solving processes." In searching for programs, variables within the control of the individual or the organization will be first considered. If a satisfactory program is not developed, then an attempt will be made to change variables not within the discretion of the problem solvers. If this fails, then the criteria may be relaxed.

The criteria for satisfactory performance are closely related to the pyschological concept of "level of aspiration." Aspiration levels change, but in general the adjustment process is a relatively slow, though constant one pressing upward. The aspiration level may be based on past organizational performance, but other bases of comparison also exert pressures. Firms compare themselves to other firms. When there is an awareness that better results can be obtained with other programs where will be a revision in the standards of satisfaction.

The rate of innovation is likely to increase when changes in the internal or external environment make existing programs unsatisfactory. These environmental changes may result from design, or by accident. A "natural" process of innovation, that is, a response to environmental stimuli, may be supplemented by organizational mechanisms to facilitate innovation. Whether or not members engage in research for new programs is a function of time pressures or deadlines attached to activities, and the degree to which clear goals can be associated with the activities.

The discovery, development, and implementation of a new program in the organization may result in the creation of a new unit to develop, elaborate, and implement it. The development phase of new programs may be a period of high activity and excitement, while the implementation phase tends to spur less interest since the program is becoming more routine. New programs may be invented, or borrowed. If a program exists outside the boundaries of the innovating organization, then it is likely that the organization will "borrow." When such is not the case, organization members will first call on their "stored" program solutions. As more people in the organization become aware of the problem, the number of available solutions will increase. The development and elaboration of these new programs is through the process of means-end analysis. The solution to the general problem is by a set of generally specified means. Each of these means becomes a subgoal, and a set of means must be discovered for achieving it. This process continues until the level of detail is such that programs exist to achieve the subgoal, for which criteria must be developed. Sensitivity to innovations is a function of the relevance of the innovation to needs of the specific unit involved. When the goal of the innovation does not "fit" with that of the reviewing organization level, it is less apt to receive high priority, or it may be referred to the appropriate level. The location of innovation is important to the power and influence structure of an organization. Organizational activity is affected by the processes that originate and evaluate proposals. The right to initiate is a source of power. It is one control over organizational activities.

March and Simon's work—*Organizations*— is described by the authors as one in which they "surveyed the literature on organization theory, starting with those theories that viewed the employee as an instrument and physiological automaton, proceeding through theories that were centrally concerned with the motivational and affective aspects of human behavior, and concluding with theories that placed particular emphasis on cognitive processes."

FIVE
ORGANIZATIONS, POWER, AND COMPLIANCE

Amitai Etzioni develops a typology of organization and examines how individual involvement with an organization and the type of power predominant in the various forms interact to explain compliance. He is concerned with why people respond in organizations and, rather than relying on concepts of "acceptance" or property rights, he describes several different bases for compliance. Essentially, he argues that the type of power that will result in compliance is contingent on the nature of the organization and why people are there.

He does not focus on authority in the traditional sense but rather develops it more fully as part of the notion of compliance structure. Compliance is related to power means and the orientation of the individual. It is the behavior of the individuals responding to power, and power may take many forms, for example, material, deprivation, and so on. Etzioni argues that it is too narrow to view legitimate authority as the reason why people comply—that nonlegitimate authority affects behavior.

Power may be grouped into three types: (1) coercive—based on physical sanctions; (2) remunerative—based on manipulation of symbolic rewards. When the individual views organization efforts to obtain compliance as legitimate and/or congruent with his expectations, he will comply.

But individuals may be involved in organizations in different ways. Etzioni suggests these may be characterized as (1) alienative, (2) calculative, and (3) moral. He says that "There are nine possible types of compliance. Three of these types (congruent types) are more effective than the other six .... Organizations are under pressure to be effective. Hence to the degree that the environment allows, *organizations tend to shift their compliance structures from incongruent to congruent types and organizations which have congruent compliance of structures tend to resist factors pushing them toward incongruent structures* (13)."

Etzioni, then, as others whose work is included in this book, finds the concept of authority as a right inadequate to explain compliance behavior. More important, however, is the manner in which Etzioni attempts to relate the notions of authority, or compliance, and different types of organizations—H.L.T.

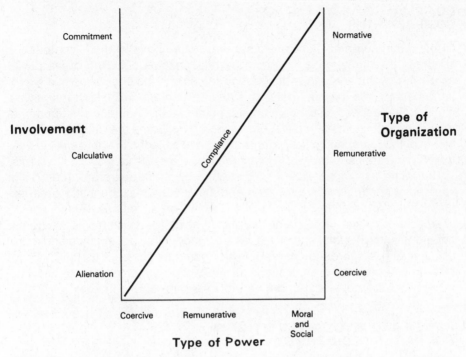

Figure 1 The relationship between power, involvement, and type of organization.

AMITAI ETZIONI'S "A COMPARATIVE ANALYSIS OF COMPLEX ORGANIZATIONS"*

ROBERT J. HOUSE

Following is a summary/review of a theory of complex organization which has been developed by Amitai Etzioni.[1] The term "organization" as used here refers to a social unit devoted primarily to the attainment of specific goals.[2] Organizations as discussed here are complex in that they involve many levels, specialization of efforts, departmentation of groups within the organization, the need for both formal and informal communication and coordination and intricate relationships of authority and responsibility. This is a study of the systematic differences among various social units classed as organizations. The theory is diagrammed in Figure 1.

*This abstract was written by Robert J. House. The material is drawn from Amitai Etzioni, *A Comparative Analysis of Complex Organizations* (New York: Free Press, 1961).

COMPLIANCE AS A BASE FOR COMPARISON

In this theory, organizations are classified on the basis of their "compliance structure." Compliance is defined as a relationship consisting of the power employed by superiors to control subordinates and the orientation of the subordinates to this power. Thus, this theory combines a structural and a motivational aspect: structural, since it concerns the kind and distribution of power in organizations; motivational, since it concerns the different commitments of the members to the organization. In this theory, Etzioni seeks to analyze organizations in terms of both social systems and personality systems.

The basic assumption underlying the theory is that there are three major sources of control whose allocation and manipulation account to a great extent for the foundation of social order within organizations. These control sources are: (1) coercion (threat and punishment), (2) economic assets (remuneration), and (3) social and moral values (recognition, acceptance and moral involvement). Accordingly, three types of compliance serve as the basis for comparison between organizations. Compliance—the organizational equivalent of social order—is the core variable, or hub, of this theory.

POWER AND INVOLVEMENT: THE COMPARATIVE DIMENSIONS

Using compliance as a comparative basis of analysis, organizations are analyzed in terms of two basic dimensions: *power,* which is applied by the organization *to* its members; and *involvement* in the organization developed *by* its members

Power

Power is referred to as a member's ability to induce or influence another member to carry out his directives by any other values which he supports. Power differs according to the means employed to make the subjects apply.

Thus, remunerative power is based on control over material resources and rewards through allocation of salaries and wages, commissions and contributions, "fringe benefits," services and commodities.

Moral and social power[3] rest on the allocation and manipulation of symbolic rewards and deprivations through employment of leaders, manipulation of mass media, allocation of esteem and prestige symbols, administration of ritual, and influence over the distribution of social acceptance and positive responses by others (e.g., recognition or approval). Thus, moral or social power rests upon the manipulation of those rewards which carry high symbolic value to the respondent.

Coercive power rests on the application, or threat, of physical sanctions such as inflation of pain, deformity, or death; generation of frustration through restriction of movements; or controlling the satisfaction of needs such as those of food, sex, comfort and the like through force.

Etzioni marshals evidence which strongly supports the proposition that most organizations tend to emphasize only one means of power, relying less on, but not completely avoiding, the other two. Most organizations, then, have both a primary and secondary compliance structure.

Involvement

The second dimension of the theory is that of involvement. Involvement is characterized in terms of intensity and direction. The intensity of involvement ranges from high to low. The direction is either positive or negative. When involvement is high, it is called commitment; when it is low, alienation. Involvement thus is a term which applies to a continuum of personal and voluntary orientation toward an organization.

CLASSIFICATION OF ORGANIZATIONS

Etzioni classified organizations according to their compliance structure as coercive, remunerative, or normative.[4]

Coercive Organizations

Coercive organizations are organizations in which coercion is the major means of control over the members, and high alienation characterizes the orientation of the members to the organization. Examples of coercive organizations would be prisoner-of-war camps, concentration camps, the large majority of prisons, traditional "correctional institutions," custodial mental hospitals, forced labor camps, and relocation camps.

Remunerative Organizations

Remunerative organizations are those in which material remuneration is a major means of control over the members. This involves a determination by the member of the amount of involvement he feels will profit him most. Thus, "calculative involvement" characterizes the orientation of the members to the remunerative organization. Those divisions of industrial organizations employing predominantly blue-collar workers or white-collar, nonprofessional workers (clerks and stenographic workers) and semiprofessional workers such as laboratory technicians and most college graduates would be placed in this category. This is true because wages, salaries, commissions, fringe benefits, working conditions, and similar rewards constitute the predominant source of control for such employees. This placement of most industrial workers into the remunerative category of organizations is in agreement with the conclusions of Stogdill[5] and Brayfield and Crockett[6] that attempts to increase performance by changing the style of supervision to a more human-relations-oriented style are in some cases reported to lead only to small increases in productivity, whereas in other cases they cause an increase in employee satisfaction but none in productivity. On the other hand, reports from industry and surveys by government bureaus generally attest to the effectiveness of wage-incentive plans in increasing productivity and achieving other objectives, assuming that such plans are not in conflict with the moral values of the employees.

White-collar employees are predominately controlled by remunerative means, but less so than blue-collar employees. Secondary, normative control, such as the manipulation of status symbols and social recognition seems to play a more important role among white-collar employees than among blue-collar employees.

Since white-collar employees have a greater tendency toward identification with the organizational objectives, and since management usually finds it difficult to manipulate esteem and prestige symbols of blue-collar workers, the use of social and moral values for purposes of influencing most industrial employees is limited.

A study of saleswomen by Lombard[7] points out behavior usually considered typical of lower-level workers. He reports, for instance, that the work groups restricts "output," limits competition among the women and enforces other norms which are in direct contrast to those supported by management.

At the same time, the manipulation of esteem and prestige symbols, which as a rule has a limited effect on blue-collar workers, seems to be more effective among white-collar employees. This point is illustrated in a study of saleswomen which emphasized the role of nonremunerative "symbolic" controls. Saleswomen who made mistakes writing out sales slips had the slips returned to them, bound with a large red rubber band, to be opened and corrected in the presence of the section manager and other saleswomen. These red bands "do not result in fines or punishments of any sort, and yet the clerks feel that to get one is a disgrace."[8] Similarly, there were "all sorts of honors bestowed upon the capable and efficient. These have small monetary value, but money is secondary to honor. To be ace—the best saleswoman in your department—is compensation enough in itself."[9]

One can imagine what the effects of similar manipulation would be if attempted with the blue-collar nonskilled worker. It is not unlikely that the person who gets the most red rubber bands would be the "ace of the day."

Normative Organizations

Normative organizations are those in which moral involvement and social acceptance is the major source of control. The orientation of members of these is characterized by high commitment to the organization. There are several frequently found types of normative organization. These are religious organizations, employing primarily professional employees such as research laboratories, law firms and medical associations. In these kinds of organizations, social power is exercised mainly through informal sanctions (e.g., social isolation or approval), through the manipulation of prestige symbols (titles, status trappings), through the personal influence of the leader or influential members of the organization, or through the manipulation of peer groups' climate of opinion.

An organization made up of professional employees utilizes mainly moral and social controls, though calculative involvement occurs here to a greater extent than in any other kind of normative organization. In this sense, professional organizations resemble white-collar industries as borderline cases, though it seems they fall on the other side of the border, whereas in professional organizations moral and social power predominates, with remunerative compliance a close second. In white-collar industries the reverse seems to be true.

Today, with increased stress placed on creative scientific work, industries find normative, or moral social control affecting larger segments of their member population. Typically, industrial firms consist of a large portion of production people who are motivated primarily by remunerative means and a small but critical, and probably growing, portion of employees who are contributing toward the creative development of the product. The same is true of newspapers which have a highly remunerative section in which the newspaper is actually produced and a highly committed, editorial wing in which it is written and edited. The editorial group may be more affected by normative power than the other sectors. Other communications industries, such as radio and television networks and advertising agencies, also have these characteristics.

The major means of control in professional organizations are based on prolonged and careful selection, education in professional value systems at universities and professional schools, or education on the job which the professional holds in the early part of his career. Examples of such jobs are the cub reporter, the law student, the intern, the novice, and the seminarian. Frequently, incumbents of these positions continue their professional education as part of the job, or on a part-time basis. Social powers, formalized in the professional code of ethics and the professional association and supported by the social bonds of the professional community and professional elites, carry great weight.

High intrinsic satisfaction from work, positively associated with voluntary involvement, characterizes the work of professionals. This commitment is sometimes disassociated from the organization and vested in the work itself, for which the profession—not the organization—serves as the reference group and the object of involvement. Thus, research scientists may be more easily persuaded by senior members of their discipline than by the managers of the firm. As one would expect from the comparatively extensive use of remunerative rewards, despite the importance of intrinsic satisfaction and other symbolic gratifications, commitment to professional organizations is not as high as it is in other normative organizations with strongly ideological overtones, such as some political parties or church organizations.

LEADERSHIP, COMPLIANCE, AND ORGANIZATIONAL SPECIALIZATION

Etzioni's theory has significant implications for management selection, the study of leadership, and organization. Organizations are often compared to task-performing, goal-oriented instruments. However, organizations which are seemingly committed to one set of goals must often pursue quite different subgoals or tasks in order to achieve those goals. These different goals and tasks frequently differ in their compliance requirements. Rarely are there two goals which can be served with optimal effectiveness by compliance structures which are precisely the same in both the predominant element and the weight given it.

It is because of the relationship between goals and compliance that multigoal or multitask "organizations" face a dilemma. Consistent emphasis on one pattern of compliance, perhaps appropriate for one sector of the organization, will cause a loss of effectiveness in the other because the pattern is congruent with only one task. If equal stress is given to two patterns or more, effectiveness may be reduced through neutralization.

However, segregation of tasks and/or personnel allows organizations to combine various compliance structures without losing effectiveness. Segregation may take the form of departmentation, thereby allowing different subunits of the organization to operate at the same time with relatively independent compliance structures. Or segregation may take place on the basis of time requirements. At any given point in time, the unit is employing only one compliance structure, but at later points in time it may switch to another. An example of this form of compliance is found in the military. During combat more reliance is placed upon moral-social pressures than during peacetime activities.

Etzioni argues that successful leadership within an organization depends upon the leader's ability to gain compliance. Abililty to gain compliance depends upon the control relationship between two levels; that is, the power applied and the kinds of involvement of the members, rather than on the substance of the work carried out. Therefore it is possible that the compliance requirements of a situation may be more important than the technological considerations of the task. This suggests that the character of compliance should be considered, as well as, or even prior to, the division of labor on the basis of task specialization. Etzioni does not deny the advantage of independent task specialization—he feels that such specialization is important, but that it should take place within major constraints imposed by the demands of the compliance structure.

There have been two opposing viewpoints concerning effective control of orgnizational performance. One point of view holds that each control relationship is a distinctive specialty to be defined in terms of performances which are controlled. The nature of the control relationship is dictated by the executive's intimate knowledge of the tasks and performances he supervises. A different position is taken by those who suggest that the control function is universal and abstract. From this point of view, control always means the ability to obtain performances through other people. The main skill required is the ability to direct the work of others and get work done by getting other people to do it. Specialized knowledge comes from experts or staff positions, not from the executive. Thus, one position maintains that control is a highly specialized function, the other that it is highly general.

Etzioni postulates that "the control function is less specialized than the performance function, it is not universal in the sense that a person who is an effective control agent in one structure will be equally effective in others . . . ." "Control differentiation is *not* based directly on the kind of performances which are supervised, but on the kind of compliance effective performance requires." Styles of leadership (here, Etzioni refers to modes of control) should be differentiated according to the kind of discipline the leader must attain, and not according to the nature of work supervised, though the two are, of course, related to some degree. Stated another way, Etzioni suggests that "the effectiveness of the mobile executive is limited to compliance areas rather than administrative or technical boundaries." Each type of compliance requires a distinctive set of personality characteristics, aptitudes, and inclinations. An individual may not have the characteristics required for more than one type of compliance. Thus, one would not expect effective combat leaders also to be effective "desk executives." Similarly, one would not expect a shop steward to be equally effective during periods of industrial harmony and in periods of labor-management conflict.

Footnotes

[1] For a more thorough discussion of this theory, see Etzioni, Amitai, *A Comparative Analysis of Complex Organization* (New York: Glencoe Free Press, 1961).

[2] The writer has taken the liberty of describing this theory in terms other than those used by Etzioni.

[3] In the original work, Etzioni refers to this kind of power as "normative power."

[4] In the original work, organizations are classified as "coercive," "utilitarian," and "normative." Utilitarian organizations are called "remunerative" organizations here.

[5] See Stogdill, R. M., *Individual Behavior and Group Achievement,* (New York: Oxford Press, 1959).

[6] Brayfield, A. H. and Crockett, W. H., "Employee Attitudes and Employee Performance" *The Psychological Bulletin,* September 1951, pp. 396–424.

[7] Lombard, G. F. F., *Behavior in a Selling Group* (Boston: Graduate School of Business Administration, Harvard University, 1955), pp. 124–130.

[8] Donovan, Frances R., *The Saleslady* (Chicago: University of Chicago Press, 1929), p. 64.

[9] Ibid., p. 192.

SIX
BUREAUCRACY: CONFLICT AND OTHER DYSFUNCTIONAL EFFECTS

Much of the criticism of classical theory has been directed at its apparent insistence on the "one best way" of organizing and managing. The principles of management and the subsequent interpretation of such notions as span of control and authority and responsibility relationships were so often violated in the everyday practice of management that they could not be called "principles." Organizations simply do not operate the way that classical theory says they should. Thus, partly due to the inadequacy of classical theory, but also because of more intensive analysis, an obsession developed in some quarters about the limitations, and the eventual demise, of organizations which approximated bureaucracy.

To Victor Thompson, the bureaucratic model is inadequate; his focus is on the problem of conflict in organizations. To him, the traditional bureaucratic structure is not compatible with rapidly developing technology, hence conflict emerges between those with the responsibility for performance and those with the capacity to make decisions.

Thompson describes outcomes of a condition in which the authority of superiors is decreasing in legitimacy, while that of specialist is increasing. For Thompson, authority in the hierarchy revolves around the question or the questions of rights and prerogatives of office. It is basic to his approach that bureaucratic authority be considered as a right of office, and similar to that presented in classical theory.

His argument is that the basis on which this right has been allocated—that is, presumed technical competence—is not appropriate. Decisions are shifting from the administrator to the specialist, yet the administrator is still held responsible. He posits a rigidity in organization structure which precludes adapting to that change, and since the structure is unlikely to be altered, and given the ever-growing gap between the right to decide and the ability to decide, the rigid structure results in a situation in which conflict is inevitable. Yet in order to maintain appearances of legitimate authority, defense mechanisms, Thompson argues, are used by both subordinates and superiors. These defense mechanisms are ideology, dramaturgy, and bureaupathology.

What Thompson presents is a dialectic dealing with power equalization in organizations that occurs when organization members are unwilling to accept the idea of legitimation and/or when the members operate in a rigid bureaucratic structure that will not change.

Sensitivity to changing technology and structural flexibility are organization conditions mandatory for effective integration of the authority and influence system in the official structure of an organization. Technology, with its concomitant increase in the number and type of specialists, generally is absorbed into the organization from external sources. This suggests that in industries or organizational groupings in which there are rapid developments and obsolence of technology, intraorganizational conflict and structural adjustment will be more critical to effectiveness than in cases where technology develops more slowly and predictably. Rapid technological change, of course, reduces the ability to predict future needs. This condition, in and of itself, implies a need for readiness for adaptation and change both in the technical and social system within the organization, but Thompson does not describe in detail alternative forms of organizations. This is done by the contingency theorists in later chapters. Nor does Thompson describe mechanisms by which this adaptation occurs. This also will be done by the contingency theorists.—H.L.T.

VICTOR THOMPSON'S "MODERN ORGANIZATIONS"

HENRY L. TOSI

Victor Thompson defines bureaucracy as a highly rationalized, impersonal integration of a large number of specialists operating to achieve some objective, upon which is superimposed a highly elaborate hierarchy of authority. The problem with which the organization must cope is securing the cooperation of specialists, and fitting specialization into a hierarchal framework. The individual is a cog in a large machine and loses some control over his destiny. He must respond to the organization. In many cases, the desired organizational response and that of the individual are opposite and problems arise.

In organizations there is a growing gap between the right to decide and the ability to decide. The right to decide is usually vested in a person performing a hierarchical role. On the other hand, the person with the greatest ability in the decision area may be performing a specialist's role. As specialization in-

*This abstract was written by Henry Tosi. It is drawn from Victor Thompson, *Modern Organizations* (New York: Knopf, 1961).

creases, this gap between the specialist and the administrator also increases. This theory is basically an analysis and an examination of the conflict between the hierarchical role and the technical role in organization and the consequence of this conflict.

THE GENERAL CHARACTERISTICS OF BUREAUCRACY

Modern organizations have emerged from earlier forms in which specialization was based on technical concepts. In early organizations, the superior usually had the ability, skill, and knowledge to make decisions. Today, by and large, the superior has *lost the ability to command, but not the right to command.* As the skills required to make decisions increase, the superior is unable to maintain a high skill level, since he must concern himself with other problems.

It is specialization which results in many characteristics which we commonly associate with bureacracy, or formal organization. As organizations grow in size, the members of the organization must be grouped into units. These units are then grouped into larger units in order to accommodate specialization and coordination. According to Thompson, the characteristics of a bureaucracy are:

1. *Rationalism.* Organizations usually seek to solve problems in the most rational manner. They are concerned with decisions which will help them achieve the organizational goal. This emphasis on rationalism in organization is largely a reflection of the increasing influence of the specialist.
2. *Appointment by merit.* In large organizations, it is necessary to promote and appoint on the basis of merit if one is to rely on highly trained specialists. To insure that the individual will stay with the organization, he must be promoted on the basis of how well he performs within his specific set of work activities.
3. *Routinization of activities.* Within organizations, activities are broken down into groups of related routines which allow the specialist to engage in the performance of his specialty.
4. *Factoring of goals.* The organizational goal is viewed in a general sense. It is broken down and factored. These, then, become the objectives, or goals, for smaller administrative or departmental units. These goals in turn are broken down and factored until concrete routines are reached. These subgoals are assigned to the lower level and become their goals. This allows lower-level units to evaluate their activity in terms of more specific criterion, rather than in terms of the general goal of the organization.
5. *Apparent inversion of ends and means.* Usually, specific activities are assigned to units. Department, or unit, members must be concerned with the performance of these activities. When other organization members

view these activities, it appears that the department members are overly concerned with the performance of those activities and the means for performing them, rather than the ends, or the objectives, which the activities are designed to achieve. For example, those who observe a budget office frequently accuse budget officers of believing the organization exists for the purpose of operating the budget procedures.

6. *Formalistic personality.* Within large organizations there are few close personal relationships among members. It is most likely that total involvement rarely occurs in interpersonal relationships.

7. *Categorization of data.* In order for the specialist to perform his activities and carry out his routines, it is necessary that he have data, and this data must be grouped into categories because of its quantity.

8. *Classification of people.* By and large, people in organizations are classified into subgroups. These subgroups, or classes of individuals, permit equal justice in policy application. Classification limits discrimination.

9. *Seeming slowness to change.* One of the major characteristics generally associated with bureaucratic organization is a tendency to react slowly, or to change slowly. This is partially due to the existence of specialists within the organization. It took time for them to acquire their skills and knowledge, therefore they may resist change which threatens them. This resistance is a kind of "cultural lag." People resist change because it upsets formal relationships and threatens the specialist with obsolescence.

10. *Concern with the monistic ideal.* In large organizations, there is a tendency to be concerned with the legitimation of the superior-subordinate relationship. Authority-responsibility relationships are stressed. The monistic emphasis is an emphasis on hierarchy. The pyramid is the resulting structure of organization that is described by the monocratic theory. The ideal application of the monistic model precludes the legitimacy of organizational conflict, divergent goals, and divergent interests of members. Since these conflicts are not legitimate, it is essential that administrators and managers spend time attempting to secure a "smooth-running organization."

As stated earlier, Thompson's analysis revolves around a study of the specialist role and the hierarchical role. The basic incongruities between these two roles and the resulting organizational consequences require discussion.

THE SPECIALIST ROLE

A bureaucracy is composed of specialized tasks developed from social processes. There are two types of specialization. The first is task specialization, a process of making activities more specific. It has to do with the division of labor. Task specialization is responsible for the repetitiveness of jobs. It occurs when an activity is subdivided into various component activities. These component activities then are grouped in some manner and assigned to an individual. Task specialization is an organizational process. It is somewhat less than completely desirable, however, since it results in limited meaning in the work to an individual.

A second type of specialization is personal specialization. It is a social process by which an individual adapts to his environment. Personal specialization makes the individual more powerful. The specific tasks he performs may be less specialized. When performance of less specialized tasks is required—that is, when the work to be done is less than routine—the result may be the specialization of the person who performs the task. Thus, the person will become a specialist. The specialization of people is a social process, prompted by the individual's welfare.

Personal specialization meets individual needs and contributes to social cohesion. Jobs which do not meet individual needs are not likely to contribute to social cohesion. Thus, highly specialized tasks, or repetitive work, may not result in great degrees of cohesion. Where there is a high degree of personal specialization in an organization, the members are forced ro recognize the interdependence of one member upon others.

As suggested earlier, one of the problems in organization is to secure the cooperation of specialists. Where personal specialization has occurred within an organization, the members are required to recognize the necessary interdependence. Where interdependence is not viewed as being necessary by members, then it must be maintained by organization power. Thus, interunit relationships may be maintained by the recognized need of members, or the exercise of organization power.

Individual activities in organization are called "programs." These are organized sets of activities that are goal directed. The individual can only learn limited numbers of them. Therefore, when new programs or activities become necessary for survival of the organization, new specialist positions within the organization must be developed.

Certain programs are combined into "instrumental relationships" to achieve externalized goals. Problems of the organization are reduced to a means-end map for solution. These problems are factored until they are reduced to a set of concrete programs. Programs are then grouped into jobs. These jobs must contain enough activity to keep their performers busy, but not so many different activities as to confuse them. The combination of programs into jobs must take into consideration the goals of the organization, the number of programs, and the extent to which the jobs fit into a supervisory unit. The number of ways that programs can be combined into jobs is limited only by the ability to perceive the possible relationships involved.

These same considerations apply to departmentalization, that is, grouping jobs into units, a unit into larger units, and so on. The kinds of departments in the organization are a function of the processes of specialization; they are the "instrumental relationships," or the exercise of hierarchical power to establish and maintain interdependencies. As tasks become more and more specialized, there is increased need for coordination. Because there is a tendency to emphasize the monistic concept of organization, relationships between specialist departments may be specified which are not in fact required. These relationships must then be supported by the use of authority.

The specialist may take many years to develop his skill. The fact that he possesses skill suggests that he may be most competent in making decisions in his skill area. Some decision-making may be passed from managers to specialists, however, and as this occurs and increases, the manager's job becomes more and more an exercise of authority without the skills necessary to make the decisions.

THE HIERARCHICAL ROLE

The hierarchy is a system of superior-subordinate roles and positions in the organization. In society, roles generally change in harmony with cultural changes. In organizations, particularly large complex bureaucracies, the advancement in specialization has brought pressure for hierarchical change. This pressure for change has been resisted, however, and, according to Thompson, the present emphasis in organization is still on the monistic concept.

In the hierarchy, the superior has certain rights. These are cultural role definitions. He may veto suggestions or proposals of subordinates. He may determine whether or not a proposal set forth by a subordinate should be implemented or forwarded to higher organizational levels. The subordinate generally has only limited rights of appeal. Obedience and loyalty of subordinates are also culturally defined rights that superiors may expect. The superior in a hierarchy generally expects his subordinates to comply with his directives. He has the right to monopolize communication between his unit and other organizational units, as well as the outside world. In general, he is responsible for communicating with higher-level officials regarding activity in his unit as well as transmitting directives from higher levels to his own unit. He has, as a result of his position in the hierarchy, a certain degree of status. He is also entitled to deference from his subordinates.

The essential nature of the rights of the superior is autocratic. He usually has the prerogative of selecting personnel within the unit, settling conflicts, determining goals of the unit (within parameters set by higher-level units) and may create nonhierarchical authority. This type of authority is a condition in which a superior may order a subordinate to comply with the influence attempts or the directives of other persons than himself.

The subordinate's role, on the other hand, is chiefly characterized by a set of duties. These duties are the correlatives of superior's rights. The subordinate's role generally requires recognition of the rights of the superior. It should be noted, however, that in most hierarchical roles, the subordinate is a superior of others. Thus, the subordinate in one relationship may be the superior in another. He therefore must concern himself with both the rights of a superior and the duties of a subordinate.

A great deal of hierarchical role behavior is concerned with deference and prestige. The hierarchy of deference in an organization is the status system. Status in an organization is important and significant when considered in conjunction with the organizational distributive system. Satisfactions, beyond market minimums, are distributed to members according to the status system. The entrance to high-status position is controlled by the hierarchy. Thus the hierarchy controls positional assignments, as well as the satisfaction and rewards that members receive. These satisfactions and rewards are distributed in a skewed fashion. Those in top positions receive a great deal more than those in bottom positions.

The amount of prestige attached to a position increases at a rapid rate as one proceeds up the organizational echelons. Prestige associated with a position is disproportionate to its absolute level. Subordinates may accord increased prestige to higher-level positions for many reasons. A subordinate may admire the boss in order to protect his own self-image. Because of the lack of hard criteria to apply to superior's role performance, the evaluation is difficult. The ambiguity attached to higher-level roles increases their prestige, suggesting that in some cases the status and prestige accorded to higher-level positions may be a result of ignorance of performance or the lack of operational performance standards for high-level officials. Also, it is highly possible that higher-level officials learn to demand deference in most cases because it is due them hierarchically.

According to Thompson, the current concept of bureacracy is "monistic." Each superior tells his subordinate what to do. Each subordinate is closely supervised by his superior and no one else. Each superior holds his subordinate responsible for performance. Authority within the organization comes down from the top. This concept of the monistic organization is based on the following assumptions. First, it is assumed that the superior is more capable than his subordinates. Second, it is assumed that the superior has the ability and the capacity to determine the results of his unit member. Third, it is assumed that nonhierarchical expertise is not relevant to the operation of the organization.

In the monistic concept, there must be a way to account for specialized activity. This is done by the concept of nonhierarchical authority, an authority created by the delegation of the superior. Thus, the staff specialist may exist, but he can only advise. It is not within the prerogative of the staff members to command. As required skills increase, more nonhierarchical authority is required in an organization. Where nonhierarchical authority exists, the right of appeal exists. This type of authority is more specific than hierarchical authority. It usually has to do with precise functions and activities. It relates to organization goals rather than personal goals. It can usually be appealed by those upon whom it is used. It can be withdrawn without destroying the function. Nonhierarchical authority is organizationally defined.

The existence and emphasis on the monistic formulation causes problems. In earlier organizations, the hierarchical roles were developed when the higher officials were the best at the job. Increasing technology makes it more difficult for those in hierarchical positions to maintain high skill levels. Organizations attempt to retain the hierarchy and fit the specialists to it. The monistic concept cannot, however, account for specialization. The concept of nonhierarchical authority is incompatible with it. The monistic concept causes a split between the right to make a decision and the ability to make it. The emphasis on a monistic concept does not provide for the legitimacy of conflict which does occur in organizations. Therefore, there must be significant effort on the part of those in the organization to smooth over such conflict.

CONFLICT

Organizations may be viewed as a factoring of broad goals to simpler and more specific sets of activities. This factoring causes the general structure of the organization. It is a function of the technology and instrumental, or goal-directed, considerations. It is determined by specialization. Factoring, along with specialization, results in the creation of nonhierarchical authority. The assignment of work to an individual, and to units, is at least initially an executive function.

The goals for which an organization can strive are technical questions. Thus, they are a function of specialization. Specialists may be viewed as persons skilled in a number of specific programs. However, the superior in the hierarchy has the right to approve organizational goals. The acceptance of innovation is probably based upon the utility of it as judged by the hierarchy in relation to the purposes or values of the organization. Yet innovation is very much a specialist function. The right to change organizational goals is a hierarchical right, but the goal which the organization is able to work toward is a technical, or specialist question.

In large, complex organizations, there is usually a need to involve many specialists, or departments of specialists, in problem-solving. This may be because of instrumental considerations or simply because of a hierarchically created relationship. At any rate, there is an increasing need to rely on specialists as the organization grows. The superior may use this need for the involvement of specialists, or coordination, to increase his power. He may delegate authority in such a manner as to create interdependencies so that he must be called in to settle differences. He is also generally able to define the problem that the group must work on. He may be protected from the influence of the group by his status and prestige, but he may at the same time have a strong influence on the group.

Organizations must also offer the individual the opportunity to satisfy his personal goals beyond the official distribution of power, capacity, and rights. The ability to achieve high levels of job satisfaction may be negatively affected by the definition of hierarchical roles. The elements required for job satisfaction may conflict with the superior's right to assign jobs and supervise them, or they may conflict with the independence of the individual. The fact that the superior can monopolize official communication may be damaging to personal satisfaction. The denial of pertinent information requirements may result in the inability of the subordinate to see the relationship between his activities and group objectives.

As one climbs higher in the organizational hierarchy, opportunity for job satisfaction decreases because of decreasing specialist content in the job. Higher-level officials generally become more oriented toward goals such as power, prestige, and money. As one proceeds up the organizational ladder, adequate operational performance standards decrease. This may result in increased anxiety for those at higher levels, and the incumbent may take some action to solidify his prestige by insisting upon hierarchical rights.

There is perhaps a more significant impact on the personal goal within organizations. The hierarchy in organization has appropriated the concept of success, or achievement of high status. To be successful culturally, one must proceed up a hierarchy. The problem, however, is that the hierarchy is able to manipulate the distributive system in large part. The resulting distribution of organization rewards and prestige is skewed, and therefore may seem unjust to those who wish to succeed. It may reduce the willingness to cooperate.

There are only a few high-status positions in the hierarchy. Admission may be based on some factors other than relevant performance. The individual most likely to get promoted may be the one who is most like those presently in hierarchical positions. Merit and ability may be overlooked. Some who should achieve success do not, and as a result do not identify with the organization. This may reduce cohesiveness, thereby losing one of the bases of cooperation. This condition essentially denies social recognition and status to many.

Conflict arises from growing inconsistencies between specialists and hierarchical roles. The existence of conflict in an organization is difficult to handle because it is not formally recognized or legitimated within a monistic system. Thus, the existence of specialist-hierarchical role conflict generates the mechanism of role defense. These role defenses are adopted by both specialists and those in hierarchical roles. Specialist role defenses are oriented primarily toward the profession, or the skill area in which the specialist functions or operates. He may seek peer support. The role defense of those in hierarchical positions is somewhat different. Generally they rely on ideology, bureaupathology, and dramaturgy. The remainder of this discussion of Thompson's view emphasizes hierarchical role defense mechanisms.

IDEOLOGY

Originally, organizations were headed by charismatic leaders. They were able to exercise authority. Members responded to their attempts to influence them. But growth of specialization has lessened the force of charisma—and made necessary the protection of the hierarchical role in the monistic system. Role definition and authority in bureaucracies must be legitimated. Three defense mechanisms have emerged. These are (1) ideology, (2) dramaturgy, and (3) bureaupathic behavior.

Power is the ability to influence others. If it is legitimate, it is called "authority." Ideas and concepts which justify power held by a person are called "ideology." Where ideology is used, the attention of organization members is usually diverted from the institutional structure. Ideology is used to justify power or authority by attempting to show that those who hold the power are the most qualified to do so, or that the incumbent authority is best for all. Thus, attention is diverted from problems which arise from the organizational structure.

The fact that the force of charisma has declined in the organization has resulted in three general methods to develop ideology. First, leadership studies have been concerned with attempting to determine the traits of leadership. Second, the field of managerial psychology has emerged. This field has attempted to fit people in organizations into existing monistic structures. Problems of intergroup conflict and divergent goals can be solved by training, communications, and reorientation of members. It is assumed that the individual can be changed to fit the structure, hence there is no need to change the present monistic form. Third, the monistic concept, the emphasis on responsibility and authority, is continued. It still holds that "specialists advise and point out the implications of their advice, while the responsibility for implementation belongs to the hierarchy." Since this is not the actual case in organizations, it is necessary to control impressions about hierarchical positions. Such control of impressions is called "dramaturgy."

DRAMATURGY

Dramaturgy is the control of information or cues imparted to others to control their impressions. Specialists, as well as those in hierarchical role positions, engage in dramaturgical behavior. The doctor's white coat and the engineer's slide rule suggest the qualifications of each of these specialists. Legitimation in the organization is especially critical because of the specialist-hierarchy gap. The greater the discrepancy, the greater the acting on the part of both members. Organizationally-defined specialties conflict with culturally-defined rights of the hierarchy. Therefore, a staff must only advise. If this advice comes in the form of commands, everyone pretends it is from a higher official. This protects the self-images of those receiving specialist's commands and communications. This is essential for maintaining the legitimacy of hierarchical roles. The impressions that the superior is supposed to convey to his subordinates are that he is industrious, busy, and loyal to the organization. The status symbols used in the organization aid in the dramaturgical process. Large offices, deep carpets, and special furniture aid in the creation of the correct impression. The superiors must be somewhat aloof and apart from lower-level members. They must have good records of performance in their job. They must be able to control their emotions, and be careful about behavior and contacts away from work.

Subordinates also engage in dramaturgy. They must be "awed" by their superiors. They must create the impression that they must be told what to do. Subordinates are supposed to look busy.

BUREAUPATHOLOGY

Individuals must adjust to organizations. Those who do, engage in "bureaucratic," or normal behavior. Some individuals, however, are unable to adjust to organizations. This inability to adjust is called "bureausis." Others may be insecure in a bureaucracy. This may result in excessive aloofness, excessive concern with routine and procedures, and resistance to change. This is called "bureaupathology."

Bureaupathology occurs when a superior appropriates the major aspects of the bureaucratic organization for satisfaction of personal needs. It is essentially exercised downward. The superior has a need to control subordinates and to make them conform to a set of preconceived standards.

Organizational success may result in insecurity and anxiety. As one proceeds up organizational levels, performance standards become less objective. The individual knows he must please his boss, but he does not know how. Anxiety may also occur when the position which an individual fills is not accepted by "significant others." The growing gap between the specialist role and the hierarchical role also produces some anxiety. The superior is in a dilemma. He must satisfy nonexplicit performance demands of his superior through subordinates whose skill and abilities he hardly understands. An insecure person may not be able to tolerate this. He may then generate pressures down the line which are passed all through the organization at lower levels. He may emphasize characteristics of the bureaucracy. This has a circular effect. As employees are subjected to greater pressures, they may deviate from the desired standards. As this occurs, the manager's anxiety is increased, and he may begin to insist still more upon the rights and prerogatives of the office he holds.

Bureaupathological behavior may result in quantitative compliance with the standards. That is, individuals may comply with the letter of the law, but not the spirit. Standards applied may be relatively trivial, but there is a need for quantitative measurement since controls can be applied only when standards are available.

Exaggerated aloofness of a superior is also another outcome of bureaupathology. Normal relationships in an organization are not warm in any case, but exaggerated aloofness protects the superiors from commitments to the subordinates so that he can require them to perform when demanded from above.

Another result of pathological behavior in organizations is resistance to change. Innovations are dangerous since they are difficult to control. Risk is involved, which the superior may be unwilling to take in any significant degree. The superior may also insist upon petty rights of office, or protocol. He may engage in close supervision and insist on exclusive contact with outsiders and higher-level officials. Bureaupathological behavior exists because of the growing insecurity of authority and the hierarchical role in organizations. Increasing specialization results in increasing incompatability with the concept of the monistic form of organization. Bureaupathological responses to insecurity are facilitated since there is a routinization of organization problem solving.

Some people are not able to adjust to bureaucracy. They view it as a curse and a condition which should not exist. Their view of organization is immature. They may engage in "bureautic" behavior. This may be viewed as the dysfunctional persistence of childish behavior patterns. The individual feels powerless in the organization. He attempts to fight the system. He feels that it does not respond to his needs, and that people may be out to "get" him. He resists "red tape" and may view the requirement to respond and comply with his superior as unnecessary.

In summary, then, there are three kinds of behavior patterns in organizations. The first is bureaucratic in nature. These patterns refer to the workings of the large, complex organization, which are determined by the nature of specialization involved. The second is bureaupathology. This involves exaggerations of behavior by insecure persons in hierarchical and nonhierarchical positions. Lastly, bureautic behavior is a reaction to modern organizations by persons who are unable to adjust to the complexity, impersonality, and impartiality of organizations. This type of behavior is viewed as immature.

COOPERATION

While management may be outwardly concerned with output, it must also be concerned with the function of obtaining cooperation of members. The methods which it may use are many. It may attempt to command, or rely heavily on a hierarchy, or obtain cooperation by means of group identification. This latter method suggests that the informal group regulates behavior. Thus, it is necessary to get the informal organization working with the formal aspect. Thompson suggests that cooperation may be most easily obtained when it is based on mutually recognized interdependence. Where there is a need to cooperate, this will be recognized. The need will be met. In addition, however, there is still the need for some legitimating devices. These must be held to a minimum. In order to secure cooperation through the recognition of mutual interdependence, it is necessary that there by equality of opportunity and distribution of rewards within the organization.

SEVEN
GROUP STRUCTURE AND ORGANIZATIONAL EFFECTS

The focus of Ralph Stogdill's work is individual behavior and group achievement. His theoretical formulation is drawn from the analysis of a large number of empirical research efforts dealing with individual, group, and organization variables as well as previous theoretical developments in groups and organizations.

Stogdill describes multiple outcomes of organizations. While others have recognized, at least implicitly, that the result of organized behavior is certainly something more than some particular product or service, Stogdill's treatment is somewhat different from those of others. For example, Argyris (1) suggests that the evaluation of organizational effectiveness should be determined in terms of the energy required to carry out the three core activities in relation to their payoffs. These activities are achievement of the objective, internal maintenance, and environmental adaption. But, unlike others, Stogdill has postulated relationships between these outcomes. He suggests what might happen to responsiveness and integration, outcome variables along with productivity, when there are efforts to increase productivity. And this is an important point, not because his statements of the relationships are necessarily correct, but rather because they represent hypotheses of a nature that are rarely advanced in organization literature. They suggest not only that trade-offs are important, but also the nature of these trade-offs when pressures are increased.

Second, Stogdill's concept of structure, one of his intervening variables, provides several interesting considerations in the manner in which it is related to the output variables. He postulates curvilinear relationships between structure and outputs. High structure is ineffective, but then so is low structure. Notice, however, that these realtionships are moderated by the nature of the work and the satisfaction of the members of the organization.

Stogdill's work is included here because it seems to be an approach which can accommodate some of the many different points of view presented earlier in this book. Stogdill acknowledges the impact of formal organization structure on behavior. On the other hand, he provides a set of concepts to deal with the problem of how individuals may alter the structure system. Thus, to use the terminology which Scott (37) attributes to the neoclassical school, formal and informal organizations, Stogdill provides a way of considering how both these aspects of organization interact to yield stable behavior patterns.—H.L.T.

RALPH M. STOGDILL'S "INDIVIDUAL BEHAVIOR AND GROUP ACHIEVEMENT"*

ALAN FILLEY

ROBERT J. HOUSE

In 1959 Stogdill published *Individual Behavior and Group Achievement* (42). It contains a theoretical model of organization behavior which synthesizes and explains the results of some 800 research studies. The theory was developed by identifying the elements of organizational behavior found in the research studies and manipulating these elements until an internally logical, predictive system emerged.

We believe the theory to be important for several reasons:

1. It resolves much of the apparent conflict and confusion between researchers and theorists who have stressed structural-functional aspects of organization and those who have emphasized behavioral aspects.
2. It offers an explanation, inferred from social science and business research findings, of (a) the relationship between organizational, group and individual objectives; (b) the interaction between formal and informal organizational behavior; and (c) the multidimensional aspects of group achievement.
3. The breadth an empirical orientation of the theory provide a basis for integrative research including several schools of thought.

Throughout his theory, Stogdill attempts to preserve internal consistency of meaning and logic and external agreement with available research. To understand its contents completely, one should follow the precise definitions of terms used in the original work and carefully read Stogdill's review of the research cited to support the theory. However, for present purposes a simple and nontechnical summary, with examples, is presented. The authors have occasionally taken the liberty of retitling some of the critical variables for

*Thanks are due the publisher and Dr. Ralph M. Stogdill for permission to use the ideas and concepts presented in *Individual Behavior and Group Achievement* (New York: Oxford University Press, 1959). Special thanks to Alan C. Filley and Robert House for their permission to use the summary they prepared.

clearer understanding. Certain relationships that are implicit in the original work are made explicit in this summary. These changes bring the inevitable risks of misinterpretation, omission, and misemphasis, for which the authors must be responsible. In general, however, every effort was made to preserve the wording, essential variables, and intent of Stogdill's theory in the summary which follows.

THE THEORY

The theoretical model is based upon nine variables which are classified into three groups: input, intervening, and output variables, as here:

Input Variables	Intervening Variables	Output Variables
Member interaction	Member satisfaction	Group responsiveness
Individual performance	Group structure	Productivity
Individual expectation	Task-oriented work	Integration

The *input variables* are (a) member interactions, (b) individual performances, and (c) individual expectations. *Intervening variables* are (a) member satisfaction, (b) group structure, and (c) task-oriented work. Intervening variables follow inputs in time, condition input variables, and are partial determinants of group achievement. *Output variables* (describing group achievement) are (a) productivity, (b) integration (cohesiveness), and (c) responsiveness (drive).

Input Variables

Interaction is defined as an action-reaction sequence in which the reaction of any member in a group is a response to the reaction of another member. Thus, where interaction takes place there is mutual reaction between two parties in the group. It is necessary to distinguish between simple reaction and the more complex interaction. Reaction is a one-way process which may be represented by the statement "A responds to B," whereas interaction is a two way process which involves both A's response to B and a reaction by B to A's response.

Stogdill defines group as an open interaction system in which actions (or reactions) determine the structure of the system and a successive interactions exert equal effects upon the identity of the system; that is, the group retains its identity and continuity even though individual members may enter or leave. The group evidences structure through the predictable actions or reactions of group members. As we shall see later, the extent to which predictable behavior is possible by group members determines the freedom of each of the members.

Group members contribute both performance and expectation to the interaction system. *Performance* is defined as one of the actions or reactions that constitute the task-oriented work of an interaction system. It is an action which identifies an individual as a member of group operations. The actor saying his lines, the lathe operator running his machine, or the manager planning work of subordinates are all exhibiting performances which identify them. Differences in performance provide the basis for differentiation of structure in groups and may be influenced by external or internal factors such as intelligence, special aptitudes, length of the working day, lighting, pacing of work, etc. Some 60 years of human engineering research has increased performance by matching the proper man to the job under proper conditions.

The expectation of group members is also an important contributing factor in the interaction system. Stogdill defines *individual expectation* as readiness for reinforcement, and says that expectation is a function of (a) drive (level of tension or reactivity exhibited by an organism), (b) the estimated probability of the occurrence of a possible outcome, and (c) the estimated desirability of the outcome. The estimates of desirability and probability may also reinforce each other if operating in the same direction and lowered probability may diminish desirability estimates. Also, probability estimates tend to be overestimated when the expected outcome is desirable (positively valued) and underestimated when the expected outcome is undesirable (negatively valued).

Probability and desirability estimates differ not only in kind but in rate of change as well. Estimated desirability rises rapidly towards its maximum value in response to initial reinforcement, and further reinforcements exert a diminishing amount of increase in desirability estimates. Estimates of probability, on the other hand, tend to rise more slowly.

Thus, one may infer that in situations where desirable group goals have been provided, perceived confirmation (reinforcement) of the likelihood of attaining these goals will elicit initial group support even if the goals actually prove to be improbable. Similarly, an individual's motivation may be regarded as a function of his drive and of the confirmation of his desirability estimates.

The group may also act upon the expectations of a member, causing him to adjust his values to the group norms or to reject the group in favor of values more suitable to him. Conformity to group norms is facilitated when the members are strongly motivated to remain in the group, when they desire group reinforcement of their own value systems, and when the group norms are clearly defined; conformity is also facilitated when the group members have access to accurate information about the norms, when the group is more highly valued by the individual than other reference groups with conflicting values, and when the group is able to reinforce expectations.

The extent to which group norms work for or against formal organization goals is strongly influenced by intervening variables, particularly that of structure.

Intervening Variables

The intervening variables of the Stogdill model influence the effectiveness with which inputs can result in a satisfactory group achievement.

The first and most important intervening variable is group structure. This variable has for a long time been recognized as a critical factor in attaining successful group action. Stogdill defines *group structure* as the differential regularities of action and reaction exhibited in the positions in a system. The position of a group member exhibits predictable patterns of performance. Group members perceive these patterns and thus confirm probability estimates of each other's performance.

In other words, the position of a member in an interaction system is defined by predictability of action and reaction. This predictability operates as a stimulus to predictable reaction by other members of a system. Thus, once structure is established and action by group members becomes predictable, then members can act upon that predictability without relying upon continuous interaction, such as checking with others for information, obtaining approval, etc. The optimum degree of structure confirms the group interaction pattern and permits the successful accomplishment of group goals, whereas less or more than optimum structure may seriously restrict group output.

A structured system thus permits members freedom. *It increases the area of freedom for its members* because the predictable individual differences in performance which define the positions in the system permit areas of action which are *not* responses to the actions of other members.

Individual freedom is highest under moderate degrees of structure. If one understands the basic doctrine and values of an organization, is allowed to interpret each situation in the light of these values, and can take discretionary action within predetermined limits, his area of freedom is both clarified and enlarged.

Individual freedom is at a minimum under extremes of high or low group structure. When group structure is too high, the individual is controlled by the system; when too low, the individual must rely upon constant interaction. If, for example, one's job is rigidly defined by repetition, procedure, or established practices, he has little freedom to act. If, on the other hand, each time one takes action he must get a new definition of policy or authority from his superior, he also has little freedom to act. This curvilinear relationship between freedom and structure is supported by a number of research studies and serves as an important link between the structural-functional school and the behavioral school of management scholars.

Group structure is composed of two subsystems, a position system and a role system. The *position system* is the more permanent of the two. It is organized by status (levels) and function (work activities). *Status* is defined as the degree of freedom granted the occupant of a position in initiating and maintaining the goal direction and structure of the system. *Function* is the general nature of the contribution that the occupant of a position is expected to make toward the accomplishment of a group purpose; this definition is analogous to the concept of general work assignment familiar to students of functional management. Both status and function create a hierarchy of positions referred to as the formal organization. Once it is established, the formal organization is quite stable; the status and function of a position remain rather fixed even though the occupant of the position may change.

The second subsystem of structure is the *role system.* The role system is an expected pattern of behavior that is attached to a person rather than to the position which he occupies. Two members holding the same position may be expected to perform different roles; for instance the subordinates of two foremen with similar status and function may expect different patterns of leader behavior from each. Expectations by group members concerning a member role are influenced by three factors: the nature of the position itself, member demands brought on changes in structural and operational requirements, and a member's perception of the kind of person that he is.

The role system is an informal structure that is less permanent than the position system. It is defined by authority and responsibility. *Authority,* as used here is defined as the degree of freedom that the occupant of a position is expected to exercise in initiating performance and interaction within a formally acknowledged structure. *Responsibility* is the set or range of performances that a member is expected to exhibit by virtue of the operational demands made upon his position in a formally acknowledged structure. It should be noted that while status and function in the formal position system and authority and responsibility in the role system are parallel concepts, they are not necessarily equal.[1]

Both the position and the role structure are determined by group interaction in the absence of any formally established relationships. When the formal organization is defined by management, however, it is adjusted to meet the needs of the role structure, the role structure adjusts to it, or both. As group members interact, their individual expectations are either confirmed and reinforced or they are not confirmed. When confirmation and reinforcement occur, a pattern of relationships is defined between members in terms of performances and expectations. If the pattern meets with the approval of group members, it is translated into a structure which defines the individual position and role of each member as related to the group purpose.

When structural patterns do not meet with member approval, adjustment is necessary if an acceptable structure is to be developed. Resolution of the conflict takes place through the interaction process. Sources of conflict are many and varied; subgroups may have conflicting goals; subgroups may expect different roles from the same position (for example, a foreman may be viewed differently by management and by his own subordinates); or role expectations may differ from position expectations.

Suitable group structure is also prerequisite to an optimum degree of the other two intervening variables, member satisfaction and task-oriented work.

Member satisfaction may be defined as the sense of personal well-being one feels when his goals or expectations are being met. (This definition is implicit in the theory.) The accomplishment of personal goals may or may not lead to the accomplishment of production goals of the formal organization. Nor does it necessarily follow that satisfied individuals create a group that is responsive to continued change and development. It is clear, however, that individual satisfaction bears curvilinear relationship to structure; that is, satisfaction is most likely to be highest under intermediate degrees of structure. Unless a member knows what is expected of him by other members of the group and how well he is meeting these expectations, he is not apt to be satisfied with his own performance or with the performance of other members of the group.

Task-oriented work also bears a curvilinear relationship to structure.[2] *Task-oriented work* is defined as all of the actions and reactions which maintain the structure and accomplish the purposes of the group. Member performances which are not directed toward group goal attainment or maintenance of the group structure are not considered part of this task-oriented work; that is, sleeping, reading, or having one's hair cut on company time (if not job connected) would meet personal but not group goals. As might be expected, task-oriented work is positively related to the achievement of total group productivity.

The relationship between the intervening variables and the various kinds of group achievement will be explained in the discussion which follows.

Types of Group Achievement

Group achievement (output) may be defined as the sum of the outcomes experienced by the group as a result of interrelated performances, interactions, and expectations of its members, as affected by intervening variables. It is essential to recognize at the outset that the output of the group is divided among three factors: productivity, responsiveness, and integration. It is not solely productivity.

Stogdill emphasizes that he has not found it possible to construct a logically consistent theory based on the hypothesis that productivity is the only achievement of organization. Rather, the achievement of an organization is divided among the three types of output.

The first of the outputs, *productivity,* is defined as the degree of change in expectancy values created by task-oriented work. Productivity measures the values created by the members for the group. While clear measures have yet to be found, productivity is generally measured in industrial organizations in terms of dollar value of output compared with dollar value of input.

Subgroups tend to develop norms which regulate productive output at a rate that is comfortable for their average members. The total group will establish a standard of productivity that can be fulfilled by all of its subgroups. For example, financial incentives have only short-term effects where they are based on quotas which are above group norms.

More lasting effects upon productivity are achieved by permitting the members of lower status positions to have role boundaries that enlarge their responsibility and authority. People tend to perform near the outer limits of their roles because they derive pride and satisfaction from demonstrating their competence to meet the expectations of others. When roles are sufficiently large, therefore, group norms are elevated to accommodate the defined area of responsibility and authority. Management literature contains many instances where job enlargement has provided an opportunity for increased responsibility and authority, resulting in positive changes in productivity and job satisfaction.

Productivity bears a curvilinear relationship to structure. It is normally highest under intermediate degrees of structure.

Structure is also curvilinearly related to another measure of achievement, responsiveness. *Group responsiveness* (drive) is defined as freedom from restraint in action toward a goal.[3] Freedom to act, freedom to interact, and freedom to reinforce expectations are examples of group responsiveness.

The responsiveness of a group may be too high or too low. If too high, as Stogdill points out, a military group may be destroyed by its willingness to charge wildly into withering enemy fire; if too low, it will fail to attack at all.

Continued favorable responsiveness is, in part, a product of success. As the group receives reinforcement of its goal expectations, it increases its responsiveness to further action. Since responsiveness is a function of structure and control, it is also closely related to group leadership.

Responsiveness is not the same as motivation. Motivation is a function of drive and confirmed desirability estimates. It provides the potential for responsiveness, which may or may not be realized, depending upon mediating factors. An individual or group may be highly motivated, yet unable to act. If motivation is to result in responsiveness, there must be attainable goal expectations, a reinforcement of those expectations by experiences of success, the necessary freedom to act, and the proper degree of structure and control.

Group integration (cohesiveness), the third output, is either positively or negatively related to the output of responsiveness. *Integration,* defined as the ability of the group to maintain structure and function under stress, meets the group's needs for structural stability, coordination, unity, and loyalty. An integrated group is characterized as having viscidity; in other words, group members function as a unit and are free from dissension, conflicting interests, and disrupting forces.

Integration is a function of intermember unity and coordination in the support of group structure, operations, and goals. It is dependent upon a clearly defined role structure that is free from role confusion and role conflict; for such conflict typically reduces the value of group members to the members, the ability of a member to act decisively and his satisfaction with the organization.

Individual satisfaction, an intervening variable, is more highly related to group integration than to productivity and responsiveness. Reinforcement of individual expectations concerning group membership simply confirms the individual's estimate of the value of membership in the group, as well as his probability estimate of experiencing further satisfaction from continued group membership. The effect of satisfying a member's expectations is to increase his support of the group, thus encouraging greater integration.

Individual satisfaction is not the same as integration, however. A group may have highly satisfied individuals but low integration if individuals are idle, playing, wasting resources, or undermining the status structure of the group. Individual satisfaction contributes to group integration only when the reinforcement of the members' expectations leads them to support the group structure, teamwork, and goals.

While member satisfaction is generally positively related to group integration, satisfaction is *not* found to be highly related to group productivity. In fact, satisfaction measures and productivity measures are found more often than not to be negatively related. This relationship is explained by the fact that satisfying experiences, such as talking to one's fellow worker or filing a grievance are often conducted at the expense of productivity. Only when meeting productivity goals is also satisfying are satisfaction and group productivity positively related. Similarly, efforts to build group integration usually takes time and resources which could otherwise be devoted to productivity.

The most frequently observed relationships between the three factors of group achievement may be summarized by the following hypotheses:

1.   Productivity and responsiveness are positively related.
2.   Responsiveness may be positively or negatively related to integration.
3.   Integration and productivity are negatively related.
4.   Productivity, responsiveness, and integration may be positively related when the group is strongly motivated in striving toward goal achievement (when inputs increase) or when motivation is very low (when inputs decrease).[4]

The organization which is successful in realizing group achievement is one which maintains a *balance of output* between the three factors mentioned. A portion of the input is used in meeting present goals; another portion is expended in maintaining the viability and responsiveness of the group so that future goals may also be reached. Only if inputs increase may all outputs be increased. Otherwise, one output may be increased at a cost of one or both of the other outputs. High or low amounts of structure and control decrease the effectiveness of performances. When structure is moderate, performances are channeled directly toward task and goal accomplishments, and group achievement is highest.

The relations between output and the other variables in the Stogdill model may be illustrated by considering two typical situations: in the first (Figure 1), work is satisfying and structure and leadership complement each other; in the second (Figure 2), work is dissatisfying and unpleasant conditions are frustrating or stress-producing.

Figure 1 illustrates the first situation. High expectations of goal achievement are supported by positive leadership patterns and structure. Group goals are defined, positions and roles are clarified, job relationships are known and accepted, and policies are stated and accepted. Reinforcement of expectations leads to individual satisfaction of group members, high motivation, and a high level of task-oriented work. The end result is a high level of achievement and a favorable balance between the outputs of the group.

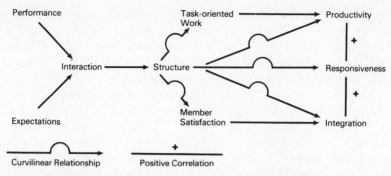

Figure 1 Group achievement when work is satisfying.

The second situation is shown in Figure 2. Here, members have adequate freedom of status and authority, but they find the work itself to be unpleasant, frustrating, or tension-producing. Under such conditions, members may evidence a high degree of group integration associated with low levels of productivity and responsiveness. If these conditions persist, inputs will also be reduced through feedback, causing all group achievement to suffer.

To illustrate the situation shown in Figure 2:

In January, 1962, British postal workers, upset by the government's anti-inflationary ban on wage increases for public employees, nearly strangled the country's postal system. The employees already earned 3.5 percent less than industrial employees and with the ban found their attempts to improve earnings frustrated.

The postal employees reacted to this frustration by a unified move to work strictly by the rule book. By common consent of both the formal and informal organization, rules had not been interpreted literally prior to the government order, yet after the ban productivity dropped precipitously when postmen refused to carry more than the regulation 35-pound load on rounds, refused to leave mail when there was no mailbox, and returned "incorrectly" addressed letters that lacked postal zone numbers.

The members had become more integrated in response to the situation diverting freedom of status and authority toward only one aspect of achievement.[5]

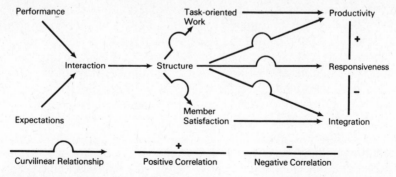

Figure 2 Group achievement when work is dissatisfying, or unpleasant, or conditions are frustrating or stress producing.

Before the government ban, there was freedom of action which permitted the achievement of both subgroup and formal goals. After their subgroup goals were frustrated, workgroups become more highly integrated and used literal interpretation of workrules as a means of restricting productivity and responsiveness toward organizational goals.

In summary, leadership which strives only for maximum production is overlooking two important elements: responsiveness and integration. Stogdill's theory emphasizes that a leader must seek the optimum balance of group achievement among all three outputs. Undue emphasis upon productivity, if it reduces expectations and integration, may have the effect of actually deteriorating the structure of the group and, therefore, its capacity for future productivity.

IMPLICATIONS OF THE THEORY FOR THE FIELD OF MANAGEMENT
Provides a Basis of Reconciliation Between Behavioralists and Structural-Functionalists

Now that a summary of Stogdill's theory has been presented, let us consider some of its implications for the field of management. One of the most important contributions is its reconciliation of much of the current controversy between the structural-functional and behavioral schools of thought. The functional school has traditionally emphasized formalization of group objectives and relationships through rational, policies, procedures, instructions, job definitions, organization structure, and control systems. This school postulates that group achievement relies heavily upon the performance of legalized or appointed functions. These functions are usually classified as planning, organizing, and controlling. The functional school also states that after the group reaches a certain level of complexity, the absence of formalization will result in confusion and ineffective methods of achievement.

In contrast with the structural-functional emphasis, the behavioral school has emphasized the complexities and interrelationships of emotional human beings operating within a viable group system. The behavioralists argue that the functional theory is primarily a mechanical explanation of organized behavior, suffering from the invalid assumption of an economic, rational man. They believe that in assuming complete rationality and overlooking the consequences of emotional and social choice, the functional theorist disregards many essential variables of organized behavior. Some behavioral scientists even imply that the very presence of formal structure will have unhealthy effects on an individual's personality development and, therefore, inhibits the attainment of group objectives.

Both schools show the bias of their origins and early training in their research designs. The functional school emphasizes the standardization, description, and measurement customary to engineering; the behavioralist stresses variations in value, perception, and choice in keeping with his psychological or sociological background. The functionalist searches primarily for determinants of efficiency; the behavioralist looks for determinants of member satisfaction. Yet both frequently identify different effects of the same independent or dependent variables; for example, the rational aspects of policy formulation versus its social or psychological consequences.

Consider the differences in taste and method of the two schools, it seems that most of their findings are noncomparable, rather than contradictory. For example, the economic value of formal organization is not disproved by proving that group members show sociometric preference or that formal organization forces members to achieve personal satisfactions (and perhaps even self-realization) off the job rather than as part of the job. Only when such effects impede the accomplishment of the organizational objectives do they raise questions of validity concerning formal organizational theory. Similarly, the importance of social systems is not negated by proving the importance of formal organization in meeting business objectives. Unfortunately, this type of inference is found in the literature of both schools of thought.

The hope for reconciliation of the two schools seems to lie in theoretical and empirical work which integrates organizational and behavioral variables into a single system.[6] Stogdill's theory is designed to accomplish this objective.

Stogdill's theory is not only logically structured; it derives it hypotheses from empirical evidence from social science literature in general, including business literature. Stogdill, a social psychologist of note, demonstrates a thorough knowledge of functional theory and research, as well as behavioral. He is one of the few organizational theorists trained in the behavioral sciences who is free from the criticism that he lacks understanding of the classical management viewpoint.

Explains Relationships Between Leader Behavior, Management Functions and Informal Organization

Stogdill also makes an important contribution to management theory when he shows that the ideal leader behavior is one which succeeds in harmonizing individual expectations and organizational objectives by reinforcing desired member behavior and by encouraging or withholding confirmation of member expectations. Ideal managerial behavior requires the performance of management functions (planning, organizing, and controlling) which provide needed structure to group members. When this structure is absent, members operate under conditions of uncertainty. If structure is properly organized, it provides the necessary basis for realization of expectations and allows members to make decisions and exercise initiative.

The freedom provided by formal structure is an important factor in providing concomitant informal activities which contribute to both productivity and individual satisfaction. This relationship is supported by research which shows that when individual and organizational objectives are harmonious, informal activity facilitates attainment of formal objectives. Informal interaction and formal structure, therefore, can be mutually supportive and provide benefits to both the individual and the organization. It follows that maximum benefit is obtained when both the formal and the informal structure are gradually and continually modified according to desirable patterns of interaction.

Although the presence and importance of the formal and informal organizations are not new concepts to management students, the combination of the two by Stogdill, bringing out their role as mediators of interaction and expectations, provides a way to view organization behavior.

Reconciles Apparent Contradictions in Empiric Research

The theory is also important in its explanation of the relationship between member satisfaction and group productivity. It illustrates why behavioral research has shown that member satisfaction and productivity do not necessarily vary positively. It also explains the conditions under which positive and negative variances can be predicted. Relating satisfaction to integration, Stogdill shows that while integration may impede the attainment of short-run productivity, it is necessary for the achievement of long-range business objectives. The sharing of output between productivity and integration is necessary in order to provide a viable, unified group capable of continued effort under conditions of threat or stress. This relationship has important implications for organizations operating under conditions of change, external threat, or internal frustration.

It should also be noted that productivity, integration, and individual satisfaction can receive the best effects of inputs at intermediate degrees of structure. Too little or too much structure will restrict group achievement; this fact should be considered both by those who seek to avoid the definition of structure in business organizations and by those who seek to reduce all activities to routine procedure.

Footnotes

[1] Stogdill's terms should be used as defined. Some have a different usage from that in general management literature. The distinction between status and authority (as used here) also points up a source of conflict between management theorists today: *status* is the level of freedom prescribed by the formal organization (often called "legal" or "formal authority") while *authority* in the Stogdill model refers to the level of freedom that is acceptable to the group (on a social or political basis) based on the "consent of the governed" rather than formal delegation.

[2] The phrase "task-oriented work" was chosen rather than Stogdill's term "operations" in order to clarify the meaning and intent of the variable.

[3] Stogdill uses the term "morale" rather than "responsiveness" for this factor. This use of the term is consistent with writings several decades ago, but it is confusing to

those who associate "morale" with any one of its many contemporary usages. The term "responsiveness" seems to retain Stogdill's meaning and avoids potential confusion.

[4]When these hypotheses are taken together they appear to be anomalous at one point: If responsiveness increases when productivity increases and productivity increases when integration decreases, then responsiveness should increase when integration decreases. Yet Stogdill says that responsiveness may vary positively or negatively with integration. Since the positive relationship is thus not accounted for in this syllogism, the need for research to explain the inconsistency is suggested. Stogdill himself recognizes that exceptions to each of the relationships posited may occur and recommends further investigation to account for these exceptions.

[5]"Rebellion by the Rules," *Time,* vol. LXXIX, no. 3 (Jan. 19, 1962), p. 35.

[6]For example, the authors are engaged in a study of the relationship between organization and behavior in the research and development divisions of three large manufacturing companies. We are exploring the relationship between such independent variables as number of superiors, organization level, type of work, span of control, attitude flexibility, intelligence, age education, time with company, and time in job; with such dependent variables as delegation of responsibility, perceived authority, leader behavior, job satisfaction, performance of managerial unit, and degree of role conflict.

EIGHT
MARKETS AND ORGANIZATION

The concepts used most frequently in organization theory are taken primarily from sociology and psychology. Little has been drawn from the field of economics, although there has been some suggestion that economics might be fruitful source of ideas (25).

Williamson's work, however, does draw heavily from economics. Williamson, an economist, tempers standard economic assumptions about rationality by using March and Simon's (23) concept of bounded rationality. He uses transaction costs, environmental certainty, and opportunism to explain how hierarchies (organizations) emerge to manage conditions where markets are not efficient regulating mechanisms.

This approach has another important feature. It redirects attention to the market, an important environmental sector which has not received the attention as technology—H.L.T.

"THE MARKETS AND HIERARCHIES AND VISIBLE HAND PERSPECTIVES"

The Markets and Hierarchies Program of
Research: Origins, Implications, Prospects
OLIVER E. WILLIAMSON AND WILLIAM G.
OUCHI

Although organization theory has its origins in sociology and is principally identified with that field, the subject matter is interdisciplinary to an unusual degree, and is incompletely informed by exclusive reliance on any single social science. We contend that organization theory is seriously underdeveloped with respect to its economic content, and argue that it needs greater appeal to economics, although economics of a nontraditional kind. Specifically, we suggest that organization theory in general and organizational design and

Reprinted by permission of the authors and the publisher from Andrew Van de Ven and William Joyce, *Perspectives on Organization Design and Behavior* (New York: Wiley, 1981).

assessment in particular need to be more sensitive to transaction costs and to the importance of economizing on those.

But economics and organization theory have a reciprocal relation (Ouchi and Van de Ven, 1980). Economics stands to benefit by drawing upon organization theory. This applies both to the refurbishing of its behavioral assumptions, which tend to be stark and sometimes implausible, and to the level of analysis, which in economics tends to be rather aggregative. The Markets and Hierarchies (M&H) program of research is based precisely on such a strategy. Thus it draws on organization theory to enrich its behavioral assumptions, and it regards the transaction, rather than the firm or market, as the basic unit of analysis.* Joining these behavioral assumptions and microanalytic focus with the economizing concepts and systems orientation characteristic of economics yields new and deeper insights into economic and social organization. This chapter reviews the origins and applications of the Markets and Hierarchies approach with special emphasis on its organization theory aspects. It develops the ramifications for organizational design, and addresses research agenda issues of special interest to organization theory specialists.

ORIGINS

It is rarely possible to do justice to earlier work on which subsequent research relies; nevertheless the following brief statement indicates the origins and background of our research.

Where to begin is somewhat arbitrary, but one decisive contribution to the evolution of the M&H approach was the interdisciplinary program of research and teaching at Carnegie Tech (now Carnegie-Mellon) in the early 1960s. The central figures at Carnegie were Richard Cyert, James March, and Herbert Simon. Williamson was a student in the economics program at Carnegie during this period and was greatly influenced by the prevailing interdisciplinary research atmosphere. The strategy of using organization theory to inform economics in the study of firm and market structures is evident in his work on managerial discretion and in other early papers (see Williamson, 1964, 1965, 1967).

It was not until later that the possibility of accomplishing a genuine synthesis between economics† and organization theory become evident. Two papers were of special significance. The first of these was "The Vertical Integra-

---

*J. R. Commons (1934) had urged such an approach much earlier, but both his efforts and those of other institutionalists were outside the mainstream of economic analysis and, except as they are dealt with in the study of economic thought, have been neglected.

†This was economics of a nontraditional kind. An efficiency orientation was maintained, but attention shifted from neoclassical production function issues to the study of transaction costs, in the spirit of J. R. Commons (1934), R. H. Coase (1937), and K. J. Arrow (1969).

tion of Production: Transaction Cost Considerations" (Williamson, 1971), which was an effort to assess the question of make-or-buy in a fully symmetrical way. Ronald Coase, In a remarkably insightful paper, had posed this issue in 1937 and recognized that transaction costs were central to its resolution. Coase observed that vertical integration permitted the firm to economize on the "cost of negotiating and concluding" many separate intermediate product market contracts by substituting a flexible employment agreement (Coase, 1952: 336). But because the factors that were responsible for differential transaction costs in the intermediate product market were not identified, the argument lacked testable implications. Why not use a flexible employment agreement to organize all transaction costs rather than just some? Until such a time as the transaction cost argument was able to explain the organization of transactions in a discriminating way, it remained rather tautological (Alchian and Demsetz, 1972). Coase's observation, some 35 years later, that his 1937 article was "much cited and little used" (Coase, 1972) is presumably explained by the failure to make the issues operational over that interval.

If, as Coase asserted, differential transaction costs were responsible for decisions to organize some activities one way and some another, a level of analysis that was sensitive to transaction cost differences was evidently needed. Williamson accomplished this by (1) making the transaction the basic unit of analysis, (2) expressly identifying alternative market and internal modes of "contracting," (3) identifying the critical dimensions with respect to which transactions differed, (4) tracing out the transaction cost ramifications, and (5) matching modes to transactions in a discriminating way. Once the vertical integration problem had been made operational in this way, a variety of related applications followed. In this sense, the puzzle of vertical integration was a paradigm problem that, once solved, provided a research strategy that could be repeated. Any problem that could be posed, directly or indirectly, as a contracting problem could be assessed in terms of the identical conceptual apparatus.

These paradigm features were not entirely evident, however, until the paper "Markets and Hierarchies: Some Elementary Considerations" took shape (Williamson, 1973). This paper had its origins in a class discussion of market failures, with special emphasis on Arrow's classic statement of the problem (Arrow, 1969). For each type of market failure that was identified (public goods problem, appropriability problem, information asymmetry, small numbers exchange, etc.), the object was to move the explanation for the condition back to a statement of primitives. The same basic human and environmental conditions that arose in assessing vertical integration kept reappearing. *Bounded rationality* and *opportunism* were the recurring human factors. The environmental factors were *uncertainty-complexity* and *small numbers exchange*. The patterned way in which these human and environmental factors were paired is shown in Figure 1.

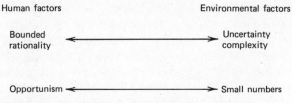

Figure 1 The organizational failures framework.

CONCEPTUAL FRAMEWORK

The rudiments of the conceptual framework upon which the Markets and Hierarchies program of research relies have now been identified. What follows is an elaboration on these.

Behavioral Assumptions

Bounded rationality and *opportunism* are the key behavioral assumptions. These assumptions about the characteristics of human actors are joined with the assertion that viable modes of organization (market, quasi market, or internal) are ones that serve to *economize* on transaction costs. While organization theory specialists related easily to the concept of bounded rationality, many economists resist it. By contrast, economizing is a much more congenial notion to economists than it is to organization theorists. Opportunism is a concept of which both are wary.

Arrow has characterized an economist as one who "by training thinks of himself as the guardian of rationality, the ascriber of rationality to others, and the prescriber of rationality to the social world" (Arrow, 1974: 16). Given this commitment, any assumption that appears to be at variance with rationality is apt to be dismissed out of hand. If it is not rational, it must be nonrational or irrational, and these are matters for other social sciences to grapple with.

As Herbert Simon has pointed out, however, economists exaggerate the extent to which nonrationality is emphasized by other social sciences. Although economists are the only social scientists who invoke hyperrationality assumptions, rationality is nevertheless a common theme throughout all of the social sciences (Simon, 1978: 2–4). The issue thus is not whether human agents are rational or not. Rather the question is whether the assumption of hyperrationality is needed or if weaker rationality assumptions will suffice.

Partly this is a matter of taste in choosing between strong and weak assumptions where both yield the same implications (Simon, 1978: 8). But there is more to it than tastes. Conceptualizing a problem one way rather than another can have a profound effect on the follow-up research agenda. Thus organization structure is of little important and hence can be disregarded if hyperrationality assumptions are maintained, which explains why the neo-classical theory of the firm describes the organization as a production function rather than a complex hierarchy. The opposite assumption, that human agents are so overwhelmed by complexity that they are incapable of planning, likewise reduces the study of organizational design to insignificance. This appears to be close to the view of March and Olsen (1976) and Mintzberg (1973).

The Markets and Hierarchies approach avoids both of these extremes. An intermediate degree of bounded rationality is attributed to human agents. Organizational design takes on economic significance precisely because the productive utilization of this intermediate capability is of crucial importance. But there is more to organizational design than economizing on bounded rationality. Issues of opportunism also arise and need to be addressed.

Opportunism extends the usual motivational assumption of self-interest seeking to include self-interest seeking with guile. Thus, whereas bounded rationality suggests decision making less complex than the usual assumption of hyperrationality, opportunism suggests calculating behavior more sophisticated than the usual assumption of simple self-interest. Opportunism refers to "making false or empty, that is, self-disbelieved threats or promises," cutting corners for undisclosed personal advantage, covering up tracks, and the like. Although it is a central behavioral assumption, it is not essential that all economic agents behave this way. What is crucial is that *some* agents behave in this fashion and that it is costly to sort out those who are opportunistic from those who are not.

Faced with bounded rationality on the one hand and the proclivity for some human agents to behave opportunistically on the other, the basic organizational design issue essentially reduces to this: organize transactions in such a way as to economize on bounded rationality while simultaneously safeguarding those transactions against the hazards of opportunism.

The Governance of Contractual Relations

The governance of contractual relations warrants careful attention in the degree to which economic agents are subject to bounded rationality *and* are given to opportunism. In the absence of either, the ubiquitous contracting model goes through.

Thus suppose the absence of bounded rationality among opportunistic agents. Mind-boggling though it is to contemplate, such agents will engage in "a single gigantic once-for-all forward 'higgle-haggle' in which all contingent goods and services (i.e., all goods and services at each possible time-cum-environmental condition) are bought and sold once and for all now for money payments made now" (Meade, 1971: 166). Propensities to behave opportunistically will simply be of no account.

Suppose alternatively that agents are subject to bounded rationality but are free of opportunism. Autonomous contracting again applies, though the reasons here are different. Since each party can depend on his or her opposite to honor the spirit as well as the letter of an agreement, successive adaptations can and will be implemented as contingencies unfold. Bridges are thus crossed when they arise, whereas the unbounded rationality model stipulates bridge crossings exhaustively in advance. Adaptive, sequential decision making by nonopportunistic parties will nevertheless reach the same joint profit optimizing result.

The fact is, however, that human agents are neither unboundedly rational nor reliably free of opportunism. Interesting transaction cost issues thereby arise, and organizational design is a relevant concern precisely for this reason. But a predictive theory of efficient organizational structure requires more than an acknowledgment that human actors are subject to bounded rationality and given to opportunism. A schema for framing the dimensions of transactions is needed and must be joined with a description of alternative modes for organizing transactions. In addition, a strategy for matching organizing modes (governance structures) to transactions needs to be devised.

The rudiments of such an approach have been set out elsewhere (Williamson, 1979b). The critical dimensions for describing transactions are (1) uncertainty, (2) the frequency with which transactions recur, and (3) the degree to which durable transaction-specific investments are required to realize least-cost supply. The main governance modes to which transactions need to be matched are (1) markets (with varying degrees of adjudicatory support); (2) internal organization; and (3) an intermediate form of bilateral exchange referred to as "obligational market contracting."

Our principal interest here is internal organization. Internal organization is well-suited to transactions that involve recurrent exchange in the face of a nontrivial degree of uncertainty and that incur transaction-specific investments. Since internal organization requires the development of specialized governance structure, the cost of which must be amortized across the transactions assigned to it, it is rarely economical to organize occasional transactions internally. Likewise, transactions for which uncertainty is low require little adaptation, hence little governance, and thus can organized by market contracting. Except, however, as transaction-specific investments are involved, neither frequency nor uncertainty—individually or in combination—justifies the creation of internal organization (with its associated transaction specific governance structure).

Considering the importance that we attach to transaction-specific investments, some explication is needed. The crucial issue is the degree to which durable, nonmarketable expenses are incurred. Items that are unspecialized among users pose few hazards, since buyers in these circumstances can easily turn to alternative sources, and suppliers can sell output intended for one buyer to other buyers without difficulty. (The argument also turns on the degree to which inputs can be diverted from one use to another without loss of productivity.) Nonmarketability problems arise when the *specific identity* of the parties has important cost-bearing consequences. Transactions of this kind will be referred to as idiosyncratic.

Occasionally the identity of the parties is important from the outset, as when a buyer induces a supplier to invest in specialized physical capital of a transaction-specific kind. Inasmuch as the value of this capital in other uses is by definition much smaller than the specialized use for which it has been intended, the supplier is effectively "locked into" the transaction to a significant degree. This is symmetrical, moreover, in that the buyer cannot turn to alternative sources of supply and obtain the item on favorable terms, since the cost of supply from unspecialized capital is presumably great.* The buyer is thus committed to the transaction as well.

Ordinarily, however, there is more to idiosyncratic exchange than specialized physical capital. Human-capital investments that are transaction-specific commonly occur as well. Specialized training and learning-by-doing economies in production operations are illustrations. Except when these investments are transferable to alternative suppliers at low cost, which is rare, the benefits of the set-up costs can be realized only so long as the relationship between the buyer and seller of the intermediate product is maintained.

Additional transaction-specific savings can accrue at the interface between supplier and buyer as contracts are successively adapted to unfolding events, and as periodic contract-renewal agreements are reached. Familiarity here permits communication economies to be realized: specialized language develops as experience accumulates and nuances are signaled and received in a sensitive say. Both institutional and personal trust relations evolve.

In consideration of the value placed upon economies of these kinds, agents who engage in recurring, uncertain, idiosyncratic transactions have a strong interest in preserving the exchange relation. Autonomous contracting modes give way to internal organization as the value associated with exchange continuity increases. The continuity advantages of internal organization over markets in these circumstances are attributable to its more sensitive governance characteristics and its stronger joint profit maximizing features.

APPLICATIONS

A theory is judged to be more fruitful the "more precise the prediction, the wider the area within which the theory yields predictions, and the more additional lines of future research it suggests" (Friedman, 1953: 10). The basic exchange paradigm that was originally worked up to address the issue of vertical integration across successive manufacturing stages has proved to be remarkably robust. Although this was not evident at the outset, it quickly became apparent that any organizational relation that can be reformulated as a contracting problem can be addressed in substantially identical terms. Applications of the exchange paradigm include: assessments of the employment relation (Williamson, Wachter, and Harris, 1975; Hashimoto and Yu, 1979); franchise bidding for natural monopolies (Williamson, 1976); the efficacy of capital markets (Williamson, 1975: Chapter 9); oligopoly (Posner, 1969;

---

*This assumes that it is costly for the incumbent supplier to transfer specialized physical assets to new suppliers. On this, see Williamson (1976).

Williamson, 1975: Chapter 12); vertical market restrictions (Williamson, 1979a); and aspects of inflation (Wachter and Williamson, 1978).

Other applications include: a restatement of contract law in transaction cost terms (Williamson, 1979b: 235–254); the uses of transaction cost reasoning by marketing specialists (Carman, 1978); possible applications to the study of comparative economic systems (Campbell, 1978); and uses of the exchange paradigm to examine noneconomic phenomena—family law being an example (Williamson, 1979b: 258). Of special interest here are the applications of the Markets and Hierarchies approach to matters of internal organization. These design issues are developed in the following section.

Empirical tests of three kinds have been used to assess predictions of the Markets and Hierarchies approach: cross-sectional studies, experimental studies, and case studies. The cross-sectional studies that have been performed test what is referred to as the multidivisional form hypothesis (Williamson, 1975: 150):

> The organization and operation of the large enterprise along the lines of the M-form favors goal pursuit and least-cost behavior more nearly associated with the neoclassical profit maximization hypothesis than does the U-form organizational alternative.

Three studies have been done in which organization form is used as an explanatory variable in studies of business performance. The studies by Peter Steer and John Cable (1978) of British firms and by Henry Armour and David Teece (1978) of U.S. petroleum corporations both confirm the importance of organization form. Teece has since extended the analysis from petroleum firms to assess the ramifications of organization form differences among the principal firms in 15 industries and obtains results that confirm the hypothesis (Teece, 1979).

Richard Burton and Borge Obel (1980) have tested the M-form hypothesis by examining the ramifications of organizational design for profitability in the context of a linear programming model of the firm in which the Danzig-Wolf decomposition algorithm was used. Two different technologies, one more decomposable than the other, were studied. The M-form hypothesis is confirmed for both technologies, the profit difference being greater for the more decomposable technology—which is also an implication of the theory.

Case studies of several kinds have been performed. The most complete of these involves an assessment of franchise bidding for natural monopolies. Demsetz (1968), Posner (1972), and Stigler (1968: 18–19) have argued that franchise bidding is an attractive alternative to rate-of-return regulation in dealing with natural monopolies. An abstract assessment of the contracting ramifications of franchise bidding discloses, however, that the purported benefits of franchise bidding are suspect where market and technological uncertainty are great and incumbent suppliers invest in specialized, long-lived equipment and acquire idiosyncratic skills (Williamson, 1976). A case study of franchise bidding for CATV in Oakland, California, confirmed this. Not only were general ramifications of the contracting approach borne out by the study, but the study corroborated contracting details as well.

ORGANIZATIONAL DESIGN

Consistent with the general thrust of the Markets and Hierarchies approach, organization design is addressed as a transaction cost issue, and economizing purposes are emphasized. The general argument is this: except when there are perversities associated with the funding process, or when strategically situated members of an organization are unable to participate in the prospective gains, unrealized efficiency opportunities always offer an incentive to reorganize.

Inasmuch as these perversities are more common in noncommercial than in commercial enterprises, the argument has stronger predictive force for the latter. Indeed our attention in this section is restricted entirely to the commercial sector. We nevertheless believe that the spirit of the analysis carries over to nonprofit enterprises and government bureaus, which we include in our discussion of the research agenda.

Although the main organizational design "action" entails economizing on transaction costs, this is not to say that technology is irrelevant. But technology by itself rarely has determinative organizational consequences for more than a small group of highly interdependent workers. Indeed, except when the transaction costs of adapting interfaces between technologically separable work stations are great, markets will be the governance mode by which the exchange of intermediate product is accomplished. Internal organization not only has little to offer in these circumstances but incurs unneeded costs.

However, in circumstances in which autonomous contracting is costly and hazardous, governance structures of an internal organizational kind arise. Three applications of this general argument follow, after which we summarize the implications and go on briefly to consider other organizational design traditions and contrast them with the approach favored here.

Vertical Integration*

The recent monograph by Alfred Chandler, Jr. (1977), describing marketing developments during the late nineteenth century provides strong support for the proposition that transaction costs are sufficiently significant to affect the structure of industries sometimes motivating firms to integrate forward from manufacturing into the distribution stage.

Chandler's Findings. Chandler's description of forward integration into distribution by American manufacturers distinguishes between the developments of infrastructure and the induced distributional response. The appearance of the railroads and the telegraph and telephone systems in the latter part of the nineteenth century permitted wider geographic areas to be served in a reliable and timely way. The "reliability and speed of the new transporta-

---

*The argument here follows Williamson (1979a, pp. 968–972).

tion and communication" permitted greater economies of scale to be realized in factory organization (Chandler, 1977:245). These economies of scale at the factory level were latent, in the sense that the technology was there waiting to be exploited. Because it is not manufacturing cost but delivered cost that matters, however, it became profitable to realize these scale economies only when a low-cost distribution system appeared. That is, so long as transportation expenses were great, the most efficient way to serve markets was by dispersing factories.

Once the new transportation and communication infrastructure was in place, the stage was set for the distributional response. A crucial question was how to devise a coordinated manufacturing-distribution response. In principle, both stages could have remained autonomous: manufacturers could have remained specialized and built larger-scale plants while specialized distributors could have responded simultaneously, either on their own initiative or by contract, by assembling the requisite distribution network. In many industries, however, "existing marketers were unable to sell and distribute products in the volume they were produced . . . . Once the inadequacies of existing marketers became clear, manufacturers integrated forward into marketing" (Chandler, 1977:287). An administrative override was evidently needed.

Not all industries integrated forward, however, and when they did it was not to the same extent. Some industries linked manufacturing only with advertising and wholesaling; retail integration was not attempted. Nondurable industries that had recently adopted continuous process machinery—cigarettes, matches, cereals, and canned goods are examples – were in this category (Chandler, 1977:287). More ambitious and interesting were producer and consumer durables that required "specialized marketing services— demonstration, installation, consumer credit, after-sales service and repair," services that existing middlemen "had neither the interest nor facilities to provide" (Chandler, 1977:288). Examples here included sewing machines, farm machinery, office machines, and heavy electrical equipment.

A Transaction Cost Interpretation. The new transportation and communication infrastructure permitted manufacturers to serve larger markets in a low-cost way. The effects of these infrastructural developments on plant size are displayed in Figure 2. (On the motivation for this, see Scherer, Beckenstein, Kaufer, and Murphy, 1975.)

The APC curve shows the average cost of production as plant size increases. These average costs decrease over a wide range due to assumed economies of scale. The curve ADC_1 shows the original average distribution cost of delivering products from a plant. This curve increases throughput because greater sales require marketing to a larger geographic region. The curve ADC_2 shows the average distribution cost after the new infrastructure is put in place. It is consistently lower than ADC_1 but also rises throughout. ATC_1 and ATC_2 are average total cost curves that are given by the vertical

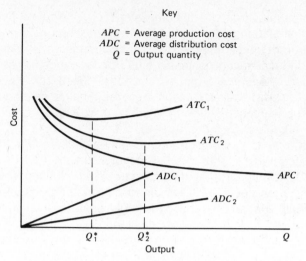

Key

APC = Average production cost
ADC = Average distribution cost
Q = Output quantity

Figure 2 Effects of average distribution cost on average total cost.

summation of *APC* with *ADC₁* and *ADC₂*, respectively. Average total costs reach a minimum at Q_1^* and Q_2^*, where Q_2^* is necessarily larger than Q_1^*, given the stipulated shift in average distribution costs. An increase in plant scale and the extension of service to larger geographic markets are thus indicated.

Problems of implementation, however, are not addressed by this cost curve apparatus. How are the linkages between manufacturing and distribution to be forged? They are not created automatically. If existing middlemen respond in a slow and faltering way to the opportunities that the new transportation and communication infrastructures afford, the stage is set for someone, in this instance the manufacturers, to experiment with new organizational structures.

The issues here are of a transaction cost rather than of a production cost kind. Although a definitive analysis of the "inadequacies of existing marketers" reported by Chandler (1977:287) would require further research, we conjecture that these distributional difficulties are due to goal incongruence coupled with the hazards posed by small numbers supply relations between autonomous parties. It was difficult for marketers who were accustomed to operating in a local market regime to perceive the opportunities that awaited them. And there was no obvious way to signal these opportunities by relying upon decentralized pricing (Malmgren, 1961). Moreover, even if manufacturers and distributors both perceived the opportunities that the new transportation and communication infrastructure afforded, and if each responded independently in reliance upon the other, problems of divergence woud arise if each recorded or interpreted the data differently. Such goal incongruence would exist, moreover, at both an aggregate and a disaggregate level.

In principle, manufacturers could have taken the initiative and effected goal congruence by contract. Coordination by contract is costly, however, where the two parties are great. The hazards to which we refer have been discussed elsewhere in the context of idiosyncratic exchange. Such problems arise when investments in specialized human or physical assets are required in order to complete the transaction in an economical way. With respect to the issues of concern to Chandler, the problems were especially severe when the mass production and sale of consumer or producer durables were contemplated. Distributors here would have to be induced to make specialized (product-and-brand specific) investments and, once these investments were made, manufacturers and distributors would thereafter often be dealing with each other in what essentially was a bilateral exchange arrangement. Given the hazards of opportunism that arise in such circumstances, both parties were reluctant to rely on autonomous contracting.

Note in this connection that Chandler did not observe vertical integration occurring in uniform degree in all industries. This is precisely what one would anticipate when vertical integration is assessed in transaction cost terms. Thus vertical integration into distribution was negligible in some industries—standardized nuts and bolts being an example. In others, integration involved advertising and wholesaling but not retailing—branded consumer nondurables being in this category. In still others, integration included retailing and related support services—certain branded nondurables being among these. This progression is marked by the degree of transaction-specific investment, which is an implication of transaction cost theory. Other theories of vertical integration, by contrast, are silent on these matters.

This substitution of bureaucratic for market governance occurred in response to profit opportunities. But social cost savings also resulted. In the absence of other factors, net social as well as net private gains accrue when such organizational innovations appear.

Becoming Multidivisional. The transformation of the modern corporation from a functional to a multidivisional structure has been documented in Chandler.* This transformation is treated prominently in the *Markets and Hierarchies* volume (Williamson, 1975: Chapters 8–9). Only a few comments are offered here.

Chandler characterizes the reasons for the success of the multidivision structure thus:

> The basic reasons for its success was simply that it clearly removed the executives responsible for the destiny of the entire enterprise from the more routine operational

---

*The path-breaking book here is Chandler's *Strategy and Structure* (1966). Williamson's shift of emphasis from the factors that were responsible for managerial discretion to the factors, including especially internal organization, that served to attenuate managerial discretion was much influenced by this book.

activities, and so gave them the time, information, and even psychological commitment for long-term planning and appraisal . . . .

[The] new structure left the broad strategic decisions as to the allocation of existing resources and the acquisition of new ones in the hands of a top team of generalists. Relieved of operating duties and tactical decisions, a general executive was less likely to reflect the position of just one part of the whole (Chandler, 1966: 382–383).

If Chandler is correct, this organizational change from a functional to a multidivisional structure served both to economize on bounded rationality, by relieving top executives of the more routine operational activities and simultaneously to reduce subgoal pursuit, which is a manifestation of opportunism. Inasmuch as most institutional choices involve trade-offs rather than Pareto-superior moves, this is surely quite remarkable. How was this accomplished?

The difficulties that the functionally organized firm encountered as it grew in size and diversity were attributable to diseconomies of agglomeration. The centralization of what are effectively decomposable parts has adverse operating consequences of three kinds. First, attempts to achieve unneeded coordination generate overhead costs. Second, forced interdependencies give rise to congestion and other spillover costs. Third, opportunistic subgoal pursuit is more difficult to detect and control as the degree of interconnectedness increases. Operating cost increases thus arise out of a failure to recognize essential decomposability. But the deficiencies of the functional structure went beyond these operating cost features. The functional form also served to confuse organizational purpose by failure to separate strategic from operating decision making.

Although becoming multidivisional would not have been feasible without decomposability, the benefits of reorganization required more than an assignment of semiautonomous standing to natural subunits within the firm. Becoming multidivisional further required the development of a strategic decision-making capability in the central office—indeed would have been hazardous to implement without this capability. The assignment of investment resources to high yield uses could be reliably accomplished only as the general office (1) had a sense of direction, (2) was able to evaluate the merits of investment proposals originated by the operating divisions, and (3) had the capacity to audit and assess operating division performance.

Removing top management from the operating affairs of the enterprise meant that, whereas bureaucratic control processes had governed previously, operating divisions were now governed in quasi-market fashion. Thus divisions were assigned the status of quasi firms, and the central office assumed functions of review and resource allocation ordinarily associated with the capital market. As a consequence of these changes the goal confusion (or incongruence) that had previously reigned was supplanted by subgoal clarity that was meaningfully related to enterprise objectives. The self-interest seeking that, when coupled with goal incongruence, had once drained the energies of the enterprise was now turned to productive purposes.

It is noteworthy that the transformation of the functional to the multidivisional form had little if any relation to technology. Organizational structure was altered, but the underlying technology remained the same in most instances. Thus although efficiency purposes were served, the economies driving the change and the economies that were realized were of a transaction cost rather than technological kind.

Bureaucracies and Clans

The shift from functional to divisional structure has for the most part been completed in large U.S. corporations (Teece, 1979) and has been proceeding rapidly in Europe (Franko, 1972). But a further question is what management "style" ought to be practiced in the large multidivisional enterprise. Issues relating to the "economics of atmosphere" (Williamson, 1975: 37–39) arise in this connection. Ouchi has addressed the merits of bureaucratic versus clan-type management styles in a series of recent papers on this subject (Ouchi, 1978, 1979, 1980).

To put the issue one way: What form of contracting ought to prevail within an organization? As with market modes of contracting, there are two general options, which we designate as "hard" and "soft" contracting, respectively. Under hard contracting, the parties remain relatively autonomous, each is expected to press his or her interests vigorously, and contracting is relatively complete. Soft contracting, by contrast, presumes much closer identity of interests between the parties, and formal contracts are much less complete. This is the clan-type management style.

Although contract law specialists, sociologists, and others have long recognized soft contracting practices, the study of soft contracting has only recently come under scrutiny. Ian Macneil's (1974, 1978) work on "relational contracting" is especially instructive. While it is beyond the scope of this paper to review the literature here, we nonetheless think it important to elaborate on the special problems that soft contracting encounters if it is introduced in an alien culture.

The basic argument is this: Soft contracting, to be viable, needs to be supported by a more elaborate informal governance apparatus than is associated with hard contracting. Thus, whereas the latter relies heavily on legal and economic sanctions, the former rests much more on social controls. As compared with hard contracting, soft contracting appeals more to the spirit than to the letter of the agreement.

Four points are relevant in this regard. First, not all transactions need the additional supports afforded by soft contracting. Economizing considerations would dictate that a distinction be made between those that do and that do not, and that each be organized appropriately. Second, the immediate parties to soft contracts are the ones who stand most to benefit from preserving the exchange. Accordingly, they have incentives to develop a bilateral (transaction-specific) trust relation. Third, the institutional infrastructure within which soft contracts are embedded also influences the viability of this type of exchange. And fourth, the design of transactions is a decision variable: depending on their confidence in the trading relation, parties will vary the degree to which trading hazards are introduced.

Trading hazards differ with the degree of transaction-specific investment and with uncertainty. The first of these hazards is obvious: Where investments are of a transaction-specific kind, parties will be unable to divert these assets to alternative uses of an equally productive kind. Accordingly, as the degree of asset specificity increases, additional governance supports are needed. The same applies as uncertainty is increased. The argument here is that the occasions to adapt the transaction to new circumstances increase as the degree of uncertainty increases. Since the incentive to defect from the spirit of the agreement increases as the frequency and magnitude of the indicated adaptations are increased, greater hazards are thereby posed.

Although the degree of uncertainty is commonly beyond the control of the parties, the degree of asset specificity is often theirs to determine. Thus, assume that a particular transaction is subject to an intermediate degree of uncertainty and the parties are attempting to optimize with respect to its transaction-specific features. Specifically, assume the following:

1. The transaction in question involves an employment relation.
2. Two different job designs are under consideration, one of a hard contracting and the other of a soft contracting kind.
3. Human capital skill acquisitions are involved for each job design: Under hard contracting the skills acquired are of a general purpose kind, while under soft contracting they are of a special kind.
4. Physical capital expenditures are identical whichever job design is adopted.
5. Assuming contractual continuity, the more productive job design is the one that involves special-purpose skill acquisition.

Whether this more productive job design is adopted, however, is problematical. In contrast to employees with general-purpose skills, employees who have acquired task-specific skills will be able to move to alternative employment only by experiencing a nontrivial productivity sacrifice in the process. In consideration of these added hazards, employers will be successful in inducing employees to acquire specialized skills only when the workers are either adequately compensated in advance for the hazards or when the job is adequately protected against opportunism during the course of task execution.

Holding governance structures constant, the wage premium needed to compensate workers against the added hazards may easily render the task-specific job design competitively nonviable, especially if workers are risk averse. The question then is whether this potentially more productive job design can be salvaged by surrounding it with transactional safeguards. This brings us back to the matter of bilateral trading relations and the institutional matrix within which trading takes place.

The "special problems" of soft contracting to which we referred earlier are particularly great when soft contracting is introduced into an alien culture. The reason for this is that the entire burden of providing contractual safeguards falls entirely on the immediate parties to the transaction if background cultural supports are missing. Should one of the parties choose to defect, there is no further support for sustaining the transaction to which either can appeal. In contrast, where individual soft contracts are embedded in a soft contracting trading culture, defection is subject to added sanctions. The incentives to defect are accordingly reduced.

To some extent, the parties to the transaction may be able to devise procedural safeguards themselves. One example is the development of "internal labor markets" whereby wages are assigned to jobs rather than to individuals, promotion ladders are defined, a sensitive grievance structure is devised, and so on (Doeringer and Piore, 1971; Williamson, Wachter, and Harris, 1975). But societal safeguards may provide additional security. This varies among economic systems. The "clan" form of organization that Ouchi (1978, 1979) has studied is much more viable in some cultures (e.g., Japanese) than in others (e.g., American).

The limitations of hard contracting are nevertheless great as the need progressively increases for successive adaptations to be made in response to uncertainty. Contracts simply fail to provide adequately for the appropriate responses in advance, and employees may engage in strategic bargaining. The more cooperative work relations associated with soft contracting have a clear advantage in these circumstances. The problem then is how to bring this off. This is a matter for which future research is plainly needed.

Other Organizational Design Traditions

The literature on organizational design is vast, and we address only a small part of it here. Jeffrey Pfeffer's (1978) recent book on this subject distinguishes between longitudinal studies, managerial studies, and the power approach. He observes that most of the longitudinal studies have been preoccupied with measurement to the exclusion of theory (Pfeffer, 1978: xiv). The work of Jay Galbraith (1973) and of Paul Lawrence and Jay Lorsch (1967) is in the managerial tradition. Pfeffer contends that this work is preoccupied with efficiency and effectiveness and neglects power and influence (Pfeffer, 1978: xv). Pfeffer's preferred approach is to regard organizations "as coalitions with ill-defined and inconsistent preferences" (Pfeffer, 1978: xvi), a tradition that he associates with Cyert and March 1963), Karl Weick (1969), and March and Olsen (1976). Organizational design issues are then addressed in terms of control, influence, and power.

Other organizational design approaches that go unmentioned by Pfeffer are the organizational ecology approach (Hannan and Freeman, 1977; Aldrich, 1979) and the theory of organizational structures advanced by Kenneth Mackenzie (1978). Inasmuch as efficiency figures prominently in both of these last two approaches, both are complementary to the Markets and Hierarchies approach. The power approach to organizational design, by contrast, is a very different tradition.

The neglect of power by the M&H approach is not to suggest that power is either uninteresting or unimportant. We submit, however, that power considerations will usually give way to efficiency—at least in profit-making enterprises, if observations are taken at sufficiently long intervals, say a decade. Thus the powers of heads of functional divisions and of their subordinates were vastly altered when functionally organized firms shifted to a multidivisional strucutre. Were power the only or the main organizational design factor, it is difficult to believe that large American and subsequently European businesses would have undergone such a vast organizational transformation over the past thirty years. From transaction cost and ecological points of view, however, the transformation, once started, was predictable.

Or consider Pfeffer's assertion that if "the chief executive in a corporation always comes from marketing . . . there is a clue about power in the organization" (Pfeffer, 1978:23). Viewed from a power perspective, the argument evidently is that the marketing people in this corporation have "possession of control over critical resources", have preferential access to information, and are strategically located to cope with "critical organizational uncertainty" (Pfeffer, 1978: 17–28). We do not disagree with any of this but would make the more straightforward argument that the marketing function in this organization is especially critical to competitive viability.

Thus our position is that those parts of the enterprise that are most critical to organizational viability will be *assigned* possession of control over critical resources, will *have* preferential access to information, and will be *dealing* with critical organizational uncertainties. In some organizations this may be marketing, in others it may be R&D, and in still others it may be production. Failure to assign control to that part of the enterprise on which viability turns would contradict the efficiency hypothesis but would presumably be explained as a power outcome.*

Inasmuch as power is very vague and has resisted successive efforts to make it operational, whereas efficiency is much more clearly specified and the plausibility of an efficiency hypothesis is buttressed by ecological survival tests, we urge that efficiency analysis be made the center piece of the study of organizational design. This does not imply that power has no role to play, but we think it invites confusion to explain organizational results that are pre-

---

*Thus suppose that, from a competitive effectiveness viewpoint, marketing is the most important functional area. Suppose further that the founder and his progeny are engineers, and that each has worked his way up through manufacturing. Inasmuch as they have an ownership lock (power) on the system, the chief executive and his principal aides are appointed from these ranks. Although this has the efficiency benefit of coupling ownership and control, the firm may be vulnerable to market developments in relation to its rivals. Power explains the inefficiency (vulnerability) condition.

dicted by the efficiency hypothesis in terms of power. Rather power explains results when the organization sacrifices efficiency to serve special interests. We concede that this occurs. But we do not believe that major organizational changes in the commercial sector are explained in these terms. The evidence is all to the contrary.

THE RESEARCH AGENDA

The Markets and Hierarchies approach to the study of organizational issues is relatively new as compared with other research traditions. Neither its power nor its limits have been fully established. Applications to date, however, have been numerous and mainly encouraging. Our discussion here merely suggests additional theoretical, empirical, and public policy applications.

General

As noted earlier, any problem that arises as a contracting problem or can be recast as one can usefully be examined in Markets and Hierarchies terms. This is not to suggest that the contracting paradigm should be applied to the exclusion of other research traditions. We nevertheless believe that insights not easily derived from alternative approaches can often be obtained by assessing transaction cost features. While sometimes these insights may be of a fragmentary kind, often they relate to core issues.

Inasmuch as transaction costs have reference to the costs of running the economic system, the useful comparisons are between alternative modes rather than between a proposed mode and a frictionless ideal. Given that an explicit or implicit exchange is to be accomplished or a coordinated adaptation is to be affected, how should the transaction be organized? For many purposes, the analysis can be thought of as interface management. This applies within and between markets and firms.

Some Specifics

Business History: Markets to Hierarchies. Transacation cost economics can be applied advantageously to the study of changing organizational structures through time. This is true both of organizational changes since the industrial revolution (Chandler, 1966, 1977) and also preindustrial changes (North, 1978). A richer understanding of the economics of institutions is sure to emerge as business historians, industrial organization specialists, economic theorists, and organization theorists apply their collective talents to the systematic study of institutional issues. Transaction cost economizing is, we submit, the driving force that is responsible for the main institutional changes (for an interpretation of Chandler's recent book in transaction cost terms, see Williamson, 1980). Applications will include product market organization and also changing labor and capital market forms of organization through time.

Bureaucracies. Applications of Markets and Hierarchies to commercial bureaucracies will be concerned with interface governance. Specific organizational design applications (possibly with special reference to particular functions such as research and development) as well as general applications (again, the matrix form is in need of interpretation) should be possible. Additional empirical tests of the M-form of other hypotheses can also be anticipated. Perhaps most important, the limits of internal organization are poorly understood in relation to the limits of markets. The transaction cost approach appears to have much to offer for such an assessment. The ramifications are of interest both to worker-managed and to capitalist enterprises (Fitzroy and Mueller, 1978). Whether recent developments involving employee participation in Europe constitute a contradiction to the efficiency hypothesis also warrants scrutiny.

Clans. The organization of economic activity by greater reliance on clan-type structures requires study. Both the limitations of clans as well as the discriminating application of clan forms of organization deserve attention. As between alternative forms of *internal* organization, the clan appears to realize greater advantage in circumstances in which uncertainty is great. The argument needs to be elaborated and specific applications attempted, to service industries, high technology industries, and others characterized by extreme performance ambiguity.

The proposition that clan forms join high productivity with emotional well-being (low levels of alienation) deserves further scrutiny. As with other organizational panaceas, we believe that this is too simplistic. Rather the argument needs to be made in a more discriminating way that recognizes transaction cost distinctions. The proposition that defection hazards are greater for clan forms, and that such forms are viable only when accompanied by additional governance supports, also warrants further study. Comparative international studies, in which hard versus soft contracting cultures are scrutinized, may be useful.

Public Policy Toward Business. Public policy applications will also continue. This includes both antitrust and regulation. In the antitrust area, issues of strategic behavior and fairness will come under special scrutiny. What has been referred to as the Decision Process Approach, which makes operational "procedural rationality" (Simon, 1978), would appear to hold promise for the microanalytic study of regulatory issues (Williamson, 1979c).

Nonprofit Organizations. The organization of nonprofit enterprises, which are growing in economic importance (Weisbord, 1979), is intriguing and has hitherto evaded explanation of more than a partial or ad hoc kind. Whether the transaction cost approach will be illuminating remains to be seen. One of the problems, with transactions in many nonprofit organizations, as in service businesses, is that they are amorphous. Also the viability tests for nonprofit organizations are often much weaker—partly because product market competition is weak, but also because an effective capital market displacement mechanism (takeover) is missing.

The study of government bureaus suffers from many of these same limitations. Once progress is made in studying nonprofit organizations from a transaction cost (or any other) point of view, follow-up applications to government bureaus should be easy.

CONCLUSION

The Markets and Hierarchies program of research is relatively young in comparison with other research traditions in organization theory. Being young, it has its skeptics. We would not have it otherwise.

For one thing, we are inclined to be eclectic. No single approach applies equally well to all problems, and some issues are usefully addressed from several points of view. For another, we believe that most of the challenges can be met. Sometimes this may require extending the theory to apply to new circumstances. Sometimes it will require sharpening or qualifying parts of the argument. Formalizing aspects of the argument may sometimes be needed and appears to be feasible. (See the paper by Hashimoto and Yu, 1979, for developments of this last kind.)

The distinctive powers of the approach are attributable to its reliance on transaction cost reasoning and its unremitting emphasis on efficiency. While the particulars differ, the same approach to the study of transactions applies quite generally. The core methodological properties are these:

1. The transaction is the basic unit of analysis.
2. Human agents are subject to bounded rationality and self-interest.
3. The critical dimensions for describing transactions are frequency, uncertainty, and transaction-specific investments.
4. Economizing on transaction costs is the principal factor that explains viable modes of contracting; it is the main issue with which organizational design ought to be concerned.
5. Assessing transaction cost differences is a comparative institutional exercise.

The approach is able to deal symmetrically with market and nonmarket modes of organization and has successfully addressed a wide variety of organizational issues in a coherent way.

Those who prefer methodology and those who are averse to efficiency analysis will insist, with cause, that there is more to organization theory than economizing on transaction costs. We agree. We sumbit, however, that efficiency analysis is important to the study of all forms of organization and is absolutely crucial to the study of commercial organizations. And we furthermore contend that the main test of a theory is its implications. So long as alternative theories are evaluated on this standard, we are confident that the Markets and Hierarchies approach will fare well in the comparison.

REFERENCES

Alchian, A. A., and H. Demsetz (1972). "Production, Information Costs, and Economic Organization," *American Economic Review* 62, 12:777–795.

Aldrich, H. E. (1979). *Organizations and Environments,* Englewood Cliffs, N.J.: Prentice-Hall.

Armour, H. O., and D. J. Teece (1978). "Organization Structure and Economic Performance: A Test of the Multidivisional Hypothesis," *Bell Journal of Economics* 9:106–122.

Arrow, K. J. (1969). "The Organization of Economic Activity," *The Analysis and Evaluation Public Expenditure: The PPB System,* Joint Economic Committee, 91st Cong., 1st Session, pp. 59–73.

Arrow, K. J. (1974). *Limits of Organization,* New York: Norton.

Burton, R., and B. Obel (1980). "Analysis of the M-Form Hypothesis for Contracting Technologies," *Administrative Science Quarterly* 25,3:457–466.

Campbell, R. W. (1978). "New Concepts in the Study of Economic Systems," unpublished manuscript.

Carman, J. M. (1979). "Paradigms for Marketing Theory," in *Research in Marketing,* Greenwich, CT: JAI Press.

Chandler, A. D., Jr. (1966). *Strategy and Structure,* Cambridge, Mass.: MIT Press.

Chandler, A. D., Jr. (1978). *The Visible Hand: The Managerial Revolution in American Business,* Cambridge, Mass.: Harvard University Press.

Coase, R. H. (1952). "The Nature of the Firm," *Economica N. S.,* 1937 4:386–405, reprinted in G. J. Stigler and K. E. Boulding, Eds., *Readings in Price Theory,* Homewood, Ill.: R. D. Irwin.

Coase, R. H. (1972). "Industrial Organization: A Proposal for Research," in V. R. Fuchs, Ed., *Policy Issues and Research Opportunities in Industrial Organization,* New York: Columbia University Press.

Commons, J. R. (1934). *Institutional Economics,* Madison: University of Wisconsin Press.

Cyert, R. M., and J. G. March (1963). *A Behavioral Theory of the Firm,* Englewood Cliffs, N.J.: Prentice-Hall.

Demsetz, H. (1968). "The Cost of Transacting," *Quarterly Journal of Economics* 82, 2:33–53.

Doeringer, P., and M. Piore (1971). *Internal Labor Markets and Manpower Analysis,* Lexington, Mass.: D. C. Heath.

Fitzroy, F. R., and D. C. Mueller (1977). "Contract and the Economics of Organization," Discussion Paper 77–25, International Institute of Management, Berlin.

Franko, L. G. (1972). "The Growth, Organizational Efficiency of European Multinational Firms: Some Emerging Hypotheses," *Colloques International Aux C.N.R.S.* 549, 335–366.

Friedman, M. (1953). *Essays in Positive Economics,* Chicago: University of Chicago Press.

Galbraith, J. (1973). *Designing Complex Organizations,* Reading, Mass.: Addison-Wesley.

Goffman, I. (1969). *Strategic Interaction,* Philadelphia: University of Pennsylvania Press.

Hannan, M., and J. Freeman (1977). "The Population Ecology of Organizations," *American Journal of Sociology* 82, 3:929–964.

Hashimoto, M., and B. T. Yu (1980). "Specific Capital, Employment Contracts and Wage Rigidity," *Bell Journal of Economics* 2: 536–549.

Lawrence, D., and J. Lorsch (1967). *Organization and Environment,* Homewood, Ill.: R. D. Irwin.

Mackenzie, K. D. (1978). *Organizational Structures,* Arlington Heights, Ill.: AHM Publishing.

Macneil, I. R. (1974). "The Many Futures of Contract," *Southern California Law Review* 47, 5:691–816.

Macneil, I. R. (1978). "Contracts: Adjustment of Long-Term Economic Relations under Classical, Neoclassical, and Relational Contract Law," *Northwestern University Law Review* 72, 1:854–905.

Malmgren, H. (1961). "Information, Expectations and the Theory of the Firm," *Quarterly Journal of Economics* 75:399–421.

March, J. G., and J. P. Olsen (1976). *Ambiguity and Choice in Organizations,* Bergen: Universitetsforlaget.

Meade, J. E. (1971). *The Controlled Economy,* Albany: State University of New York Press.

Mintzberg, H. (1973). *The Nature of Managerial Work,* New York: Harper and Row.

North, D. C. (1978). "Structures and Performance: The Task of Economic History," *Journal of Economic Literature* 16:963–978.

Ouchi, W. G. (1977). "The Relationship between Organizational Structure and Organizational Control," *Administrative Science Quarterly* 22:95–113.

Ouchi, W. G. (1978). "The Transmission of Control through Organizational Hierarchy," *Academy of Management Journal* 21:248–263.

Ouchi, W. G. (1979). "A Conceptual Framework for the Design of Organizational Control Mechanisms," *Management Science.* 29, 9:833–845.

Ouchi, W. G., and A. H. Van de Ven (1980). "Antitrust and Organization Theory," in O. E. Williamson, Ed., *Antitrust Law and Economics,* Houston: Dame Publications.

Pfeffer, J. (1978). *Organizational Design,* Arlington Heights, Ill.: AHM Publishing.

Posner, R. A. (1969). "Natural Monopoly and its Regulation," *Stanford Law Review* 21, 548–564.

Posner, R. A. (1972). "The Appropriate Scope of Regulation in the Cable Television Industry," *Bell Journal of Economics* 3:98–129.

Scherer, F. M., A. Beckenstein, E. Kaufer, and R. Murphy (1975). *The Economics of Multiplant Operation: An International Comparison Study,* Cambridge, Mass.: Harvard University Press.

Simon, H. A. (1978). "Rationality and Process and Product of Thought," *American Economic Review* 68:1–16.

Steer, F., and J. Cable (1978). "Internal Organization and Profit: An Empirical Analysis of Large U. K. Companies," *Journal of Industiral Economics* 27:13–30.

Stigler, G. J. (1968). *The Organization of Industry,* Homewood, Ill.: R. D. Irwin.

Teece, D. J. (1979). "Internal Organization and Economic Performance," unpublished manuscript, Stanford, Cal.

Wachter, M., and O. E. Williamson (1978). "Obligational Markets and the Mechanics of Inflation," *Bell Journal of Economics* 9:549–571.

Weick, K. E. (1969). *The Social Psychology of Organizing,* Reading, Mass.: Addison-Wesley.

Weisbrod, B. (1979). "Economics of Institutional Choice," unpublished manuscript.

Williamson, O. E. (1964). *The Economics of Discretionary Behavior: Managerial Objectives in a Theory of the Firm,* Englewood Cliffs, N.J.: Prentice-Hall.

Williamson, O. E. (1965). "A Dynamic Theory of Interfirm Behavior," *Quarterly Journal of Economics,* November.

Williamson, O. E. (1967). "Hierarchical Control and Optimum Firm Size," *Journal of Political Economy* 75:123–138.

Williamson, O. E. (1971). "The Vertical Integration of Production: Market Failure Considerations," *American Economic Review* 61:112–123.

Williamson, O. E. (1973). "Markets and Hierarchies: Some Elementary Considerations," *American Economic Review* 63:316–325.

Williamson, O. E. (1975). *Markets and Hierarchies: Analysis and Antitrust Implications,* New York: Free Press.

Williamson, O. E. (1976). "Francise Bidding for Natural Monopolies-in General and with Respect to CATV," *Bell Journal of Economics* 7:73–104.

Williamson, O. E. (1979a). "Assessing Vertical Market Restrictions: Antitrust Ramifications of the Transaction Cost Approach," *University of Pennsylvania Law Review* 127:953–993.

Williamson, O. E. (1979b). "Transaction-Cost Economics: The Governance of Contractual Relations," *Journal of Law and Economics* 22:233–262.

Williamson, O. E. (1979c). "Public Policy on Saccharin: The Decision Process Approach and Its Alternatives," unpublished manuscript.

Williamson, O. E. (1980). "Emergence of the Visible Hand: Implications for Industrial Organization," in A. D. Chandler, Jr., Ed., *Managerial Hierarchies,* Cambridge, Mass.: Harvard University Press, pp. 183–202.

NINE
EARLY CONTINGENCY APPROACHES

This chapter focuses on some of the early writings of contingency approaches to organization. This approach is concerned with the organization as a unit in interaction with its environment. In this approach, the organization is considered as a complex set of interdependent parts interacting with one another and dependent in whole on some larger environment. Organizational survival is the goal and the organization will adapt in such a way as to achieve it. Thompson notes that "dysfunctions are conceivable, but it is assumed that the offending part will adjust to produce a net positive contribution or be disengaged or else this system will degenerate (43)." Thompson does not, however, as others have done, dismiss the other strategies of organization analysis, that is, the closed system methods. He suggests that both these approaches lead to some "truth, but neither alone affords an adequate understanding of complex organization."

The first selection, a summary/review of Selznick's work, is consistent with this natural system point of view. Selznick focuses on external organizations and how they may be fundamentally important in defining the nature of the organization. Cooptation is an adjustment process which facilitates the probabilities of survival of the organization. Cooptation is a mechanism used when the structure of the organization is inconsistent with the external environment imposing pressures on it. It is the process of absorbing new elements into leadership or policy-determination positions.

Selznick also points to the unanticipated consequences of individual activities in an organization. Some have suggested that the classical theorists presuppose away the notions of conflict and dysfunction by designing organization structure rigidly. While this may have been done in theory, it is impossible to do in fact. Selznick highlights the problems that could occur.

Selznick, however, does not describe alternative organization forms that might be appropriate in various types of environment. He simply describes the need for adaptation and some mechanisms by which it might occur. Burns and Stalker provide important insights into alternative organization forms. While there have been a number of critics of classical theory and the theory of bureaucracy, the major alternative form proposed by most tends to approximate a democratic organization. Yet when this organization form is put against the realities of the world, it is as ill fitting as bureaucracy in many instances. Burns and Stalker suggest that the important variable to be considered is the environment. Essentially they believe that in a relatively stable situation, a mechanistic (or bureaucratic) structure may be substantially more effective than one which approaches a democratic ideal. In a highly variable, or volatile environment, however, more flexible forms, which they call "organic," would be appropriate.

Borrowing from Burns and Stalker, and in an attempt to increase the understanding of organizational/effectiveness relationships, Joan Woodward and her associates undertook a research project which may well mark a turning point in the development of theory about organizations. An empirically based work that examined a large sample of British firms, her study provides strong evidence for the intuitive criticism that there is no *one* best way to organize. Woodward's work points sharply to some prescriptions that might be useful to the practitioner.—H. L. T.

SELZNICK'S "TVA AND THE GRASS ROOTS"*

HENRY L. TOSI

Selznick's basic aim in *TVA and the Grass Roots* is to present an approach to analyzing organizations. He is concerned with behavior that is internally relevant to them, and attempts to examine structural conditions which influence that behavior.

The organization is an adaptive social structure. It is a technical instrument for mobilizing human energies and directing them toward set aims. It is a mechanism which adapts to its environment. It is molded by forces tangential to its rational, ordered structure and stated goals. The organization may be viewed as a dynamic conditioning field which shapes the behavior of those at its helm (and implicity other members). It is a tool which has a life of its own separate from that of the members, yet mobilizing units which must come to terms with the environment. Organization behavior can best be understood when it is traced to the needs and structure of the organization as a living social institution.

Organizations have certain needs generated by the organization itself which command the attention and the decisions of those in power. In order to satisfy these needs, the organization must be adaptive to the environment in which it operates. These needs are:

1. The security of the organization in the social environment—this requires some continuity of policy and leadership.

*Summarized from Philip Selznick, *TVA and the Grass Roots* (Berkeley: University of California Press, 1953). I assume full responsibility for the interpretation herein.

2.   Maintenance of the stability of lines of communication and authority.
3.   A homogeneous outlook of participants regarding the meaning and role of the organization.
4.   The achievement of continuous support and participation on the part of the members.
5.   The stability of informal relations within the organization.

The formal and informal structure of activities within the organization develops in response to these needs. The organization can continue to exist only when it satisfies these needs and comes to terms with the environment. An informal structure develops within the formal structure of the organization. This informal structure reflects attempts of individuals and subgroups to control the conditions of their existence. It contains an informal control and communications mechanism, or system. This informal structure may be useful to the formal leadership as a communication device, but it extracts a cost for its existence; some power is taken from the formal system.

EXTERNAL ORGANIZATIONS

The characteristics of the organization may be determined by the constraints of other organizations in the environment. External organizations or groups sometimes have a special relationship to the organization. This may require that both the organization and the external body support each other in some way. The organization may have some responsibility to the external units, such as clients, customers, or the public. The character of this external group tends to define and shape the character of the organization. Somehow, it must be represented. It may be formally represented. The organization may recruit external unit members as organization members. They may also absorb them into the leadership structure of the organization. When the outside organization is not formally represented, it must rely on the ideology (to be discussed later) or some other mechanism to maintain the relationship. These external relationships affect the character and policy of the organization since adjustment to them is required.

COOPTATION

One way that the organization comes to terms with the environment it through the mechanism of cooptation. Cooptation is an adjustment, or coping, mechanism which enhances the chances of survival of the organization. It is needed when formal authority is out of balance with the institutional environment. It is the process of absorbing new elements into the leadership or policy-determining structure of the organization as a means of averting threats to the organization's stability and existence. It is an attempt to accommodate to the existing environment. In effect, power is shared with other interested groups.

Cooptation may be viewed in both formal and informal dimensions. Formal cooptation occurs when those absorbed into the policy-making and leadership structure share in the power as well as the burdens of administration. This happens when the organization publicly absorbs new elements. It is required when it is necessary to enhance or increase the legitimacy of the governing group, or where there is need for self-government within the organization.

Cooptation may be, however, a response to specific power centers. Informal cooptation is an internal response to the specific pressures of power within the community or the organization. In this case, the coopted elements share only in the power. It is an internal adaptation of the system when the formal authority structure is threatened. The power nucleus of affected groups may be absorbed into the organization to appease or reduce the opposition of other groups. Informal cooptation is a recognition of and a concession to the human resources in the organization. This type of cooptation may *not* be formally acknowledged.

Cooptation reflects the existing tension between social power and formal authority. When formal authority and social power exist together, there is no need for it. Cooptation broadens the leadership and has an important effect on the governing body. It restricts alternatives available to them. There is a need to accommodate the organization to those who have been coopted.

Cooptation is, in fact, a form of delegation. Those who coopt (the leaders) must be concerned with objectives and the means for achieving them. But they must also be concerned with those whom the organization affects. When either formal or informal cooptation occurs, the organization commits itself to activities supported and reinforced by the coopted elements. Thus, it must reach an equilibrium with those coopted, the objectives, the means of achieving them, and the environment. Thus cooptation, even though relatively slight, exerts pressure throughout the organization.

As a result of cooptation, a flow of information may be provided to those who have been coopted. Additionally, the organization is provided with the group resources of those coopted members. Cooptation also allows adaptation of decisions to lower, or local levels of the organization. Therefore, other organizations within the environment which have been coopted shape the characteristics and the nature of the coopting organization.

IDEOLOGY

Organizations are like people, searching for stability and meaning. Instability in the environment results in the development of a sustaining ideology, especially when the organization is threatened by the surrounding environment. It is necessary that this ideology be based on accepted political and moral values. The organization ideology serves as a parameter for decisions.

Ideology, or doctrine, arises as a special need of the organization. The source of ideology in the organization may be (1) from the influence of other institutions, and/or (2) the result of the need for internal communications to develop stability and homogeneity of attitudes.

Ideology facilitates the decentralization of management to lower levels. It shapes the views of new members as well as uniting technical experts within the bounds of the organization rather than toward their professions. Ideology may also emerge as organization members defend it against outsiders. Thus, doctrine, or ideology, satisfies internal needs but also provides an adjustment mechanism for the organization through which it can interact with other segments of the environment. It does not, however, provide a complete adjustment mechanism.

Ideology most probably is stated in laugauge which is ambiguous to the members. The meanings of concepts included in it may be different for different members. For instance, the concept of "increased effectiveness" might suggest reduced operating costs to a production foreman, while it may mean a more restrictive quality control policy to the quality-control staff executive. These ambiguities, however, mean something to members in terms of the specific activity in which they engage. The diverse meanings of ideology begin to take shape and become concrete through administrative decisions. Decisions must be made within discretionary bounds of the executive. Discretion has to do with the selection of alternatives. When it is used it involves, in some cases, intervention in the activities of other people. It is necessary therefore to consider the interests of those whom the decisions affect.

Decisions must be made within "ideology." The existence and use of abstract philosophies and ideologies to control organization result in problems. Ideology is abstract and action is specific. The resolution of this dilemma is an ongoing activity. Specific action programs must be developed to achieve these abstractions. The activities generally required to achieve abstractions may in practice be difficult to implement. Additionally, the delegation process separates planning functions (which may be derived from the philosophy or ideology) from the operating or specific activity.

Decisions made within the discretion bounds are inhibited by pressure groups within and outside the organization. Some policies may be highly dependent upon the connection the organization has with external organizations. For instance, the return goods policy of industrial manufacturers may be a function of "real control" that the buyer has over the seller.

UNANTICIPATED CONSEQUENCES

Lower-level officials of the organization must make decisions. In some cases, when there is ambiguity regarding the job content of these lower-level officials, their decisions may be based on their own values and norms. These may be inconsistent with, or different from, those of others in the organization. They may also be inconsistent or different from the objectives of the organization. Policy and doctrine attempt to generate action which is intended to be rational. Decisions within the discretion boundaries of administrators, however, require that they act selectively within their environment, which is conditioned by their own interests, values, or internalized norms. These decisions may yield results other than those intended within the concept of the ideology.

There are several reasons why these unanticipated consequences may occur. First, the individual may have commitments to other places or other organizational units which exert pressures contrary to the ideology. The external commitments of groups or members, (basic values, norms, and loyalties) may result in the inability of that organizational component to adjust to other aspects of the organization and to the organization's structure. This is most likely when these various commitments and norms are divergent.

Decisions made by higher-level organization members may commit lower levels to specific actions which the lower levels may not deem desirable. The interests of subgroups or departments must be viewed in light of the social situations within which their activities are carried on and the long-run consequences to the organization. Some activities necessary to maintain the organization may have, then, undesirable consequences for subordinate units. Some acts are simply required, such as procedures, which may become ends in themselves to these lower-level units. When this happens the unit may become more concerned with the performance of the function rather than the end which is desired as a result of performance. This preoccupation with means rather than ends may be harmful to the organization, yet these commitments may be enforced by the social environment and institutionalization.

The individual's personality also must be considered in obtaining unanticipated results. His needs, personal history, and experiences may result in a personality which rejects the demands of others, yet he must conform to some degree. Resistance to change and conflict may develop.

The organization strives, however, for a unified pattern of responses. This requires unity, or homogeneity, of outlook of members. As unity is approximated, the organizational character emerges. This may be essentially described as the way people live together in an organization. Those who cannot tolerate this character leave the organization.

The discretion of an executive is related to the organization character in the following manner. By increasing and integrating the many responses within an organization, it can be invested with a character. Precedent and custom then tend to preserve this character. When organizational conflict exists, the process of decisions, or the use of discretion, will be closely scrutinized. The administrator's decision will be infused with a high degree of self-consciousness.

The internal pressures toward unity are generated by the interests, values, and ideas which characterize the social environment of the organization. Once the organization has selected from the many alternative philosophies and values available, the organization reflects on its own character and sentiment to which it becomes aligned. These philosophies and values are available in the social environment, or context, within which the organization operates.

Additionally, different philosophies and values may be representative of various groups within the organization. This may be an unanticipated result of cooptation of members with divergent views. As each group attempts to make its basic philosophy predominant, a struggle for influence may ensue. The internal struggle between these groups is important in the concept of organizational leadership. The struggle results in the evolution of "organization character." This means that if the organization character changes, the leadership which stands for those ideals may be placed in a power position. Or leadership may change the character of the organization by gaining unity of thought regarding a particular ideology.

Another paradox for leadership in an organization should be considered. Leadership, by its nature, is involved with conflicting goals and problems. If it ignores the participation of the members, then the cooperation level may be threatened. If it encourages participation, however, its leadership position may be threatened by the acceptance of another ideology by other organization members.

"THE MANAGEMENT OF INNOVATION"*

T. BURNS
G. M. STALKER

. . . The utility of the notions of "mechanistic" and "organic" management systems resides largely in their being related as dependent variables to the rate of "environmental" change. "Environmental," in this connection, refers to the technological basis of production and to the market situation. . . . The increasing rate of technological change characteristic of the last generation could plausibly be regarded as a function of fundamental changes in the relationship of production to consumption.

If the form of management is properly to be seen as dependent on the situation the concern is trying to meet, it follows that there is no single set of principles for "good organization," an ideal type of management system which can serve as a model to which administrative practice should, or could in time, approximate. It follows also that there is an overriding management task in first interpreting correctly the market and technological situation, in terms of its instability or of the rate at which conditions are changing, and then designing the management system appropriate to the conditions, and making it work. "Direction," as I have labelled this activity, is the distinctive task of managers-in-chief. . . .

*Excerpted with permission of the publisher from T. Burns and G. M. Stalker, *The Management of Innovation* (London: Tavistock Publications, 1961).

For the individual, much of the importance of the difference between mechanistic and organic systems lies in the extent of his commitment to the working organization. Mechanistic systems (namely "bureaucracies") define his functions, together with the methods, responsibilities, and powers appropriate to them; in other words, however, this means that boundaries are set. That is to say, in being told what he has to attend to, and how, he is also told what he does not have to bother with, what is not his affair, what is not expected of him, what he can post elsewhere as the responsibility of others. In organic systems, the boundaries of feasible demands on the individual disappear. The greatest stress is placed on his regarding himself as fully implicated in the discharge of any task appearing over his horizon, as involved not merely in the exercise of a special competence but in commitment to the success of the concern's undertakings approximating somewhat to that of the doctor or scientist in the discharge of his professional functions . . .

MECHANISTIC AND ORGANIC SYSTEMS

We are now at the point at which we may set down the outline of the two management systems which represent for us . . . the two polar extremities of the forms which such systems can take when they are adapted to a specific rate of technical and commercial change. The case we have tried to establish from the literature, as from our research experience . . ., is that the different forms assumed by a working organization do exist objectively and are not merely interpretations offered by observers of different schools.

Both types represent a "rational" form of organization, in that they may both, in our experience, be explicitly and deliberately created and maintained to exploit the human resources of a concern in the most efficient manner feasible in the circumstances of the concern. Not surprisingly, however, each exhibits characteristics which have been hitherto associated with different kinds of interpretation. For it is our contention that empirical findings have usually been classified according to sociological ideology rather than according to the functional specificity of the working organization to its task and the conditions confronting it.

We have tried to argue that these are two formally contrasted forms of management system. These we shall call the mechanistic and organic form.

A *mechanistic* management system is appropriate to stable conditions. It is characterized by:

1. The specialized differentiation of functional tasks into which the problems and tasks facing the concern as a whole are broken down.
2. The abstract nature of each individual task, which is pursued with techniques and purposes more or less distinct from those of the concern as a whole (i.e., the functionaries tend to pursue the technical improvement of means, rather than the accomplishment of the ends of the concern).
3. The reconciliation, for each level in the hierarchy, of these distinct performances by the immediate superiors, who are also, in turn, responsible for seeing that each is relevant in his own special part of the task.

4. The precise definition of rights and obligations and technical methods attached to each functional role.
5. The translation of rights and obligations and methods into the responsibilities of a functional position.
6. Hierarchic structure of control, authority and communication.
7. A reinforcement of the hierarchic structure by the location of knowledge of actualities exclusively at the top of the hierarchy, where the final reconciliation of distinct tasks and assessment of relevance is made.[1]
8. A tendency for interaction between members of the concern to be vertical (i.e., between superior and subordinate).
9. A tendency for operations and working behavior to be governed by the instructions and decisions issued by superiors.
10. Insistence on loyalty to the concern and obedience to superiors as a condition of membership.
11. A greater importance and prestige attaching to internal (local) than to general (cosmopolitan) knowledge, experience, and skill.

The *organic* form is appropriate to changing conditions, which give rise constantly to fresh problems and unforeseen requirements for action which cannot be broken down or distributed automatically arising from the functional roles defined within a hierarchic structure. It is characterized by:

1. The contributive nature of special knowledge and experience to the common task of the concern.
2. The "realistic" nature of the individual task, which is seen as set by the total situation of the concern.
3. The adjustment and continual re-definition of individual tasks through interaction with others.
4. The shedding of "responsibility" as a limited field of rights, obligations and methods. (Problems may not be posted upwards, downwards or sideways as being someone else's responsibility.)
5. The spread of commitment to concern beyond any technical definition.
6. A network structure of control, authority, and communication. The sanctions which apply to the individual's conduct in his working role derive more from presumed community of interest with the rest of the working organization in the survival and growth of the firm, and less from a contractual relationship between himself and a nonpersonal corporation, represented for him by an immediate superior.
7. Omniscience no longer imputed to the head of the concern; knowledge about the technical or commercial nature of the here and now task may be located anywhere in the network; this location becoming the *ad hoc* center of control authority and communication.
8. A lateral rather than a vertical direction of communication through the organization, communication between people of different rank, also, resembling consultation rather than command.
9. A content of communciation which consists of information and advice rather than instructions and decisions.

10. Commitment to the concern's tasks and to the "technological ethos" of material progress and expansion is more highly valued than loyalty and obedience.

11. Importance and prestige attach to affiliations and expertise valid in the industrial and technical and commercial milieux external to the firm.

One important corollary to be attached to this account is that while organic systems are not hierarchic in the same sense as are mechanistic, they remain stratified. Positions are differentiated according to seniority (i.e., greater expertise). The lead in joint decisions is frequently taken by seniors, but it is an essential presumption of the organic system that the lead (i.e., "authority,") is taken by whoever shows himself most informed and capable (i.e., the "best authority"). The location of authority is settled by consensus.

A second observation is that the area of commitment to the concern—the extent to which the individual yields himself as a resource to be used by the working organization—is far more extensive in organic than in mechanistic systems. Commitment, in fact, is expected to approach that of the professional scientist to his work, and frequently does. One further consequence of this is that it becomes far less feasible to distinguish "informal" from "formal" organization.

Thirdly, the emptying out of significance from the hierarchic command system, by which cooperation is ensured and which serves to monitor the working organization under a mechanistic system, is encountered by the development of shared beliefs about the values and goals of the concern. The growth and accretion of institutionalized values, beliefs, and conduct, in the forms of commitments, ideology, and manners, around an image of the concern in its industrial and commercial setting make good the loss of formal structure.

Finally, the two forms of system represents a polarity, not a dichotomy; there are . . . intermediate stages between the extremities empirically known to us. Also, the relation of one form to the other is elastic, so that a concern oscillating between relative stability and relative change may also oscillate between the two forms. A concern may (and frequently does) operate with a management system which includes both types.

The organic form, by departing from the familiar clarity and fixity of the hierarchic structure, is often experienced by the individual manager as an uneasy, embarrassed, or chronically anxious quest for knowledge about what he should be doing, or what is expected of him, and similar apprehensiveness about what others are doing. Indeed, as we shall see later, this kind of response is necessary if the organic form of organization is to work effectively. Understandbly, such anxiety finds expression in resentment when the apparent confusion besetting him is not explained. In these situations, all managers some of the time, and many managers all the time, yearn for more definition and structure.

On the other hand, some managers recognize a rationale of nondefinition, a reasoned basis for the practice of those successful firms in which designation of status, function, and line of responsibility and authority has been vague or even avoided.

The desire for more definition is often in effect a wish to have the limits of one's task more neatly defined—to know what and when one doesn't have to bother about as much as to know what one does have to. It follows that the more definition is given, the more omniscient the management must be, so that no functions are left wholly or partly undischarged, no person is overburdened with undelegated responsibility, or left without the authority to do his job properly. To do this, to have all the separate functions attached to individual roles fitting together and comprehensively, to have communication between persons constantly maintained on a level adequate to the needs of each functional role, requires rules or traditions of behavior proved over a long time and an equally fixed, stable task. The omniscience which may then be credited to the head of the concern is expressed throughout its body through the lines of command, extending in a clear, explicitly titled hierarchy of officers and subordinates.

The whole mechanistic form is instinct with this twofold principle of definition and dependence which acts as the frame within which action is conceived and carried out. It works, unconsciously, almost in the smallest minutiae of daily activity. "How late is late?" The answer to this question is not to be found in the rule book, but in the superior. Late is when the boss thinks it is late. Is he the kind of man who thinks 8:00 is the time, and 1 is late? Does he think that 8:15 is all right occasionally if it is not a regular thing? Does he think that everyone should be allowed a 5-minutes grace after 8:00 but after that they are late?

Settling questions about how a person's job is to be done in this way is nevertheless simple, direct, and economical of effort. . . .

One other feature of mechanistic organization needs emphasis. It is a necessary condition of its operation that the individual "works on his own," functionally isolated; he "knows his job," he is "responsible for seeing it's done." He works at a job which is in a sense artifically abstracted from the realities of the situation the concern is dealing with, the accountant "dealing with the costs side," the works manager "pushing production," and so on. As this works out in practice, the rest of the organization becomes part of the problem situation the individual has to deal with in order to perform successfully (i.e., difficulties and probelms arising from work or information which has been handed over the "responsibility barrier" between two jobs or departments are regarded as "really" the responsibility of the person from whom they were received). As a design engineer put in, "When you get designers handing over designs completely to production, it's their responsibility now. And you get tennis games played with the responsibility for anything that goes wrong. What happens is that you're constantly getting unsuspected faults arising from characteristics which you didn't think important in the design. If you get to hear of these through a sales person, or a production person or somebody to whom the design was handed over to in the dim past, then, instead of being a design problem, it's an annoyance caused by that particular person, who can't do his own job—because you'd thought you were finished with that one, and you'ie on to something else now."

When the assumptions of the form of organization make for preoccupation with specialized tasks, the chances of career success, or of greater influence, depend rather on the relative importance which may be attached to each special function by the superior whose task it is to reconcile and control a number of them. And, indeed, to press the claims of one's job or department for a bigger share of the firm's resources is in many cases regarded as a mark of initiative, of effectiveness, and even of "loyalty to the firm's interests." The state of affairs thus engendered squares with the role of the superior, the man who can see the wood instead of just the trees, and gives it the reinforcement of the aloof detachment belonging to a court of appeal. The ordinary relationship prevailing between individual managers "in charge of" different functions is one of rivalry, a rivalry which may be rendered innocuous to the persons involved by personal friendship or the norms of sociability, but which turns discussion about the situations which constitute the real problems of the concern—how to make products more cheaply, how to sell more, how to allocate resources, whether to curtail activity in one sector, whether to risk expansion in another, and so on—into an arena of conflicting interests.

The distinctive feature of the second, organic system is the pervasiveness of the working organization as an institution. In concrete terms, this makes itself felt in a preparedness to combine with others in serving the general aims of the concern. Proportionately to the rate and extent of change, the less can the omniscience appropriate to command organizations be ascribed to the head of the organization; for executives, and even operatives, in a changing firm it is always theirs to reason why. Furthermore, the less definition can be given to status, roles, and modes of communication, the more do the activities of each member of the organization become determined by the real tasks of the firm as he sees them than by instruction and routine. The individual's job ceases to be self-contained; the only way in which "his" job can be done is by his participating continually with others in the solution of problems which are real to the firm, and put in a language of requirements and activities meaningful to them all. Such methods of working put much heavier demands on the individual. . . .

We have endeavored to stress the appropriateness of each system to its own specific set of conditions. Equally, we desire to avoid the suggestion that either system is superior under all circumstances to the other. In particular, nothing in our experience justifies the assumption that mechanistic systems should be superseded by organic in conditions of stability.[2] The beginning of administrative wisdom is the awareness that there is no optimum type of management system.

Footnotes

[1]This functional attribute of the head of a concern often takes on a clearly expressive aspect. It is common enough for concerns to instruct all people with whom they deal to address correspondence to the firm (i.e., to its formal head) and for all outgoing letters and orders to be signed by the head of the concern. Similarly, the printed letter heading used by Government departments carries instructions for the replies to be addressed to the Secretary, etc. These instructions are not always taken seriously, either by members of the organization or their correspondents, but in one company this practice was insisted upon and was taken to somewhat unusual lengths: *all* correspondence was delivered to the managing director, who would thereafter distribute excerpts to members of the staff, synthesizing their replies into the letter of reply which he eventually sent. Telephone communication was also controlled by limiting the numbers of extensions, and by monitoring incoming and outgoing calls.

[2][A] instance of this assumption is contained in H. A. Shepard's paper addressed to the Symposium on the Direction of Research Establishments, 1956: "There is much evidence to suggest that the optimal use of human resources in industrial organizations requires a different set of conditions, assumptions, and skills from those traditonally present in industry. Over the past twenty-five years, some new orientations have emerged from organizational experiments, observations and inventions. The new orientations depart radically from doctrines associated with 'Scientific Management' and traditional bureaucratic patterns.

"The central emphases in this development are as follows:

"1. Wide participation in decision-making, rather than centralized decision-making.

"2. The face-to-face group, rather than the individual, as the basic unit of organization.

"3. Mutual confidence, rather than authority, as the integrative force in organization.

"4. The supervisor as the agent for maintaining intragroup and intergroup communication, rather than as the agent of higher authority.

"5. Growth of members of the organization to greater responsibility, rather than external control of the member's performance or their tasks."

WOODWARD'S "INDUSTRIAL ORGANIZATION"*

DONNA G. GOEHLE

Joan Woodward's book, *Industrial Organization* (50) represents the results of nearly a decade of empirical study of British industry located in South Essex. The research was undertaken by the Human Relations Research Unit at the South East Essex College of Technology beginning in 1953, with the major part of the field work completed in 1958. Additional research, utilizing se-

*This abstract was prepared by Donna G. Goehle. It is based on Joan Woodward, *Industrial Organization: Theory and Practice* (London: Oxford University Press, 1965).

lected firms and aimed toward in-depth analysis of preliminary findings, was begun in 1960.

The general objective of the research workers in initially approaching the study was that, "a project had to be devised, which, although problem centered, might make a contribution to the field of industrial sociology." According to Woodward, preliminary findings indicated that in the "final formulation of the project industrial firms would have to be studied as complex social systems and line-staff relationships looked at as parts of a whole rather than in isolation." Moreover, the wide differences between firms indicated that it would be necessary to include as many of the nearby firms as possible; however, such a broadening of the effort brought about additional possibilities for superficial results, and therefore it was decided that the project should first concentrate on making a broad survey of the whole area, and then additional in-depth studies could be undertaken if there were sufficient time and resurces made available. Woodward's text presents an account of the studies themselves and the conclusions drawn from an analysis of the data.

THE SURVEY AND INITIAL CONCLUSIONS

In the first study of 100 industrial firms conducted between September 1954 and September 1955, the researchers attempted to obtain information regarding the formal organization and operating procedures. It was felt that the large number of firms involved in the first phase of the study would preclude attempts to find out very much about the informal social relationships within the firm; therefore, the information sought by the research unit was limited to the following categories:

1. History, background, and objectives.
2. Description of the manufacturing processes and methods.
3. Forms and routines through which the firm was organized and operated.
4. Facts and figures that could be used to make an assessment of the firm's commercial success.

In evaluating the information regarding history, background and objectives, it became evident that although all firms were engaged in manufacturing, there were substantial differences among them. "The nature of their markets, the type of customers they served, the methods they employed, and the targets they set for themselves differed considerably." The differences in manufacturing processes were also noticeable and were grouped according to the following "technical variables": "the density of production, the flexibility of production, facilities, the diversity of products, the time span of operations, and the way in which production programs were initiated and controlled." (This classification of technical variables related to production types becomes a critical element throughout the entire period of the study.)

In reference to the third category of information sought, the research workers obtained organizaton charts where they were available, and tried to construct them through interviewing when they were not. Information in this category focused on determining the pattern of prescribed relationships as well as a duties and responsibilities of each office studied. In addition, they studied "the history and responsibilities of the principal staff and specialist departments, including sales, research, development, personnel, inspection, maintenance, and purchasing; they examined the documentation associated with planning and control procedures and the methods used in costing and budgetary control." Considerable attention was also given to analyzing the labor structure for each firm.

Since the researchers were not only interested in determining how the various firms were organized and operated, but also in discovering whether particular forms of organization were associated with managerial efficiency and success, they also attempted to assemble information regarding the ways in which a firm's success might be evaluated internally and externally. Some of the factors taken into account in assessing the "success" of the enterprise included such things as market position and market share, annual reports and financial statements for a five-year period, fluctuations in the market price of the firm's stock, reputation among competitors and labor unions, and internally generated information thought to be significant in explaining the relationship between internal operations and enterprise success.

In developing a measure of commercial success which could be used in testing the relationship between organizational form and that success, the methods used by the researchers seem to be imprecise and are not treated as rigorously as some of the other variables utilized. Internal efficiency, although mentioned, does not appear to be fully developed in either of the studies; however, some oblique references to the efficiency of certain production technologies does appear in the analysis of both studies. Aside from grouping the firms on the basis of the general categories of "average," "above average," and "below average," the researchers did not concentrate their analysis on linking more specific measures of commercial success to particular organizational forms.

In their analysis of organization, Woodward and her colleagues focused primarily on the types of organization traditionally associated with the "classical" school of organizational thought; line organization, functional organization, and line-staff organization. They divided the firms into these categories and found the following distribution of types among the firms surveyed: 35 predominately line organization; 2 functional organization; 59 line-staff organization; and 4 unclassifiable.

A considerable degree of variation, especially in the manner in which specialist departments evolved, existed among the firms surveyed; however, there seemed to be no consistent pattern of evolution which held true across the sample. In addition, firms rated at both ends of the success continuum illustrated diverse organizational forms. According to the study, there did not appear to be a direct interrelationship between organizational structure and commercial success. When other variables were examined, such as the length of the command hierarchy, the sizes of the span of control at various levels, the size of the firm based on total employees, the industry type, and managerial qualifications, no link between one or more variables and commercial success could be established.

Woodward and her associates also utilized Burns' approach to classifying industrial organizations as "mechanistic" and "organic" systems. Applying this classification to the firms being studied they found that "Organic systems, both those consciously planned on organic lines and those planned on mechanistic lines but operated on organic principles, outnumbered mechanistic systems by approximately two to one," The results of the analysis of the participating firms, based on the criteria Burns' work suggested, seem to substantiate his earlier findings. Woodward reports the results in the following manner:

> As a result of his researches he came to the conclusion that mechanistic systems are appropriate to stable conditions and organic systems to conditions of change. It will be recalled that South Essex is an area in which the newer and developing industries predominate, and it might therefore be expected that organic systems would predominate (p. 24).

Having reached these general conclusions in their initial analysis of the data, the researchers turned to a more detailed examination of the technical variables. Although some social scientists, including Weber and Veblen, have suggested a link between technological circumstances and the structure and behavior of social systems, there had been relatively little empirical work undertaken which would delineate this suggested relationship. In the absence of such a framework, Woodward's researchers initially grouped the firms on the basis of similarities in manufacturing processes and methods. Once the initial classification was complete, they were able to determine that "firms with similar goals and associated manufacturing policies had similar manufacturing processes—the range of tools, instruments, machines and technical formulas was limited and controlled by the manufacturing policy." The first breakdown of firms studied included those enterprises "where production was 'one of a kind' to meet customers' individual requirements, and those where production was standardized."

This initial breakdown quickly developed into many more categories based on the size of the unit being produced, the technical complexity of the product being produced, and the diversity of products being manufactured, to mention only a few. It became obvious to the researchers that each of the manufacturing processes was unique in some way; therefore, some method of systematizing the firms according to technical variables had to be developed. "It was felt that the system of division normally used by production engineers into the three categories of jobbing, batch, and mass production were inadequate. . . ." Consequently, a more expanded grouping of eleven categories, based on these basic production types, was devised. Figure 1 represents the distribution of firms by production system.

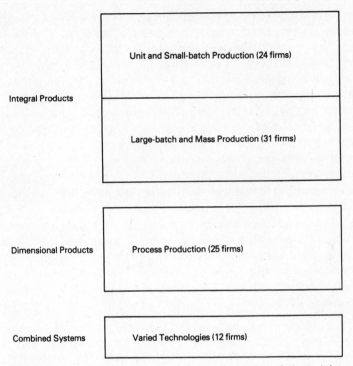

Figure 1 Production systems of firms in the study (adapted from Joan Woodward).

In relating the production categories to the ways in which the various firms were organized and operated, the first significant pattern emerged. It was determined that, "firms with similar production systems appeared to have similar organizational structures." According to Woodward, the differences between some of the firms placed in the same category were not as significant as the differences observed between the various categories. Furthermore, "the figures relating to the various organizational characteristics tended to cluster around the medians, the medians varying from one category to another." Based on these observations, the following conclusions were drawn:

Therefore, the main conclusion reached through this research project was that the existence of the link between technology and social structure first postulated by Thorstein Veblen (1919) can be demonstrated empirically (p. 50).

Although Woodward is careful to note that the research did not prove technology was the *only* important variable in determining the organizational structure, it was one which could be isolated for further study without too much difficulty. In addition, "the only variable found to be demonstrably related to variations in organization was the system of production in operation." In examining this relationship, the following characteristics were also considered: "the length of the line of command; the span of control of the chief executive; the percentage of total turnover allocated to the payment of wages and salaries; and the ratio of managers to total personnel, of clerical and administrative staff to manual workers, of direct to indirect labor, and of graduate to non-graduate supervision in the production departments."

Throughout this phase of the report. Woodward distinguishes the predominant characteristics of firms operating at both ends of the production continuum as well as in the middle ranges and relates them in a systematic fashion to the variables. She then continues by developing a discussion of the relationship between technology, organization, and success. Since one of the objectives in conducting the study was to determine whether or not management principles were being applied in practice and whether they were influential in ensuring business success, the researchers wanted to determine what type of organizational system might prove to be most appropriate for a particular production system. On the basis of analyzing the preceding organizational characteristics—number of levels in the chain in of command, labor costs, and various labor ratios—with measures of organizational success, Woodward concludes that:

> The fact that organizational characteristics, technology and success were linked together in this way suggested that not only was the system of production an important variable in the determination of organizational structure, but also that one particular form of organization was most appropriate to each system of production. In unit production, for example, not only did short and relatively broadly based pyramids predominate, but they also appeared to ensure success. Process production, on the other hand, would seem to require the taller and more narrowly based pyramid (p. 71).

Woodward also found that "successful firms inside the large batch production range tended to have mechanistic management systems. On the other hand, successful firms outside this range tended to have organic systems."

In explaining the observations of the Woodward team and their relationship to the concepts associated with classical management theory, she makes the following statement:

> In general, the administrative expedients associated with success in large-batch firms were in line with the principles and ideas on which the teaching of managment subjects is based. In all successful large-batch production firms there was not only a clear definition of duties and responsibilities of the kind already referred to, but also an adherence to the principles of unity of command; a separation (at least on paper) of advisory from executive responsibilites, and a chief executive who controlled no more than the recommended five or six direct subordinates.

> The tendency to regard large-batch production as the typical system of modern industry may be the explanation of this link between success and conformity with management theory. The people responsible for developing management theory no doubt had large batch production in mind as they speculated about management. In general, the experience on which their generalizations were based had been obtained in large-batch production industry (pp. 71–72).

In summarizing the results of the survey, Woodward states that "While at first sight there seemed to be no link between organization and success, and no one best way or organizing a factory, it subsequently became apparent that there was a particular form of organization most appropriate to each technical situation." According to the survey, "within a limited range of technology this was also the form of organization most closely in line with the principles and ideas of management theory. . . . Outside this limited range however, the rules appear to be different, the most suitable form of organization being out of line with these ideas." It should be noted that Woodward carefully states that the researchers found a link between organization, technology, and success, but that a *precisely defined causal* relationship was not claimed nor established by this phase of the research.

Examining the link between organization and technology, the researchers were also interested in evaluating the relationship between technology, social structure, and administrative practices in general. Viewing the firm as a social system within a larger social system, Woodward defines social structure as the "framework on which the system operates." According to Woodward, the variables in the system include: "occupational structure, the enterprise consisting of members of different occupational groups in the community; formal organization (i.e., the stable and explicit pattern of prescribed relationships designed to enable those employed to work together in the achievement of objectives) and informal organization (i.e., the pattern of relationships which actually emerges from day-to-day operations"). Since the researchers were interested in determining to what degree management theory, as it was being taught, was being applied in designing and administering organizations, it was natural that the analysis would probably move in the direction of further defining the link between technology and organization.

From the information obtained in the survey, Woodward and her colleagues determined that formal organization was considerably affected by technical factors. Although they found that there was less conscious planning of formal organizations in the firms they studied than one would expect, given the findings of several other social scientists in the industrial field, they did discover that some interesting relationships between formal planning of organizational structure, formalization of the informal structure, and the type of production being employed in the enterprise. In the successful firms of the first group (utilizing formal organizational planning), "unit and small-batch production and continuous-flow production predominated, while the majority of successful firms in the second category were in the large-batch production category." This finding would tend to suggest that "conscious planning produces better results in some kinds of industry than in others."

Since other social scientists have frequently assumed that "formal organization is the part of social structure least affected by technology," the conclusions drawn by Woodward seem especially interesting: "the survey findings suggested that the link between technology and organization persists in spite of, rather than because of, the conscious behavior or deliberate policy, and in defiance of the tendency in management education to emphasize the independence of the administrative process from technical considerations." Through her analysis of these findings, she suggests that technical environments can and do affect the structure of both the formal and the informal organization of the enterprise. Furthermore, she contends that "technology, because it influences the roles defined by formal organization, must therefore influence industrial behavior, for how a person reacts depends as much on the demands of his role and the circumstances in which he finds himself, as on her personality." Woodward goes on to state that "there can be occasions when the behavior forced on him by his role will conflict with his personality." To her way of thinking, the individual will resolve the conflict in one of two ways—modifying his personality to conform to the role considerations or leave the organization. In light of the hypothesized relationship between technical variables and organizational roles and the concomitant possibilities for conflict for the individual, Woodward concludes that perhaps top managers are brought to the upper levels of the organization through having those "personalities which best fit the technical background in which they have to operate."

Although explicit causal relationships were not defined, Woodward and her associates suggest that a number of other initial observations could be made from analyzing the results of this first survey. It was determined, for instance, that certain technical environments seem to impose greater strains than others might on members of all levels of the hierarchy. In addition, intermanagerial and employee-employer relationships appeared to "be better at the extremes of the scale than they were in the middle; pressure was greatest in the middle and it seemed more important to build mechanisms into the organizational structure which would resolve the conflicts likely to occur." At this stage of the research Woodward summarizes the findings and their implications for formulating the next stage of the study.

> Thus it seems that an analysis of situational demands could lead not only to the development of better techniques for appraising organizational structure and for conscious planning, but also to an increased understanding of the personal qualities and skills required in different industrial situations, and to improved methods of training directed towards giving those concerned a better understanding of the strains and stresses associated with the roles they are likely to occupy (p. 80).

THE CASE STUDIES

In order to investigate some of their initial observations, the group undertook a more detailed case study of 20 selected firms in which manufacturing methods were either changing or mixed. It was felt that if technology and organization were linked in the manner suggested by the earlier findings, more difficult organizational challenges and problems would arise in firms with these characteristics. Therefore, they wanted to examine firms which were characterized as undergoing a change in production systems (caused by technological developments) and which might require that the formal organization be modified to a new set of situational demands.

Firms utilizing mixed production systems were also chosen for additional study because of the possibilities they presented for studying potentially incompatible situational demands arising from the technology. If those organizations were found to have conflicting situational demands, study of the organizational structure might reveal the way in which these demands might be reconciled. Thus, this phase of the study was intended to evaluate in more detail the relationship between the technology of production and the associated organizational pattern. Consequently, the three main aspects of organization selected for examination in this phase of the study were: "the type of organization with particular reference to the breakdown between line and staff roles; the relationships between the three main functions of manufacturing— research and development, production, and marketing; and the organization of production, including the way in which results were predicted and controlled."

The researchers began by examining the relationship between situational demands arising from the technology and the organizational structure. In general, the "follow-up studies confirmed that in many firms the conscious process of organization-building proceeds independently of technical change and development, and that the link between technology and organization was not the product of conscious behavior or deliberate policy." In face, many of those interviewed seemed to feel that there was no one best way for organizing a firm and that there were a number of alternatives which could potentially be as effective as the one they happened to be using. It appeared in some firms, that there were changes in organization which followed a change in technology and resulted from the apparent inability of the preceding organization to cope with that change.

Although the observations made in the second phase of the research seemed to support the conclusions of the initial study, a number of interesting points emerged in the more detailed phase of analysis. "The research workers realized as they studied firms more deeply that not only the type of organization but also the functions of the organization were linked with technology." Although the organization is often thought of as having a dual function in serving both technical and social ends, Woodward and her colleagues found rather substantial differences between the functions of organization required for one type of firm (or production process) and those of a firm utilizing a less advanced system of production. They discovered that "in the process industry, the design or mechanism for coordinating work is intrinsic in the plant itself, and in some of the mass production firms they studied, the control system fulfilled a similar function." Consequently, "in both these systems, production emerged almost automatically once the production process had been set in motion." Summarizing the relationship between organization structure, functions, and technology among observed firms, Woodward states:

> This means that in the technically advanced firm organization serves primarily social ends, its function being to define roles and relationships within a social system. This means that the organization planner can concentrate on establishing the network of

relationships which is best for people. Moreover, because coordination is independent of organization, the form of organization is not likely to have a critical effect on business success.

In the less advanced systems of production, where organization serves both technical and social ends, there is likely to be a much closer link between business success and the form of organization, and the two functions can come into conflict. The network of relationships best for production is not necessarily best for people (p. 123).

Based on these observations, Woodward suggests that the initial step in designing an organizational structure compatible with the situational demands imposed by the technology is to determine the purposes of the organization. Unfortunately, according to Woodward's view, classical management thought is inadequate in relating organizational structure to business success in this manner, particularly when considered in light of the situational demands imposed by a particular technology.

After having made the distinction between task and element functions and their relationship to organizational structure, Woodward turned her analysis toward examining the relationship between the task functions and the personnel charged with carrying them out. This phase of the analysis focused on the relationship between task functions and the three major manufacturing tasks mentioned earlier: manufacturing, marketing, and development. In evaluating the task functions associated with each of these functions, Woodward and her colleagues discovered that in the technically advanced systems, the functions could be separated quite easily; however, in the unit and small-bath process firms, the separation between these three functions was much more difficult to achieve.

In addition, they determined that "the relative importance of the various functions was also related to the system of production," and that within each production organization, one task element seemed to be central and critical to both success and survival. Although they recognized that this difference in emphasis between firms could certainly be due to more than a dependency on a certain type of technology, they concluded that "in the long run, technology remained the dominant factor in the determination of the critical factor."

Through their analysis of the status system, they observed that the successful firms accorded adequate recognition to the importance of the critical function. They also discovered that the department in which the chief executive had previously worked was also the department with the highest status. Taking this link between the status system and technology as well as the background of the chief executive, they concluded that "there was a tendency for firms whose chief executive had been closely associated with the critical function earlier in his career to be the more successful ones."

The general outcome of this phase of the study can be summarized as follows:

As we have seen, in unit production and large-batch and mass production, organization has to serve both technical and social ends; the coordination of basic activities depends upon organization, the difference between these two types of production being that whereas in unit production there is no conflict between technical and social ends, in large-batch and mass production such conflict can and does arise.

Process production is different again. This is the type of industry where organization does not have to provide a mechanism for the coordination of work; its main purpose is therefore social.

The fact that organization does not provide the mechanism for the coordination of work may be the fundamental reason why relationships between development, production, and marketing were more harmonious in process firms than in large-batch and mass-production firms even though roles were in general less clearly defined (p. 127).

When the researchers turned their attention from the overall organizational structure to the more detailed elements of planning and controlling production, they found that the link between technology and organization was not always as apparent. When production organization was considered, it did not appear to be as closely related to technology as some of the other aspects of organization. In evaluating this situation further, Woodward and her colleagues observed that "there was greater variation in the way production operations were planned and controlled in the firms in the middle ranges of the scale . . . . As far as the organization of production was concerned, situational demands impose themselves more rigidly and obviously at the extremes than in the middle ranges of the scale.

It appeared that at either end of the continuum, the possible ranges in organizational choice were much more confined by the type of production technology than in the middle ranges; consequently, those in the middle ground had much more latitude in determining organizational issues related to production. In fact, it was determined that within this middle range, even an unsuitable organization had relatively little immediate impact on the success of the enterprise. Therefore, Woodward concludes that, in the case of firms in the middle ranges of the production spectrum, technology was an important variable; however, other variables were equally important.

It was in her analysis of the production organization that Woodward seemed to find classical management theory most noticeably inadequate for analyzing and understanding the behavior and the relationships associated with complicated production processes. Although the conventional line-staff classifications were evidently useful to the researchers in identifying and categorizing some of the problem areas in organization, they were unable to utilize these concepts in fully explaining the nature of their findings. This seemed to be particularly evident in those situations where they were attempting to evaluate the relationship between control systems and the human relations problems they observed in several situations.

THE FOLLOW-UP INVESTIGATIONS

Throughout their extensive study of manufacturing organizations in the South Essex area, Woodward and her associates had demonstrated and evaluated the existence of a link between technology and organizational characteristics. They were not interested in deepening their understanding of the apparent interaction between technical and behavioral factors. To this end, additional and and more intensive studies of three firms were begun. The researchers now wanted to refine the instrument used in classifying technology and detail the appropriate technical technical characteristics for the various production processes considered earlier. In addition, they wanted to further examine the relationship between technology and organization in those enterprises undergoing technical changes. One other objective of the study was to further examine the effects of formalization on control procedures.

The analysis of the control system was, to some degree, meant to serve as a basis for further studies in the area, and some comments on the background of this aspect of the project seem appropriate.

> Briefly, this project is based on the assumption that when the management of a firm makes a decision to manufacture a product or series of products a control system is automatically brought into existence. Objectives have to be determined in relation to the product and a sequence of activities planned in order to achieve these objectives. Plans then have to be executed and information generated to enable the results to be assessed. If activities are to be repeated, corrective action may have to be taken or the objectives modified in the light of the result obtained. For those concerned with the product at all levels of the hierarchy, the control system is the framework in which they operate, determining the amount of discretion they have in the organization of their own activities. It is hoped that some way of describing control systems in terms of such parameters as degrees of formalization, complexity, and fragmentation will be found, and the behavior associated with them analyzed (p. 186).

The researchers discovered that substantially less organizational disturbance and modification had resulted in the one firm which experienced a change in moving from process production to automated, continuous-flow production than occurred in the two plants characterized as having substantially different production technologies. This would seem to support their initial hypothesis that: "Technical changes involving a change in the nature of the production system have the greatest effect on organization and behavior."

In continuous-process production plants, the commercial success of the enterprise was more closely linked to the assurances of a long-range market potential for its products; therefore, the "number of imponderables was relatively few and the consequences of taking a particular course of action could be predicted with a certain degree of certainty." Although Woodward does not elaborate on the topic of uncertainty in markets as it might affect intra-firm organizational issues, she seems to suggest that the problems faced by some of the other firms—having different production technologies—may be related to the uncertainties in marketing of products and the interrelationship of those uncertainties with production scheduling, control, and plant organization and administration.

The role of the chief executive also differed among the three types of companies. Again, because of the rigid framework of control provided by the production process itself in process industries, relationships were characterized as being less stressful than those in the other two firms. In addition, although the members of the organization were working under a relatively rigid framework of control—based on the process technology—there appeared to be fewer complaints in this organization regarding limitations on individual action and authority. Interestingly, chief executives in the process production industry were observed as spending less time on purely technical matters than their counterparts in other firms. Since technical decisions in crisis situations were delegated to those which technical expertise and long-range planning decisions were too important to be left to one man, the observers felt that the chief executive in this industry was more involved in the social organization of the firm than his counterparts in other types of production plants.

In evaluating the other two plants which were moving into the batch-production type of technology from opposite ends of the continuum, results concerning the effect of change on these two organizations indicated that the most "recalcitrant problems of organization and behavior are likely to be found in the batch-production area of technology." Since it was anticipated that the problems in adjusting to change in each of these organizations would probably take a greater period of time than in the process industry and might prove to be more costly, the researchers were interested in examining further the relationship between the degree of adjustment required and the duration of the period of tension accompanying these changes. Since the researchers sought to study a "before and after" situation, and already had considerable data on these firms, these studies allowed the researchers to control the experiment somewhat by holding the factors other than technology constant.

In analyzing the results of this phase of the study, the researchers concluded that their initial predictions of the effect of technological change on organization and behavior were substantiated. In brief, they determined that the batch-production technology brought with it some of the most difficult problems in both behavior and organization. "Moreover, the differences in the ease with which firms adapted to technical change could be explained in terms of the senior managers' ability to anticipate these problems, and the initiative shown in simultaneous planning of organizational and technical change." According to Woodward, the results of this phase of the study:

> Provided a further demonstration of the main thesis put forward . . . , i.e., that meaningful explanations of behavior can be derived from an analysis of the work situation. It seemed that in identifying technology as one of the primary variables on which behavior depended, a step forward had been made in the determination of the conditions under which behavior becomes standarized and predictable (p. 208).

In evaluating the effects of technical change on organization and behavior, the researchers also examined the relationship between informal and formal organization within the firms being studied and found that the organizational objectives were frequently achieved by the informal organization. Furthermore, they found that "a disfunctional organization could be compensated by contributive informal relationships," and that this observation was particularly notable when viewed in relation to technical change.

When technical change was introduced, the researchers found that organizations varied in the way in which the formal and informal organizations responded to the new requirements. In some firms, where technical change and organizational change were simultaneously planned and initiated, adjustment of the informal to the formal organization seemed much more rapid. Conversely, where organizational change and technical change were not simultaneously introduced and/or planned for, the informal organization was the primary means by which the organizational goal was effected. It was only later that the adjustment was made in the formal organization. The possible advantages in control gained through proper attention to planning both organizational and technical change seem evident and appear to be supported by Woodward's analysis.

CONCLUSIONS

Certainly, the conclusions reached in the study tend to support the view that the "rules of classical management theory do not always work in practice"; however, classical theory was not dismissed as useless in the analysis of organizations.

Woodward concluded that the existing classical theory was deficient in its ability to incorporate the formal and informal aspects of organizational behavior. She also found the human relations school to be inadequate in explaining the complexities of organization and behavior. Consequently, "far from casting away management principles altogether, one of the more significant factors in the research findings was the confirmation that these principles were postively linked to business success in one particular area of technology." But there is still the absence of clearcut guides for application in differing settings which would enhance both stabililty in application and improved predictability.

TEN
LATER CONTINGENCY MODELS

The selections in the previous chapter represent a good deal of the important conceptual bases for later theoretical development. Further development of these notions is provided in James Thompson's approach. Thompson is especially concerned with the lack of "good" theory for use by researchers. He attempts to integrate concepts from a wide range of social science literature to deal with the important questions of how organizations adapt to and cope with the environment.

Perrow presents detail not developed in the early literature. His formulation includes the extreme ends of the organization spectrum, but he also describes "mixed" forms and some attendant problems for participants in them. His concept of variability of particular environmental sectors, and the way this is linked to structure, is important for it makes abundantly clear that structure decisions may not be at the complete discretion of individuals inside the organization.

Henry Mintzberg elaborates the organization form even more. He outlines a typology of five "pure types" of organization. Each of these has a configuration of structural elements which differs from others. These different structures emerge in response to the environment and as a result of managerial decisions about the design of the organization.

Finally, the last selection by Tosi outlines an approach which draws heavily from organization theory and organizational behavior. This model is based on the premise that different types of organizations will attract different types of people, thus giving rise to the need for different managerial approaches.—H.L.T.

JAMES D. THOMPSON'S "ORGANIZATIONS IN ACTION"*

DONNA G. GOEHLE

James D. Thompson, in prefacing his *Organizations in Action* (43), states that a "central purpose of the book is to identify a framework which might link at important points several of the now independent approaches to understand-

*This abstract was prepared by Donna F. Goehle. It is based on James Thompson, *Organizations in Action* (New York: McGraw-Hill, 1967).

ing organizations." In developing primarily a theoretical inventory of concepts and propositions about the ways in which those concepts might be related in explaining complex organizations, Thompson does not attempt to test his formulations empirically; rather, he suggests that the framework he advances may be useful for others in generating those hypotheses. In contrast to Woodward's work, Thompson has included a wide range of organizational types which he generally characterizes as being "instrumental organizations which induce or coerce participation" and has excluded only those organizations of a "voluntary" nature such as some religious groups and ideological associations. From the outset, Thompson makes it clear that he is interested in focusing on the behavior of organizations and only tangentially in considering individual behavior within organizations.

Thompson has attempted to meld many of the various approaches to the study of organizations arising out of the various fields and disciplines which deal with observing and understanding complex organizations. According to Thompson, these interdisciplinary approaches have yielded useful concepts and propositions regarding organizations, though their contributions to the general field or organizational study have been limited by fragmentation. Therefore, rather than focusing entirely on one approach discarding critical elements of several different ones, Thompson suggests ways in which the approaches and concepts can be reconciled and used in building a more comprehensive theoretical framework which more accurately assists in explaining the complex phenomena involved in organizational analysis.

STRATEGIES FOR STUDYING ORGANIZATIONS

Thompson begins his book by reviewing the complexities of organizations and the various conceptual approaches which have been developed in attempting to explain and understand the phenomena associated with complex organizations. He discusses the inherent conflict between the "closed-system" and "open-system" models and their apparent limitations in application. Finding both of these models lacking in comprehensiveness—the closed system in that it does not accommodate environmental influences and the open system in that it perhaps overemphasizes adaptability to the neglect of more controllable elements—Thompson indicates that the Simon-March-Cyert stream of study provides some means of overcoming the conflict between the two approaches. However, he also feels that this latter approach is lacking in that it tends to omit some of the useful information garnered from studies utilizing the older approaches.

Consequently, Thompson also attempts a synthesis of the closed and open systems approach in his treatment of organizational behavior. Thompson says, "For purposes of this volume then, we will conceive of complex organizations as open systems, hence indeterminate and faced with uncertainty, but at the same time subject to criteria of rationality, and hence needing determinateness and certainty." The remainder of the first section of his book is devoted to explaining the nature of the conflict between these two approaches and the necessity of viewing organizations in relation to concepts advanced in both the open and closed systems approahces. He recognizes that much of the literature illustrates the adaptiveness of organizations to their environment, and also recognizes the weakness of such approaches in application to organizational design and administrative practice. Therefore, he seeks some means of building upon these concepts while holding rationality as a criteria upon which the theory must also be judged.

He does not suggest that the two approaches are equally incompatible at all ranges of organizational phenomena, but that the problems associated with each tend to fall into one of Parson's three categories of responsibility and control—"technical, managerial, and institutional." For each of these levels, Thompson indicates that a different approach may be most suitable. For instance, "if the closed-system aspects of organizations are seen most clearly at the technical level, and the open-system qualities appear most vividly at the institutional level, it would suggest that a significant function of the managerial level is to mediate between the two extremes and the emphasis they exhibit." Since organizations are usually forced to interact with their environment in both resource-acquisition and output disposal, Thompson argues that the organization will attempt to isolate its "technical core" as much as possible from the uncertainties generated by this interaction with the environment.

Because uncertainties may arise from either the technology or the environment, and since there are substantial numbers of variations observable in both categories, Thompson argues that organizations will also differ in their methods of coping with these different combinations. Since the three levels (technical, managerial, and institutional) are interdependent, organizational differences in coping with uncertainty of various types will also create differences in these levels across organizations as efforts are made to reduce uncertainty.

RATIONALITY IN ORGANIZATIONS

In his chapter on rationality in organizations, Thompson attempts to develop a framework from which the relationship between "technical rationality" and "organizational rationality" can be understood, compared, and related to the actions of complex organizations.

According to him, "instrumental action is rooted on one hand in desired outcomes and on the other hand in beliefs about cause-effect relationships. Given a desire, the state of man's knowledge at any point in time dictates the kinds of variables required and the manner of their manipulation to bring that desire to fruition." In Thompson's view, "technical rationality" represents "the extent to which these activities thus dictated by man's beliefs are judged to produce the desired outcomes." The measures of technical rationality can be evaluated in terms of whether or not the desired outcome is achieved (instrumental) and whether the results were achieved with the least expenditure of resources (economic). Both of these criteria are essential to a discussion of the ways in which technology may be employed by complex organizations, and consequently, its potential influence on the organization itself.

Since there are numerous technologies available in society which may be employed by organizations, three general categories of technology are proposed which are sufficiently distinct for purposes of illustrating Thompson's point. They are: *"long-linked* (involving serial interdependence); *mediating* (requiring operating in standardized ways and extensively with multiple clients or customers widely distributed in time and space); and *intensive* (a custom technology which depends on the availability of potentially necessary resources and their suitable application in an individual case or project.)"

According to Thompson, since technical rationality is an abstraction concerning beliefs about cause and effect relationships, "it is only instrumentally perfect when it becomes a closed system of logic." Since organizations are forced to implement these technolgoies in action, the logic of the closed system does not accurately reflect the requirements nor the alternatives characterizing particular situations. Therefore, although every organization can be described as having a "core technology," the "technical core is always an incomplete representation of what the organization must do to accomplish deisred results." And according to Thompson:

> Technical rationality is a necessary component but never alone sufficient to provide *organizational rationality* which involves acquiring the inputs which are taken for granted by the technology, and dispensing outputs which again are outside the scope of the core technology.
>
> At a minimum, organizational rationality involves three major component activities: (1) input activities, (2) technological activities, and (3) output activities. Since they are interdependent, organizational rationality requires that they be appropriately geared to one another. The inputs acquired must be within the scope of the technology, and it must be within the capacity of the organization to dispose of the technological production (p. 19).

Given this interdependence, it is obvious that the input and output activities require an open-system type of logic and do impinge on the closed-system logic of the technology. Because of this interdependence, it is impossible to completely "seal-off" the technological core in the sense of a closed-system. Therefore, organizations will seek to minimize the influences of the environment through such techniques as buffering, leveling, forecasting, and rationing. The elements within the environment which Thompson feels are an influence on organizational action can be classified as "constraints" and "contingencies." Constraints are those fixed conditions which the organization cannot control. Contingencies are those factors which may or may not vary but are not subject to the arbitrary control of the organization. Organizational rationality is, therefore, some combination of constraints, contingencies, and the controllable variables cited previously.

Because it is assumed that organizations will seek some types of control over environmental interdependence and will engage in various types of action to gain that control where possible, Thompson suggests that the direction of those actions as well as the nature of them must also be examined. In order to accomplish that task, he introduces the concept of organizational "domain."

DOMAINS OF ORGANIZED ACTION

Organizations must establish some type of domain in terms of the "range of products, the populations served, and the services offered." Thompson then goes on to consider the relationship between domain, dependence, and environment. In Thompson's words "The results of organizational action rest not on a single technology, but upon a technological matrix. A complicated technology incorporates the products or results of still other technologies. Although a particular organization may operate several core technologies, its domain always falls short of the total matrix."

With such a concept, Thompson illustrates the interlocking relationships among modern organizations in general, and commercial enterprises in particular. Given these overlaps within the system, "the organization's domain identifies the points at which the organization is dependent on inputs from the environment." The nature of the dependencies, for a particular organization, will be primarily determined by the composition of the environment and the location of various organization-serving capacities within it. Thus, the organizational interfaces with the environment—such as sources of raw materials and markets for products—can be viewed as being dispersed, concentrated, or somewhere between the two extremes. According to Thompson, each organization will have a unique set of input and output relationships depending on the environment which it encounters and operates within.

Since environment can be taken to mean almost everything beyond the internal organization, he suggests that William R. Dill's concept of "task environment," which defines task environment as "the parts of the environment which are relevant or potentially relevant to goal setting and goal attainment," is more useful conceptually. Among the elements of task environment are the following: customers, suppliers, competitors, and regulatory groups. In the same way that no two organizational domains are exactly alike, neither are two task environments. In Thompson's view, "which individuals, which other organizations, and which aggregates constitute the task environment for a particular organization is determined by the requirements of the technology, the boundaries of the domain, and the composition of the larger environment."

In examining the relationship between task environment and domain, he argues that domain-consensus is reached through mutual expectations regarding the roles of various organizations. This consensus "defines a set of expectations both for members of the organization and for others which whom they interact about what the organization will and will not do." This appears to be one of the weaker arguments in the discussion thus far, since Thompson does not deal with the fact that different elements of the task environment may have widely divergent views regarding the domain of other elements. For example, he mentions regulatory agencies as being one of the elements of a firm's task environment along with customers, suppliers, competitors, etc., but he argues that domain consensus arises from mutual expectations about what others will and/or will not do. It would seem that each of these elements may have very different expectations about what the firm will or will not do. In fact, perhaps, it is this lack of consensus on specifics which requires the existence of regulatory agencies to continually redefine the boundaries of the firm's domain. On the other hand, the firm may have very different expectations of the appropriate domain for regulatory agencies and for its intermediate customers, to mention only two areas of potential disagreement.

Still, each organization must exchange with several elements of its task environment, each of which is also involved in a network of interdependencies characterizing its own domain and task environment. In this process of multiorganizational interaction, one or more elements in the task environment of one organization may choose to discontinue its support of that organization. Thus, according to Thompson, task environments also impose contingencies for organizations. In addition, they may also impose constraints, such as those encountered by a local high school which can only draw on the surrounding community for certain inputs. Since both constraints and contingencies can interfere with the attainment of rationality, Thompson argues that "organizations that are subject to the norms of rationality will attempt to manage dependency."

In order to manage that dependency, organizations must have some kind of power. To Thompson, power is the obverse of dependence. In his view, "an organization has power relative to an element of its task environment to the extent that the organization has capacity to satisfy the needs of that element and to the extent that the organization monopolizes that capacity." An organization's "net power" results from the interaction of the organization with the various elements comprising the pluralistic task environment. In this view, organizations with relatively little control over inputs will seek to gain power on the output side of the equation.

Some organizations will also be characterized as being powerful or weak in their ability to control *both* inputs and outputs; however, those organizations gaining control over both inputs and outputs may find that countervailing power may arise within the task environment to reduce the discretion with which that power might be applied (i.e., regulatory agencies). Thompson also argues that power should not be treated as a zero-sum game in that increased interdependence among equally powerful elements may result in increased power for both parties.

Organizations want to manage the dependency of their task environment, and there are several strategies they can follow to avoid becoming subservient to any of the elements in that environment. The organization may attempt to maintain alternatives (as in the case of suppliers), acquire "prestige" (one of the "cheapest" means of gaining power since it does not increase dependency), enlarge the task environment, and engage in cooperative strategies for managing interdependencies (such as contracting, coopting, and coalescing). In attempting to manage interorganizational relations and maintain a viable domain, organizations are seeking an "optimal point between the realities of interdependence and the norms of rationality." Since the maneuvering necessary to reach that optimum point can be both costly and disruptive, organizations "subject to norms of rationality [Would] seek to design themselves so as to minimize the necessity of maneuvering and compromise."

ORGANIZATIONAL DESIGN

In addition to dealing with contingencies through developing strategies for interaction with the elements of the task environment, Thompson argues that organizations may also be able to remove or reduce those contingencies through organizational design. Since the domain of an organization is influenced by technology, the population being served and the services being rendered, a substantial change in organizational design would involve a modification of the "mix" of these elements. Some of the ways in which this modification might be achieved include vertical integration (especially with long-linked technologies), increases in the size of the populations being served (as in mediating technologies), and incorporating the object or the client into the organization (as in the case of intensive technologies). Not all of these alternatives are viable for an organization at any one time since organizations may be constrained by capital requirements, the ability of the market to absorb additional production output, and/or legal restrictions, to mention only a few.

Nevertheless, if we assume there are pressures being exerted on the organization which encourage it to grow, Thompson argues that the direction of growth will "not be random but will be guided by the nature of the technology and the task environment. Consequently, if organizations vary in design, they must also vary in structure."

TECHNOLOGY AND STRUCTURE

In introducing the topic of organizational structure, Thompson states:

> The major components of a complex organization are determined by the design of that organization. Invariably these major components are further segmented, or departmentalized, and connections are established within and between departments. It is this internal differentiation and patterning of relationships that we will refer to as structure (p. 51).

He is particularly interested in considering those components of the organization which appear to be most protected from environmental influences—the technical core. (The combined effects of both environment and technology are dealt with later in his work.) Since "structure is a fundamental vehicle by which organizations achieve bounded rationality," some coordination of effort, along with protection of the technical core is achieved.

> By delimiting responsibilities, control over resources, and other matters, organizations provide their participating members with boundaries within which efficiency may be a reasonable expectation. But if structure affords numerous spheres of bounded rationality, it must also facilitate the *coordinated* action of those *independent* elements (p. 54).

Thus, according to Thompson, before organizational structure can be understood, the meaning of, and different types of interdependence and coordination must be considered. Three types of internal interdependence described by Thompson include "pooled interdependence," "sequential interdependence," and "reciprocal interdependence." These three types, in the order introduced, contain increasing degrees of contingency and are, therefore, more difficult and costly to coordinate. The three methods of coordination, each most appropriate for dealing with the different types of interdependence, are "standardization," "coordination by plan," and "coordination by mutual adjustment." Since coordination is necessary, but may also be costly, Thompson argues that organizations will seek to minimize coordination costs. "It is the task of structure to facilitate the appropriate coordinating processes."

Operating under norms of rationality and in attempting to minimize coordination costs, organizations will localize and make "conditionally autonomous, first reciprocally then sequentially interdependent ones, and finally grouping positions homogeneously to facilitate standardization." Hierarchy is introduced because of the fact that first groupings do not totally take care of interdependence. Therefore, the organization must find some means of linking the groups involved into higher-order groups, or, in effect, establishing a hierarchy. Any interdependence not included by these arrangements will then require the establishment of committees or task forces to overcome the problems of coordination.

ORGANIZATION AND STRUCTURE

Since complex organizations must interface with their environment, yet cannot fully control the influences arising from those interdependencies, the structure of the boundary-spanning units within an organization must allow for the necessary adjustments to continue to be made. In this section of his book, Thompson deals with the way in which environment also influences organizational structure (especially in the structure of the boundary-spanning units) as well as the way in which both technology and environment together influence the overall structure of the organization.

Although Thompson recognizes that the elements of the task environment vary for different organizations and, therefore, introduce certain constraints which are unique to that organization, he argues that generally the nature of those constraints can be classified within two major categories: "geographic space" (such as the costs involved in transportation) and in the "social composition" of their task environment. The social composition of the task environment can be viewed as being homogeneous or heterogeneous and stable or shifting. According to Thompson, "all organizations face task environments which are simultaneously located somewhere on the homogeneous-heterogeneous continuum and the stable-shifting continuum."

In summarizing the impact of the task environment on the structure of boundary-spanning units, Thompson states:

> The more heterogeneous the task environment, the greater the constraints presented to the organization. The more dynamic the task environment, the greater the contingencies presented to the organization. Under either condition, the organization seeking to be rational must put boundaries around the amount and scope of adaption necessary, and it does this by establishing structural units specialized to face a limited range of contingencies within a limited set of constraints. The more constraints and contingencies the organization faces, the more its boundary-spanning component will be segmented (p. 73).

Having considered the influences on the structure of the units comprising the "technical core" and the "boundary-spanning" units, the concern then becomes the means by which these elements are combined to result in the overall organizational structure. Those organizations characterized as having "technical cores and boundary-spanning activities which can be isolated from each other will be centralized with an overarching layer of functional divisions." Where those activities are reciprocally interdependent rather than isolated, an organization will tend toward arranging these units in self-sufficient clusters, each having its own domain; "this is the major form of decentralization."

Thus, in Thompson's view, the organization faces internal requirements for coordinating the technical core and externally-generated requirements for adjustment of the boundary-spanning units to the contingencies and constraints of the environment. Therefore, the major purpose of structure is to allow for the satisfaction of both internal and external organizational requirements. Because he assumes bounded rationality is necessary, Thompson argues that organizations facing heterogeneous task environments will not only attempt to identify homogeneous elements in that environment but also will establish structural units capable of dealing with each type. In this way, Thompson attempts to tie together the structural implications of the apparently incompatible close-system and open-system requirements.

THE VARIABLE HUMAN

Thompson then turns to a discussion of the characteristics of individuals and how they relate to organizations. He considers such things as the extent to which organizations can increase predictability of the behavior of their members and/or others in the task environment. He also discusses, in considerable detail, the exercise of discretion on the part of organizational members. A central argument is that "the ability or opportunity to exercise discretion is not uniformly distributed throughout the organization—that technology, task environment, design, and structure result in patterns of discretion." Thompson is interested in identifying the participants who exercise discretion, the relationships among those individuals, what "discretion" implies, and how it might be expressed or exercised.

Since Thompson has indicated from the outset that his focus is primarily on the behavior of organizations in a general sense, rather than on the behavior of specific individuals within those organizations, this second section of his text builds extensively on the preceding organizational concepts and relationships which have already been discussed.

In viewing organization members, Thompson sees them as having certain aspirations and beliefs about cause and effect relationships and postulates that they (the individuals) bring these with them to an organizational setting which provides compatible opportunities and constraints. Culture, in his view, tends to be an "homogenizing" force which limits the range of diversity of these beliefs and aspirations and allows for the "channeling" of these individuals into relevant sectors of the labor market. He argues that the composition of the inducements/contribution contract is influenced by these factors and that the I/C contract itself further limits the range of behavior an individual will exhibit in an organizational setting. All of these factors, when taken together, tend to reduce the potential for heterogeneity of expression among organizational members.

Given these observations, the individual's range of discretion can be viewed in the context of "spheres of action." These action spheres also, "differ according to the technologies in which these jobs are imbedded." By locating jobs within technological contexts, individuals are therefore presented with patterned spheres of action. Since a job is "both a unit in the organization and a unit in the career of the individual, the joining of the two is a result of bargained agreement or inducements/contribution contract." Given the duality of the expectations, "it is then only reasonable to expect the resulting behavior to be patterned."

Proceeding from these initial assumptions regarding the nature of the individual behavior in an organizational setting, Thompson further illustrates the ways in which these patterns of behavior are influenced by technological factors, environmental constraints and contingencies, and the individual's position within the subunits of the organizational structure. He builds on the concepts of interdependence and power to describe the range of discretion and/or authority for an individual. In this manner, Thompson integrates a logical framework of individual behavior within the overall framework already established for the organization.

The administrative process is considered in terms of two types of administrative action necessary for the organization to survive. They are "adaptive" and "directive." Adaptive actions are necessitated primarily by environmental influences, and directive actions arise out of the basic internal requirements of the organization. Recognizing that both types of action are necessary, they must be coordinated in such a way as to allow the organization to manipulate "strategic variables" in order to survive. This manipulation of strategic variables should, therefore, result in a "viable coalignment" with other elements in the environment. Given the fluidity of the task environment, it is apparent that the types of co-alignment are continually changing; therefore, a major task of administration, in Thompson's view, is to reduce the uncertainty involved in the process through achieving coalignment "not merely of people (in coalitions) but of institutionalized action—of technology and task environment into a viable domain, and of organizational structure appropriate to it." As a result, "the administrative process must reduce uncertainty but at the same time search for flexibility."

CONCLUSIONS

Thompson concludes that the fundamental problem faced by complex organizations is coping with uncertainty. Coping with uncertainty is therefore the essence of the administrative process. The sources of uncertainty for an organization arise from three areas, two are external to the organization and one is internal. "External uncertainties stem from (1) *generalized uncertainty* or lack of cause/effect understanding of the culture at large, and (2) contingency, in which the outcomes of organizational action are in part determined by the actions of elements of the environment." The third source of uncertainty is internal; the *interdependence of components.* The way in which these uncertainties are resolved is:

> Solution of the first type [generalized uncertainty], provides a pattern against which organizational action can be ordered. Solution of the second type [contingency] affords organizational freedom to so order the action against the pattern. Solution of the third [interdependence of components] results in the actual ordering of action to fit the pattern (p. 160).

This is the way Thompson summarizes the general nature of his view of organizations as having certain aspects of closed systems and of open systems within a context of internal and external uncertainty. Given the assumed necessity of rationality, both must be taken individually and together in explaining the behavior of complex organizations in a contemporary setting.

"ORGANIZATION ANALYSIS: A SOCIOLOGICAL POINT OF VIEW"*

CHARLES PERROW

THE MIXED MODEL

Let us assume, for a moment, that we are talking about organizations where all three of the following functions are important: research, production, and marketing. Though industrial terminology is being used here, it should be recognized that all organizations have, to at least some limited extent, all these functions. A correctional institution, an employment agency, the social security administration, or various military units all not only produce products but must also market them in some form or other. The manner in which they produce and market these products is based upon an appropriate technology. To find, change, develop, and improve the technology constitutes a research function, as does the determination of what the new products will be. Of course, for some organizations, marketing is a minor problem, while for others it is a major one, and the same is true of research and even of production. Assuming all three are important, however, how should they be organized?

The organizational form will depend upon the state of the art in each function and the changes required by the environment. Preferably production and marketing would be routinized: even fairly routine research functions would be preferred . . . . If all three are routine (or nonroutine), the organization has little difficulty in determining the best method of organizing the whole. All can be structured alike and integration problems are minimized.

However, it is far more common to find varying degrees of routinization among the three functions. Typically, production is fairly routine and exists in a stable environment; research is nonroutine; and marketing is in-between. This situation presents problems of coordination beyond those normally encountered when there are different units, since the three units will think differently and will be accustomed to different ways of getting things done. Production, for example, may think only in terms of the very short run. This is the basis upon which this function is judged; the unit is not responsible for, nor in a position to anticipate, new products or techniques. Marketing, however, must take a somewhat longer perspective. (If the marketing function is not developed, and only a sales division exists, its perspective may be as short-range as production.) Development, and especially research, however, should have a relatively long perspective compared to production and marketing. Time perspectives establish priorities, and thus the units may clash. They will disagree about such matters as the allocation of resources or the urgency of solving a particular problem. Not only perspectives are involved, but also ac-

---

*From *Organizational Analysis: A Sociological View* by Charles Perrow, © 1970 by Wadsworth Publishing Company, Inc., Belmont, California 94002. Reprinted by permission of the author and the publisher, Brooks/Cole Publishing Company.

tual structures. With its short-range perspective and precise goals which can be measured, production is likely to have highly specialized subunits, clear lines of authority, precise rules and procedures. Research, at the other extreme, may depend more upon lateral and diagonal communication among its members, resulting in a good deal of informal contact; there may be few intermediate measures of productivity and few binding rules or procedures. It may be difficult for members of these two departments to work together, or even to communciate information easily, because of their different "styles."

TECHNOLOGY MODELS

So far we have been content with a simple polar contrast between bureaucratized organizations or units and nonbureaucratized units. The key to the distinction has been the kind of work performed in the organization or unit of the organization: its degree of routine or lack of routine. But if we analyze the term "routine" more closely, it appears that we mean that two conditions are present—there are well-established techniques which are sure to work, and these are applied to essentially similar raw materials. That is, there is little uncertainty about methods and little variety or change in the tasks that must be performed.

Similarly, nonroutineness means that there are a few well-established techniques; there is little certainty about methods, or whether or not they will work. But it also means that there may be a variety of different tasks to perform, in the sense that raw materials are not standardized, or orders from customers ask for many different or custom-made products.

The operations of some firms may have little variety, yet quite a bit of uncertainty; others may have little uncertainty, but a great deal of variety. These two types are neither highly routine nor highly nonroutine. They are in the middle somehow, but they are not in the same middle; they themselves differ from one another. So it is possible to be nonroutine in one sense and not another, or routine in one sense but not in another . . . .

Variability and Search

. . . . Organizations are designed to get some kind of work done. To do this work they need techniques or technologies. These techniques are applied to some kind of "raw material" which the organization transforms into a marketable product. It doesn't matter what the product is; it may be reformed delinquents, TV programs, advertising symbols, governmental decisions, or steel. But some technology is required, not only in the actual production process, but also for procuring the input of materials, capital, and labor and disposing of the output to some other organization or consumer, and for coordinating the three "functions" or "phases" of input-transformation-output.

How does one think about, or conceptualize technology so that it may be analyzed in this way, as a means of transforming raw materials (human, symbolic, or material) into desirable goods and services? In this view of technology, machines and equipment are merely tools; they are not the technology itself. Indeed, the personnel man uses a technology that has little to do with tools. Nor can we use the actual techniques such as are found in production manuals, for these are too specific to the particular organization. Instead, let us consider the individual who is assigned to do a specific task.

He receives stimuli (orders, signals) to which he must respond. Even the decision to ignore the stimulus or not even to "see it" is a response. He "searches" his mind to decide what kind of response to make. So far we have two concepts with which to work: the stimulus and the response. The response is conceived of as "search behavior": If the stimulus is familiar and the individual has learned in the past what to do in the face of it, little search behavior is required. He may respond automatically or after a moment's thought . . . .

If the stimulus is unfamiliar, however, and the individual decides not to ignore it or to panic, considerable search behavior must be instituted, and the search is of a different kind. The problem presented by the stimulus is not immediately analyzable; search must take place without manuals, computers, or clerks who have the requisite information and programs . . . .

If we substitute a more general term for stimuli—raw material—we can see that the nature of the search procedure depends a good deal upon what is known about the material that one is to transform through techniques. If a good deal is known that is relevant to the transformation process, search can be quite routine and analyzable . . . .

The other dimension of technology which will be used here is the variability of the stimuli presented to an individual—the variety of problems which may lead to search behavior. Sometimes the variety is great and every task seems to be a new one demanding the institution of search behavior of some magnitude (whether analyzable or unanalyzable). Sometimes stimuli are not very varied and the individual is confronted chiefly with familiar situations and a few novel ones. Note that, in industrial firms, this is not necessarily a distinction between a great or small variety of products. Automobile firms produce an amazing variety of models and a staggering variety of parts, but these are not novel situations requiring search behavior (except in the design and engineering of model changes).

Note also that the difference between analyzable or routine search is not necessarily the same as the distinction between technologically advanced and technologically backward industries. Some semiconductors, such as auto diodes, are a product of advanced technology but they can be made in a quite routine fashion. Certain kinds of ferro castings for the auto industry—a technologically "backward" process—cannot be made on a routine basis. To routinize production would require the solution of problems that have yet to be analyzed.

We now have two dimensions, the degree of variability of stimuli and the degree to which search procedures are analyzable. Let us refer to the first as simply the number of *exceptions* encountered by the individual. If we dichoto-

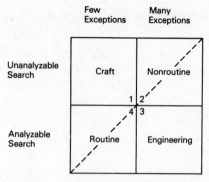

Figure 1   Technology variables.

mize and then cross-classify these there are four possibilities which, in Figure 1, we have labeled craft, nonroutine, routine, and engineering.

A factory manufacturing a standard product like heating elements for electric stoves (cell 4), and an engineering firm building made-to-order machines such as drill presses or electric motors (cell 3), may both be routine to the extent to which search behavior is analyzable. Still, they differ in the variety of occasions when search must be instituted—rarely in the factory, and quite frequently in the engineering firm. The engineering firm must continually modify designs and introduce modifications to meet the customers' needs. In a firm making fine glassware (cell 1), search may be as unanalyzable as in the factory which makes nuclear-propulsion systems (cell 2). Yet the variety of the stimuli in the glassware factory is small, while the varying requirements of the customers of the other firm present a great variety of problems or stimuli. The work of the nuclear fuel system firm would be highly nonroutine, combining unanalyzable problems with great variability of problems; the operations of a heating-element factory or a mill making reinforcing bars for concrete structure would be highly routine—a small variety of problems, while those which do occur would be subject to analyzable search procedures. The glass firm is low on variability but high on unanalyzable search procedures (therefore, referred to as a craftsman model). The engineering firm is high on variability but has analyzable search procedures—an engineering model.

Note that if one were discussing only routine and nonroutine companies or bureaucratic and nonbureaucratic structures, only cells 4 and 2 would be relevant. These are represented by a two-dimensional continuum characterized by a broken line; this is the sort of operation to which we have previously limited our discussion. However, organizations can fall into the categories represented by cells 1 and 3 though they probably would cluster rather close to the center of the figure.

The same kind of analysis can be used for people-changing organizations. . . .

Technology and Structure

What, then, does technology have to do with the *structure* of the organization? The answer has already been strongly hinted at in the discussion of non-bureaucratic and bureaucratic structures. But now it is possible to be a little more specific. We must assume here that, in the interest of efficiency, organizations wittingly or unwittingly attempt to maximize the congruence between their technology and their structure. Many which fail to make such a match should be more or less bureaucratically organized than they are. But let us assume that they have all studied the sociology of complex organizations and have adapted their structures to fit their technology. What would the four types of firms look like?

There are many, many ways to conceptualize structure. For our purposes here let me choose the following variables: the discretion of subgroups; their power; the basis of coordination within a group; and the interdependence of groups. For the moment, let us also deal only with production, although these concepts are equally applicable to marketing and perhaps even to the research aspects of organizations. If we single out middle and lower management we can make some predictions about the organization of each group and the relationship between them. Middle management here will, in general, mean the people who are concerned with the administration of production; we will call this the technical level. Lower management is concerned with the supervision of production.

Figure 2 suggests some of the structural characteristics of the four types of firms. In the nonroutine type of firm—characterized by unanalyzable search procedures and the need to deal with many exceptions—both discretion and power are high in both groups; in both, coordination is through feedback (mutual adjustment) rather than through advance planning (programmed), and finally, the interdependence of the groups is high. What this means is that the supervisors of production work closely with the technical people in the administration of production since the latter cannot call the shots for the former on the basis of routine information sent upstairs. Indeed, job descriptions may be such that it is difficult to distinguish the supervisory level from the technical level. Both groups are free to define situations as best they can. Therefore, both have considerable power with respect to such matters as resources and organizational strategies.

This model resembles what others have called the organic as opposed to the mechanistic structure, or the professional or collegial as opposed to the bureaucratic structure. This type of structure is probably efficient only for highly nonroutine organizations. There are few of these, even though they are quite visible and attractive to social scientists who see in them reflections of their academic institutions and values.

Most firms fit into the quite routine cell. It is in their interest to fall in this category because it means greater control over processes and much more certainty of outlook (we are ignoring market situations). In routine firms, the discretion allowed to both supervisors of production and administrators of

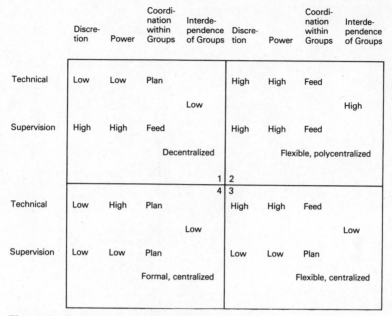

Figure 2 Task structure—task-related interaction.

production is minimal—there is little ambiguity in these situations. The power of the technical middle-management level, however, is high, for it controls the supervisory level on the basis of routine reports. In both cases coordination within the levels comes through planning (giving further power to the technical level) because events can be foreseen. Interdependence between the two groups is likely to be low. This arrangment approaches the bureaucratic model. Where it is appropriate, it is undoubtedly the most efficient.

In the engineering model—characterized by analyzable problems with many exceptions—the technical-level functions more like the nonroutine firm. There is great discretion in choosing among programs and considerable power, and coordination is achieved through the feedback of information for problem solving. But on the shop floor, discretion and power are—should be—minimal. Planning is the basis of coordination here, and there is little interdependence between the two levels—designs are sent down and executed. In the craftsman model—characterized by unanalyzable problems and a few exceptions—it is the supervisory level which has discretion and high power and coordinates through feedback. The technical level is weak, responds to the supervisors of production, and needs little discretion and little power. Coordination is on the basis of planning in the technical level. Interdependence of the two levels can be low.

To become even bolder in our speculation, Figure 3 may be revised to include two more unusual types of industrial organizations—the research and development firm or unit, which would be very nonroutine, and the continuous

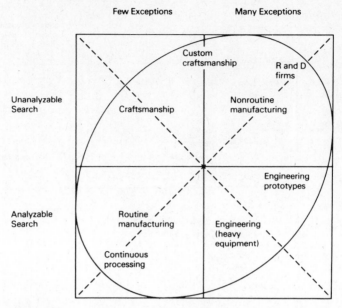

Figure 3

processing industry, such as oil or chemicals, or, to some extent, beer and other beverages, which would be very routine. Other examples of craft and engineering firms can also be added. (See Figure 3.)

The elliptical character of the model suggests that it is somewhat unusual to find organizations at the extreme of the axis represented by the dotted line. Still, examples do exist on that continuum. The distinction is not simply between routine and nonroutine or between bureaucratic and nonbureaucratic, as represented by the broken line.

This analysis is, admittedly, entirely speculative.[1] However, research is proceeding along these lines, and there may be some support for the specific models and predictions. We have gone into this particular theory in such detail in order to suggest at least one way of conceptualizing differences among organizations and to show that these differences indicate different kinds of strategies, none of which are either good or bad in themselves. As noted, most social scientists consider the nonbureaucratic, or nonroutine organization to be good and the bureaucratic or routine organization to be bad (it impedes progress, is old fashioned, is hard on its employees, etc.).[2] But this judgment is debatable. One of the purposes of the R and D firm, or the nonroutine organization, is to generate ways of routinizing production and building better bureaucratic controls into organizations. Furthermore, for routine work, the bureaucratic structure may be both the most efficient and the most humane. Not all people prefer the hectic, open-ended, and uncertain character of nonroutine tasks, not even top management.

In addition, this little exercise in speculation suggests a way of looking at problems in organizational structure. For example, going back to Figure 1, to simplify matters, if an organization in cell 1 (craft) hires an engineer at the middle-management level who is used to working an organization in cell 3 (engineering), and if he tries through the use of discretion and personal power to coordinate the work in his unit by means of on-the-spot feedback, he is likely to be in for for trouble. In this type of firm, many production problems have no analyzable solution. An engineer cannot dictate the solution of such problems nor can he exercise a high degree of discretion in helping or controlling staff members at the supervisory level. Furthermore, because problems vary very little and exceptional occasions seldom occur, he will find that he must do a great deal more advance planning within the technical group in order to support the supervisory level. He cannot expect supervisors to coordinate their own activities primarily through advance planning because of the unanalyzable nature of the problems which do occur.

Or, suppose that a successful production supervisor from a firm in cell 4 (routine) is moved to a position in a different division of the company where the work is more characteristic of cell 2 activities (nonroutine). Such a supervisor might find it quite difficult to become accustomed to exercising a high degree of discretion and power within this supervisory level. He might also be unable to adjust to coordination achieved through on-the-spot discussion when he has been used to coordination by means of fairly routine advance planning.

However, these examples relate to the problems of individuals. A more striking instance might be a case involving the recommendations of a management consultant firm which is accustomed to dealing with organizations within cell 4 (routine). Should the consultants try to apply their customary solutions to an organization in one of the other cells, they well might fail. (The Hoover Commission, charged with reorganizing much of the federal government, consistently made this error.) Similarly, a management-training program designed to increase the independence and autonomy of managers and the interdependence of groups could be quite successful in cell 2 (nonroutine), but be a waste of time in cell 4. To cite a final example: We have noted that organizations may attempt to move into cell 4 by reducing the number of exceptions that may occur, by decreasing the variability of raw materials, and by finding analyzable ways of solving their problems. However, this victory may be short-lived. If the market suddenly changes, or the technology changes, such an organization may find itself back in cells 3, 2, or 1. It would be well to be prepared to change the organizational structure when such events occur.

More important than the specific examples or recommendations, however, is the perspective illustrated here. This view holds that organizations are not all alike and that the way in which they may vary is in terms of their technology. Two aspects of technology—exceptions and search—are abstracted and analyzed independently and concurrently. Whether or not the scheme just presented is verified by empirical research, and whether or not it proves to have predictive value, matters less than this: before an organization's problems can be solved, it is essential to determine the nature of the organization. Once the determination is made, some administrative and management proverbs may apply very well but others may be irrelevant or even invalid.

The social-structure view of organizations is only beginning to generate such perspectives. To add to the few now current, many more will probably develop in time. Any two may have a compelling logic in themselves but may not be compatible with each other. This should not cause great alarm, since an organization can generally be viewed from several quite different viewpoints or positions and each can yield some useful truths.

The Woodward Model

For example, the first major attempt to apply a technological perspective to organizations differs in several respects from the one just outlined but is quite viable in its own right. In addition, it touches upon some important practical matters not covered by the previous scheme. Joan Woodward, working at the time out of a technical college in South Essex, England, conducted a study of 100 firms in an industrial area in attempting to test the utility of "classical management theory." She was interested in such matters as ideas concerning types of organizational structure (functional, line, or line-staff); degree of specialization of functions; the optimum span of control and number of hierarchical levels; and staff-worker ratios. None of these factors had any particular significance in relation to organizational success. As she says, this was a disconcerting finding for a group attempting to teach management principles in a technical college. Only after the firms were grouped according to their typical mode of production did the data fall into place. In its more simplified form she uses three types of production systems: unit and small-batch (e.g., made-to-order items, such as custom suits, prototype electronic equipment, custom furniture, and machine tools), large-batch assembly, and mass production (e.g., large bakeries, mass-produced clothing, industrial equipment, autos), and process production (e.g., oil, chemicals, and pharmaceuticals). Simply stated, the three systems may be called unit, mass, and process. She describes the whole scale as roughly equivalent to increasing technical complexity, or technical advance in historical terms.

Considered in this way it appeared that firms with similar production systems had similar organizational structures—despite the variety of products involved . . . .

. . . The critical function is different for each type of organization. Unit firms tend to be dominated by engineering personnel; mass-production firms by production people; process firms by marketers. Similarly, the relationships between these groups, the amounts and kinds of stresses, the difficulties of integration and cooperation vary in rather complex ways in each type. But the most important conclusion is that there is no evidence to prove that sales, production, or development is most important in all organizations. The importance of a function depends upon the specific technology employed.

With a comparative perspective like this, which shows that there is no "one best way" of doing things in all organizations, many well-accepted and even commonplace generalizations are challenged. Instead of applying to all or most cases, such generalizations hold true only for specific types, as we have just seen in terms of the importance of sales or production . . . .

Only when we began to look at the differences between organizations and to categorize them in some meaningful way, such as by technology (though there are undoubtedly other ways), can be begin selectively to apply the multitude of insights offered by organizational analysis.

Footnotes

[1]For technical articles discussing these ideas see Perrow (27, 28, 29).

[2]For example, see Bennis (3), McGregor (24), Likert (21), Gouldner (15), Crozier (7), and V. Thompson (44).

HENRY MINTZBERG: "THE STRUCTURING OF ORGANIZATIONS"*

JANICE H. ZAHRLY

The Structuring of Organizations presents a contingency theory of organizations. Mintzberg bases the model on a review of over 200 articles and book extracts relating to organization structure.

An organization is driven toward a particular natural cluster, or configuration, based on the strength (power) of the various parts of the organization, the ways in which the parts of the organization coordinate their work, the structural design parameters, and contingency factors such as age, size, and environment. Five pure type organization structures are described, each with particular dimensions, parameters and significant contingency factors. Structural hybrids occur when the organization is drawn toward more than one configuration but the five configurations form the basis of this approach to organizations.

ELEMENTS OF THE BASIC ORGANIZATION STRUCTURES

The variables in Mintzberg's organization structure model are the various parts of the organization, mechanisms to coordinate the diverse tasks, and design parameters. The design parameters are used by the organization to establish formal and informal relationships.

---

*This abstract was prepared by Janice H. Zahrly. It is based upon Henry Mintzberg, *The Structuring of Organizations*. (Englewood Cliffs, N.J., Prentice-Hall, 1979)

Coordinating Mechanisms

Mintzberg defines the organization structure as the "sum total of the way in which it divides its labor into distinct tasks and then achieves coordination among them." Coordination is the basic element of structure, that which holds an organization together. There are five coordinating mechanisms.

Direct supervision results when one individual has the responsibility for the work of others and gives them direct orders which coordinate their work. The quarterback on a football team, for example, engages in direct supervision when he gives direct orders by calling the plays.

Standardization of work processes occurs when the content of the work, the actual process, is specified or programmed. Typically, assembly lines have most work processes specified, leaving the operator with little discretion in performance of the task.

Standardization of outputs is the coordinating mechanism whereby the results of the work (e.g., the dimensions of the product or the performance) are specified. A craftsworker may be told to make picture frames of a particular size but is not given instructions about how to make them or a plant supervisor is told to reduce costs by 10 percent but it is not told how—only the desired outcomes are specified.

Standardization of skills is the coordinating mechanism when the type of training required in order to perform the work is specified. Individuals learn how to coordinate before they perform the task. The surgeon and anesthesiologist know what to expect of each other as a result of their training. They, therefore, spend little time communicating with each other before or during an operation.

Mutual adjustment occurs when two or more people communciate informally to accomplish a task. This type of coordination occurs in very simple situations such as two people in a canoe, or in organizations such as a small shop where the owners are also operators. Mutual adjustment may also occur in the most complicated, dynamic organizations such as NASA, where highly skilled people design and build complex machines and equipment.

When the various coordinating mechanisms are placed on a task complexity continuum as in Figure 1, mutual adjustment is at each end of the continuum. Direct supervision is near mutual adjustment on the least complex end, followed by standardization of work, standardization of output, and standardization of skills. Skill standardization is near mutual adjustment on the most complex end of the continuum, with standardization of the work process and output near the center.

Task Complexity

LOW					HIGH
Mutual adjustment	Direct supervision	Standardization of work processes	Standardization of output	Standardization of skills	Mutual adjustment

Coordinating Mechanisms

Figure 1 Task complexity/coordinating mechanisms.

Parts of the Organization

The simplest organization has almost no division of labor and relies on mutual adjustment to coordinate the work procedures that lead to a product or service. However, as the organization grows, there are needs for formal coordinators (i.e., managers), an administrative hierarchy, analysts to plan and manage the standardization, and support staffs. There are five distinct parts of the organization, each with a particular function (see Figure 2).

The **operating core** of an organization is composed of operators who perform the basic work directly related to the production of goods and services. It is that part of the organization which produces essential outputs to keep the organization alive. The operating core has several functions—to secure inputs, to transform inputs to outputs, to distribute outputs, and to provide direct support for the input, output, and transformation processes. The professor is part of the operating core in a university as is the machine operator who stamps out aluminum can tops in the factory. Standardization of any type (work process, output, or skill) is the usual means of coordination in the operating core.

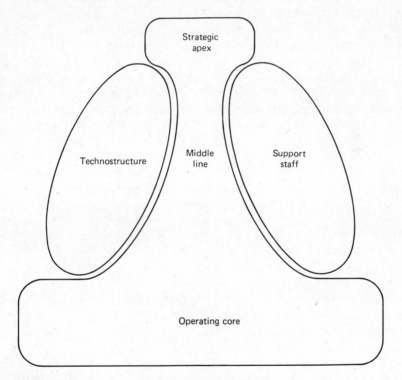

*Figure 2 The five parts of the organization.

*Figures 2–8 are reproduced with the permission of the publisher from Henry Mintzberg; *The Structure of Organizations* (Englewood Cliffs, N. J., Prentice-Hall, 1979).

The **strategic apex** is at the top of the organization. It is "charged with ensuring that the organization serve its mission in an effective way, and also that it serve the needs of those people who control or otherwise have power over the organization (such as owners, government agencies, unions of the employees, pressure groups)." Functions of the strategic apex include direct supervision, management of the organization's relations with the environment, and development of organization strategy.

Strategy formulation is the most important role of this part of the organization. Strategy formulation is the determination of how the organization can and must deal with the environment. Work activities in the strategic apex are characterized by long decision cycles, little routine and standardization, and the members have much discretion. Mutual adjustment is the major coordinating mechanism.

The **middle line** is the formal authority chain which joins the strategic apex to the operating core. Direct supervision is the usual coordinating mechanism in this segment. Usually middle line employees are called managers or supervisors. The functions of this part of the organization, in addition to direct supervision, are feedback (including upward communication of information), management of boundary conditions for the environment relevant to the individual units, and other managerial duties, which are part of supervising a particular unit (e.g., figurehead, liaison role, and allocator of resources).

The middle line manager's job can vary dramatically, depending on where the manager is in the chain of authority. At lower levels of the organization and administration, tasks are detailed and elaborate, less abstract, and more focused on work flow. The work is more structured as it approaches the operating core. When these positions are near the strategic apex they are more abstract and have less structure.

As the organization becomes larger, it relies more on all types of standardization as a means of becoming more efficient. The **technostructure** is composed of control analysts who seek to increase standardization. The control analysts, who coordinate their work by mutual adjustment, influence the work of others by designing or changing work procedures, planning work flows, training employees for certain tasks. Control analysts do not actually produce the outputs that keep the organization alive in the marketplace. They perform a support function. The technostructure is effective if it makes the work of other parts of the organization more effective.

There are three types of control analysts. The workstudy analyst (such as an industrial engineer) standardizes work processes; the planning and control analyst (such as the accountant) standardizes outputs; the personnel analyst (such as a recruiter or trainer) standardizes skills.

The function of the technostructure varies according to the organization level with which it operates. For the operating core, control analysts might standardize the operating work flow or the quality control system. The intellectual work of the middle level might be standardized by training middle managers. At the strategic apex, the control analysts might develop strategic planning models or financial systems which control the individual units.

Finally, the **support staff** exists to provide support to various organization units outside the operating work flow. Examples of support staff are company cafeterias, legal services and public relations departments. The support staff does not directly produce the product or service, but makes it easier for other units to do so. The support systems are often self-contained (i.e., a mini-organization) and are found at all levels of the organization. Although they use a variety of coordinating mechanisms most support units, because they are highly specialized and rely on professional people, coordinate by means of skill standardization.

Design Parameters

In order to establish stable patterns of behavior, organizations use formal and semiformal methods, called design parameters, to differentiate and coordinate work activities. Their particular configurations establish the structure of each organization. There are nine design parameters that are grouped into four categories. The choice and configuration of design parameters determine the structure of the organization.

The **design of positions** is the first category of decisions concerning the organization structure. Job positions are designed by *job specialization, behavior formalization,* and *training and indoctrination.*

Job specialization reflects the division of labor (the number of tasks assigned to a worker) and the worker's control over the assigned tasks. A job may be horizontally specialized or vertically specialized. In horizontal specialization the worker has a few narrowly defined tasks. In vertical specialization, work performance is separated from the administration, giving the worker little or no control over the task. Job enlargement increases the number of tasks performed (i.e., worker control).

Managerial jobs tend to be less specialized than most other jobs. Unskilled jobs are usually highly specialized, both vertically and horizontally. Complex jobs which are specialized horizontally but not vertically are called professional jobs.

Another way to design positions is through *behavior formalization.* Behavior is regulated by the standardization of work content. This regulation will result in formalization of the job (where behavioral specifications of the job are listed), formalization of the work flow (such as imposition of operating instructions), or formalization by rules and regulations. Bureaucratic organizations rely primarily on standardization. Organic organizations have little standardization. Behavior formalization is most common in the operating core, making it bureaucratic. The strategic apex tends to have an organic structure. As work progresses down the hierachy, it usually becomes more formalized. Organizations use behavior formalization to reduce variability of performance. This means that it is easier to more accurately predict and to control behaviors.

A third method of designing positions is through *training and indoctrination.* Training occurs when job related skills and knowledge are taught. Indoctrination, or socialization, is the process of acquiring organizational norms. Training is a major design parameter for the operating core, the technostructure, and for staff units. However, indoctrination is the major approach at the strategic apex and middle line portions of the organization.

Training and behavior formalization are often substitutable. Both seek to control, organize, and promote standard behavior. While the technostructure within the organization designs the work activities of the unskilled employee, outside institutions often direct the behavior of the professional. The professional learns norms as well as skills while in educational institutions, which are controlled by other professionals. By the time the professional gets to the work organization most of his behaviors are set.

The **design of the superstructure** is the second category of design parameters which fashion the structure of an organization. Included in this category are decisions about *unit grouping* and *unit size.*

Unit grouping is the basic means of clustering positions to coordinate work. It establishes a system of common supervision among positions and units, requires the sharing of common resources, creates common measures of performance, and encourages mutual adjustment. But unit grouping also creates the problem of coordination among units. When significant interdependencies among units occur, such as sequential or reciprocal interdependencies, coordination becomes costly.

Units can be grouped on the bases of knowledge, output, client, and work process, but the fundamental grouping bases are function and product. Functional grouping is concerned with the work process and scale interdependencies. This occurs when some unit autonomy is sacrificed to obtain economies of scale, such as the installation of a company data processing system that processes all records in a central location. This method of grouping lacks a built-in mechanism to coordinate the work flow. This approach tends to be bureaucratic.

Unit grouping by product is more flexible, less bureaucratic, has fewer economies of scales and is less efficient. There is a concern for work flow coordination at the expense of process specialization. Functional grouping is more common at the lower levels of the organization, particularly in the operating core, while unit grouping by product occurs more often at higher levels. Support staff and analysts will usually be in functional units.

The second consideration when designing the superstructure (i.e., the structure of the entire organization) is the *unit size,* or the number of positions contained in a single unit. In general, the larger the unit size the greater the use of standardization for coordination. Conversely, the greater the reliance on mutual adjustment as a coordinating mechanism, the smaller the size of the work unit. The work unit can be quite large if there are no sequential or reciprocal interdependencies. In most organizations, the operating core will have the largest units. Staff units may be large or small. Unskilled staff such as cafeteria workers will be large units and operate in a bureaucratic manner. Skilled staff will be professional and will be grouped into small units which tend to be organic.

The redesign of the superstructure can come from two directions. First, if the organization's goals and missions change, structural redesign is initiated from the top downward. Second, if the technical system of the operating core changes, the redesign proceeds from the bottom up.

The **design of lateral linkages** is the third design parameter. Organizations are able to influence their structures by designing specific coordinating procedures for lateral relationships. The design of these linkages is accomplished by *planning and control systems* and *liaision devices.*

The purpose of *planning and control systems* is to standardize outputs. Action planning specifies the desired results of specific activities, such as the particular dimensions of holes to be drilled. Action planning occurs before the activity is undertaken. Work-flow interdependencies often require action planning.

Performance control systems regulate the overall results of a given unit, for example such a system may seek a 10 percent increase in sales for the total organization. Performance control systems are used with pooled interdependencies. They specify the desired results of many activities after the fact. That is, activities are not specified. Only final objectives are detailed.

Another way to design lateral linkages is to use *liaison devices.* Liaison positions may be created in the formal structure, such as the design engineer who moves between the development lab and the preproduction engineering group. Temporary task forces and permanent standing committees may be part of the formal structure. Integrating managers (such as brand, project, or program managers) bring together representatives from many functional areas.

The matrix organization structure is an example of the most complex liaison device. While a dual authority structure is created, the matrix organization has proven most effective in coordinating complex interdependencies and in responding rapidly to uncertainty in the environment.

Liaison devices encourage informality and more organic structures. In general, the more liaison devices, the smaller the unit. When work is horizontally specialized, complex, and highly interdependent, liaison devices are necessary. They are best suited for work at the middle levels of the organization. Liaison devices are rarely found in the operating core. The exception is found where professionals make up the operating core, as in the university. The strategic apex does not often use liaison devices.

The **design of the decision making system,** or *vertical* and *horizontal decentralization,* is the last category of design parameters. A centralized system gives the decision making power to one or a few persons near the top of the organization. Decentralization disperses authority to make decisions among many organization members at lower levels.

The organization decentralizes because the underlying factors of decisions cannot be understood by one person or even a small group. Decentralization allows a quick response to relevant environmental conditions. On the other hand, centralization places all decision making activities (e.g., information gathering, determining alternatives, analyzing the information, etc.) into one person or unit. In general, centralization will often lead to higher efficiency but may also contribute to lower morale since organization members may feel they no longer control their work lives.

Vertical decentralization is the delegation of decision making down the chain of authority. When decision-making power shifts laterally to nonmanagers, this is called horizontal decentralization. Vertical decentralization may be selective (for specific decisions or groups of decisions) or parallel, such as a market-based organization that is divided into divisions. Each division may vertically decentralize to differing degrees. Horizontal decentralization may shift the decision making authority to a single person in a particular organization position, to analysts (who standardize), to experts (who have the technical expertise) or to the members.

Centralization may be related to other design parameters. Behavior formalization often exists when there is centralization. Training and indoctrination lead to decentralization. Liaison devices are used in decentralized organizations; planning and control systems are preferred in centralized organizations.

CONTINGENCY FACTORS

Situational or contingency factors are viewed as independent variables, influenced by mediating variables such as the predictability or diversity of work. The structural variables, or design parameters, are the dependent variables in this model. Mintzberg hypothesizes that "effective structuring requires a consistency among the design parameters and contingency factors." Significant contingency factors that influence structure are age, size of the organization, the technical production system, environment, and the organization's power system.

Age and Size

The organization's age and size particularly affect behavior formalization and the administrative structure at the middle level. The size of an organization often changes incrementally; transition is seldom smooth. It is often disruptive. The first stage of organization development usually is a craft or entrepreneurial situation. The organization is small, informal, and organic with owners as both operators and managers. In the next stage, ownership is separated from management, bureaucracy begins to occur, and standardization emerges. If organizations move beyond the bureaucratic stage, they become divisionalized, that is, with several functional bureaucracies. Each of these functional bureaucracies has an operating core to serve a unique market. The final developmental stage is a matrix organization with grouping by two or more bases (such as function, product, geography, client, etc.) and a return to a more organic structure.

In general, there is more formalized behavior in older organizations. Organization structures often reflect the age of the industry. Job specialization and the use of professionals in staff positions are related inversely to the age of the industry. For example, farming (an old industry) has little job specialization and few staff positions, and few professionals to fill them. On the other hand, areospace is a young industry. NASA has high job specialization and many staff positions filled with professionals.

Larger organizations will tend to have more elaborate structures (more specializations, more differentiation, etc.), larger work units, and more formalized behavior. As organizations grow, the proportion of line managers decreases and the proportion of staff specialists increases.

The Technical System

The organization's technical system is the second contingency factor that will influence structure. It is closely associated with the operating core. The technical system is composed of the collective instruments used by operators to complete their work. Two dimensions of this system are the degree of regulation (the influence of the technical system on the operators) and the degree of sophistication (complexity).

The regulation imposed by the technical system is the extent to which the operator's work is controlled by the instruments or machinery which he or she uses. The surgeon's use of a scalpel is an example of the case where the "instrument" imposes only a minimal amount of regulation. On the other hand, the machinery in an oil refinery exerts a high degree of regulation, and extensively controls the operator's work. Technical system sophistication determines the difficulty of understanding the work process. Flying a giant modern aircraft requires more complex cognitive processes than does baking a cake.

In general, if the technical system is highly regulated, the work processes will be more formalized and the structure of the operating core will be more bureaucratic. As the technical system becomes more sophisticated (more complex), the administrative structure becomes more elaborate, there is more selective decentralization to the staff, and more liaison devices are used. However, if the operating core is automated, there is little need for rules and procedures (formalization). The administrative structure may be organic and the operators and first line supervisors are specialists.

The Environment

A third contingency factor is the organization's external environment. This is more important at the strategic apex where strategies and policies are established. Relevant environmental dimensions are the degree of stability, degree of complexity, market diversity, and degree of hostility toward the organization.

As the environment becomes more dynamic, the structure becomes more organic. Extreme hostility in the environment drives the administration to temporarily centralize control, whereas disparities in the environment lead the organization to decentralize selectively to various differentiated work groups. If the organization's markets are diversified, there is a propensity to divisionalize, or split the organization into market-based units.

The more complex the environment, the greater the need for decentralization. The relationship between environmental complexity and stability suggest four types of structures, shown in Figure 3.

Power

The final contingency factor includes external control, personal power needs, and the style of power that is fashionable. The more an organization is controlled externally, the more its structure will be centralized and bureaucratic. If the CEO is held accountable by external decision makers, he or she will tend to centralize in order to control more carefully. Also, because the organization must justify its actions to outsiders, there will be greater behavior formalization.

Excessive individual power needs in top executives will lead to unwarranted centralization. Moreover, the organization structure preferred by those with power is often adopted—even if it is inappropriate for the particular organizational circumstances.

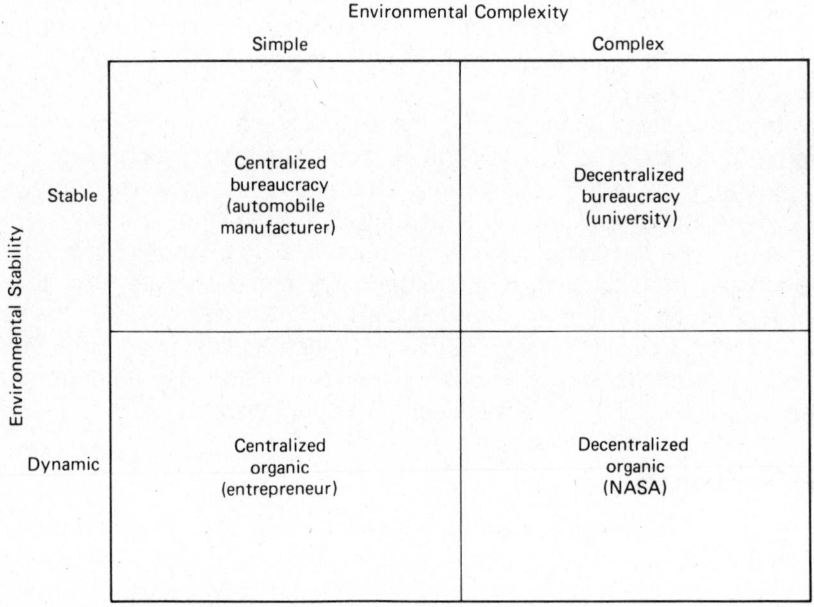

Environmental Complexity

	Simple	Complex
Stable	Centralized bureaucracy (automobile manufacturer)	Decentralized bureaucracy (university)
Dynamic	Centralized organic (entrepreneur)	Decentralized organic (NASA)

(Environmental Stability)

Figure 3 Environmental complexity and stability.

STRUCTURAL CONFIGURATIONS

Relating the organization elements (coordinating mechanisms, parts of the organization, and the design parameters) with the contingency factors, five natural clusters or configurations of organization structure emerge. That is, certain types of coordination are used more often with certain levels of decentralization, and certain parts of the organization have more strength when particular lateral linkages are used, etc. The five basic structures are (1) the simple structure, (2) machine bureaucracy, (3) professional bureaucracy, (4) divisionalized form, and (5) adhocracy.

The Simple Structure

The simple structure is illustrated in Figure 4. The strategic apex is the most important organizational part in the simple structure. Little or no technostructure and support staff exist. The managerial hierarchy is small. There is almost no division of labor and minimal differentiation occurs between units. Most coordination is a result of direct supervision and decision making is highly centralized. Formal planning, training, and liaison devices are unnecessary. The organization is organic with flexible work flow and decision making processes. The entrepreneurial firm is an example of the simple structure.

Simple, dynamic environments are conducive to simple structures. Simple structures tend to be small. A simple structure often describes the formative years of many organizations. Organizations may revert to a simple structure in times of crisis. Leaders in the simple structure are often autocratic or charismatic.

There are several important facets of the simple structure. The strategic apex is usually involved in both production and strategy. While this allows rapid reaction to any change, the entrepreneur/owner/manager is the center of the firm and all relevant knowledge rests in one person. This structure has high risk in that it is dependent on one person or, at best, only a few persons. Furthermore, the decision maker (i.e., the owner) may not recognize the need for growth, for staff, for technical expertise, and so forth.

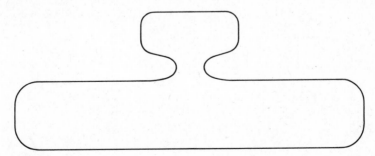

Figure 4 The simple structure.

Technical systems are, in general, nonsophisticated and nonregulating. A major advantage of this structure is that it is easy to transmit a sense of mission to those in the organization. The owner and employees know the goals of the firm and work toward them. This structure also allows a great deal of flexibility that is not present in other organization structures.

The Machine Bureaucracy

The machine bureaucracy, shown in Figure 5, is a performance organization, not a problem-solving one. Production is the goal, not problem solving. There are always specific tasks leading to a particular performance. The operating core is characterized by standardization of work processes, formalized behavior, and narrow, specialized jobs. The administrative hierarchy (the middle line) is tall and fairly narrow. Because of the standardization of work, the technostructure is the dominant part of the organization. The support staff is also large and has much informal power. Line and staff are sharply differentiated in that there is a clear division between them.

Rules and regulations permeate the organization. Formal authority structures and formal communication systems exist and are fully utilized. There is an inflexibility and an obsession with control. In an attempt to remove uncertainty, the operating core is often sealed off from external influences. The support staff increases in an attempt to remove all uncertainty. This structure inherently promotes conflict, because of the line-staff division, the specialized narrow work which is routine, and the extreme division of labor.

Even though the technostructure is dominant, the strategic apex also maintains great power. Strategy tends to be transmitted from the top down with a heavy emphasis on action planning. Decision making is vertically centralized with selective horizontal decentralization to the technostructure. The strategic apex delegates some power to parts of the technostructure when appropriate.

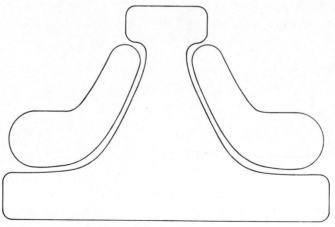

Figure 5 The machine bureaucracy.

There is only a small administrative component because many rules and regulations control the organization.

The machine bureaucracy operates in large, mature organizations. The environment is simple and stable and the technical systems are regulating. This structure is typified by mass production firms, often with much external control. This external control may be exercised by owners (i.e., stockholders) as in industrial firms or by a government agency as the nature of control over the U. S. Postal Service. While the machine bureaucracy is a dominant structure today, it is not a fashionable or popular design. However, it is an indispensable configuration, particularly in a society that demands mass-produced goods where full automation is not yet possible or reasonable.

The machine bureaucracy is the most effective structure for mass production because it is the most efficient system for the performance of routine tasks. Because of a propensity to treat workers as machines, coordination is difficult. Only vertical communication is allowed, which can lead to an abuse of power (e.g., the supervisor who insists on controlling *all* communication). This will certainly lead to centralization. It also often leads to information overload on the part of supervisors and managers. The strategic apex is overburdened with superfluous data and incomplete or old information which is often used as the basis for significant decisions.

The Professional Bureaucracy

The operating core of the professional bureaucracy (see Figure 6) is made up of professionals and is the most significant component in this structure. Tasks are specialized horizontally. The professionals have much control over their work and they often work closely with clients. This is very different from the machine bureaucracy where the work processes are routine and which attracts unskilled or semiskilled workers.

Coordination is accomplished by standardization of skills. Such standardization occurs after much training and indoctrination. Professionals are extensively trained by institutions other than the employing organization. Therefore, standards are usually set by the professions, outside the organization. This is

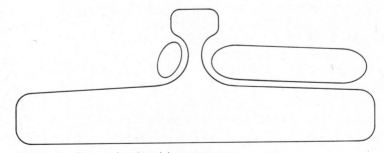

Figure 6 The professional bureaucracy.

in contrast to the machine bureaucracy where the technostructure sets work standards.

The professional bureaucracy is, however, bureaucratic in nature. There are many rules and regulations, authority is based on expertise, organizational tenure is pervasive.

The operating core is large and there is a large support staff to support that operating core. The middle line and technostructure are small, as is the strategic apex.

Horizontal and vertical decentralization characterize this structure. The tasks performed by the professional are too complex to be directly supervised or standardized. The diagnosis of the situation is a fundamental task in the professional bureaucracy and that requires the operator (i.e., the professional) to be well versed in relevant areas. Since the professional has expertise, he or she derives some power from this expertise and his or her professional services are often in great demand. Because of expert power, the professional is allowed high autonomy. He or she may be subject to little outside control but is subject to the censure of colleagues should the professional behave in an inappropriate manner.

The administrative hierarchy is made up of professionals, often serving at the pleasure of the professional operators. The organization is very democratic. Information and decisions tend to flow from the bottom up. The professional administrator is both a negotiator, handling disturbances within the organization, and a boundary spanner, interacting with external people and organizations. Strategies are often formulated by individuals within the system, professional associations, or external entities with control, such as the board which controls state university systems.

The environment is the most significant contingency factor for the professional bureaucracy. A stable and complex environment leads to standardized skills. This structure has no typical age or size. The technical system (i.e., the system of instruments used to apply knowledge) is not highly regulated or complex. However the technology (i.e., the knowlege base) is sophisticated but not regulated. Power rests with the operator.

Issues unique to the professional bureaucracy are based on the professional as an operator. No other structure claims democracy for its workers. The operators have more autonomy than in any other type of organization. Unfortunately, because there is little outside control, professionals can be quite unproductive, yet often keep their positions and salaries. The profession often ignores problems and, in so doing, ignores the needs of both clients and the organization. Conflict is rampant between the support staff and the operator/professionals. Professionals are often unable to deal with incompetent and unconscientious colleagues, leaving the client or organization to bear the brunt of the unprofessional behavior. Professional bureaucracies are inflexible structures. They are not suited to innovation and can be very inefficient by retaining old policies or procedures that are no longer useful.

The Divisionalized Form

The divisionalized form, shown in Figure 7, is a structure that is superimposed on several division structures, with each division being driven toward a machine bureaucracy. Market grouping is the usual basis for the divisionalization. Usually the separate divisions have duplicate operating functions. The divisions are quasi-autonomous and loosely coupled to the superstructure, which permits limited vertical decentralization to division managers. However, divisions may be quite centralized within themselves. This structure is often a result of mergers and consolidations.

Performance control systems, which focus on outputs and standards, are the predominant control devices. In turn, the primary coordinating mechanism is standardization of outputs. The middle line (i.e., the division managers) is the critical part of this organization. Division managers have great power and often have standardized skills. In essence, they are chief executive officers for their divisions.

The sharp division of labor between the strategic apex (headquarters) and the divisions occurs because the divisions control operations and determine the strategies for specific markets. However, headquarters manages the overall strategy and resources, designs the performance control system and monitors divisional performance while remaining small relative to the divisional units. The technostructure and support staff are small while the operating core is very large, since it is composed of the actual divisions.

Market diversity leads to divisionalization, but this structural form is only possible when the organization's technical system can be segmented, with each division controlling a different segment. The divisionalized structure tends to be an older, larger organization. The environment is similar to that of a machine bureaucracy—stable, simple with horizontal diversification. However, hybrid structures tend to develop when the environment is dynamic or complex. Hybrids also develop when coordinating mechanisms other than standardization of output exist. These hybrid structures take parts of the five pure structures and must be classified in terms of their unique characteristics, rather than as one of the five aggregate structural forms.

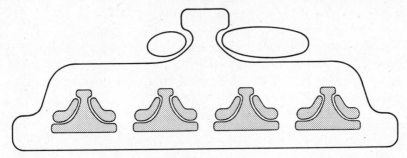

Figure 7 The divisionalized form.

The divisionalized form is most effective in the private sector. It seems to be ill suited for the nonbusiness sector since it operates best with machine bureaucracy divisions and it needs quantifiable goals with the performance control system.

There are several unique aspects of the divisionalized form. Economic advantages of divisionalization are that it encourages efficient allocation of capital within the division, trains general managers as they move through the divisions, diversifies risk, and is strategically responsive to the market. These can be disadvantages if they are abused, however. Headquarters managers have a tendency to usurp divisional powers, to centralize, and to design stronger performance control systems. In turn, the quantitative nature of the control system can drive the firm to act in socially unresponsive or irresponsible ways. This concentration of power in headquarters can lead to anticompetitiveness and is the basis for the tendency to move toward machine bureaucracy.

The divisionalized form has the narrowest range of any of the structures in that it is only applicable in limited circumstances. It can occur in any environment but tends to move toward the simple, stable environment. The economic advantages occur only because of fundamental inefficiencies in the capital markets, the finished goods markets, and stockholder control systems. Mintzberg suggests that this structure is perhaps the "ideal type"—one that is approached but never reached. It is positioned to adapt rapidly to environmental changes, yet has the superstructure for support.

The Adhocracy

The most complex structure, and the one most appropriate for organization innovation, is the adhocracy (see Figure 8). It is an organic structure with little formalization of behavior, highly trained specialists, and multidisciplinary project teams or matrix teams with functional and market grouping. The many managers (project, functional, integrating, etc.) coordinate by mutual adjustment using several liaison devices. The managers themselves occupy liaison roles much of the time. It is difficult for one person to become powerful in this dynamic organizational environment. There is selective decentralization, both horizontal and vertical.

There are two types of adhocracies, differing as a function of the ultimate consumer: the operating adhocracy and the administrative adhocracy. The operating adhocracy innovates and solves problems directly on behalf of its clients. Examples are the creative advertising agency or the design engineering firm which makes prototypes for clients. Output of an operating adhocracy is similar to output from a professional bureaucracy. In actuality, there is a professional bureaucracy that corresponds to each operating adhocracy. Both organizations produce the same product, but use different structures. For example, an experimental theater company is an adhocracy while the permanent theater company, which works to improve or perfect its standard fare, is a professional bureaucracy. Yet both provide theatrical entertainment. The area above the dotted line in Figure 8 is an operating adhocracy.

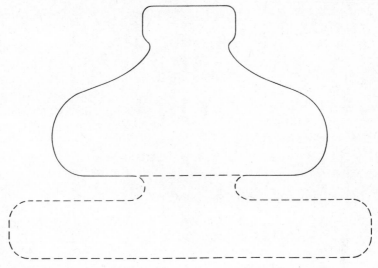

Figure 8 The adhocracy.

The administrative adhocracy differs from the operating adhocracy in that it engages in project work on its own behalf. There is a sharp distinction between the administrative and operating components, which is shown as the complete figure in Figure 8. The administration is organic but the operations (1) are carried out by a separate part of the organization, (2) are contracted out, or (3) are automated. Magazine production is an excellent example of the administrative adhocracy. While the creation of the copy, the marketing, and the strategy are highly dynamic, the actual printing of the magazine is routine, and usually delegated to a machine bureaucracy.

The support staff is the most significant part of the adhocracy, but it does not stand alone as a separate organization element. All parts of the organization blend together. The line-staff distinction is blurred, and the strategic apex tends to blend with the middle line and the operating core. Strategy and planning tend to be dynamic and continuous.

Environments conducive to the use of adhocracies are dynamic and complex. These allow organic, relatively decentralized operations. Frequent product changes drive the firm toward adhocracy. Many hybrid adhocracies exist, particularly with multinational interdependent organizations. The adhocracy is fashionable, perhaps because it is so suited for innovative work.

Adhocracies tend to be young and are the least stable structure of the five configurations. The operating adhocracy is particularly prone to a short life in that lack of success will cause the firm to disappear, but success breeds stability and bureaucracy.

The administrative adhocracy has a tendency to grow large while the operating adhocracy is often small or midsize. The technical systems are different—the operating adhocracy has a simple, nonregulating system while

Table 1 Dimensions of the Five Configurations

	Simple Structure	Machine Bureaucracy	Professional Bureaucracy	Divisionalized Form	Adhocracy
Key coordinating mechanism Key part of organization	Direct supervision Strategic apex	Standardization of work Technostructure	Standardization of skills Operating core	Standardization of outputs Middle line	Mutual adjustment Support staff (with operating core in operating adhocracy)
DESIGN PARAMETERS Specialization of jobs	Little specialization	*Much horizontal and vertical specialization*	*Much horizontal specialization*	Some horizontal and vertical specialization (between divisions and HQ)	*Much horizontal specialization*
Training and indoctrination	Little training and indoctrination	Little training and indoctrination	*Much training and indoctrination*	Some training and indoctrination (of division managers)	Much training
Formalization of behavior Bureaucratic/organic	Little formalization *Organic*	Much formalization *Bureaucratic*	Little formalization *Bureaucratic*	Much formalization (within divisions) *Bureaucratic*	Little formalization *Organic*
Grouping Unit size	*Usually functional* *Wide*	*Usually functional* *Wide at bottom, narrow elsewhere*	Functional and market Wide at bottom, narrow elsewhere	*Market* *Wide (at top)*	*Functional and market* *Narrow throughout*
Planning and control systems	Little planning and control	Action planning	Little planning and control	*Much performance control*	Limited action planning (esp. in administrative adhocracy)
Liaison devices	Few liaison devices	Few liaison devices	Liaison devices in administration	Few liaison devices	*Many liaison devices throughout*
Decentralization	*Centralization*	*Limited horizontal decentralization*	*Horizontal and vertical decentralization*	*Limited vertical decentralization*	*Selective decentralization*
CONTINGENCY FACTORS Age and size	Typically young and small	Typically old and large	Varies	Typically old and very large	Typically young (operating adhocracy)
Technical system	Simple, not regulating	Regulating but not automated, not very complex	Not regulating or complex	Divisible, otherwise typically like machine bureaucracy	Very complex, often automated (in administrative adhocracy); not regulating or complex (in operating adhocracy)
Environment	Simple and dynamic; sometimes hostile	Simple and stable	Complex and stable	Relatively simple and stable; diversified markets (especially products and services)	Complex and dynamic; sometimes disparate (in administrative adhocracy)
Power	Chief executive control; often owner-managed; not fashionable	Technocratic and external control; not fashionable	Professional operator control; fashionable	Middle line control; fashionable (especially in industry)	Expert control; very fashionable

the technical system for the administrative adhocracy is sophisticated and often automated.

Power goes to the experts but is not concentrated in one area. Adhocracy is unique in that it is the most political structure of the five forms. Task ambiguity, high expert power, and matrix formats combine to institutionalize conflict, leading to the many managers and coordination by mutual adjustment. This structure is inefficient, loses economies of scale, and sacrifices the advantages of specialization. The high cost of communication and integration make the structure prohibitive in some situations. Adhocracy is best suited for performing complex, ill-structured programs.

CONCLUDING OVERVIEW

An organization is driven toward one of the configurations based on the contingency factors and the strength of the organizational parts. The strategic apex moves toward direct supervision and centralization. Standardized work processes are urged by the technostructure while standardized skills are promoted by operators. The middle managers want to have autonomy to manage their individual units and have standard outputs. The pull by the support staff, and by operators in the operating adhocracy, is for collaboration and mutual adjustment. Each structure is unique in that different parts of the organization are strong, different design parameters are significant and different contingency factors are important. Table 1 indicates how the several factors differ among the various structures.*

Hybrid structures emerge when the organization responds to more than one force at the same time. This is reflected in one of two ways. Either the structure adopted will be a mixture of two configurations or different units in the organization will have different structures. Organizations usually begin with a simple structure or an operating adhocracy and make transitions to other forms based on the design parameters and contingency factors. Structural transitions often lag behind the new conditions that evoke them. There is no one best structure. There are only structures that are internally consistent and in harmony with the contingency factors.

"MANAGEMENT PROCESS CONTINGENCY THEORY" †

HENRY L. TOSI

The theoretical formulation presented here is drawn from a wide range of ideas, many of which have been presented earlier in this book. The theory integrates concepts from organization theory and organization behavior and

---

*From: Henry Mintzberg "Configurations of Organization Structure" in H. Meltzer and Walter R. Nord, *Making Organizations Humane and Productive.* New York: Wiley, 1981. Reprinted by permission of the publisher.

†This is an original selection written for this book.

then states some general propositions about how to manage organizations effectively. In this sense, this is a theory of management practice.

The basic premise is that some managerial approaches are more effective than others, but that is so only as a function of circumstances. In order to determine what approach is most effective, managers must consider two factors. These are (1) the organization structure and (2) the personnel in the organization.

The first factor, the organization structure, is the pattern of relationships among the individuals in the organization. In some organizations, the work is very repetitive, and the structure is fixed and fairly rigid. In other organizations the work is more creative and less repetitive, and the structure of the organization is accordingly more flexible, there is more looseness, more freedom in defining what employees do.

Some organizations exist in environments characterized by more uncertainty than others. Research suggests that when there is a great deal of environmental uncertainty, a less rigidly structured organization works best. In such an environmental setting, the work of individuals will be less repetitive, perhaps more creative. We call this kind of structure a dynamic, or flexible, organization.

When there is a high degree of environmental certainty, a highly structured organization works best. Such organizations, operating in a more certain environment, are called hierarchical or bureaucratic. In them, work is more routine and repetitive than it is in the dynamic organzation.

The second factor is the personnel. Organizations, structured in certain ways, will attract, and be choosen by, individuals with certain kinds of skills and personality characteristics. For instance, people with a need for a great deal of freedom and latitude in determining what they do seek to avoid bureaucratic organizations.

A person's attitude toward work is a function of early experiences at home as a child, and later on in schools. The manager must try to understand the personality structures that result from these early experiences in order to deal effectively with subordinates. The different reactions of individuals in different types of organizations should determine the nature of interpersonal relationships between managers and subordinates.

In the sections that follow we will examine these two factors in some detail. We show how organization structure emerges from environmental pressures and from human decisions. The different orientations of individuals to work and how these orientations exist in the various types of organization is also shown. Finally, we speculate about motivation, performance evaluation, and leadership and decision making in effective organizations.

ORGANIZATION ORIENTATIONS

Through socialization a culture, society, or an institution conditions the behavior and attitudes of individuals. The unique set of values, attitudes, and behaviors of individuals in their adult lives begin their formation in early childhood experiences. From birth, a person is subjected to the pressure of group norms and values, cues, and reinforcements that, over a period of time, develop and shape behavior and attitudes. Certain modes of adapting to situations which are encountered emerge. This pattern of adaptation is called "personality."

Personality is the unique pattern of psychological and behavioral characteristics of an individual. Many believe that once formed, personality is resistant to change. Certain aspects of the personality take on special importance in the world of work. For example, people differ in their reaction to authority. Since all organizations have pervasive authority systems, how one reacts specifically and generally to them will affect the persons adaptation to work and, perhaps, his or her performance.

It is useful to categorize various orientations that people have toward organizations and work because it provides some understanding about a person's motivational and behavioral tendencies. Some people are highly committed to the organization, others seem to have little interest in their work or the organization. Still others seem to be extremely interested in what they do, they have little commitment to the organization in which they work (Presthus, 1978). The following categories are a typology of organizational personality orientations. They are useful because these different personality types exist in different proportions in different types of organizations. In addition, these orientations reflect different motivational propensities and predispositions. Such a typology is necessary if prescriptive statements are to be a basic part of a theory.

The Organizationalist*

The "organizationalist" is a person highly committed to the *place* of work. He or she seeks organizational rewards and advancement and identifies with the system. The person's self-concept is inextricably tied to the organization. The organizationalist has high morale, high job satisfaction, and an extremely low tolerance for uncertainty. He or she wants to know what her job is, for what he or she is responsible, and to whom he or she is accountable. The organizationalist is very concerned with the effectiveness and efficiency of the organization.

Organizational success is important because it is reflective of personal success. An organizationalist is highly committed to the organization's goals. Identifying with a superior and he or she finds it easy to rationalize organizational pressures for conformity and performance, since this type is seeking promotion and other rewards from the system. Organization status is very important. Life values may be defined, or reflected by, the level one has achieved in the organization. Because this is so important, the organizationalist probably experiences a great deal of status anxiety, or fears that his or her position in the organization is threatened in reality or potentially.

*The following discussion of work orientations draws heavily from the work of Robert Presthus (1978).

The organizationalist avoids controversy, tending to stay within the "channels" of the system, not readily going outside them to handle problems.

The Socialization of the Organizationalist. The organizationalist develops an early respect for authority figures. Early experiences lead to the recognition of the importance of authority, realizing that authority figures have power to dispense rewards and/or impose sanctions. Presthus (1978) has suggested that the organizationalist comes from a family in which rewards and sanctions are applied primarily by a dominant father figure.

Externally Oriented Persons

Some people seem to work just for the pay they receive. Jobs are not a critical part of their lives. They may perform well but are not highly committed to the organization. They may be managers, lower-level employees, or highly trained professionals. Such persons do not seek organization rewards or strive for higher position. They accept what they have.

Given a choice, they would rather be doing other things. They seek satisfaction of higher-order psychological needs outside the organization through activities that are not related to where they work or what their work is. This is in marked contrast to the organizationalist, who seeks need satisfaction from a connection with the firm.

The externally oriented person generally withdraws from work. He or she may be alienated by the tedium of the work itself. There is no extensive involvement with the work organization. An externalist participates in it only minimally beyond work requirements. There are other, more important things in life than the job and the company. Rather than emphasizing traditional Western values of work, as does the organizationalist, the externalist seems more concerned with leisure.

Status and prestige associated with the job are rejected. Work is separated from the more meaningful aspects of the person's life. The externalist adapts to the work environment by withdrawing from it as much as possible, seeking psychological satisfaction from neither the work itself nor the organization.

The Socialization of the Externally Oriented. Presthus (1978) suggests that the externally oriented person generally comes from the lower middle class. A limited education restricts opportunities for advancement, so the person is highly likely to remain in that group.

We must not assume, however, that only lower-level personnel are externalists. Certainly we would expect to find fewer externalists at higher levels, but it is not uncommon to find them in the upper management ranks. Managers may develop such a view in the following way. Early in one's career, a manager may be highly committed to the organization, actively seeking its rewards and advancement opportunities. However, in middle age and in later life, the person may find that he or she has been passed over several times for promotion. When this happens, positive reinforcement is sought elsewhere. Organization promotion practices may turn managers from highly committed organizationalists to externally oriented types.

Often a person, whether a manager, a specialist, or an operative worker turns the substance of his or her life to other things. Employees who once followed orders without question may change. This may be due to a basic shift in values, but more often it is because the organizationalist is passed over for promotions or experiences other negative events in his or her career.

It does necessarily follow, from the discussion so far that the externalist is a less effective employee than an organizationalist. The orientation, no matter what, is a state of mind. It may be only indirectly related to competence or quality of performance. The externalist with high skill levels may perform extremely well since ability is an important component in determining level of performance.

The Professional

Professionals also have external orientations but they are preoccupied with their jobs or, more specifically, their careers. While the organizationalist's self-concept is linked to *where* he or she works, the professional is tied to *what* he or she does.

Professionals generally experience very intense occupational socialization. Such socialization experiences condition the professional to believe that it is important to perform extremely well. However, there must often be compromises with the needs of the organization. When the professional is subjected to managerial pressure to conform to organization demands that are inconsistent with his or her professional values, the professionally oriented person may believe that such directives are not rational.

Professionals tend to be dissatisfied when they perceive themselves to be in a situation where they cannot most effectively utilize all their skills. The professionals feel underutilized and their self-esteem may be threatened because there is no opportunity to do the things which they have been trained to do.

Professionals are often not concerned with organizational status. They look outward to other professional colleagues for approval. The professional would rather not be in the organization, but would prefer to be operating independently. Yet an organization is necessary, since it is imperative to have a place to work, a base of operations, and a source of income. The professional must adapt in some way to these inconsistent demands, and accommodating to these demands are often high conflictful.

The Socialization of the Professional. The professionally oriented person often has a middle-class background and has become successful through either higher education or by personal efforts to increase skills (Presthus, 1978). He or she is likely to have a strong "ideological" orientation and to be extremely concerned that he or she does well in his or her chosen field. Professional success is usually defined in terms of personal achievement, more than likely measured by recognition from external colleagues rather than by organizational rewards. Organizational rewards have some value however, since they represent one way that a professional may judge the importance of his or her professional contribution relative to others in the system.

ORGANIZATION SUBSYSTEMS*

The Katz and Kahn (1978) concept of systems provides a way to conceptualize a wide range of different organizations. A system is a set of bounded and interrelated components. Inputs are drawn from other systems and transformed into outputs. These may become inputs for other systems.

Complex organizations are open systems. They interact with and adapt to an outside environment. For example, a business organization must react to changes in the environments from which it takes its inputs or resources (e.g., suppliers of raw materials), and to changes in the environments in which it delivers outputs or goods and services (i.e., to clients or customers). Organization may try to influence or exert control over environments. For example, a firm may decide to buy another which is a supplier in order to have a guaranteed source of raw materials. But no organization has complete power over its environments, and all are influenced by their environments in a number of ways.

A system may be considered to be made up of subsystems. Organization subsystems are related groups of activities which various units perform to meet the objectives of the organization. The organization subsystems are (1) production subsystems, (2) adaptive subsystems, (3) boundary-spanning subsystems, (4) maintenance subsystems, and (5) managerial subsystems.

Production Subsystems.   The production subsystem is the technical core of the organization, producing the product, service, or ideas which are bought, or otherwise consumed, by the public. Every organization has a production subsystem. There is a tendency to equate the production subsystem with manufacturing firms. This is too narrow a view. In a business firm, the production system is the task-oriented work which creates the product or service—for example, an assembly line, a transaction system for tellers in a bank, or those activities in a retailing outlet which take place after goods are bought but before they are sold.

This subsystem is important since it is most likely to be a high-cost subsystem; that is, large sums will be required to build, create, or otherwise develop it. This large investment produces pressures for effective and efficient utilization. Procedures and approaches are designed to protect it from unpredictable fluctuations in the environment. There are different types of pro-

*This discussion draws extensively from Daniel Katz and Robert Kahn, *The Social Psychology of Organizations.* New York: Wiley, 1978.

duction subsystems. Thompson (1967) proposes a general classification scheme of production technologies: long linked, mediating, and intensive. (These are discussed in more detail on pages 170 to 173.)

Boundary-spanning Subsystems. Boundary-spanning subsystems carry on the environmental transactions in procuring the input, disposing of the output, or assisting in these functions. The activities themselves are performed within the organization, but they connect it with external points of contact. They are one type of link between the organization with the relevant environment. A major portion of activities of sales unit of a firm and the purchasing department are illustrations of boundary-spanning functions.

Adaptive Subsystems. Adaptive subsystems are another link between the organization and the environment. These are activities within an organization which monitor the relevant environment. These are crucial for organization survival. If the environmental context changes, the organization must change.

Research and development are one kind of adaptive subsystem activities. Lobbying to influence government policy in areas which might affect the organization are also adaptive activities. Financial and other control activities to monitor and control the level of efficiency and performance of a firm to see that it is profitable enough to acquire capital for future investment are also adaptive activities.

Maintenance Subsystems. Maintenance subsystem activities seek to smooth out the problems of operating the other subsystems, and to monitor their *internal* operation. The general concern of the maintenance subsystem is insuring predictability of the rest of the organization. One important function of the maintenance subsystem is to enhance cooperation and commitment from members. This is accomplished through activities such as indoctrination, socialization, training activities, and administering the compensation system, the performance appraisal system, and other human resource management activities.

Maintenance activities also focus on setting performance standards for tasks, raw materials standards, and product or service quality standards. Surveillance or evaluation activities are carried out to insure that such standards are met. The maintenance subsystem devises and monitors adherence to preestablished rules and norms.

Managerial Subsystems. "Managerial subsystems," say Katz and Kahn (1978), "comprise the organized activities for controlling, coordinating, and directing the many subsystems of the structure. They represent another slice of the organizational pattern and . . . deal with coordination of subsystems and adjustment of the total system to its environment." The managerial subsystem handles general policy questions such as determining general policy and strategy to interact with the environment to insure long-term survival. The resolution of internal conflict between departments is also one of its functions, as is the use of the authority structure to disseminate directives and to resolve conflict.

THE RELEVANT ENVIRONMENT OF THE ORGANIZATION

Organizations interact with other organizations which provide inputs, make use of outputs, exert pressures for certain kinds of decisions, and in general affect in some important fashion the focal organization.

The relevant environment is made up of those groups, or institutions, beyond an organization's boundaries which provide immediate inputs, exert significant pressure on decisions, or make use of the organization's output. This means that at any one point in time, there are some external organizations which are closer and have a more significant effect on what goes on in a firm than do others.

Circumstances could bring other institutions or organizations into the relevant environment. When other sectors of the environment begin to impose pressures, they may threaten the existence of the organization. Any outside force which generates sufficient pressure to create pressures within an organization either in the managerial structure, the production structure, or the boundary-spanning structures must be of necessity be defined as part of the relevant environment because the organization must adapt to it.

The Environmental Sectors

Two sectors of the environment which are of most use in analyzing problems in the management of business organizations are the market and technological environmental sectors. It should be noted that other sectors may be more critical in different organizations. They would, however, have similar effects as we will outline here.

The Market Environment. Organizations produce some commodity, product value, or service for a particular set of individuals, the consumers of the output. Within an organization, there is also a "market" for outputs of subunits (or departments). The notion of organization subsystems suggests, for example, that the output of the production subsystem becomes an input for the boundary-spanning market subsystem. Departments in organizations provide some sort of product or service to other units. Demands of these users may range from specific tangible products such as subassemblies, completed units, memoranda or reports, to services, ideas, or other more abstract values.

The Technological Environment. The technological sector of the environment has two components. The first is the availability of techniques and processes which the organization can obtain to form the production system. In this sense, technology refers to available hardware. How this is absorbed, organized, and set up internally defines the production subsystem described earlier—which means that internal production systems cannot be any farther advanced than the technology available, although it is also quite possible that production systems may not come close to using all available technology advances.

The second aspect refers to the ideas or knowledge underlying the processing or the distribution of the service; that is, the translation of science to useful application. Every organization makes use of some knowledge base, some science, in its subsystems.

Characteristics of the Environment

Defining the relevant environment only indicates where an organization operates. What causes the organization to take the structure that it does is the degree of environmental change.

The degree of change is a very important aspect of the environment as it affects an organization's structure. Degree of change may be conceived of as a continuum. At the opposite ends are (1) stability and (2) volatility. These two states of the environment have important implications for the internal structure of the organization, the type of individual who is likely to join a particular operation, and the shaping of perceptions, attitudes, and values in the organization. Most important, however, is that the environment has a significant effect on the degree to which internal subsystems of the organization take on highly routine or stable characteristics. For example, when there is a large steady market for a product and a well-developed technology, a firm may invest large sums in plant and equipment to serve it. Where the market demands vary, equipment with more general use may be most appropriate.

The Stable Environment. In the stable environment changes are not severe, occurring in small increments, with a minimal impact on the structure, processes, and output of the organization. Environmental changes are likely to be in size (e.g., the amount of beer consumed or insurance sold) rather than in kind.

For the organization, the effect of changes in the stable environment will be primarily on the size of the membership of the organization. Since the product is unlikley to change significantly, there will be little need to significantly alter the production subsystem.

With stability, it is likely that there will be extensive investment in plant, equipment, and distribution methods, and when there are increases or decreases in the market, the method of adaptation can be a short-term one, consisting of reducing or increasing the work force. Alterations in the production system come rather slowly. If there is a shift in demand, say a drop, then the mode of accommodation is not to seek new products, but rather to lay off personnel until demand increases, or perhaps to permanently adjust to lower sales levels.

The stable environment is characterized by high levels of predictability. Fairly accurate predictions of the market level can be made on some fairly common set of change measures, or indexes. For instance, the level of automobile sales may be predicted reasonably well if there are reasonably accurate data available on changes in population, income, and interest rates.

The Volatile Environment.   The volatile environment is likely to be turbulent, with more intense changes than in the stable environment. Changes are more rapid and random, and prediction is difficult. When the market is volatile, the customers may change or the level of demand may vary widely. When the technology is volatile, new concepts and ideas are being rapidly generated, and these new ideas affect either the manner in which the production processes are carried out or the nature of the processes themselves.

TYPES OF ORGANIZATIONS

Structures of different organizations will vary according to the conditions of the environment. That is, the relationships among organization's subsystems (production, adaptive, etc.) will depend on whether the market and/or technology is stable or volatile. Using the concepts about subsystems, their interface with the environment, and the character of the environment, we can describe different types of organizations. The basic model is shown in Figure 1. One axis is the technological dimension of environments; the other axis is the market dimension. Both dimensions are characterized by levels of uncertainty; stability and volatility are the extreme ends. These two points are used only for analytical purposes, but they are adequate for our analysis and discussion.

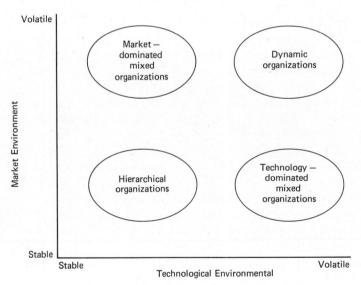

Figure 1   The relationship between environment and type of organization.

The five subsystems can be expected to vary within each organizational type. These relationships are theoretical and general tendencies. Nevertheless, organizations of all types do exhibit certain similar general structures and characteristics when their environments are similar.

The Hierarchical, Bureaucratic Organization

The hierarchical organization is the most appropriate form of organizational adaptation when the environment is very stable. It will emerge whenever the market and the technology are stable and predictable.

Production Subsystems.   Tasks are likely to be highly repetitive. That is, a standard way of performing work is established and routinized. All those who perform the tasks are then supposed to do them in the prescribed way.

There will also be extreme division of labor. Since the work activities can be standardized, they can be reduced to relatively small and simple work units. This often results in the situation in which each employee has only limited knowledge of how his or her work contributes to the total production process.

The low level of worker skill can lead to a high level of dependence of the individual on the organization. Workers are easy to replace because a large labor pool is available with people who can perform the work and because the individual who does the work has little control over how he or she produces or what he or she does. This lack of job security gives rise to a need for some protective mechanism. In bureaucratic organizations, there is often an external agent such as a union or the civil service system which provides some degree of job security against arbitrary actions of managers.

Boundary-spanning Subsystems.   The two major boundary-spanning activities are, first, a mechanism which distributes the product and/or service and, second, the procurement mechanisms that secure the raw materials or the resources required to produce the product or service.

Marketing and distribution activities will be well defined and standardized because the market for the hierarchical organization is relatively unchanging. The organization itself will have a great deal of influence over the distribution system.

It is likely that the products manufactured or the services of organizations in an industry characterized by hierarchical organizations will be fairly similar in terms of function and use. Therefore, a consumer may use any one of several products from different firms to obtain the kind of satisfaction he needs. This means that a marketing strategy might be based on pricing or product differentiation achieved through advertising and promotion.

The procurement function will draw inputs from well-developed and well-defined sources. In large industries, such as the auto industry, firms may have captive suppliers. A captive supplier is a firm which sells a large portion of its product to just one other firm. It depends primarily on one customer for the bulk of its business. This gives the customer the capacity to influence such things as price and production techniques to such an extent that the supplier may well be considered as a subsidiary.

With a highly repetitive production subsystem and well-defined sources of supply, boundary-spanning activities are particularly important in minimizing production cost. Repetitive production subsystems operate most efficiently when they can function at a fairly level rate. Since even in a stable market and with a stable technology there are minor fluctuations, a level rate of production activities may be sustained by maintaining inventories of both raw materials and finished goods.

Other boundary-spanning functions also exist. These are activities which bring other type resources into the organization. For example, recruiting by the personnel department is a boundary-spanning activity.

Adaptive Subsystems. In a stable environment, adaptive activities will be relatively simple. This is because interpreting the environment is relatively easy. In such a case there will be set rules for interpreting changes in the environment because the experience of the organization will be such that it has learned what parts of the environment it should monitor and how to adapt to them. It will have a fairly good information base to be used in making decisions. An organization operating in a stable environment may be able to use standard census data, for example, or other similar market research information as a basis for deciding how to adapt.

In hierarchical organizations fairly simple ways of adapting internally to changes in the environment will emerge. It is usually possible to develop a fairly systematic procedure which can be implemented when the environment changes.

The stability of the environment facilitates long-range planning. Long-term commitments of resources may be made with a great deal more certainty than in less stable environments. This may in turn facilitate the acquisition of the required capital at costs lower than where more risk is involved. The more stable the environment, the more likely that the firm will be able to make use of borrowed sources of capital rather than equity capital. Investors assume less risk and the organization can make long-term commitments to pay for the use of the borrowed capital.

Research and development is an important adaptive subsystem. Here the concern is with assessing changes in technology which may lead to a change in the production subsystem. However, since by definition technological changes are relatively minimal in an organization that is in a stable environment, engineering and research and development activities in such a situation are more likely to focus on applications engineering than on advancing the science or state of the art. Thus, the job of the engineer in the stable organization will be more concerned with product improvement within the existing technology than with trying to develop a new product or different production processes.

Maintenance Subsystems. These subsystems will be fairly stable. Historically developed information that has achieved organizational credibility will be used for control purposes. Even in organizations in which no measures of profitability are available, historical costs which have been associated with activities will come to be regarded as acceptable measures.

The focus of the maintenance subsystems will be on measuring performance outcomes. Those who carry out these activities will become extremely involved with performing the measurement function, perhaps at the expense of not placing proper emphasis on the achievement of organization objectives. This is called *the inversion of means and ends.* The purpose of the maintenance subsystem is to increase internal effectiveness, which means they are support systems; they should provide benefits to the organization, not cause problems. This, however, does not occur when there is "means-ends" inversion.

In a hierarchical organization, employees in maintenance activities will be extensively involved in performance evaluation, especially of managers. Because there is much cost and other performance information available, there is a tendency to rely on "hard criteria." Having such information gives a department—say personnel—a great deal of power, and its power can have a significant effect on decisions made in other parts of the firm. Auditing and budgeting units have the same potential power. When information is centralized and controlled, those who have it are extremely influential. Since information is localized in maintenance subsystems, these subsystems have a great deal of organization influence.

Since the production subsystem is highly repetitive and the work is divided into small activity units, personnel testing may be a very effective selection tool. That is, as mentioned earlier, in a stable organization with jobs having lower skill requirements than in other types of organizations, a larger labor pool is probably available. When there is a large number of workers it may be more effective to screen them with some sort of performance test than attempt to make subjective evaluations of their abilities or to test them later when they get on the job.

High morale and motivation are especially difficult to maintain when the work is routine, repetitive, or programmed. Rank-and-file workers in the hierarchical or bureaucratic organization will experience boredom and alienation.

Managerial Subsystems. This subsystem will be characterized by a highly centralized control. The nature of the information is such that it can be quickly collected and transmitted to the higher levels, so that decisions can be made about operations at lower levels without requiring a great deal of involvement of managers at those levels. There will be close control and monitoring of operations centralized at higher levels. Lower-level managerial discretion is likely to be relatively low.

The bureaucratic organization is characterized by a fairly rigid hierarchy by appealing to executives at higher levels (i.e., using the formal hierarchical system as a problem-resolution mechanism).

One of the major problems for the managerial subsystems is the conflict between the "management" group and operating employees. In industrial organization this will take the form of union-management bargaining, and in public organizations by the relationship between the administrative staffs and civil service agencies.

People will move to top-level managerial position after fairly long careers. There will be a relatively small portion of managers relative to the number of workers. The number of positions at higher levels will be relatively small. If this is true, and since the managers at the higher levels make promotion decisions, it is likely that there will be a high degree of similarity in point of view among high-level executives. Promotions will be based not only on performance, but also because one has the "right" point of view.

This form of promotion policy can create a special problem with individuals with high needs for achievement who are employed by such a firm. They will find promotion opportunities limited, leading them to go elsewhere to satisfy advancement needs.

In the hierarchical organization, managerial control will be based on position power. Generally, there will be fairly well-defined goals. It is unlikely that the organization will be seeking to provide products or services different from its current capability. The major decision about goals will be how much and when the product or service is to be provided. This will be relatively easy to forecast, since the market is stable.

The Flexible, Dynamic Organization

The flexible, dynamic organization is found where the market and technological sectors are highly volatile. It is one in which the structure, relationships, and jobs are more loosely defined, so that the process of adapting to change is relatively easy.

Production Subsystems. The production subsystem is composed primarily of general-purpose equipment or technology. Essentially, it is job-shop oriented so that the various production elements can be rearranged, when necessary, in order to perform the particular kinds of activities necessary to provide the required outputs as the market or the technology changes. Thus, the production subsystem itself will be in a fairly constant state of change. This as intensive technology, one in which the sequencing of operations will vary from project to project which makes it relatively difficult, if not impossible to develop routine, repetitive production procedures (see pages 170 to 173).

Boundary-spanning Subsystems. The method of getting the product or service to customers will vary from customer to customer. Channels of distribution will be relatively unstructured and will change from time to time. This means, essentially, that the organization will probably have to handle its marketing by itself. Since the distribution function cannot be routinized, highly skilled indivdiuals in both the technical and marketing functions will be needed.

Those involved with the procurement function must constantly seek and find different types of raw materials and resources, because both the level and type of raw material inputs will change from time to time.

Adaptive Subsystems. These activities will be performed by individuals in marketing and distribution functions, procurement, as well as in engineering and research development. They must be highly skilled at interpreting the environment. Whereas in the hierarchical form there are fairly well-defined cues which trigger internal organizational adjustments, for the flexible organization information which might cue an internal change in the subsystem will vary from time to time and may occur in random fashion. Thus, individual skill is essential to make some assessment as to the nature of the organization change, since it is practically impossible to specify in advance what specific aspect of the environment must be monitored.

Similar clinical, analytical skill is required of those who must restructure the organization in response to external changes. In the hierarchical form of organization, a minor change in one of the external indicators may trigger a specific type of internal change. In the flexible organization, however, the process of adjustment and the resulting set of relationships will nearly always vary. This variation will be a function of different sets of circumstances and, thus, it will differ according to the circumstances. This means that the individuals in the adaptive subsystem in a flexible organization will be very influential in decision making, policy making, and strategy formulation.

Marketing activities will usually take the form of both extensive market research and a subjective assessment of what the data mean. In research and development, the adaptive processes will likely be more toward the side of pure, rather than applied, research.

Members performing adaptive activities must, of necessity, continually update their skills and abilities to maintain them at a high level. In some cases, the organization's strategy to maintain the required skill levels may be to hire individuals with the required capability, rather than following a training or development approach. And since, by definition, these skills may be rapidly changing, there may be a fairly high level of turnover among those involved in the adaptive processes.

Since the cost of developing adaptive skills is usually too high for an organization to bear, individuals who have acquired these skills on their own will be recruited. This means that those who come to an organization and function in an adaptive capacity are likley to be more highly trained or more highly skilled than those performing other functions. This will have important implications for the levels of compensation in organizations. In the flexible organization, individuals are as likely to be paid for the level of education and training they bring to the job as for the level of importance of their job within the organization.

Borrowing capital for a firm of this sort is difficult, since there is high risk involved. With a great degree of unpredictable fluctuation in an environment investors are less willing to take the risk of lending capital at a fixed rate. Investors tend to desire equity participation. The capital structure will be weighted toward equity sources which would provide great potential gain attendant with the high risk.

Maintenance Subsystems. Here, the utility of historical data for control purposes is minimal since there may be little history to go by. Therefore, cost standards for project evaluation will come from forecasted estimates. This means that performance control and evaluation will be much more likely to be subjective than be based on "objective" performance measures. In flexible organizations it is likely that "end results" will be less frequently used for assessment than in bureaucratic organizations, and there will be greater focus on the *manner in which individuals go about performing their work.*

The control function will reside in either the person with expertise in a particular area or the person with the greatest financial interest. The expert will have great influence simply because of his or her capabilities. If expertise is the predominant power base, the influence pattern will shift from time to time, depending on the nature of the project or activity and who is the house expert at a particular point in time. When influence derives from the level of financial interest, the owner or the major stockholder makes the decisions. In this case, the organization will be an extension of that person's interests.

Personnel in these organizations are likely to have a short-range commitment to the organization. They will focus on their area of professional expertise or on their self-interest in promotion and advancement, since in a flexible organization there may be relatively few long-term activities to provide a basis for lengthy tenure. Individuals will be brought into the organization when they are required. When their services are no longer needed they may be terminated or they may move on voluntarily. This may make it undesirable and, from an individual point of view, unwise to be highly committed to the organization.

This career uncertainty may not pose a particular problem for the individual or for the organization. It is likely that people who accept employment in flexible organizations have learned that relatively rapid movement is part of the game. Professionals may be willing to work in any number of different organizations as long as they are able to do what they have been trained to do and what they believe to be important.

Managerial Subsystems. The managerial subsystem will be relatively less structured than in other forms of organizations. There will be few policy guidelines to use in the decision-making process, because the variability of the environment will preclude well-defined, set policies over time.

The organization structure will be flexible, one where individuals may be moved from project to project as the need for their skills arise, with the authority structure different for each project. Individuals will move from superior to superior, depending on what needs to be done. Teams will be composed of individuals who will work on particular projects. When the project is completed, the individuals on a team may move to different teams. If their skills are no longer required in the organization, they may be terminated either willingly or unwillingly. This mobility can cause problems unless the individual has a high tolerance for ambiguity and for role conflict.

In a flexible organization, the individual may report to several superiors because he or she may be assigned to more than one project at a time. This will cause situations in which there are conflicting demands. This is almost certainly to be the case with different leadership styles.

Flexible organizations are likely to be relatively small compared with hierarchical forms. This small size facilitates adaptability to the environment. As an organization grows, however, it will begin to develop some degree of procedural rigidity and hierarchy. This may mitigate against effective adaptation to environmental changes.

Flexible organizations will generally move to a more stable environment sector. This will increase the degree of certainty in which they operate. This makes planning and control easier. If it can make such a move, the organization will be able to make longer-term commitments to its members, perhaps facilitating recruitment since persons may be willing to join an organization where they can make a "career."

This last point may be especially important when individuals have a high degree of career anxiety. While a person might have a great deal of confidence in his or her own skills and abilities as a professional, the uncertainty of where he or whe will be working can pose a problem. This uncertainty is probably related to lower levels of organization commitment, which in turn would make it difficult to obtain high levels of compliance from individuals.

Technology-dominated Mixed Organizations

In technology-dominated mixed (TDM) organizations, the major threat to survival and effectiveness stems from uncertainty in the technological environment. The market environment of these organizations is relatively stable. Scientific breakthroughs, new production technology, or other new concepts can provide their creator or an early adopter with a significant competitive advantage. Therefore, it is important to monitor the technological sector of the environment carefully and make changes in the organization system when necessary.

The TDM organization will have one major structural component with hierarchical characteristics, and another component which will be less tightly structured. This case presents the problem of achieving good relationships with clear lines of authority and responsibility. Often problems will be solved between these two different components of the organization. Attempting to resolve conflicts between them by using the position authority of higher management levels is likely to be ineffective, since it is improbable that individuals in the managerial hierarchy or the marketing sector will have a level of technical expertise as high as those in the technical sector or that is acceptable to the latter. The professionals, that is, are likely to react negatively to administrative decisions.

Organizational members in the more structured market sector are likely to be either externally oriented or organizationally oriented as opposed to the professional orientation of those in the more flexible technical sectors. This will result in different reactions to pressures from the maintenance system seeking to impose regularity through standardized procedures and methods.

Production Subsystems. The production subsystem in a TDM organization will likely use intensive technology. Equipment will have unpredictable life, making investment in special-purpose machinery highly risky. The tendency will be to use, where possible, general-purpose processes to increase the productive life expectancy of equipment. Personnel who work in the production subsystem are likely to be highly skilled crafts workers who have spent relatively long times developing skills on particular types of equipment. They might have done this in apprenticeship programs, or through vocational training.

Boundary-spanning Subsystems. Channels of distribution will be fairly well set in place. Products will perhaps change technologically, but they will be distributed as they had been before any new product developments.

Boundary-spanning units in contact with outside firms in the technological environment must be able to change with technology. New sources of supply will be needed as raw material requirements change.

In the early stages of technology change, product pricing will take advantage of the innovation and price will be high. However, if competitors enter the market with similar but lower-priced products, there will be some adaptation problems in the rigid marketing section. Customers may be reluctant to buy until there is more price stability.

Adaptive Subsystems. Major policy and strategy influence will come from those in the technological sectors. In this group, individual skill and ability will be important in assessing the environment. Research and development activities will be more extensive than applications engineering, thus placing more emphasis on advanced knowledge and skills than on pragmatic issues of design.

Market research activities will be fairly simple. They will most probably focus on existing, or easily collectible, data which have become fairly widely accepted indicators to be used in decision making.

Maintenance Subsystems. These subsystems face a paradoxical problem. Since they exert pressures for stability and predictability, the market sector will develop systematic marketing and distribution processes. This will result in "bureaucratic" marketing unit. For the organization's technological activities, however, a rigidly structured system may cause problems, since freedom to adjust and react to the changing environment requires that individual discretionary limits must be relatively broad.

For control and evaluation purposes, other problems exist for the maintenance subsystems. For example, because of the stable market it may be easy to develop a good, acceptable set of distribution cost estimates. This results in quantified, objective "cost" estimates against which actual costs can be compared. When "objective" data such as these are available, they become the basis for performance evaluations. A manager will therefore be able to measure marketing efficiency with some accuracy.

There is a different performance evaluation problem in the technological sector. At the volatile boundary, the individual has little control over what outside people and organizations do. In addition, since the determination of a need for change, the internal implementation of the change, and the resulting effects on organization performance may cover a long period of time, it is difficult to develop end result performance outcome criteria as we can for, say, marketing or production costs because individuals and/or groups must be evaluated before results can be known. Performance criteria here will be more subjective. Therefore, there will be two different types of criteria used in different parts of the organization. This may induce perceptions of inequity because members may feel that the other type of criteria is better than one against which they are assessed.

In personnel recruitment, emphasis will be on acquiring highly skilled and trained professionals for the technological sector. The level of organization commitment of this group will probably be lower than that of those in the more stable sections of the organization, since they will identify to some extent with their professional group. This identification with other professionals outside the company should be of value to the organization, however, since such contacts are a valuable source of ideas.

Managerial Subsystems. The authority structure of a TDM organization will be varied. For instance, in the marketing sector we would expect to find fairly well-defined job responsibilities, accountability to specific superiors for work, and limited discretion for decisions. On the other hand, in the technological sector, there will be more latitude of action. The production subsystem is likely to be caught in the middle, between pressures from research and engineering to adopt newer production methods and the marketing unit's desire to maintain the product relatively as is.

Market-dominated Mixed Organization

In the market-dominated mixed (MDM) form organization, major policy influence will be from the marketing unit because of the need to stay in close touch with a constantly changing, unpredictable environmental consumer or client group.

Production Subsystems. The type of environment confronting MDM organizations leads to programmed production tasks performed with a stable technology. Skill requirements for those in this system will be moderately low, and job security will probably result from union protection. The performance of the production system will be measured by relatively objective cost measures. There will be considerable pressure from the marketing segment to change the product to meet changing consumer preferences.

Adaptive Subsystems. The relatively placid condition of the technological external environment calls for little scientific research or development in the MDM organization. Technical functions will probably be of an applied nature.

In the marketing sector, there will be extensive market research devoted to uncovering new markets. More than likely, those performing this function will rely on clinical assessments of markets. Experience, intuition, and judgment will be more useful in determining what and where markets will be than research efforts using standard market information sets such as population data, income estimates, or traditional buying patterns.

Boundary-spanning Subsystems. In general, product changes of an MDM firm will be style or design changes, rather than changes in what the product will do. Therefore, in MD mixed organization the acquisition of inputs will only be a significant problem when they may directly change the character of the output, or if the market requires a product with different raw material requirements. That is, if the market requires a different type of raw material, then purchasing must seek new sources of supply. For instance, when a dress manufacturer finds that new materials are selling in the market and they must be used in manufacturing, the purchasing staff will have to seek out new sources of supply.

Product pricing will be controlled by the marketing subsystem, since it will need latitude and discretion in price setting to market effectively. The marketing staff can probably best be characterized as "promoters" rather than as sales managers.

Maintenance Subsystems. Primary organizational control problems will be found in the marketing segment of the firm. Consequently it is difficult to develop internal control approaches satisfactory to those who perform maintenance functions. The flexible and varied nature of the marketing and distribution system will make collection of historical and relevant cost data difficult, since distribution systems may be changing.

Some difficulties will occur as a result of the applied nature of the required technical activities. While engineers and scientists may have been socialized through an education which has taught them to value research activities, their jobs may focus on more applied problems. This can lead to disillusionment, dissatisfaction, and similar attendant problems. These problems may be especially acute because of the higher status of the marketing group in the organization.

Managerial Subsystems. A hierarchical authority structure will prevail in the technical sectors of the market-dominated firm. A more loose authority structure will exist in the marketing and distribution sectors, which will have more individual discretion and freedom in decision making. Control systems to monitor changes in and adapt to the environment will be developed in such a way as to be triggered by decisions made in the marketing sector. It is highly likely that the head of this type of mixed organization will be someone with marketing or sales background.

As in a technologically dominated firm, there will be problems in coordinating the stable and dynamic segments of the organization. The well-defined structure of the technical sector may not only pose adjustment problems for the professionals who work in it, but also may present difficulties when it is interrelated to the more flexible organization structure in the marketing sector.

ORGANIZATION TYPES AND INDIVIDUAL ORIENTATIONS

Thus far we have outlined concepts which focus on individuals and organizations. At this point we speculate about how these two sets of concepts are related to each other. This is an important and unique aspect of this formulation because it embeds theoretical ideas about individuals into an organization context.

Organization Socialization and the Psychological Contract

To a large degree, work orientations (professional, external, organizational) are shaped before a person begins a work career. Early socialization experiences are the bases for values, expectations, and beliefs about what one should do at work. These are, however, only one side of the issue. Organizations have expectations about what members should do, how a person should act relative to organization norms. This set of mutual expectations between an individual and the work organization is called the psychological contract.

The initial form of the psychological contract results from what a person knows about an organization before he or she joins it and the person's work orientation. The new member comes with a set of beliefs about working conditions, mode of supervision, and the type of work assignments. Those in the organization expect the new member to learn and comply with critical norms of attitude, behavior, and performance.

The psychological contract is continually and informally negotiated over time through organization socialization. A person may find a divergence between initial personal expectations and what is actually occurring. A period of adjustment and change takes place. As the organization's expectations become more clear, the individual's side of the contract may change. If there is a great divergence, the person may leave.

Personnel Structure of Hierarchical Organizations

In a hierarchical organization, the largest proportion of employees will be rank-and-file workers—blue collar in manufacturing, for instance, and white collar in, say, insurance companies or government agencies (see Figure 2). Most of this group can be characterized as having an external orientation. They tend, in general, not to be highly committed to work and/or the organization. They tend to seek psychological satisfactions outside the workplace. This is partly due to their narrow job definitions; that is, the tasks are not extremely challenging, and there is relatively little opportunity for advancement to positions where rewards are greater. One reason why promotion opportunities are limited is that there are fewer positions at the higher levels. Another is that often the requisites for promotions include advanced education, which the lower-level group is less likely to have.

The middle management and specialist groups in the hierarchical organization will also contain a large number of externals—in this case managers who have reached career plateaus and have little opportunity for advance-

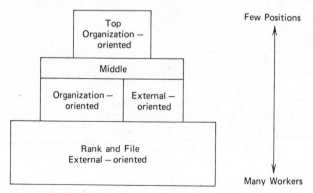

Figure 2 Orientations as a function of level in a hierarchical organization.

ment. They became increasingly committed to their life away from work rather than to the work of organization.

We can also expect, at the midlevels, to find a group of "organization-oriented" managers and specialists, people on the way up who seek the values and rewards of the system itself, high in achievement orientation and loyal to the organization.

At the highest level of the organization, we expect to find mostly organization-oriented types. This is so because it is likely that one of the major promotion criteria is organizational loyalty.

The Personnel Structure of Dynamic Organization

In the dynamic organization the mixture of organizational orientations will tend to be as shown in Figure 3. At the lowest level of the organization there will be a professionally oriented group of specialists, highly trained and skilled. The externalists will probably be a smaller group of operating personnel charged with carrying out routine tasks. They will be longer-term employees.

At the midlevels, the mixture of types changes. Two groups of roughly the same size will be found, one of organizationally oriented managers and one of professionally oriented managers. The organizationalists will be administrators who are making a managerial career. The professionally oriented group will be specialists who have been promoted to managerial positions because of their high competence, but who have retained their original value system.

The distribution of types changes again at the top level, which will have a preponderance of organizationalists. This occurs because selection decisions for higher managerial ranks are made by those already in high positions, and they are likely to place more value on the organization, as such, than on professional commitment. Technical skills are still important at this level, however, and some of the top management group will have a professional orientation.

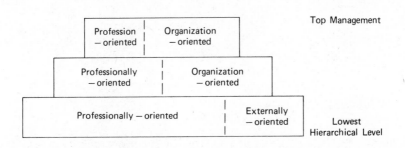

Figure 3 Representation of different orientations as a function of organization level in the dynamic organization.

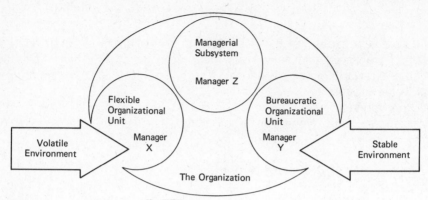

Figure 4 A representation of the organizational orientation case in the mixed organization.

The Personnel Structure of Mixed Organizations

Figure 4 represents the mixed organization. It shows two organizational units, one flexible and one bureaucratic. Manager X of the flexible unit will need to operate with a loose structure, make decisions under uncertainty, and often must manage highly trained personnel such as engineers, or marketing professionals. On the other hand, it is likely that manager Y of the bureaucratic unit will find that he or she is responsible for a highly routine systems with well-defined decision rules and policies. These differences between the organizational units may create problems for manager X and manager Y—and also for manager Z who must manage the interface between the units.

The factor determining the severity of this interface problem is the amount of interdependence between the units. In the mixed organization, it is likely that in some units the work flow requires that the two units must work closely together. Obviously the greater the interdependence, the higher the need for integration.

The staffing patterns of the mixed organization will be of a combination form. The bureaucratic segment will be staffed as is the bureaucratic organization (see Figure 2). The flexible segment will be staffed in a pattern such as the dynamic organization (see Figure 3). At the top levels of the mixed organization we expect that the key executives will come from the segment of the organization at the volatile boundary and that the mix of work orientations at that level will be as that in the dynamic organization.

MAJOR DECISION AREAS LINKING ENVIRONMENTS AND ORGANIZATIONS

Organizations become what they are because of the environment *and* choices made by the members. Two important decision areas which affect organization structure and effectiveness are choices about strategy and organization design.

Strategic choices are those which (1) seek to locate the organization with respect to the specific environment and (2) choose methods to operate within that environment. Consider first the issue of the choice of the environmental niche. Individuals (and groups) may select a particular site in the environment. For example, the market for women's clothes ranges from high fashion to traditional styles. A manufacturer may choose to operate in one or the other, or perhaps both. For all practical purposes, selecting one environmental sector over another minimizes adapting problems (i.e., variations in the sector not selected will have no direct effects in the focal firm).

Firms may also seek to affect the characteristics of the environment, (i.e., the degree of stability). Market environments may be made increasingly volatile through advertising or new product introduction. A firm may engage in extensive research efforts which, if successful, will increase the uncertainty of the technological environment in which it exists with similar firms. If an organization can shift the character of the environment in a direction to which the organization's capacity is presently directed, it stands to gain a competitive advantage.

The second strategic choice issue is the determination of proactive approaches to operate in the environment, the "tactics" for surviving in the environmental niche. Snow and Hrebiniak's study (1980) may be useful here. They examined the general relationships between strategy and organization performance in four industries in environments with widely different degrees of uncertainty. They classified managers as (1) defenders, (2) prospectors, (3) analyzers, and (4) reactors. Essentially they found that "different types of organization strategy . . . can occur contemporaneously in the same industrial environment, apparently reducing the effects of natural selection." They conclude from this research that the environment does not determine the type of strategies that can be used. This suggests that there is a wide range of alternatives that managers may use in dealing with the environment.

Organization design is the second choice area. Organization design is defined as the manner in which organization subsystems are differentiated and then integrated in departmental units. The formal design of an organization is restricted to those alternatives which are compatible with the organization systems. This means that general nature of the subsystem activities (i.e., production, boundary spanning, etc.) is driven by the specific environment, but the specific organization form is a managerial choice.

To illustrate with an example of automobile manufacturing we assume that, basically, technology and market considerations affect all manufacturers in similar ways. There are certain fundamental processes which must be performed to produce and distribute a car. Given these assumptions, *design* (or choice) now enters. These subsystems may be differentiated and integrated in different ways. Volvo has designed the subsystems so that they are somewhat flexible and susceptible to operation by work teams. Ford had designed similar subsystems into a functional organization. There is a separate production unit, marketing division, and finance department. General Motors recently designed the subsystems into a product organization form. The GM divisions were highly autonomous and virtually free-standing companies. Thus, an organization in a relatively stable environment may be designed as a product organization or as a functional organization. The choice depends on whether those making design decisions believe that profitability may be maximized by emphasizing customer service with a product organization or by increasing internal efficiencies with a functional organization (Filley, 1978).

SOME EFFECTIVENESS PROPOSITIONS

Accepting the foregoing arguments, it is possible to state a set of propositions about organization effectiveness. For sake of brevity, and for illustrative purposes, only propositions about leadership, motivation and performance, personnel selection, and decision strategies are stated. Other propositions derived from the model are stated in more detail elsewhere (Tosi and Hamner, 1982; Tosi and Carroll, 1982; Carroll and Tosi, 1977).

Leadership

Leadership propositions are based on the path-goal model (House, 1971) and Fiedler's contingency theory of leadership (1976).

Proposition 1. Effective hierarchical organizations will be dominated by consideration styles of leadership. These styles are those in which leaders show concern for workers. Managers create a climate of psychological support, warmth, helpfulness and show concern for and trust others.

Proposition 2. Effective dynamic organizations will be dominated by structuring styles of leadership. This is behavior in which the leader directs tasks, assigns responsibilities, and specifies deadlines. Structuring behavior will be seen by members as being goal-directed behavior.

Proposition 3. In effective mixed organizations, effective leadership styles will be varied. In the flexible segment, structuring behavior is the dominant form. In the hierarchical segment, consideration behavior by leaders will dominate. Those leaders who manage the interface between dynamic and bureaucratic units will primarily engage in conflict-resolution forms of activity.

Motivation and Performance

Based on the premise that performance is a function of motivation and ability ($P = M \times A$), the following propositions are offered.

Proposition 4. Organization effectiveness can be improved in hierarchical organizations through the use of job design approaches. In some instances, jobs may be expanded in order to provide task enrichment. In other cases, work may be engineered so that it is more efficiently performed.

Proposition 5. Organization effectiveness is most likely to be improved in dynamic organizations by strategies which increase individual's skills and ability. This may take the form of training and educational programs, or it may be brought about by terminating some present staff and acquiring new, better personnel.

Selecton of Personnel

Assuming that for hierarchical organizations there is a relatively large labor pool from which individuals will be selected to perform relatively narrow tasks, the following proposition is offered.

Proposition 6. Statistical selection procedures will increase organization effectiveness when used to select personnel in the production subsystems of hierarchical organizations.

A different set of assumptions is warranted for the labor pool of flexible organizations: (1) individuals must possess a wide range of professional skills and (2) the labor pool will be small.

Proposition 7. Clinical selection procedures will increase organization effectiveness when used to select personnel in the production subsystems of dynamic organizations.

Decision Making

The nature of the organization's environment is the primary determinant of the form of decision making in organizations. Volatile environments are highly uncertain and stable environments can be characterized as being high in certainty. Therefore the following proposition is offered.

Proposition 8. In dynamic organizations the decision strategies under uncertainty will be the most dominant approach. In hierarchical organizations, decision approaches under conditions of certainty and risk will be most predominant.

SUMMARY

This model of organization is based on the assumption that achieving congruency between individuals, organization, and the environment will increase effectiveness. Four types of organization structure were described. Individual orientation to organizations are also integral elements of the model. Based on these premises, a limited set of effectiveness propositions were stated.

REFERENCES

Carroll, Stephen, and Tosi, Henry, *Organizational Behavior* (Chicago, Ill.: St. Clair Press, 1977).

Fiedler, Fred, *A Contingency Theory of Leadership* (New York: McGraw-Hill, 1976).

Filley, Alan C, *The Compleat Manager* (Champaign, Ill.: Research Press, 1978).

Katz, Daniel, and Kahn, Robert, *The Social Psychology of Organizations* (New York: Wiley, 1978).

House, Robert J., "A Path Goal Theory of Leadership Effectiveness," *Administrative Science Quarterly,* 16 (September 1971), 213–230.

Presthus, Robert, *The Organizational Society* (New York: St. Martins Press, 1978).

Snow, Charles, and Hrebiniak, Lawrence, "Strategy, Distinctive Competence and Organizational Performance," *Administrative Science Quarterly,* 25 (June 1980), 317–336.

Thompson, James, *Organizations in Action* (New York: McGraw-Hill, 1967).

Tosi, Henry, and Hamner, W. Clay, *Organizational Behavior and Management: A Contingency Approach* (New York: Wiley, 1982).

Tosi, Henry, and Carroll, Stephen, *Management* (New York: Wiley, 1982).

REFERENCES

1. Argyris, C., *Integrating the Individual and the Organization* (New York: Wiley, 1964).
2. Barnard, Chester I., *The Functions of the Executive* (Cambridge, Mass.: Harvard University Press, 1938).
3. Bennis, W., *Changing Organizations* (New York: McGraw-Hill, 1966).
4. Blau, P.M., Hydebrand, W.V., and Stauffer, R.E., "The Structure of Small Bureaucracies," *American Sociological Review,* 31 (1966), 179–191.
5. Burns, T., and Stalker, G.M., *The Management of Innovation* (London: Tavistock, 1961).
6. Cohen, M.D., March, J.G., and Olsen, J.P., "A Garbage Can Model of Organizational Choice," *Administrative Science Quarterly,* 17 (March 1972), 1–25.
7. Crozier, M., *The Bureaucratic Phenomenon* (Chicago: University of Chicago Press, 1964).
8. Cummings, L.L., "Towards Organizational Behavior," *The Academy of Management Review,* January 1978, Vol. 3, No. 1, 90–98.
9. Cyert, R., and March, J., *A Behavioral Theory of the Firm* (Englewood Cliffs, N.J.: Prentice-Hall, 1963).
10. Davis, Ralph, *The Fundamentals of Top Management* (New York: Harper Brothers Publishers, 1951).
11. Dill, William, R., "Desegregation of Integration? Comments About Contemporary Research on Organizations," in Cooper, W.W. et al. (eds.), *New Perspectives in Organization Research* (New York: Wiley, 1964).
12. Dubin, R. "Theory Building in Applied Areas" in M.D. Dunnette (ed.), *Handbook of Industrial and Organizational Psychology* (Chicago; Rand McNally, 1976).
13. Etzioni, Amitai, *A Comparative Analysis of Complex Organizations* (New York: Free Press, 1961).
14. Filley, A.C., *The Compleat Manager: What Works When* (Champaign, Ill.: Research Press, 1978).
15. Gouldner, A.W., *Patterns of Industrial Bureaucracy* (New York: The Free Press, 1954).
16. Hedberg, B.L., Nystrom, P.C., and Starbuck, W.H., "Camping On Seesaws: Prescriptions For A Self Designing Organization," *Administrative Science Quarterly,* 21 (March, 1976), 41–65.

17. Katz, D., and Kahn, R.L., *The Social Psychology of Organizations* (New York: Wiley, 1978).

18. Kaufman, H., *The Forest Ranger: A Study in Administrative Behavior* (Baltimore: The Johns Hopkins Press, 1960).

19. Krupp, Sherman, *Pattern in Organization Analysis: A Critical Examination* (New York: Holt, Rinehart and Winston, 1961).

20. Lawrence, P.R., and Lorsch, J.W., *Organization and Environment* (Cambridge, Mass.: Harvard Univ. Press, 1967).

21. Likert, R., *New Patterns of Management* (New York: McGraw-Hill, 1961).

22. Likert, R., *The Human Organization* (New York: McGraw-Hill, 1967).

23. March, J., and Simon, H., *Organizations* (New York: Wiley, 1958).

24. McGregor, D., *The Professional Manager* (New York: McGraw-Hill, 1967).

25. McGuire, J., *Theories of Business Behavior* (New York: Prentice-Hall, 1964).

26. Mintzberg, Henry, *The Structuring of Organizations* (Englewood Cliffs, N.J.: Prentice-Hall, 1979).

27. Perrow, C., "A Framework for the Comparative Analysis of Organizations," *American Sociological Review,* 32 (1967), 194–208.

28. Perrow, C., "Technology and Organizational Structure," *Proceedings of the Nineteenth Annual Meeting of the Industrial Relations Research Association* (Madison, Wis.: 1967), 157–163.

29. Perrow, C., "Technology and Structural Changes in Business Firms," in Roberts, B.C. (ed.), *Industrial Relations: Contemporary Issues* (New York: Macmillan, 1968).

30. Perrow, C., *Organizational Analysis: A Sociological Overview* (Belmont, Calif.: Wadsworth Publishing, 1970).

31. Presthus, R., *The Organizational Society* (New York: St. Martins Press, 1978).

32. Reynolds, P.D., *A Primer in Theory Construction* (New York: Bobbs Merrill, 1971).

33. Rigby, Paul H., *Conceptual Foundations of Business Research* (New York: John Wiley & Sons, 1965).

34. Rubenstein, Albert H., and Haberstroh, Chadwick, Jr. (eds.), *Some Theories of Organization* (Homewood, Ill.: R.D. Irwin and the Dorsey Press, 1966).

35. Rudner, Richard S., *Philosophy of Social Science* (Englewood Cliffs, N.J.: Prentice-Hall, 1966).

36. Schumpeter, J., *Capitalism, Socialism and Democracy* (New York: Harper, 1942).

37. Scott, William, "Organization Theory: An Overview of Appraisal" *Journal of the Academy of Management,* vol. 4, no. 1, (April 1961), 7–26.

38. Selznick, P., *Leadership in Administration* (New York: Harper, 1957).

39. Selznick, P., *TVA and the Grass Roots* (Berkeley, Calif.: University of Calif. Press, 1949).

40. Snow, C., and Hrebiniak, L., "Strategy, Distinctive Competence and Organizational Performance," *Administrative Science Quarterly,* 25 (June, 1980), 317–336.
41. Stogdill, Ralph M., "Dimensions of Organization Theory" in Thompson, James D., *Approaches to Organizational Design* (Pittsburgh, Pa.: University of Pittsburgh Press, 1966).
42. Stogdill, Ralph M., *Individual Behavior and Group Achievement* (New York: Oxford University Press, 1959).
43. Thompson, James D., *Organizations in Action* (New York: McGraw-Hill, 1967).
44. Thompson, Victor, *Modern Organizations* (New York: Knopf, 1961).
45. Thompson, Victor, "Bureaucracy and Innovation," *Administration Science Quarterly,* 10 (1965), 1–20.
46. Tosi, Henry L., and Carroll, Stephen J., *Management: Contingencies, Structure and Process* (Chicago, Ill.: St. Clair Press, 1975).
47. Weber, M., *The Theory of Social and Economic Organization,* trans. by T. Parsons (New York: The Free Press, 1947).
48. Williamson, Oliver E., *Markets and Hierarchies: Analysis and Antitrust Implications* (New York: Free Press, 1975).
49. Williamson, Oliver E., and Ouchi, William, "The Markets and Hierarchies and Visible Hand Perspectives" in Van de Ven, Andrew, and Joyce, William, (eds.), *Perspectives on Organization Design and Behavior* (New York: Wiley, 1981).
50. Woodward, J., *Industrial Organization: Theory and Practice* (London: Oxford University Press, 1965).

REGENTS ENGLISH WORKBOOK

Intermediate

ROBERT J. DIXSON

2

PRENTICE HALL REGENTS, Englewood Cliffs, NJ 07632

Cover and text design: Finley/Wall Associates

Copyright © 1986 by R.J. Dixson Associates

ISBN 0-13-770934-X 01

Published by Prentice-Hall, Inc.
A Division of Simon & Schuster
Englewood Cliffs, New Jersey 07632

Printed in the United States of America

10 9 8 7

To the Teacher

There is no need here to describe the different types of exercises which this book contains or to discuss their wide variety and extent. A glance through the following pages is enough to acquaint anyone with the book's general contents.

Since this is a workbook, there is also little to say as to how it should be used. Each exercise carries its own instructions, and the students proceed accordingly. On the other hand, there are a few points of general pedagogy which the teacher using the book should keep in mind.

First, this is a workbook, and all explanatory material has been kept to a minimum. Thus, the book is not designed to be used alone or to replace completely the regular classroom text. Rather, this book should be used to supplement the regular classroom text, to give needed variety to the lesson, or to provide additional drill materials on important points of grammar and usage.

Second, as a teacher using this book, don't assume that after students have written the answers to an exercise correctly, they know the material thoroughly and can use the principle in their everyday speech. The exercise is often only the beginning. Much drill and practice are still necessary. Therefore, ask questions or introduce simple conversation involving the particular grammar principle. Also, don't hesitate to repeat the exercises in the book several times. Run over these exercises orally in class. If the students have already written the answers in their books, they can cover these answers with their hand or with a separate sheet of paper. Continue to review past exercises which seem important to you or which have given the students difficulty.

Third, don't fall into the further error of assuming that some of the exercises in this book are too easy for your particular students. Certain exercises may seem easy to you—especially if you speak English as a native—but they still represent a real challenge to anyone studying English as a foreign language. In this connection, there is one additional point of utmost importance which should be kept in mind. We are not interested in these exercises in tricking or even in *testing* the student. The exercises are not designed to find out how much a student knows or does not know. Their purpose is simply to drill the student on certain basic points of grammar and usage. The exercises are practice exercises—nothing more. They provide just another means of having students repeat materials which can be learned only through continuous use. For this reason, a good deal of direct repetition has been purposely introduced, not only in individual exercises but throughout the book.

There are three workbooks in the series. Book 1 is for the beginning student; Book 2 is for the intermediate student; Book 3 is for the advanced student. As regards the exact division of material, this plan was followed:

The exercises in Book 1 more or less parallel the development by lesson of the material in *Beginning Lessons in English* A and B. Similarly, Book 2 follows the general development of the lessons in *Second Book in English*. Book 3 reviews the material in Books 1 and 2 and focuses on special problems on the advanced level. All the books mentioned are published by Regents Publishing Company.

Regents English Workbooks are readily adaptable to many uses and can serve effectively to supplement any standard classroom textbook. A perforated answer key at the back of the book makes classroom use or self-study equally feasible.

R.J.D.

iv

Contents

1 Review:
possessive adjectives

my	our
your	your
his	their
her	
its	

I like *my* new car.   We bought *our* house last year.
She has *her* appointment today.   They drank *their* coffee quickly.

Write the correct possessive pronoun in the blanks.

1. Sylvia usually goes to school with _____ sister.   *her*

2. Frank likes _____ English class very much.   *his*

3. We spent two hours on _____ homework last night.   *our*

4. Richard and Nick always do _____ homework to-gether.   *their*

5. Mrs. Teng loves _____ children very much.   *his*

6. The dog did not eat _____ dinner.   *his*

7. _____ first name is Anne.   *her*

8. Do you always do _____ homework in the li-brary?   *your*

9. I enjoy _____ English class very much.   *my*

10. Teresa and _____ brother study in the same class.   *my*

11. We all think a great deal of _____ English teacher.   *our*

12. Mr. Lee left _____ pen on the desk.   *his*

13. Yesterday I left _____ notebook on the bus.   *my*

14. Most parents love _____ children.   *their*

15. Both boys have on _____ new suits.   *they*

16. Marianne is wearing _____ new hat today.   *her*

17. The cat pays little attention to _____ (kittens.)   *his*

18. Do you always bring _____ lunch to school?   *your*

19. Miss Wong left yesterday on _____ vacation.   *her*

20. Juan writes a letter to _____ grandparents every week.   *his*

21. He asked me to help him with _____ shopping.   *his*

1

2 **Review:** object pronouns

I	me	we	us
you	you	you	you
he	him	they	them
she	her		
it	it		

We use object pronouns as direct objects, indirect objects, and objects of prepositions.

I saw *them* in London.
Roger gave *me* his phone number.
Susan bought the record for *him*.

Change the words in italics to the correct object pronouns.

1. I met *Suzanne* on the street yesterday. _____her_____

2. She saw *Noriko and me* in the park. _____us_____

3. She left *her keys* in the car. _____you_____

4. I told *the boys* about it. _____them_____

5. I saw *you and your brother* at the movies last night. _____

6. He rode *his bicycle* to school this morning. _____you_____

7. She told *her parents* about the accident. _____you_____

8. I have *my book* with me. _____

9. We see *those girls* in the park every afternoon. _____

10. I liked *that movie* very much. _____

11. He sent *Nina* some flowers. _____

12. I wrote *your telephone number* in my notebook. _____

13. I eat lunch with *Henry and Charles* every day. _____

14. Put *the cat* outside. _____

15. I don't like to have *animals* in the house. _____

16. I heard *the president* on the radio last night. _____

17. You can go with *Marcia and me* to the party. _____

18. I gave the money to *the maid*. _____

19. Are you going to the movies with *Ali*? _____

20. He put *the money* in the bank. _____

21. She told *her friends* about it. _____

3　Review: reflexive pronouns

myself	ourselves
yourself	yourselves
himself	themselves
herself	
itself	

Reflexive pronouns refer back to the subject of the sentence when the subject and the object are the same person.

Henry hurt *himself* in the game.

Reflexive pronouns emphasize a person or a thing in the sentence.

Lisa *herself* thought of the idea.

We often use the preposition *by* and a reflexive pronoun to give the meaning of "alone" or "without help."

He prefers to do his homework *by himself*. She went to Europe *by herself*.

Write the correct reflexive pronoun in the blanks.

1. Jackie fell and hurt _____ .　　*herself*
2. I want to buy _____ a new hat.　　*myself*
3. Mr. Oguri _____ will give the principal speech.　　*himself*
4. We _____ will serve the meal.　　*ourselves*
5. They all enjoyed _____ very much at the party.　　*themselves*
6. I also enjoyed _____ very much.　　*myself*
7. The dog hurt _____ when it jumped over the fence.　　*himself*
8. Monique cut _____ with the knife.　　*herself*
9. We need to look at _____ in the mirror.　　*ourselves*
10. Most children like to look at _____ in the mirror.　　*themselves*
11. The president _____ will speak to the members of Congress.　　*himself*
12. I _____ will return the book to you.　　*myself*
13. Carlos _____ saw the accident.　　*himself*
14. Mr. Roth arranged the flowers _____ .　　*himself*
15. Did you ever cut _____ badly with a knife?　　*yourselves*
16. He considers _____ too good for the job.　　*himself*
17. I don't like to go to the movies by _____ .　　*myself*

3

4 **Review:** possessive pronouns

mine	ours
yours	yours
his	theirs
hers	
its	

Possessive pronouns are used to avoid repeating the same words in a sentence.

That glass is *my glass*.   That glass is *mine*.
This money is *our money*.   This money is *ours*.

Write the correct possessive pronouns in the blanks.

1. This coat is *her coat*.   <u>hers</u>
2. That car is *their car*.   _____
3. This pack of cigarettes is *my pack of cigarettes*.   _____
4. That umbrella is *his umbrella*.   _____
5. That dog in the yard is *our dog*.   _____
6. This desk is *his desk*.   _____
7. Those books are *your books*.   _____
8. This pencil is also *your pencil*.   _____
9. Is this magazine *her magazine*?   _____
10. Your English book is the same as *my English book*.   _____
11. Those books are *Hector and Mario's books*.   _____
12. These books are *my books and your books*.   _____
13. Both these cars are *my cars*.   _____
14. This seat is mine, and the other one is *your seat*.   _____
15. Whose pen is this? Is it *your pen*?   _____
16. It is *Angela's pen*.   _____
17. I study in my room, and Michel studies in *his room*.   _____
18. I think this notebook is *your notebook*.   _____
19. These pencils are *their pencils*.   _____
20. I found my hat, but Tomiko couldn't find *her hat*.   _____
21. Felipe left *his hat* on the bus.   _____

(5) **Review:** plural of nouns 1

Most English nouns form the plural by adding *s* to the singular form.

books   friends   days

Nouns ending in *s, sh, ch, x,* or *z* add *es* to form the plural.

church–churches   kiss–kisses   wish–wishes

Some nouns have irregular plurals.

man–men   foot–feet   mouse–mice   ox–oxen
child–children   tooth–teeth   goose–geese   woman–women

Write the plural form of the following words.

1. lunch ___lunches___
2. tie _____
3. class _____
4. teacher _____
5. beach _____
6. window _____
7. door _____
8. dress _____
9. watch _____
10. book _____
11. ox _____
12. pencil _____
13. cafeteria _____
14. student _____
15. wish _____
16. headache _____
17. box _____
18. school _____
19. child _____
20. tail _____
21. woman _____
22. brother _____

23. notebook _____
24. hand _____
25. mouse _____
26. hat _____
27. goose _____
28. loss _____
29. car _____
30. cover _____
31. bus _____
32. foot _____
33. dish _____
34. man _____
35. kiss _____
36. face _____
37. church _____
38. cousin _____
39. pen _____
40. sister _____
41. match _____
42. coat _____
43. cat _____
44. nose _____

6 **Review:** plural of nouns 2

Nouns ending in *y* form their plural in two ways:

a. **If a vowel precedes the *y*, add *s*.**

key–keys   toy–toys

b. **If a consonant precedes the *y*, change the *y* to *i* and add *es*.**

lady–ladies   city–cities

Nouns ending in *f* or *fe* usually form their plural by changing the endings to *ves*.

wife–wives   leaf–leaves   calf–calves

Nouns ending in *o*, where *o* is preceded by a consonant, form their plurals by adding *es*.

hero–heroes   mosquito–mosquitoes

Write the plural form of the following words.

1. tomato _tomatoes_
2. dish _____
3. child _____
4. city _____
5. book _____
6. knife _____
7. box _____
8. potato _____
9. class _____
10. bus _____
11. street _____
12. exercise _____
13. wish _____
14. copy _____
15. pen _____
16. key _____
17. church _____
18. hero _____

19. woman _____
20. army _____
21. half _____
22. brother _____
23. leaf _____
24. dress _____
25. sister _____
26. match _____
27. letter _____
28. hat _____
29. man _____
30. lunch _____
31. foot _____
32. pillow _____
33. company _____
34. lady _____
35. mouse _____
36. wife _____

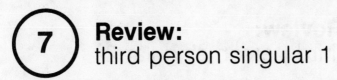

7 Review:
third person singular 1

Verbs in the third person singular, present tense, follow the general spelling rules for plural nouns.

Most verbs add *s*.

he works   she drives

If a verb ends in *y* preceded by a consonant, change *y* to *i* and add *es*.

study–he studies   carry–she carries

When a verb ends in *o*, we generally add *es*.

go–he goes   do–she does

Verbs ending in *s*, *sh*, *ch*, *x*, or *z* take *es* endings in the third person singular.

wish–he wishes   catch–she catches

Change the verb to the third person singular, present tense.

1. study _studies_
2. like _____
3. play _____
4. go _____
5. carry _____
6. teach _____
7. show _____
8. do _____
9. watch _____
10. try _____
11. speak _____
12. notice _____
13. say _____
14. pass _____
15. wash _____
16. catch _____
17. bring _____
18. leave _____
19. sit _____

20. know _____
21. think _____
22. see _____
23. laugh _____
24. match _____
25. dance _____
26. cry _____
27. pay _____
28. sing _____
29. wish _____
30. push _____
31. pull _____
32. dress _____
33. miss _____
34. use _____
35. pass _____
36. cash _____
37. fix _____
38. reply _____

8 Review:
third person singular 2

The auxiliary verbs *can*, *may*, *must*, *should*, *ought*, **and** *will* **do not change spelling in any of the three persons, singular and plural.**

I *can* go.   You *should* stay.   They *must* leave.

Change to the third person singular by changing *I* **to** *she*. **Write your answers in the blanks at the right.**

1. I know   She knows
2. I can speak   She can speak
3. I must go   _____
4. I am   _____
5. I have   _____
6. I will see   _____
7. I may study   _____
8. I have seen   _____
9. I am studying   _____
10. I will be   _____
11. I can go   _____
12. I should study   _____
13. I play   _____
14. I carry   _____
15. I go   _____
16. I ought to go   _____
17. I can wait   _____
18. I wait   _____
19. I am waiting   _____
20. I will wait   _____
21. I have waited   _____

22. I like   _____
23. I must see   _____
24. I have been   _____
25. I will take   _____
26. I am working   _____
27. I may work   _____
28. I work   _____
29. I want   _____
30. I do   _____
31. I wish   _____
32. I can meet   _____
33. I try   _____
34. I am leaving   _____
35. I use   _____
36. I wash   _____
37. I am going   _____
38. I will know   _____
39. I must try   _____
40. I have tried   _____
41. I will try   _____
42. I ought to see   _____

9 Review: simple present tense

Write the correct form of the simple present tense of the verbs in parentheses.

1. Yuriko (like) to study English.   _____likes_____
2. Pauline (have) many friends in this school. _____
3. We (study) in the same class. _____
4. Kenji also (study) in our class. _____
5. He and I (be) good friends. _____
6. Both of our English teachers (be) North Americans. _____
7. They (explain) things very clearly. _____
8. There (be) many students absent today. _____
9. I (watch) television every night. _____
10. My father (listen) to music every night. _____
11. The children (play) in the park every afternoon. _____
12. There (be) someone at the door. _____
13. Juanita (live) on Church Street. _____
14. Alma (go) to the movies almost every night. _____
15. We always (come) to school by bus. _____
16. Peter (do) his homework very carefully. _____
17. He never (make) mistakes in spelling. _____
18. You (be) older than I. _____
19. We both (want) to learn English well. _____
20. They (have) work to do today. _____
21. Nadia (have) two cars. _____
22. She (be) a very rich woman. _____
23. She generally (go) to the United States by plane. _____
24. She sometimes (stay) there for a whole month. _____

Review:
subject-verb agreement

Change the italicized words to the plural form. Make the corresponding changes in the verbs. Write only the subject and the verb in your answers.

1. The *book* is on the table.   The books are
2. *This* is mine.   _____
3. *I* am busy today.   _____
4. *She* likes to study English.   _____
5. *That book* belongs to William.   _____
6. *He* was afraid of the dog.   _____
7. The *boy* does the work well.   _____
8. *He* is writing the exercises.   _____
9. The *child* is afraid of the dog.   _____
10. *This pencil* belongs to Mary.   _____
11. The *tomato* is ripe.   _____
12. The *dish* is on the table.   _____
13. The *class* has started.   _____
14. The *woman* is waiting outside.   _____
15. *This book* is yours.   _____
16. *I* am going to study French.   _____
17. *She* is making good progress.   _____
18. The *bus* is late today.   _____
19. The *man* has left.   _____
20. *He* will leave soon.   _____
21. *She* can speak English well.   _____
22. The *boy* must study more.   _____
23. *She* was here yesterday.   _____
24. The *leaf* is falling from the tree.   _____

Vocabulary review:
opposites 1

Write the opposites of the following words.

1. young	old	25. clean	
2. high		26. absent	
3. arrive		27. beautiful	
4. inside		28. happy	
5. wild		29. easy	
6. awake		30. narrow	
7. brave		31. lose	
8. hard		32. low	
9. sharp		33. under	
10. smooth		34. east	
11. borrow		35. north	
12. forward		36. late	
13. polite		37. buy	
14. thick		38. tall	
15. before		39. often	
16. in front of		40. sweet	
17. expensive		41. cause	
18. dry		42. good	
19. false		43. summer	
20. child		44. big	
21. empty		45. find	
22. push		46. remember	
23. wide		47. future	
24. loose		48. best	

Write the correct prepositions in the blanks.

1. I explained the matter _____ her very clearly.   _____to_____

2. What is the matter _____ him?   _____

3. She seems to be _____ a big hurry.   _____

4. We went there _____ mistake.   _____

5. What has happened _____ Ted?   _____

6. This is an exception _____ the rule.   _____

7. He was absent _____ class twice last week.   _____

8. She should be ashamed _____ such poor work.   _____

9. This river is one of the longest _____ the world.   _____

10. They plan to take a trip _____ the world.   _____

11. He says that he'll be back _____ a few minutes.   _____

12. The police officer looked _____ me suspiciously.   _____

13. Angela is looking _____ the book that she lost.   _____

14. How many new words do you look up _____ your dictionary every day?   _____

15. They may stay in Europe _____ several months.   _____

16. I plan to go to San Francisco _____ plane.   _____

17. He arrived _____ school twenty minutes late.   _____

18. I do not know the first thing _____ mathematics.   _____

19. She copied her speech word _____ word from the encyclopedia.   _____

20. Be sure to write your exercises _____ ink.   _____

21. His face is familiar _____ me.   _____

22. Don't mention anything about it _____ him.   _____

23. Let's sit here on this bench _____ a while.   _____

24. She paid _____ credit card.   _____

Select the correct answer and write it in the space provided.

1. The opposite of *generous* is (kind, angry, recent, selfish). _____selfish_____

2. A synonym for *recently* is (seldom, never, lately, ultimately). _____

3. We pronounce the word *half* to rhyme with (hall, have, laugh, rough). _____

4. We pronounce the word *sew* to rhyme with (flew, know, cow, blue). _____

5. To *call up* someone is to (criticize, visit, stare at, telephone) him or her. _____

6. To *call on* someone is to (telephone, visit, admire, talk about) him or her. _____

7. To be *about to do* something is to be (interested in doing, at the point of doing, eager to do) it. _____

8. Which of these past tense forms do we pronounce as a word of only one syllable: counted, painted, talked, needed? _____

9. Which letter in the word *wrist* is silent (not pronounced)? _____

10. Which letter in the word *honest* is silent (not pronounced)? _____

11. Which of these words is not spelled correctly: February, excelent, translation, suggestion, convenient? _____

12. What is the corresponding noun form of the adjective *difficult*? _____

13. What is the corresponding noun form of the verb *explain*? _____

14. We pronounce the contraction *she's* to rhyme with (kiss, piece, sneeze, cries). _____

15. The word *possibility* has five syllables. On which syllable do we accent the word—the first, second, third, or fourth syllable? _____

16. If I say that I will be back *by* eight o'clock, this means that I will be back (exactly at eight, about eight, at eight at the latest). _____

13

General review 1

Select the correct form. Write your answers in the blanks.

1. The weather today is warmer (than, as) it was yester-
   day.   _____than_____

2. Listen! The water (is running, runs).   _____

3. They (have lived, lived) there since January.   _____

4. We (was, were) both absent from class yesterday.   _____

5. My friend sent (me, to me) a present from Singapore.   _____

6. They (have, are having) their lunch now.   _____

7. There were (many, much) students absent from class
   this morning.   _____

8. She does not speak English well, (also, either).   _____

9. I didn't hear (someone, anyone) in the room.   _____

10. He (works, has worked) in that company for many years.   _____

11. He always (is coming, comes) to school by bus.   _____

12. I spoke to him (on, by) the telephone yesterday.   _____

13. What time did you (get, got) up this morning?   _____

14. I (wrote, have written) a letter to him yesterday.   _____

15. Rose always (does, makes) many mistakes in spelling.   _____

16. Anne wants (me to go, that I go) with her to the movies
    tonight.   _____

17. It is not difficult (learn, to learn) English.   _____

18. I don't know where (does he live, he lives).   _____

19. (This, These) pencils belong to Giorgio.   _____

20. He is (a, an) honest man.   _____

21. Sue (has, have) many friends in this school.   _____

22. How many students (is there, are there) in your English
    class?   _____

14

Review:
regular verbs, past tense

The past tense of regular verbs is formed by adding *ed* to their singular form.

work–worked   play–played

If the verb ends in *e*, only *d* is added.

change–changed   close–closed

If the verb ends in *y*, preceded by a consonant, change the *y* to *i* and add *ed*.

study–studied   marry–married

If a single final consonant follows a single stressed vowel, double the final consonant before adding *ed*.

plan–planned   admit–admitted

Write the past tense form of each of these regular verbs in the blanks at the right.

1. describe __described__
2. force _____
3. study _____
4. indicate _____
5. need _____
6. learn _____
7. practice _____
8. use _____
9. marry _____
10. manage _____
11. carry _____
12. play _____
13. guide _____
14. plan _____
15. hope _____
16. cry _____
17. seem _____

18. enjoy _____
19. appear _____
20. help _____
21. travel _____
22. please _____
23. spell _____
24. face _____
25. worry _____
26. depend _____
27. decrease _____
28. remain _____
29. point _____
30. suppose _____
31. refer _____
32. insist _____
33. notice _____
34. admit _____

(16) Pronunciation of the past tense

In regular verbs ending in *t* or *d*, the *ed* is pronounced as a separate syllable.

count–count(ed)   wait–wait(ed)   land–land(ed)

When we add *ed* to regular verbs of one syllable not ending in *t* or *d*, they are pronounced as one syllable.

live-lived   close–closed   cross–crossed

Pronounce the following past tense forms. Then write the number 1 or 2 to show whether the word is pronounced as a word of one syllable or as a word of two syllables.

1. ended ____2____
2. watched ____1____
3. counted _____
4. stayed _____
5. needed _____
6. called _____
7. seemed _____
8. planned _____
9. waited _____
10. washed _____
11. wanted _____
12. walked _____
13. pushed _____
14. spelled _____
15. planted _____
16. cleaned _____
17. asked _____
18. pointed _____
19. moved _____
20. shopped _____

21. rushed _____
22. parted _____
23. cooked _____
24. rented _____
25. lived _____
26. shared _____
27. lasted _____
28. closed _____
29. helped _____
30. landed _____
31. used _____
32. hoped _____
33. handed _____
34. crossed _____
35. signed _____
36. earned _____
37. painted _____
38. dropped _____
39. burned _____
40. laughed _____

17 Review: irregular verbs, past tense 1

Review the forms of the irregular verbs below. Remember that the past tense form is the same as the past participle form for these verbs.

bring	brought	feel	felt	mean	meant
buy	bought	keep	kept	sleep	slept
catch	caught	kneel	knelt	sweep	swept
creep	crept	leave	left	teach	taught
deal	dealt	lose	lost	think	thought

Write the past tense form of the verbs in parentheses. Practice reading these sentences in the past tense.

1. I (sleep) more than ten hours last night. _____slept_____

2. He (buy) that car last year. _____

3. Rob (lose) a hundred dollars at the races yesterday. _____

4. It was after ten o'clock when she (leave). _____

5. I didn't understand what he (mean). _____

6. The police (catch) the thief last night after a long search. _____

7. Sandra (bring) her little brother to class yesterday. _____

8. They (sweep) each of the rooms carefully. _____

9. The president's speech (deal) with the subject of taxes. _____

10. Mike (teach) us English last semester. _____

11. I (think) I could not come to the lesson today. _____

12. When Annette won the prize, her family naturally (feel) very proud of her. _____

13. The dog put his tail between his legs and (creep) out of the room. _____

14. The teacher asked them to stop, but the two boys (keep) on talking. _____

15. The little girl (kneel) beside her mother and prayed. _____

16. Where did you leave your notebook? I (leave) it on the bus. _____

17. I (mean) to call you yesterday, but I forgot. _____

18. Although we did not arrive home until late, the cook (keep) the dinner hot for us. _____

19. Where did you buy your new hat? I (buy) it in London. _____

20. I (feel) very weak all day yesterday. _____

17

18 Review: Irregular verbs, past tense 2

Review the forms of the irregular verbs below. Remember that the past tense form is the same as the past participle form. The verbs below form the past tense by changing the vowel sound.

dig	dug	hold	held	shoot	shot
feed	fed	lead	led	sit	sat
fight	fought	meet	met	stand	stood
find	found	read	read	strike	struck
hang	hung	shine	shone	win	won

Hang has another past tense form, *hanged*, used only in reference to death by hanging. *Shine* also has another past tense form, *shined*. Thus, "The sun *shone*," but "John *shined* his shoes."

Write the past tense form of the verbs in parentheses. Practice reading these sentences in the past tense.

1. Our team (win) both games last week. _____won_____

2. I (find) this book on the bus yesterday. _____

3. I (meet) him several years ago in Washington. _____

4. Last year the the Republican Party (hold) its convention in Chicago. _____

5. We (sit) in the first row at the theater last evening. _____

6. The lightning (strike) two houses in our block last week. _____

7. Where did you read about the accident? I (read) about it in yesterday's newspaper. _____

8. The police worked on the case for several months before they finally (find) the thief. _____

9. The guide (lead) us down one long hall after another. _____

10. Dick (hang) up his hat and coat as soon as he came in. _____

11. Our troops (fight) well, but the enemy was too strong. _____

12. Where did you hold the meeting? We (hold) it in the school auditorium. _____

13. What did the dog dig up? He (dig) up two old bones. _____

14. The sun (shine) all day yesterday. _____

15. They (feed) the prisoners only bread and water. _____

16. We (stand) in line an hour to buy tickets for the show. _____

(19) Review: negative form 1

The negative of *to be*, **in both present and past tenses, is formed by placing** *not* **after the verb.**

He *is not* a good tennis player.　　They *were not* at our party last night.

Form the negative of sentences with auxiliary verbs (*can, must, may, will, should,* **etc.) by placing** *not* **after the auxiliary. Remember that** *can* + *not* **is spelled as one word.**

You *should not* break a promise.　　We *will not* go by boat this year.

Change the following sentences to the negative form. Include the main verb in your answer where appropriate.

1. Joe will study in our group.　　　　　　　<u>will not study</u>
2. You must tell him about it.　　　　　　　_____
3. She may return later.　　　　　　　　　　_____
4. He is very busy today.　　　　　　　　　　_____
5. They were here yesterday.　　　　　　　　_____
6. He is studying in our group.　　　　　　　_____
7. She should spend more time on that report.　_____
8. They will be back at five o'clock.　　　　　_____
9. She can speak French well.　　　　　　　　_____
10. We are going to the movies tonight.　　　　_____
11. They are old friends.　　　　　　　　　　_____
12. She is a good cook.　　　　　　　　　　　_____
13. He has gone to Chicago.　　　　　　　　　_____
14. She will telephone you tonight.　　　　　　_____
15. We were tired after the dance.　　　　　　_____
16. I am a computer expert.　　　　　　　　　_____
17. There is enough sugar in the bowl.　　　　_____
18. There were many students absent from the lesson.　_____
19. I can meet you later.　　　　　　　　　　_____
20. You must write your exercises in pencil.　_____
21. You may smoke here.

19

(20) Review: negative form 2

The auxiliaries *do* **and** *does* **+** *not* **are used to form negative sentences in the present tense. Place** *do not* **or** *does not* **before the simple form of the verb.**

I speak French well.   She works hard at the office.
I *do not* speak French well.   She *does not* work hard at the office.

To form the negative in the past tense, place *did not* **before the simple form of the verb.** *Did* **is used for all persons, singular and plural.**

He came to class early.   We ate a big dinner at noon.
He *did not* come to class early.   We *did not* eat a big dinner at noon.

Change the following sentences to the negative form. Be careful to use the correct auxiliary for the present and past tenses.

1. She comes to class on time.   does not come
2. They live near here.   _____
3. I know him very well.   _____
4. I got two rolls this morning.   _____
5. We want to learn French.   _____
6. The bus stopped on this corner.   _____
7. We ate dinner at home last night.   _____
8. She sat near me in class.   _____
9. He reads many books in French.   _____
10. He speaks to us in English.   _____
11. Tim smokes too much.   _____
12. She came with me to the lesson.   _____
13. I had a lot of work to do yesterday.   _____
14. The child drank all the milk.   _____
15. Teresa watched television last night.   _____
16. He hung his coat on the chair.   _____
17. I found my book.   _____
18. We sit in the first row at the opera.   _____
19. We learned many new words yesterday.   _____
20. They held the meeting in the school auditorium.   _____
21. The dog dug two holes in the yard.   _____

(21) Review: negative form 3

Change the following sentences to the negative form. Write the complete verb in the blanks.

1. He will return next week. will not return
2. He speaks English well. _____
3. It is raining hard. _____
4. She is a good student. _____
5. We were late for the lesson this morning. _____
6. I met Giselle on Fifth Avenue yesterday. _____
7. Our team won both games. _____
8. He will be on time this evening. _____
9. She came to class late this morning. _____
10. Adela feels much better today. _____
11. The movie last night was very good. _____
12. They are going to Spain next year. _____
13. She can speak English well. _____
14. You may smoke here. _____
15. Felipe should spend more time on his homework. _____
16. They go to the movies every night. _____
17. I like Italian movies. _____
18. She is a good teacher. _____
19. He will tell you the truth. _____
20. He called on the telephone last night. _____
21. She is wearing a brown sweater. _____
22. The train left at four o'clock. _____
23. I understand him very easily. _____
24. He speaks very slowly. _____

(22) Review: question form 1

To form questions with *to be* **in the present and past tenses, place the verb before the subject.**

    Is Lisa the best student in your class?   *Were your friends* on time yesterday?

Form questions with auxiliaries (*can, must, may, will, should, ought,* **etc.**) **by placing the auxiliary before the subject.**

    May we leave class early today?   *Will you* have time to finish before dinner?

Remember that in *there* **+** *be* **sentences,** *there* **is treated like a subject.**

Change the following sentences to the question form. Write the answer in the space provided.

1. Sam will study in our group.   <u>Will Sam study</u>
2. She can speak French well.   _____
3. She is a politician.   _____
4. He may sit here.   _____
5. They were tired after the dance.   _____
6. She is a good manager.   _____
7. He can go with us to the movies.   _____
8. He should mention it to her.   _____
9. They will be angry.   _____
10. She is studying to be a lawyer.   _____
11. Mr. Darbari has gone to Chicago.   _____
12. She will telephone us later.   _____
13. He is an excellent student.   _____
14. There were two men in the office.   _____
15. He should study more.   _____
16. They are old friends.   _____
17. They were both here yesterday.   _____
18. It is raining hard.   _____
19. They are going to a meeting.   _____
20. She will be ready soon.   _____

23 Review: question form 2

Form questions in the simple present tense by placing the auxiliary *do* before the subject. Use *does* for the third person singular.

Do we have enough gas to get home?   *Does Andy* work in your office?

Form questions in the past tense by placing the auxiliary *did* before the subject.

Did Judy drive there by herself?   *Did you* enjoy your holiday in Greece?

Change the following sentences to the question form. Write the auxiliary, followed by the subject and the main verb in the space provided.

1. She comes to class on time.   Does she come
2. They left at two o'clock.   _____
3. She studies in our group.   _____
4. He bought a new car last year.   _____
5. She drives her brother to class.   _____
6. Daniela answered the phone.   _____
7. He sat in the first row.   _____
8. He speaks English very clearly.   _____
9. They go to the movies almost every night.   _____
10. They met in Europe last year.   _____
11. The child cut his finger badly.   _____
12. She gave us some good advice.   _____
13. They live on the second floor.   _____
14. You drink milk with your meals.   _____
15. The bus stops on this corner.   _____
16. The train arrived on time.   _____
17. He writes her every week.   _____
18. They brought Steve a present from New York.   _____
19. He lost his money in Monte Carlo.   _____
20. They caught the thief after a long search.   _____
21. Valentina smokes too much.   _____

24 Review: question form 3

Change the following sentences to the question form. Write the auxiliary, followed by the subject and the main verb in the space provided. If the only verb is *to be*, reverse the order of the subject and verb.

1. She went to Chicago by plane. <u>Did she go</u>
2. He will be in the office on Tuesday. _____
3. Harriet is a good tennis player. _____
4. He works very hard. _____
5. The boys spent the afternoon in the park. _____
6. Paula plays baseball well. _____
7. His sister sings well. _____
8. The telephone is ringing loudly. _____
9. It looks like rain. _____
10. We have enough coffee for everybody. _____
11. The sun is shining now. _____
12. The weather is becoming very warm. _____
13. It rained hard last night. _____
14. Loretta can speak French well. _____
15. He must see a doctor at once. _____
16. Antonia will tell us all about it. _____
17. The man speaks English badly. _____
18. Beatrice could understand him easily. _____
19. The train left on time. _____
20. It will arrive in Philadelphia around noon. _____
21. He has a lot of work to do today. _____
22. She feels better after her operation. _____
23. He wants a better job. _____
24. They spent two weeks in Mexico City. _____

25 *The*

The **is a definite article. It refers to a particular object or to particular objects.**

The book that I bought is on the table. *The* pictures you took are excellent.

Nouns that name an indefinite quantity or an intangible quality do not take an article.

Gold is a precious metal. *Honesty* is always appreciated.

When these nouns are used to express a particular quality or quantity, they should be preceded by *the*.

The gold in this jewlery is very old. *The honesty* of that child is above question.

The **is not used before the names of persons, countries, continents, streets, cities, or towns when they are used as proper nouns. (Exceptions: *the* United States, *the* Soviet Union, *the* Dominican Republic, etc.)**

Ms. Torrence lives on *White Oak Lane*, in *Fairfax*. She's going to travel to *Europe* next summer. She'll visit *London, Paris*, and *Rome*.

When these words are used as adjectives, they are preceded by *the*.

London is a large city. *The London transportation system* is excellent.

Write the article *the*, if necessary, in the blanks. If it is not necessary, leave blank.

1. He came here directly from _____ Mexico.   (no article)

2. They say that _____ weather in Acapulco is beautiful.   the

3. Mr. and Mrs. Bielski are now traveling in _____ Brazil.   _____

4. He has always lived in _____ United States.   _____

5. Does Maria speak _____ English well?   _____

6. _____ English language is not difficult to learn.   _____

7. I like _____ tea better than coffee.   _____

8. _____ tea in your cup is Japanese.   _____

9. _____ women are important in U.S. politics.   _____

10. Do you agree that _____ gentlemen speak softly?   _____

11. We all took a walk along _____ Fifth Avenue.   _____

12. _____ Third Avenue street fair was a big success.   _____

Review:
present continuous tense

The simple present tense is used to describe an action that happens regularly or in general.

  It always *rains* in April here.   They *eat* dinner around eight o'clock.

The present continuous tense describes an action which is occurring at the moment of speaking.

  I *am typing* this document. (now)   We *are having* trouble with the computer.

Write the present continuous tense or the simple present tense of the verbs in parentheses.

1. The doorbell (ring) very often. _____rings_____

2. The doorbell (ring) now. _____

3. She (write) many letters to her parents. _____

4. Alice is busy now. She (write) a letter. _____

5. Mr. Sato (smoke) too much. _____

6. He (smoke) more than a pack of cigarettes every day. _____

7. Look! He (smoke) a cigarette now. _____

8. It (rain) a great deal during the spring months. _____

9. Look! It (begin) to rain. _____

10. Listen! Someone (knock) at the door. _____

11. The bus always (stop) at this corner. _____

12. The bus (stop) for us now. _____

13. I always (get) on the bus at this corner. _____

14. Mr. and Mrs. Gonzalez (build) a new home on Second Avenue. _____

15. We (have) English lessons three times a week. _____

16. We (have) our English lesson now. _____

17. Look! Rose (wave) to us from across the street. _____

18. Patricia always (come) to school by bus. _____

19. Be quiet or you will wake the baby. She (sleep). _____

20. She (sleep) about fourteen hours a day. _____

21. Mr. Tran (speak) English with a strong foreign accent. _____

27 Past continuous tense 1

Form the past continuous tense with the past tense of *to be* **and the present participle of the main verb.**

I was working	we were working
you were working	you were working
he was working	they were working
she was working	
it was working	

The past continuous is used to describe an action that was going on when another action took place.

I *was sleeping* when you phoned.
We *were leaving* the house when they arrived.

Write the past continuous form of the verbs in parentheses.

1. I (sleep) when you telephoned. _was sleeping_
2. We (sit) in the park when it began to rain. _____
3. The sun (shine) brightly when I got up this morning. _____
4. I (walk) down Broadway when I met him. _____
5. We (have) lunch when she called. _____
6. Bruce (study) when I went to see him last night. _____
7. He fell while he (play) in the park. _____
8. They (drive) to Chicago when the accident happened. _____
9. The teacher (write) on the board when we entered the classroom. _____
10. She fell while she (get) off the bus. _____
11. My mother (prepare) dinner when I got home. _____
12. I (have) lunch when I first felt sick. _____
13. It (rain) hard when I left home. _____
14. But when I arrived at school, the sun (shine). _____
15. Molly (talk) with Jack when I passed them in the hall. _____
16. They (watch) television when we called them. _____
17. I (have) lunch when you telephoned. _____
18. Both children (sleep) when I went into the room. _____
19. The man (suffer) greatly when the ambulance arrived. _____

(28) Past continuous tense 2

Write the correct form of the verb in the simple past or the past continuous tense for each sentence below.

1. I (sleep) well last night. _____slept_____
2. I (sleep) when the fire started. _____
3. When I got up this morning, the wind (blow) hard. _____
4. It (rain) hard last night. _____
5. It (rain) hard when I left home. _____
6. The child fell while she (play) in the park. _____
7. She (play) in the park all afternoon. _____
8. We (have) dinner when you telephoned. _____
9. I (read) two new books last week. _____
10. When we got there, Keith (read) the newspaper. _____
11. I (write) several letters last night. _____
12. I (write) a letter when you called me. _____
13. The sun (shine) brightly when I got up this morning. _____
14. The telephone (ring) just as I was leaving. _____
15. Mr. Ryan (drive) to Chicago in his new car. _____
16. The accident happened while he (drive) to Chicago. _____
17. The boys (play) baseball all afternoon yesterday. _____
18. Pedro fell and hurt himself while he (play) baseball. _____
19. We (see) Josie at the movie theater last night. _____
20. We met Yuriko just as she (leave) school. _____
21. We (wait) an hour for you after class yesterday. _____
22. While we (wait) for a taxi, Martha came along and took us home. _____

Write the correct prepositions in the blanks.

1. We arrived _____ Miami at exactly six o'clock.   ____in____

2. They live _____ Washington Avenue.   _____

3. He arrived _____ school at nine o'clock.   _____

4. They live across the street _____ us.   _____

5. He listens _____ the radio every night.   _____

6. We stayed _____ the Hotel Roma.   _____

7. She refused to shake hands _____ him.   _____

8. They are going to New York _____ plane.   _____

9. The plane flew directly _____ our house.   _____

10. She placed her coat _____ top of mine.   _____

11. The teacher distributed the papers _____ the pupils.

     _____

12. There is something wrong _____ this telephone.   _____

13. I spoke to him _____ the telephone last night.   _____

14. I'll call you back _____ twenty minutes.   _____

15. We waited for you _____ an hour.   _____

16. I'll be back _____ ten minutes.   _____

17. They weren't _____ the hotel last night.   _____

18. I am going to Bonnie's house _____ dinner.   _____

19. He is going to ask her _____ a date.   _____

20. What are your plans _____ the weekend?   _____

21. Anne will tell you all _____ our plans.   _____

22. The man died _____ a heart attack.   _____

23. What is the matter _____ John today?   _____

24. He should be more careful _____ his health.   _____

25. She lives far _____ here.   _____

30 Vocabulary review 2

Select the correct answer and write it in the space provided.

1. A person who cannot *hear* is (blind, deaf, sick, busy). _____deaf_____

2. A person who can read is (smart, legible, literate, oral). _____

3. Which one of these words is not spelled correctly: exhausted, Febuary, Wednesday, participle, anecdote? _____

4. What is the superlative form of the adjective *bad*? _____

5. What is the superlative form of the adjective *good*? _____

6. Which of these verbs is in the past tense: see, go, did, take, bring? _____

7. Which of these auxiliary verbs do we use to form the future tense: do, did, have, will, can? _____

8. Which of these auxiliary verbs do we use to form the present perfect tense: do, did, will, have, can? _____

9. What is the corresponding noun form of the adjective *dangerous*? _____

10. What is the corresponding adjective form of the noun *height*? _____

11. Which of the following words rhymes with *wrist*: fast, least, this, missed? _____

12. Which letter in the words *half, walk*, and *talk* is silent (not pronounced)? _____

13. Which of these animals has a very long neck: tiger, wolf, zebra, giraffe? _____

14. To *call up* someone is to (admire, telephone, visit, study with) him or her. _____

15. To *call off* something is to (tear, need, cancel, postpone) it. _____

16. *Once in a while* means (often, seldom, occasionally, just once). _____

17. Which one of these verbs is an irregular verb: walk, refer, take, want, count? _____

18. Which one of these verbs is a regular verb: see, bring, know, do, pull? _____

19. The opposite of *full* is (big, open, narrow, empty). _____

Select the correct form. Write your answers in the blanks.

1. They came to class earlier (than, as) we.   _____than_____

2. She asked me where (I lived, did I live).   _____

3. There (was, were) many students absent from class.   _____

4. He is (a, an) athlete.   _____

5. The last lesson was (a, an) easy one.   _____

6. (This, These) books belong to my brother.   _____

7. The boy (run, ran) from the room.   _____

8. Olga was sick yesterday and (can, could) not come to class.   _____

9. Does Ms. Eng (smoke, smokes) very much?   _____

10. Listen! The stereo (plays, is playing).   _____

11. He has lived in that same house (since, for) many years.   _____

12. I (saw, have seen) that movie last week.   _____

13. When I arrived, they (ate, were eating).   _____

14. Penny always (comes, is coming) to school by bus.   _____

15. He sent (her, to her) a beautiful bouquet of flowers.   _____

16. Look! Isn't that Carmen who (crosses, is crossing) the street?   _____

17. It (rained, was raining) hard when I got up this morning.   _____

18. He (works, has worked) for that firm since January.   _____

19. He doesn't know her, and I don't, (also, either).   _____

20. She wants (us to wait, that we wait) for him.   _____

21. We (was, were) all late for the meeting.   _____

22. He says that he has (saw, seen) that movie.   _____

32 *Have to:* present tense

Must and *have to* **express obligation or need. We use** *have to* **more often than** *must*.

You *must* study for this exam.

Harry *must* leave town on business.

You *have to* study for this exam.

Harry *has to* leave town on business.

Change the words in italics to the correct form of *have to* **+ verb.**

1. They *must prepare* their exercises more carefully. <u>have to prepare</u>
2. She *must go* to Chicago tonight. _____
3. She *must leave* at once. _____
4. I *must be* there before four o'clock. _____
5. We *must learn* at least ten new words every day. _____
6. I *must have* more spending money. _____
7. Everyone *must work* eight hours a day. _____
8. He *must go* to the hospital to see his friend. _____
9. You *must wait* in the reception area. _____
10. I *must go* to the bank. _____
11. He *must spend* more time on his homework. _____
12. I *must go* to the dentist. _____
13. He *must be* in his office before nine o'clock. _____
14. We *must leave* before Hugh gets here. _____
15. You *must write* your exercises in ink. _____
16. Everyone *must write* a composition for tomorrow's lesson. _____
17. They *must remain* there all afternoon. _____
18. I *must get* there before three o'clock. _____
19. She *must remain* in bed for at least three weeks. _____
20. After that, she *must visit* the doctor every week. _____

Must has no past or future tenses. We use *have to* to express obligation or need in the past, future, or present perfect tenses.

I *have to* leave early tonight.
I *had to* leave early last night.
I'll *have to* leave early tomorrow.
I *have had to* leave early every day this week.

A. **Change the following sentences to the past tense.**

1. I have to write many letters.   had to write

2. He has to leave for school at eight o'clock.   _____

3. She has to work very hard.   _____

4. They have to get up early every morning.   _____

5. We have to walk to school.   _____

6. I have to learn many new words every day.   _____

7. I have to have more money.   _____

B. **Change the following sentences to the future tense.**

1. He has to work very hard.   will have to work

2. You have to return later.   _____

3. We have to do this right away.   _____

4. She has to be there before nine o'clock.   _____

5. I have to buy the tickets first.   _____

6. We have to wait at least an hour for him.   _____

7. She has to make an appointment with him.   _____

C. **Change the following sentences to the present perfect tense.**

1. We have to speak clearly.   have had to speak

2. Peter has to learn to drive.   _____

3. You have to go on a diet.   _____

4. They have to return from their vacation early.   _____

5. I have to take another flight.   _____

6. Angela has to cook for twenty guests.   _____

7. You have to buy new shoes.   _____

34 *Have to:* negative form

To form the negative with *have to,* **place** *do not, does not, did not,* **or** *will not* **before** *have.* **The contracted forms** *don't, doesn't, didn't,* **and** *won't* **are normally used.**

I *have to* catch the seven-thirty train.	I *don't have to* catch the seven-thirty train.
Lisa *will have to* stay with you.	Lisa *won't have to* stay with you.
They *had to* help me.	They *didn't have to* help me.

Change the following sentences to the negative form. Use contractions.

1. She has to work late tonight.   doesn't have to work
2. He had to leave early. _____
3. We have to study hard for our next exam. _____
4. I have to write that letter at once. _____
5. I had to wait a long time to see him. _____
6. She has to spend more time on her homework. _____
7. I have to return later. _____
8. He has to be at his office before eight o'clock. _____
9. They have to leave before Wednesday. _____
10. We had to walk to school. _____
11. You will have to send him a telegram. _____
12. You have to wait for me. _____
13. We had to pay the doctor for her services. _____
14. I had to go the bank. _____
15. I have to cash his check today. _____
16. We will have to invite Mary to the party. _____
17. She has to take an exam in English. _____
18. He had to join the navy. _____
19. She has to leave for Mexico this week. _____
20. We have to write a composition every week. _____
21. We had to write a letter to the lawyer. _____

35 Have to: question form

To form questions with *have to*, place *do*, *does*, *did*, or *will* before the subject.

Sally *has to* play in a tennis match.   *Does* Sally *have to* play in a tennis match?

We *will have to* be ready early.   *Will* we *have to* be ready early?

Change the following sentences to the question form.

1. John has to stay home tonight. <u>Does John have to stay</u>
2. He had to stay home last night, too. _____
3. The students have to learn many new words. _____
4. They will have to write a composition each week. _____
5. She had to wait for him for an hour. _____
6. You have to return later. _____
7. She had to go to the doctor. _____
8. She has to take another exam. _____
9. We had to invite Eric to the party. _____
10. He has to leave for Europe next week. _____
11. We will have to write our exercises in ink. _____
12. They have to arrive at school before nine o'clock. _____
13. Tom has to get up early every morning. _____
14. Sue has to help her mother. _____
15. She had to prepare the dinner. _____
16. She has to work very hard. _____
17. They had to stay home last night and study. _____
18. He has to go the hospital for an operation. _____
19. I have to sign my name at the bottom of the page. _____
20. We had to send him a telegram. _____
21. We have to save every cent possible. _____

36 *Say, tell*

Say is used in direct quotations.

> Joseph *said*, "It's too early to leave for the theater."
> She *said* to me, "Your computer print-out is ready."

Say is used for indirect quotations where the person to whom the words are spoken is not mentioned.

> Harvey *said* that he could not come tomorrow.

Tell is used for indirect quotations when the person to whom the words are spoken is mentioned.

> Harvey *told me* that he could not come tomorrow.

Tell is used in the following expressions: to tell the truth, to tell a lie, to tell a story, to tell time, to tell a secret, to tell about something.

The word *that*, when used to introduce a subordinate clause as in these sentences, is often dropped in everyday speech. We may say "She said that she was busy" or "She said she was busy." Both forms are correct.

Write the correct form of *say* or *tell* in the blanks.

1. She _____ both of us (that) she was going to get married.   told
2. Roger _____ (that) he was busy after class. _____
3. He _____ (that) he always ate lunch in the cafeteria. _____
4. Sally _____ (that) it was the truth. _____
5. I _____ you (that) the car belonged to George. _____
6. Martin _____ him (that) the house was for sale. _____
7. Susan _____ (that) she could teach me to paint. _____
8. Robert _____ , "The book is from the library." _____
9. Can you _____ me where Ms. Nomura's office is? _____
10. He _____ (that) he understood Polish. _____
11. Dolores _____ (that) she felt ill. _____
12. I _____ the teacher (that) I already knew how to type. _____
13. He _____ me (that) Marc was in the hospital. _____
14. Annette _____ us (that) it was a good hotel. _____

I have worked	we have worked
you have worked	you have worked
he has worked	they have worked
she has worked	
it has worked	

The present perfect tense is for an action that began in the past and is still continuing.

She *has owned* her house since 1984. (She still owns it.)
We *have known* Bill for years. (We know him now.)

Remember that the simple past tense describes an action which happened at a definite time in the past.

We *went* there last year.

Write the simple past tense or present perfect tense of the verbs in parentheses.

1. We live on 72nd Street, where we (live) for almost five years. ___have lived___

2. From 1975 to 1980, we (live) on 96th Street. _____

3. Marie-France (begin) to study English as soon as she arrived in the United States. _____

4. She (study) English continuously since then. _____

5. Ricardo (study) French when he was in high school. _____

6. The First World War (begin) in 1914 and ended in 1918. _____

7. It (last) for four years. _____

8. We (be) in California last winter. _____

9. They (live) in California since 1974. _____

10. My last car was a Chevrolet. I (have) it for four years. _____

11. My present car is a Buick. I (have) it for two years. _____

12. Sonia and I are good friends. In fact, we (be) good friends for more than ten years. _____

13. We (become) friends when we were students in the university. _____

14. Dr. Pavlik (be) our family doctor ever since we moved to this town. _____

37

Write the full form of the items which appear below.

1. 6 oz.   six ounces
2. 1 lb. _____
3. 1 mi. _____
4. 7 a.m. _____
5. 6 p.m. _____
6. .6 _____
7. ½ _____
8. ¼ _____
9. 6% _____
10. #5 _____
11. 68° _____
12. AC _____
13. DC _____
14. etc. _____
15. 1 gal. _____
16. TV _____
17. C.O.D. _____
18. qt. _____
19. pt. _____
20. yd. _____
21. in. _____
22. & _____
23. Inc. _____
24. 2 yrs. _____

25. 4 ft. _____
26. 96th St. _____
27. Ave. _____
28. Blvd. _____
29. Rd. _____
30. Bldg. _____
31. Feb. _____
32. Aug. _____
33. Dec. _____
34. sq. ft. _____
35. 1st _____
36. 3rd _____
37. 7th _____
38. Thurs. _____
39. Wed. _____
40. NBC _____
41. NY _____
42. CA _____
43. IL _____
44. WA _____
45. CT _____
46. OH _____
47. MI _____
48. TN _____

(39) Present perfect continuous tense

The present perfect continuous tense is formed with *have/has been* and the present participle of the main verb.

I have been working	we have been working
you have been working	you have been working
he has been working	they have been working
she has been working	
it has been working	

The present perfect continuous tense is used to describe an action that began in the past and is continuing in the present.

We *have been living* here for eight years.
Bruce *has been studying* law since last year.

Write the present perfect continuous tense of the verbs in parentheses.

1. She (study) English for two years.   has been studying
2. We (live) in this house since last March.   _____
3. I (try) to reach you by phone for the last hour.   _____
4. He (drive) that same old car for at least ten years.   _____
5. She (feel) much better recently.   _____
6. He (sit) on that bench for several hours.   _____
7. Rose (work) on that same problem for several days.   _____
8. They (talk) on the telephone for over an hour.   _____
9. She naturally speaks English well because she (speak) it all her life.   _____
10. He (work) in that same office ever since I first met him.   _____
11. Ms. Russo (teach) school for many years.   _____
12. They (go) together for almost a year.   _____
13. I (wait) here for you for almost an hour.   _____
14. It (rain) all day long.   _____
15. You (whistle) that same tune for the last hour.   _____
16. She (study) music since she was a child.   _____
17. She (wear) that same hat for more than a year.   _____
18. They (work) there for a long time.   _____
19. We (plan) this trip for many months.   _____

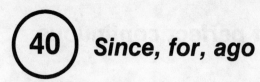

(40) *Since, for, ago*

For **shows the length of time of the action in the present, past, and future tenses.**

We have lived here *for* six years.   She'll stay in Europe *for* a year.

Since **tells when the action began.**

They have lived here *since* 1978.

Ago **refers to how much time back in the past something happened.**

My ancestors arrived in this country 175 years *ago*.

Write *since*, *for*, or *ago* in the blanks.

1. I met him on the street about two weeks _____ .   <u>ago</u>
2. He has been studying English _____ last January.   _____
3. She has been studying English _____ two years.   _____
4. I visited them in Miami about six months _____ .   _____
5. He stayed with us _____ about six months.   _____
6. Clara has lived in that same house _____ many years.   _____
7. They have lived there _____ 1984.   _____
8. She has never been the same _____ he went away.   _____
9. He has been sick _____ several days.   _____
10. She has been sick _____ Wednesday.   _____
11. How long _____ did the accident happen?   _____
12. I haven't seen Chris _____ last Christmas.   _____
13. We talked _____ about two hours.   _____
14. She has been in the hospital _____ July.   _____
15. He left for Chicago three days _____ .   _____
16. I haven't talked with her _____ yesterday.   _____
17. I talked with her _____ a few minutes yesterday.   _____
18. Mr. Pelli has been teaching English ever _____ he returned to the United States.   _____
19. She first began to teach English about three years _____ .   _____
20. She has been teaching English _____ many years.   _____

41 **Past perfect tense**

To form the past perfect tense, use *had* and the past participle of the main verb.

I had finished   we had finished
you had finished   you had finished
he had finished   they had finished
she had finished
it had finished

The past perfect tense is used to tell about an action which began and ended in the past before another past action. It is used with the past tense, either stated or implied.

By the time you arrived, they *had* already *left*.
It *had burned* down before the first fire trucks arrived.

Write the past perfect tense of the verbs in parentheses.

1. He told me that he (visit) Miami several times.   <u>had visited</u>
2. I thought it was the stranger who (steal) the money.   _____
3. I saw that we (take) the wrong road.   _____
4. She said that she (have) her lunch.   _____
5. I thought he (find) his keys.   _____
6. I told him that I (see) the movie.   _____
7. When we arrived, they already (leave).   _____
8. I visited many of the places where I (play) as a boy.   _____
9. We got there just ten minutes after he (leave).   _____
10. She (live) there two years when the war began.   _____
11. He said that he (look) everywhere for it.   _____
12. She told us that she already (take) the money to the bank.   _____
13. I was sure that he (have) the same trouble before.   _____
14. The police said that they (receive) several similar reports the same evening.   _____
15. What did he say he (do) with the money?   _____
16. He said that he (put) it back where he had found it.   _____
17. By the time we got there, all the other guests (leave).   _____
18. We saw, as soon as we arrived home, that someone (break) into the house.   _____

41

Change the following sentences to the negative form.

1. He knows English well.   does not know

2. She left yesterday for California.   _____

3. Anne is a very good student.   _____

4. I wanted to take a walk.   _____

5. He has studied English for many years.   _____

6. He told her all about his plans.   _____

7. They will return on Wednesday.   _____

8. He is having his lunch now.   _____

9. They have left for the station.   _____

10. She can speak French well.   _____

11. You must tell him about it.   _____

12. They are going to the movies with us.   _____

13. It is a beautiful day.   _____

14. It was a very pleasant day.   _____

15. She has worked in that office for many years.   _____

16. They have been living there for a long time.   _____

17. She has to work tonight.   _____

18. She had to go to the hospital to see a friend.   _____

19. He came to the lesson yesterday.   _____

20. They are making good progress in their studies.   _____

21. He told me to wait for him.   _____

22. She prepares her lessons carefully.   _____

23. They were playing tennis at the time.   _____

24. Julia has finished that work.   _____

Review: question form 4

Change the following sentences to the question form.

1. She works on the tenth floor. <u>Does she work</u>
2. He gave her the message. _____
3. She is a good friend of hers. _____
4. We are going to the movies tonight. _____
5. They will return home on Wednesday. _____
6. He left his keys at home. _____
7. Marcia can swim very well. _____
8. She is going to study French next year. _____
9. He has read that novel before. _____
10. She has been studying English for many years. _____
11. She is very eager to learn English well. _____
12. We have to have more practice in conversation. _____
13. Robert had to leave for New York yesterday. _____
14. He will return in a few days. _____
15. They were having lunch at the time. _____
16. They built that bridge last year. _____
17. They will deliver the merchandise tomorrow. _____
18. She was here at three o'clock. _____
19. It is almost three o'clock. _____
20. The wind is blowing very hard. _____
21. There were many people in the park. _____
22. The child cut herself badly. _____
23. The boy ran between the two cars. _____
24. The doorbell is ringing now. _____

Write the correct prepositions or particles in the blanks.

1. The exercise was too difficult _____ him to do. ___for___

2. It was kind _____ you do that for her. _____

3. She is worried _____ her husband's health. _____

4. They are putting _____ several new buildings in that block. _____

5. The bus doesn't stop _____ this corner. _____

6. Have you heard _____ Sally's new baby? _____

7. Nora wants to go _____ a diet. _____

8. What are they laughing _____ ? _____

9. What was he talking _____ ? _____

10. He has been studying English _____ three years. _____

11. She has worked in that office _____ last year. _____

12. We hung the pictures _____ the fireplace. _____

13. The temperature dropped from ten degrees above zero to ten degrees _____ zero. _____

14. Why don't you sit _____ a more comfortable chair? _____

15. That building seems to be _____ fire. _____

16. The elevator is not running today. It is _____ of order. _____

17. What is the matter _____ him? _____

18. I make many mistakes _____ spelling. _____

19. I see Josie in the cafeteria _____ time to time. _____

20. I will get _____ touch with you next week. _____

21. He seems to be _____ a hurry. _____

22. She was absent _____ class twice last week. _____

23. He came to school _____ spite of the fact that he was not feeling well. _____

24. This book belongs _____ Nancy. _____

45 Vocabulary review 3

Select the correct answer and write it in the space provided.

1. The opposite of *sharp* is (new, funny, dull, necessary).   *dull*

2. *I'd rather go* means that I (want to, prefer to, had better, seldom) go.   _____

3. Which of these words is not spelled correctly: breakfast, secretary, committee, entrence?   _____

4. What is the corresponding noun form of the verb *to agree*?   _____

5. What is the corresponding verb form of the noun *explosion*?   _____

6. Which one of these verbs has the same form in the past tense as in the present tense: go, walk, take, put, see?   _____

7. Which of these is a past participle: find, thank, saw, been, went?   _____

8. We pronounce the word *comb* to rhyme with (come, sum, tomb, home).   _____

9. We pronounce the word *axe* to rhyme with (fix, fast, lacks, first).   _____

10. If a man does something *by himself*, he does it (well, hurriedly, to himself, alone).   _____

11. A synonym for *besides* is (alongside, near, in addition to, close).   _____

12. What is the corresponding noun form of the verb *to advise*?   _____

13. The opposite of *frequently* is (often, new, seldom, now).   _____

14. *Lately* means (often, very soon, recently, later).   _____

15. *I'm kidding* means I'm (smiling, joking, crying, laughing).   _____

16. Which letter in the word *answer* is silent (not pronounced)?   _____

17. Which letter in the word *listen* is silent (not pronounced)?   _____

The items in boldface are mistakes. Change them to make the facts correct, and write your answers in the blanks.

1. There are **thirteen** months in a year.   twelve

2. The capital of the United States is **Philadelphia**.   _____

3. Ten divided by two is **four**.   _____

4. We pronounce the word *talked* as a word of **two syllables**. _____

5. Tigers and lions are **domestic** animals.   _____

6. We use the indefinite article *an* before words which begin with a **consonant**. _____

7. We accent the word *television* on the **fourth** syllable.   _____

8. We call those verbs which form their past tense by adding *ed* to the present tense **irregular** verbs. _____

9. The next to the last month of the year is **October**.   _____

10. The sun always **sets** in the east.   _____

11. There are **four** pints in a quart.   _____

12. There are **eighteen** ounces in a pound.   _____

13. In the United States, we always celebrate Thanksgiving Day on a **Tuesday**. _____

14. Canada lies **east** of the United States.   _____

15. The auxiliary verb which we use in English to form the present perfect tense is **will**. _____

16. The coldest season of the year in the United States is **autumn**. _____

17. There are **fifty-six** weeks in a year.   _____

18. The verb *take* is the kind of verb called **regular**.   _____

19. The past participle of *take* is **took**.   _____

20. The English alphabet has **twenty-four** letters.   _____

21. On a watch or clock, the minute hand is **shorter** than the hour hand. _____

22. Abraham Lincoln was president of the United States during the **Revolutionary War**. _____

Select the correct form. Write your answers in the blanks.

1. Maria has worked in that office (for, since) many years. _____for_____

2. Tony said that he (saw, had seen) that movie. _____

3. When we arrived, Alice (read, was reading) the newspaper. _____

4. This book is mine, and that one is (your, yours). _____

5. We (must, had to) go to the hospital last night to see a friend who is sick. _____

6. We (haven't to, don't have to) work tomorrow because it is a holiday. _____

7. We (have been, were) in California for two months last winter. _____

8. I saw that we (take, were taking) the wrong road. _____

9. I said that we (needed, were needing) a map. _____

10. What time did you (leave, left) home this morning? _____

11. Hurry! The bus (comes, is coming). _____

12. They (have, are having) their dinner now. _____

13. The teacher explained (us, to us) the meaning of the word. _____

14. Rita wants (me to go, that I go) to the movies with her. _____

15. He gave (me, to me) all the money he had. _____

16. The wind (is blowing, blows) very hard during the month of March. _____

17. I didn't hear (someone, anyone) in the next room. _____

18. We (went, have gone) to the movies last night. _____

19. We (are, have been) friends for many years. _____

20. Julio (said, told) that he could not come to the lesson. _____

21. Listen! The birds (sing, are singing). _____

22. He is (a, an) old friend of hers. _____

48 **Review:** contractions

To be
I'm	we're
you're	you're
he's	they're
she's	
it's	

Certain auxiliaries are also commonly used in the contracted form: *I'll (I will), I've (I have), you've (you have), she'd (she had),* **etc.**

Remember that we usually use the contracted form with negatives and auxiliary verbs.

  isn't, wasn't, won't, can't, don't, didn't, haven't, etc.

═══

Change the words in italics to the contracted form.

1. *I am* very busy today.   I'm
2. *You are* a good friend of his.   _____
3. *She is* going to the movies with us.   _____
4. *It is* raining.   _____
5. *She is* the best student in the class.   _____
6. *We are* very old friends.   _____
7. *They are* having their lunch now.   _____
8. *There is* someone in the next room.   _____
9. *You are* here too early.   _____
10. *I will* meet you at six o'clock.   _____
11. *You will* be late if you don't hurry.   _____
12. *She will* return next week.   _____
13. *We will* be back at five o'clock.   _____
14. I *do not* know her well.   _____
15. He *does not* speak English.   _____
16. They *did not* come to the meeting last night.   _____
17. I *will not* be able to meet you tomorrow.   _____
18. Nancy *will not* return until Wednesday.   _____
19. They *are not* going to the movies with us.   _____
20. I *have not* seen that movie.   _____

(49) Expressions of purpose

Use *in order to* or *to* followed by the simple form of the verb to express purpose. The short form (*to*) is more common in everyday conversation.

> We went to the hospital *in order to* see our friend.
> We went to the hospital *to* see our friend.

For is used before nouns to express purpose.

> I went to the store *for* some ice cream.
> She's shopping *for* a new stereo.

Use *to* or *for* to complete the following sentences.

1. She went to town _____ buy some gas. _____to_____

2. She has gone to the corner store _____ some vegetables. _____

3. He went to the bank _____ some money. _____

4. He went to the bank _____ get some money. _____

5. He is going to go to Florida _____ his health. _____

6. Barbara came _____ the books that you promised to lend her. _____

7. I have to go to the post office _____ mail a letter. _____

8. He first came to this country _____ visit his relatives. _____

9. I'll stop at the theater _____ the tickets that you bought. _____

10. I'll stop at the theater _____ pick up the tickets that you bought. _____

11. We are going to the airport _____ meet some friends. _____

12. Martha is coming to our house tonight _____ dinner. _____

13. He is coming to the United States just _____ study English. _____

14. Some friends came _____ visit us last night. _____

15. He often waits after class just _____ talk with the teacher. _____

16. She went to the florist's _____ buy some flowers. _____

Review:
indirect object position

If the indirect object follows the direct object, the preposition *to* or *for* is used. If the indirect object precedes the direct object, we do not use a preposition.

He handed the phone *to me*.
I bought a new tennis racquet *for* Ruth.

He handed *me* the phone.
I bought *Ruth* a new tennis racquet.

Some verbs that function this way are *give*, *send*, *bring*, *tell*, *write*, **and** *buy*.

Change the following sentences so that the indirect object comes before the direct object. Write only the main verb and the indirect object in the spaces provided.

1. He gave the money to her.   _____gave her_____

2. I gave the tickets to Antonia. _____

3. I sent some money to him for his birthday. _____

4. Don't show these things to Rudy. _____

5. She paid the money to the landlord. _____

6. He sold the books to his friend. _____

7. I took the flowers to her. _____

8. She brought a box of candy to me. _____

9. He bought a new car for his wife. _____

10. She brought many presents to us from abroad. _____

11. I will write a letter to you next week. _____

12. She gave the money to her father to put in the bank. _____

13. We sent some flowers to Ms. Pappas. _____

14. I told the whole story to Sharon. _____

15. He gave a piece of the candy to each of us. _____

16. He lent a large sum of money to his brother. _____

17. Please hand those plates to me. _____

18. She sent a postcard to each of them. _____

19. The teacher gave a good mark to Mike. _____

20. They will send the merchandise to us next week. _____

21. He lent his car to us for the afternoon. _____

22. She may bring a present for me from Bali. _____

(51) Review: irregular verbs, past participle

Study and memorize the following list of irregular verbs. This list shows many of the verbs that end in an *n* sound in the past participle form.

bite	bit	bitten	eat	ate	eaten
blow	blew	blown	fall	fell	fallen
break	broke	broken	fly	flew	flown
choose	chose	chosen	freeze	froze	frozen
do	did	done	get	got	gotten
draw	drew	drawn	give	gave	given
drive	drove	driven	go	went	gone

Write the correct form of the verbs in the sentences below.

1. Yesterday the wind (blow) down the tree in front of our house. _blew_

2. All the birds have (fly) south for the winter. _____

3. He told us that he had (drive) the car more than a hundred thousand miles. _____

4. Last night thieves (break) into our neighbor's home. _____

5. It is the third time that someone has (break) into her home. _____

6. While he was skating in the park yesterday, Alex (fall) and hurt himself. _____

7. He has (fall) many times before but never hurt himself. _____

8. We (do) some exercises similar to these last week. _____

9. I went to the bank this morning and (draw) out all my money. _____

10. Someone told me that Alice has (go) back to California for good. _____

11. We (eat) lunch in the school cafeteria yesterday. _____

12. It was so cold last winter in Europe that more than a hundred people (freeze) to death. _____

13. I met Tom yesterday and (give) him the money that I owed him. _____

14. At the meeting last night, we (choose) Nina as the new president of our club. _____

15. That dog has (bite) several people. _____

16. Have you (do) your homework yet? _____

51

(52) Future tense with *going to*

In addition to *will* + the simple form of the verb to express the future tense, we form the future tense with the appropriate form of *to be going to* and the simple form of the verb. The contracted forms are normally used.

I *am going to* see (*I'm going to* see)   we *are going to* see
you *are going to* see (*you're going to* see)   (*we're going to* see)
he *is going to* see (*he's going to* see)   you *are going to* see
she *is going to* see (*she's going to* see)   (*you're going to* see)
it *is going to* see (*it's going to* see)   they *are going to* see
                                (*they're going to* see)

We generally shorten such sentences as "He *is going to go* to Mexico on his vacation" to "He *is going* to Mexico on his vacation."

Write the correct form of *to be going to* and the simple form of the verb. Use the long form of *to be going to go*.

1. He (wait) for us after the lesson.   is going to wait
2. Michel (teach) me how to swim.   _____
3. Hurry! We (be) late for the lesson.   _____
4. She (meet) us after the theater.   _____
5. We (stay) home and watch television tonight.   _____
6. He (go) to Mexico on his vacation.   _____
7. She (take) engineering in college.   _____
8. We (go) to the beach this afternoon.   _____
9. The paper says that it (rain) tomorrow.   _____
10. We (eat) out tonight.   _____
11. Martin (have) dinner with us.   _____
12. After dinner we (go) to the theater.   _____
13. She (get) married in June.   _____
14. They (spend) their honeymoon in Bermuda.   _____
15. Tom (ask) Juanita for a date.   _____
16. You (be) late for class if you don't hurry.   _____
17. We (go) to the movies tonight.   _____
18. They (fly) to Rangoon.   _____
19. He (study) English by himself.   _____

53 **_Going to:_** past tense

The past form of _going to_ indicates an action that was planned but did not happen. To form the past tense, use the correct past tense form of _to be going to_ and the simple form of the verb.

I was going to move	we were going to move
you were going to move	you were going to move
he was going to move	they were going to move
she was going to move	
it was going to move	

We generally shorten such sentences as "I _was going to go_ **shopping this afternoon" to "I** _was going_ **shopping this afternoon."**

Write the correct form of the past tense of _to be going to_ and the simple form of the verb. Use the long form of _to be going to go._

1. We (play) bridge last night, but our guests never arrived.

   were going to play

2. I (go) shopping this afternoon, but I had too much work to do at home.

   _____

3. She (study) abroad last year but finally changed her plans.

   _____

4. We (go) to the beach yesterday, but it rained too hard.

   _____

5. I (call) you last night, but I was too busy.

   _____

6. He (see) a doctor about the pain in his back, but suddenly the pain disappeared.

   _____

7. We (buy) a new television set but decided to wait until next year.

   _____

8. They (visit) us last night but later changed their plans.   _____

9. He always said that he (be) a doctor when he grew up, but he finally went into business.

   _____

10. We (eat) out last night, but the weather was too bad.   _____

11. I (send) him a telegram but later decided to telephone.

    _____

12. She (lend) me the money, but her husband was opposed to it.

    _____

13. He (let) me know when he arrived, but he failed to do so.

    _____

(54) Sequence of tenses

When the main verb of the sentence is in the past tense, all dependent verbs are generally in the past tense, too.

Jerry *says* he *will* come to the party.

Jerry *said* he *would* come to the party.

I *know* this test *will* be difficult.

I *knew* this test *would* be difficult.

Note the irregular past tense form of the following auxiliary verbs:

will	would
can	could
may	might
have	had

Choose the correct word to complete the following sentences.

1. Sarah said that she (will, would) be late for the lesson.   _would_

2. I thought it (is, was) going to rain. _____

3. He didn't think he (can, could) go with us. _____

4. The newspaper said that the weather today (will, would) be cold. _____

5. He said that his first name (is, was) Robert. _____

6. I asked him where he (lives, lived). _____

7. She said her name (is, was) Brigitte. _____

8. I asked him whether he (likes, liked) New Delhi. _____

9. The man told me that he (lives, lived) in Mexico. _____

10. He also said that he (can, could) speak Spanish well. _____

11. I thought I (will, would) be late for the lesson. _____

12. She said she (may, might) go with us to the movies tonight. _____

13. I didn't know what his last name (is, was). _____

14. She told me she (has lost, had lost) her pocketbook. _____

15. She explained to me what the word (means, meant). _____

16. I asked the boy how old he (is, was). _____

17. He told me that he (will, would) help me with the work. _____

18. I thought I (may, might) be too late to see her. _____

19. I saw at once that he (is, was) a serious student. _____

20. I asked him what time it (is, was). _____

54

The letter *s* is pronounced *s* in words such as *pass*, *this*, *see*, and *ask*. The letter *s* is pronounced *z* in words such as *his*, *does*, *rose*, and *goes*.

Practice listening to and pronouncing the different *s* sounds. Write *s* or *z* or show how the letter is pronounced.

1. easy _____z_____
2. pass _____s_____
3. mouse _____
4. bus _____
5. news _____
6. raise _____
7. seat _____
8. does _____
9. comes _____
10. eats _____
11. rose _____
12. class _____
13. bus _____
14. peas _____
15. tennis _____
16. knows _____
17. nose _____
18. books _____
19. eyes _____
20. pens _____
21. dress _____
22. closed _____

23. this _____
24. these _____
25. those _____
26. kiss _____
27. his _____
28. goes _____
29. some _____
30. first _____
31. cousin _____
32. tries _____
33. brings _____
34. likes _____
35. puts _____
36. dogs _____
37. cats _____
38. was _____
39. case _____
40. movies _____
41. plays _____
42. tries _____
43. cost _____
44. is _____

(56) Pronunciation of *ed* in regular verbs

The final *ed* in the past tense of regular verbs takes two different pronunciations:

a. When *ed* is added to a verb ending in an unvoiced consonant (p, t, f, k, s, etc.), the final *d* is pronounced *t*.

b. When *ed* is added to a verb ending in a voiced consonant (b, d, v, g, z, l, etc.) or in a vowel sound, the final *d* is pronounced *d*.

Write *t* or *d* to show the pronunciation of the *ed* in each word.

1. lived	_d_	22. boiled	_____
2. picked	_t_	23. finished	_____
3. jumped	_____	24. burned	_____
4. placed	_____	25. filled	_____
5. hurried	_____	26. passed	_____
6. rushed	_____	27. excused	_____
7. smoked	_____	28. mailed	_____
8. killed	_____	29. slipped	_____
9. looked	_____	30. liked	_____
10. dropped	_____	31. used	_____
11. turned	_____	32. changed	_____
12. crossed	_____	33. worked	_____
13. entered	_____	34. studied	_____
14. stopped	_____	35. talked	_____
15. earned	_____	36. spelled	_____
16. knocked	_____	37. thanked	_____
17. saved	_____	38. washed	_____
18. played	_____	39. poured	_____
19. wished	_____	40. walked	_____
20. showed	_____	41. pulled	_____
21. closed	_____	42. tried	_____

57 *To get*

Idiomatic Meanings:

To get (someplace) means "to arrive."
I *got* home late last night.   Her flight *gets* here at ten P.M.

To get means "to buy."
He *got* a new suit on sale.   We're *getting* a word processor for the office.

To get, with various adjectives, means "to become."
Gabriela *got* angry when you said that.   I always *get* hungry at this time of day.

To get is used in many idiomatic expressions, for example, *to get up, to get on, to get in, to get over.*

In the following sentences, substitute the proper phrase with a form of *to get* for the words in italics.

1. He *became angry* with us because we left so early.   <u>got angry</u>
2. I didn't *arrive home* until almost eight o'clock.   _____
3. He *entered* the elevator as soon as the door opened.   _____
4. How long will it take you to *prepare* for the party?   _____
5. The plane *arrives in* Washington about noon.   _____
6. She always *boards* the bus at this corner.   _____
7. She always *leaves* the bus at 79th Street.   _____
8. I *become very tired* if I have to walk too far.   _____
9. Helen *became excited* when she heard the good news.   _____
10. It took her several months to *recover from* the death of her friend.   _____
11. John *entered* the automobile first, and then I followed him.   _____
12. I usually *arrive at* my office at about nine o'clock.   _____
13. I seldom *reach home* before seven o'clock.   _____
14. Mr. Smith drank so much wine that I thought he was going to *become drunk*.   _____
15. They plan to *marry* in June.   _____
16. I always *become nervous* before an examination.   _____

58 Silent letters

For each of the words below, write the consonant that is written but not pronounced.

1. knife	k	26. write		
2. answer	w	27. fasten		
3. handsome		28. castle		
4. Christmas		29. hymn		
5. island		30. scissors		
6. doubt		31. lamb		
7. knee		32. gnaw		
8. wrestle		33. limb		
9. honest		34. wrong		
10. often		35. wrist		
11. knew		36. listen		
12. sign		37. sword		
13. dumb		38. comb		
14. match		39. knot		
15. walk		40. kneel		
16. could		41. czar		
17. talk		42. half		
18. knock		43. ghost		
19. know		44. whistle		
20. Wednesday		45. scent		
21. pneumonia		46. calf		
22. climb		47. ledge		
23. should		48. hour		
24. aisle		49. scene		
25. whole		50. thumb		

The items in boldface are mistakes. Change them to make the facts correct, and write your answers in the blanks.

1. There are **fifty-six** weeks in a year. <u>fifty-two</u>
2. The opposite of *thick* is **narrow**. _____
3. To board a train is to **get off** it. _____
4. Grass is generally **red** in color. _____
5. The word *sleepy* is **a noun**. _____
6. December is the **tenth** month of the year. _____
7. The opposite of *loose* is **find**. _____
8. The opposite of *safe* is **careless**. _____
9. In the word *wrist* the letter **r** is silent (not pronounced). _____
10. A triangle is a geometrical figure having **four** sides. _____
11. To *call on* someone is to **telephone** him or her. _____
12. The Pacific Ocean lies **east** of the United States. _____
13. The sun always rises in the **west**. _____
14. Grapes grow on **trees**. _____
15. We always buy and sell eggs by the **pound**. _____
16. The term of office of the president of the United States is **six** years. _____
17. There are **thirty-nine** inches in a yard. _____
18. **Mr.** is a title for a married or unmarried woman. _____
19. A common English proverb is "A stitch in time saves **eight**." _____
20. Columbus discovered America in **1482**. _____
21. The past participle of the verb *to be* is **was**. _____
22. The past participle of the verb *to see* is **saw**. _____

60 Prepositions 4

Write the correct prepositions or particles in the blanks.

1. He is not interested _____ English. _____in_____

2. We arrived _____ Boston at exactly six o'clock. _____

3. She lives far _____ the station. _____

4. We went to the beach in spite _____ the bad weather. _____

5. Sue sits _____ front of me in chemistry class. _____

6. The police officer ran _____ the thief but could not catch him. _____

7. Roger is mad _____ me because I won't go to the beach with him. _____

8. Ana is always trying to borrow money _____ someone. _____

9. I'll be back _____ an hour. _____

10. It is dark in this room. Please turn _____ the light. _____

11. The wind blew my hat _____. _____

12. The dog tried to jump _____ the fence, but the fence was too high for him. _____

13. The man died _____ pneumonia. _____

14. They called off the game because _____ rain. _____

15. Her English is improving little _____ little. _____

16. The teacher crossed _____ several words in my composition. _____

17. The vending machine is not working today. It must be out _____ order. _____

18. Al did not do very well _____ his last exam. _____

19. Maureen is very enthusiastic _____ her new job. _____

20. He left his hat _____ the chair. _____

21. He likes to walk _____ the rain. _____

22. Rosemary plays the piano _____ ear. _____

23. We plan to go to Chicago _____ plane. _____

24. She is the girl I spoke to you _____. _____

Select the correct answer and write it in the space provided.

1. We pronounce the contraction *he'd* to rhyme with (head, need, had, nod).   <u>need</u>

2. Tomatoes grow (on trees, on vines, in the ground, on bushes).   _____

3. We pronounce the word *please* to rhyme with (police, this, cease, breeze).   _____

4. To *get over* something means to (end, return to, need, recover from) it.   _____

5. What is the corresponding noun form of the verb to *succeed*?   _____

6. Which of the following animals is used mainly in the desert: giraffe, elephant, camel, cow?   _____

7. Which of the following is a popular dessert in the United States: roast beef, apple pie, chocolate milk, celery?   _____

8. We pronounce the word *said* to rhyme with (laid, sad, made, bed).   _____

9. Which of the following past tense forms do we pronounce as a word of only one syllable: counted, wanted, asked, needed, planted.   _____

10. Which letter in the word *ghost* is silent (not pronounced)?   _____

11. Which letter in the word *knit* is silent (not pronounced)?   _____

12. Which of these past tense forms do we pronounce as a word of two syllables: asked, changed, burned, pointed?   _____

13. In an airplane, which section is the cheapest: business class, coach, first class?   _____

14. The word *exhausted* has three syllables; on which of these three syllables do we accent the word?   _____

15. *Lately* means (very late, hardly ever, recently, seldom).   _____

16. Which one of these words is not spelled correctly: berth, shouted, garantee, reservation, interpreter?   _____

17. Which of these is a past participle: went, came, saw, did, gone?   _____

62 General review 4

Select the correct form. Write your answers in the blanks.

1. They (was, were) both sitting in the park when I saw them. _____were_____

2. When I met him, he already (has had, had had) his lunch. _____

3. Ali (saved, has saved) $500 since January. _____

4. Last night, while we (went, were going) to the movies, we met some old friends. _____

5. Nina (went, has gone) to the dance last night with Sal. _____

6. With (who, whom) did you go to the movies last night? _____

7. Orchids, (who, which) are very beautiful, are difficult to grow. _____

8. She asked (me to wait, that I wait) for her. _____

9. He (said, told) that he would be back at six o'clock. _____

10. She said her last name (is, was) Castro. _____

11. He said that he (will, would) wait for us after the lesson. _____

12. Ruth sat (between, among) Sachiko and Stephanie. _____

13. Liz always (sits, is sitting) at this desk. _____

14. Look! It (begins, is beginning) to snow. _____

15. (Not, No) one student from our group attended the meeting. _____

16. He asked me what (was my name, my name was). _____

17. She spends (much, many) time on her English. _____

18. He has always been a good friend of (her, hers). _____

19. Yesterday I met an old classmate of (me, my, mine). _____

20. He (said, told) us that he would meet us at noon. _____

21. Chris was sick yesterday and (can, could) not come to class. _____

22. When I got there, they (were having, had) dinner. _____

62

63 **Passive voice 1**

In the passive voice, the subject receives the action of the verb. Form the passive voice by using the appropriate form of *to be* and the past participle of the main verb.

Active Voice	*Passive Voice*
He repairs my shoes.	My shoes *are repaired* by him.
He repaired my shoes.	My shoes *were repaired* by him.
He will repair my shoes.	My shoes *will be repaired* by him.
He has repaired my shoes.	My shoes *have been repaired* by him.

Change the following sentences from the active to the passive voice. Write complete sentences. Put all adverbial expressions at the end of the sentence.

1. Mr. Dodd teaches this class.   This class is taught by Mr. Dodd.

2. She writes many newspaper articles. _____

3. The maid cleans the room every day. _____

4. Everyone hears their quarrels. _____

5. The letter carrier delivers the mail. _____

6. The secretary writes all the letters. _____

7. Everyone enjoys her speeches. _____

8. They sell the magazine everywhere. _____

9. She corrects our exercises at home. _____

10. Joe prepares dinner every night. _____

11. They deliver the mail at ten o'clock. _____

12. A messenger brings urgent information. _____

13. They sign the papers in ink. _____

14. She brought presents from Hong Kong. _____

15. The teacher corrects our compositions. _____

16. They print the books in Boston. _____

17. He cuts the grass once a week. _____

18. They send the letters by air mail. _____

19. The lawyer prepares the contracts. _____

20. The foundation provides the money. _____

(64) Passive voice 2

The passive voice in the past perfect tense is formed in the following way:

Akira Kurosawa had directed the movie.
The movie *had been directed* by Akira Kurosawa.

Change the following sentences from the active to the passive voice. Write complete sentences. Put all adverbial expressions at the end of the sentence.

1. Mr. Sato taught the class yesterday.

   The class was taught by Mr. Sato yesterday.

2. Someone took the money. _____

3. The letter carrier had delivered the mail. _____

4. He has signed the letters. _____

5. She has written many books. _____

6. Marianne paid the bills by check. _____

7. They will finish the work tomorrow. _____

8. He had finished the work in time. _____

9. They have planned the party. _____

10. Native Americans grew corn in Mexico. _____

11. He has designed several buildings. _____

12. He had signed the contract previously. _____

13. She broke the plate while she was washing it. _____

14. Julia saw the accident on her way home from work. _____

15. They had bought the tickets. _____

16. They have found the child at last. _____

17. Sonia planted the trees. _____

18. They prepared the dinner. _____

19. She will send it immediately. _____

20. He used the key to open the door. _____

65 Passive voice 3

Form the passive voice of *can*, *have to*, *may*, *must*, *ought to*, and *should* with *be* and the past participle of the main verb.

I *must* finish this work quickly.　　This work *must be finished* (by me) quickly.

You *can* protect the plants with plastic bags.　　The plants *can be protected* (by you) with plastic bags.

She *should* do her work on a word processor.　　Her work *should be done* (by her) on a word processor.

Form the passive voice with infinitives by using *be* and the past participle of the main verb.

He has *to do* it today.　　It has *to be done* (by him) today.

They are going *to take* it.　　It is going *to be taken* by them.

Form the passive in the continuous tenses with *being* and the past participle of the main verb.

She *is watering* the flowers.　　The flowers *are being watered* by her.

If it is not important to state the doer of the action, the *by* phrase can be omitted.

Change the following sentences from the active to the passive voice. Write complete sentences. Leave out the *by* phrase if the subject is a pronoun. Put all adverbial expressions at the end of the sentence.

1. We can finish this today.　　This can be finished today.
2. The museum may keep it for two weeks.　　———————
3. You can pay the bill later.　　———————
4. We have to deliver it tomorrow.　　———————
5. They can't put those things there.　　———————
6. They must send it at once.　　———————
7. They should deliver it today.　　———————
8. You ought to write it now.　　———————
9. Kevin must study these exercises.　　———————
10. They may bring it later.　　———————
11. Linda can use this room.　　———————
12. She has to do it soon.　　———————
13. The police may hold him for several days.　　———————

66 Passive voice: negative form

Form negatives in the passive voice by placing *not* after the auxiliary verb. We generally use the contracted forms.

The book *was not written (wasn't written)* by Ian Fleming.
The film *will not be shown (won't be shown)* until next week.

Change the following sentences to the negative form. Write the complete verb in the blanks.

1. The book was published in France.   was not published

2. The books will be delivered on Wednesday.   _____

3. These letters must be signed in pencil.   _____

4. The thief was shot by a police officer.   _____

5. This class is taught by Ellen Marks.   _____

6. The package was wrapped very neatly.   _____

7. The house was struck by lightning.   _____

8. The mail has been delivered.   _____

9. The war was followed by a serious economic depression.   _____

10. The screams were heard by everyone.   _____

11. This room can be used for our lesson.   _____

12. The book was printed in Mexico.   _____

13. The letters were sent by regular mail.   _____

14. The merchandise will be delivered tomorrow.   _____

15. The bill can be sent after the first of the month.   _____

16. The money was taken by one of the visitors.   _____

17. We were disappointed by the music.   _____

18. The report will be prepared by Joe Trumbull.   _____

19. All the work has been finished.   _____

20. The house had been decorated by a New York firm.   _____

67) **Passive voice:** question form

Form questions in the passive voice by placing the auxiliary verb before the subject.

> *Will* that film *be shown* on TV this year?
> *Was* the best actor award *won* by Robert De Niro?

Change the following sentences to the question form. Write the subject and the complete verb in the blanks.

1. The man was shot by a police officer.   Was the man shot

2. The thief was captured by the police.   _____

3. The lecture will be attended by many important people.   _____

4. The dinner has been served by the host.   _____

5. We are invited to David's party.   _____

6. The work will be done by a Santa Fe firm.   _____

7. The city was destroyed by fire.   _____

8. These letters must be signed at once.   _____

9. America was discovered in 1492.   _____

10. The house has been struck by lightning.   _____

11. The tree was blown down by the wind.   _____

12. They were arrested by the police.   _____

13. The book will be published next month.   _____

14. This work must be finished today.   _____

15. The mail is delivered at exactly nine o'clock.   _____

16. The letters are written by Connie.   _____

17. The car was destroyed in the accident.   _____

18. Their engagement will be announced soon.   _____

19. They will be married in New York.   _____

20. The meeting was held in Paris.   _____

21. It was attended by all the foreign ministers.   _____

22. All these books can be borrowed from the library.   _____

(68) Review: articles

Write the definite or indefinite article in the blanks. If no article is necessary, leave blank.

1. They say that _____ climate of Mexico is very pleasant.   the

2. I bought my new suit at _____ Macy's.   _____

3. I have such _____ headache that I can hardly see.   _____

4. How do you like that kind of _____ weather?   _____

5. I enjoy walking along _____ Ocean Avenue.   _____

6. _____ Bank Street pier is popular on weekends.   _____

7. May I have a glass of _____ cold water?   _____

8. _____ water in this glass is not cold.   _____

9. This is one of _____ longest rivers in the world.   _____

10. Susan is _____ engineer.   _____

11. I will meet you in front of _____ Grand Central Station.   _____

12. _____ United States sent three astronauts to the moon in 1969.   _____

13. Have you ever visited _____ England?   _____

14. _____ English fought bravely in World War II.   _____

15. _____ English language is not difficult to learn.   _____

16. It was so hot _____ day that we had to stop work.   _____

17. It was such _____ hot day that we had to stop work.   _____

18. We walked along Fifth Avenue as far as _____ Central Park.   _____

19. In general, it takes several years to learn _____ foreign language.   _____

20. He is _____ Frenchman.   _____

21. This is _____ Dominique's book.   _____

22. _____ Dominican Republic lies east of Cuba.   _____

23. We took a trip around _____ Mediterranean.   _____

24. _____ President Grey had a serious heart attack.   _____

25. _____ president will speak on TV tonight.   _____

Study and memorize the list of irregular verbs below. Note that they terminate in an *n* sound in the past participle form.

grow	grew	grown	speak	spoke	spoken
hide	hid	hidden	steal	stole	stolen
know	knew	known	take	took	taken
lie	lay	lain	tear	tore	torn
ride	rode	ridden	throw	threw	thrown
see	saw	seen	wear	wore	worn
shake	shook	shaken	write	wrote	written

Write the correct form of the verb in the sentences below.

1. Someone broke into our house last night and (steal) our new television set.   <u>stole</u>
2. Look! You have (tear) your coat.   _____
3. The dog has always (lie) in that position.   _____
4. I have (know) Franco for many years.   _____
5. After Michael introduced us, we (shake) hands.   _____
6. Michel (speak) to me about that matter yesterday.   _____
7. The child has (grow) more than six inches in the last year.   _____
8. Pedro got angry and (throw) the book on the table.   _____
9. The child ran and (hide) behind a tree.   _____
10. She has (wear) that hat every day for months.   _____
11. Last night I stayed at home and (write) several letters.   _____
12. Carlos (take) Monique to the dance last night.   _____
13. I haven't (ride) in Sachiko's new car yet.   _____
14. He was born in Mexico but (grow) up in California.   _____
15. I haven't (see) Nina in several weeks.   _____
16. Clara (tear) up the letter and then threw it away.   _____
17. Grace and Jane have not (speak) to each other for several months.   _____
18. Paul (know) Spain well because he had been there many times before.   _____
19. I believe he has (know) about it for a long time.   _____
20. Giselle (wear) a nice ski outfit yesterday.   _____

Vocabulary review:
opposites 2

Write the opposites of the following words.

1. loser   _winner_
2. strong   _____
3. everyone   _____
4. alive   _____
5. false   _____
6. polite   _____
7. careful   _____
8. stop   _____
9. remember   _____
10. wrong   _____
11. early   _____
12. never   _____
13. slow   _____
14. effect   _____
15. smooth   _____
16. loosen   _____
17. wholesale   _____
18. brave   _____
19. sell   _____
20. quiet   _____
21. dry   _____
22. tight   _____
23. forward   _____
24. complicated   _____
25. empty   _____

26. sweet   _____
27. tall   _____
28. useless   _____
29. increase   _____
30. follow   _____
31. parent   _____
32. front   _____
33. raise   _____
34. tragedy   _____
35. same   _____
36. east   _____
37. rise   _____
38. depart   _____
39. lost   _____
40. domestic   _____
41. presence   _____
42. temporary   _____
43. victory   _____
44. private   _____
45. enemy   _____
46. lend   _____
47. subtract   _____
48. guilty   _____
49. common   _____
50. winter   _____

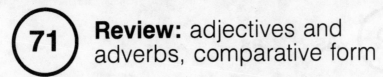

(71) Review: adjectives and adverbs, comparative form

The comparative form of one-syllable adjectives and adverbs adds *er*.

cold–colder   fast–faster

The comparative form of adjectives and adverbs of more than one syllable usually uses *more*. However, two-syllable adjectives that end in *y* or *ow* add *er*. The *y* is changed to *i* before the *er* is added.

expensive–more expensive   needy–needier
rapidly–more rapidly   shallow–shallower

Remember the irregular forms of the following adjectives and adverbs:

good–better   well–better
bad–worse   badly–worse

Write the comparative form of the following adjectives and adverbs + *than*.

1. Tokyo is (big) Chicago.   *bigger than*
2. Carmen is (intelligent) her sister.
3. He arrived (early) we expected.
4. This book is (interesting) that one.
5. The Amazon River is much (wide) the Orinoco River.
6. This exercise is (easy) the last one.
7. She sings (beautiful) her sister.
8. She drives even (fast) her father.
9. He returned (soon) we expected.
10. Some people speak English (clear) others.
11. He goes there (often) I.
12. Your pronunciation is (good) Clara's.
13. The weather today is (cold) it was yesterday.
14. She is (busy) she has ever been before.
15. Diego works (hard) the other students.
16. She prepares her lessons (careful) they.
17. They go to the movies (often) we.
18. I got up this morning (early) usual.
19. Oranges are (sweet) lemons.
20. Prices are (high) they have ever been.

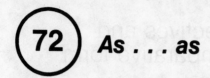

72 As . . . as

As . . . as expresses equality. The phrase may be used with both adjectives and adverbs.

Lisa is *as* tall *as* Doug.
Martin can run *as* fast *as* you can.
I left the office *as* soon *as* I could.

Supply the phrase *as . . . as*, and change adjectives to their corresponding adverb form where necessary.

1. Tomiko is (tall) her brother.   <u>as tall as</u>
2. This book was (expensive) that one.   _____
3. Mario is not (old) I.   _____
4. She can speak English (good) the teacher.   _____
5. Amanda can't swim (fast) I.   _____
6. I will be there (soon) possible.   _____
7. I did (good) I could on the examination.   _____
8. The boy ran home (fast) his legs could carry him.   _____
9. Telephone me (soon) you get home.   _____
10. I don't think it is (cold) it was yesterday.   _____
11. He came to the office (quick) he could.   _____
12. She can do the work (easy) I.   _____
13. I am not (tired) I was yesterday.   _____
14. She doesn't work (hard) the other students.   _____
15. Your pronunciation is certainly (good) mine.   _____
16. We go to the movies (often) we can.   _____
17. Naturally, I cannot speak English (rapid) the teacher. _____
18. I do my homework (careful) I can.   _____
19. She plays the piano (beautiful) anyone I have ever heard. _____
20. He is almost (rich) the queen.   _____
21. She visits us (often) she can.   _____
22. I telephoned you (soon) I could.   _____

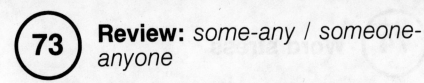

(73) Review: *some-any* / *someone-anyone*

Use *some* in affirmative sentences. Use *any* in negative sentences.

We took *some* money with us.   We didn't have *any* money with us.

Use *someone, somebody, something, somewhere* in affirmative sentences.
Use *anyone, anybody, anything, anywhere* in negative sentences.

I saw *someone* standing in the shadows.   The witness said she hadn't seen *anything*.

Choose the correct form, and write it in the blanks.

1. He doesn't have (some, any) friends there.   _____any_____

2. The police found him (somewhere, anywhere) in Central Park.   _____

3. I didn't see (someone, anyone) in Ms. Stein's office.   _____

4. I didn't have (some, any) time to prepare my homework last night.   _____

5. Irene has (some, any) very pretty Persian carpets.   _____

6. Don't tell (someone, anyone) about this.   _____

7. Rita didn't say (something, anything) to me about it.   _____

8. I gave the old man (some, any) money.   _____

9. He met her (somewhere, anywhere) in Europe.   _____

10. I didn't have (some, any) money with me at the time.   _____

11. My aunt didn't send me (something, anything) for my birthday.   _____

12. I hear (someone, anyone) in the next room.   _____

13. Juan said that he hadn't seen (someone, anyone) in the room.   _____

14. There are (some, any) people waiting to see you.   _____

15. The police refuse to let (someone, anyone) see the prisoner.   _____

16. Mr. and Mrs. Garcia don't have (some, any) children.   _____

17. We didn't see (someone, anyone) we knew at the concert.   _____

18. I lost my purse (somewhere, anywhere) between here and 79th Street.   _____

Study and memorize the pronunciation of each word listed below. Write the number of syllables of each word in the first column. Write an ordinal number in the second column to tell which syllable of each word is stressed (accented).

	Number of Syllables	*Stressed Syllable*
1. tomorrow	3	2nd
2. newspaper		
3. cafeteria		
4. communicate		
5. continuous		
6. admiration		
7. discovery		
8. president		
9. dangerous		
10. medicine		
11. repeated		
12. appeared		
13. imagination		
14. government		
15. announced		
16. disappointed		
17. important		
18. suggestion		
19. returned		
20. discovered		
21. unable		
22. popularity		
23. carriage		

Write the correct verb form in each of the following sentences.

1. They (have) dinner when we arrived. <u>were having</u>

2. I saw clearly that, a few miles back, we (take) the wrong road. _____

3. Eric always (get up) at the same time every morning. _____

4. I (see) Helen at the airport yesterday. _____

5. But I (not see) her since then. _____

6. Sally, who is in the hospital, (be) there for more than a month. _____

7. We (live) in Palo Alto from 1965 to 1975. _____

8. What _____ you (do) when I telephoned you? _____

9. Listen! Someone (knock) at the door. _____

10. When we lived in San Diego, we often (take) trips by car to Mexico. _____

11. Please be more quiet. The baby (sleep). _____

12. The sun always (rise) in the east. _____

13. Up to now, I (not be) farther west than Chicago. _____

14. Lee said that he already (see) that movie. _____

15. I met a friend yesterday whom I (not see) in five years. _____

16. We (live) in France when the war broke out. _____

17. Columbus, when he died, did not realize that he (discover) a new continent. _____

18. Look! The tree (begin) to bloom. _____

19. Isn't that Antonia who (cross) the street? _____

20. We (arrive) at school every morning at eight o'clock. _____

21. I was frightened because people (run) and screaming all around me. _____

22. Ruth Davila (teach) in that school ever since she graduated from college. _____

23. Art says that he (come) back again tomorrow. _____

24. Gabriela said that she (come) back again tomorrow. _____

25. I (see) him when I return. _____

76 Vocabulary review:
mistakes of fact 3

The items in boldface are mistakes. Change them to make the facts correct,
and write your answers in the blanks.

1. The last month of the year is **November**. <u>December</u>
2. There are **fourteen** inches in a foot. _____
3. The section which we call New England is situated in the **northwestern** part of the United States. _____
4. The longest river in the United States is the **Hudson River**. _____
5. We accent the word *invitation* on the **fourth** syllable. _____
6. We accent the word *composition* on the **second** syllable. _____
7. The word *quickly* is an **adjective**. _____
8. In the United States, Independence Day is celebrated on **November 27**. _____
9. The verb *see* is the kind of verb called **regular**. _____
10. Canada lies **south** of the United States. _____
11. The largest state in the United States is **California**. _____
12. The smallest state in the United States is **Delaware**. _____
13. To form the present perfect tense in English, we use the verb *have* as an auxiliary verb, and to this auxiliary we add the **present participle** of the main verb. _____
14. The past tense of the verb *lie* is **laid**. _____
15. The past tense of the verb *sit* is **set**. _____
16. The past participle of the verb *go* is **went**. _____
17. In the United States, Thanksgiving is celebrated in the **spring**. _____
18. We pronounce the word *walked* as a word of **two syllables**. _____
19. The superlative form of the adjective *bad* is **worse**. _____
20. March is the **fourth** month of the year. _____
21. In the United States, we celebrate Abraham Lincoln's birthday in **May**. _____
22. In the United States, when we speak of the Father of His Country, we are referring to **Abraham Lincoln**. _____

76

Write the correct prepositions or particles in the blanks

1. Both Alice and Marianne were absent _____ school yesterday.

from

2. Lucia bought a ticket _____ Chicago at the station.

_____

3. I'll be over to see you _____ Wednesday night.

_____

4. We have decided to put _____ our trip until next month.

_____

5. What is the word _____ eggs in Spanish?

_____

6. He plans to take a trip _____ the world next year.

_____

7. A scarecrow is supposed to drive birds away _____ the garden.

_____

8. What time do you get home _____ school every day?

_____

9. Our team was playing _____ the team from the next town.

_____

10. He stuck the stamps _____ the envelope.

_____

11. This is an exception _____ the rule.

_____

12. He threw a stone and hit me _____ the eye.

_____

13. He took the child _____ the hand and helped her to cross the street.

_____

14. You can always depend _____ Rose.

_____

15. He asked the druggist to give him something _____ a headache.

_____

16. He doesn't understand a word _____ English.

_____

17. I met Catherine _____ my way to school.

_____

18. They laughed _____ the story I had told.

_____

19. The buses are always crowded _____ this time of day.

_____

20. The woman who waited _____ us was very polite.

_____

21. The package was too heavy _____ her to carry.

_____

22. He smiled _____ me in a very friendly way.

_____

23. We could see them _____ the distance.

_____

Select the correct answer and write it in the space provided.

1. If someone goes somewhere *for good*, he or she goes there (on a vacation, for health reasons, for a change, permanently).

   <u>permanently</u>

2. *On account of* has the same meaning as (instead of, in front of, in need of, because of).

   _____

3. *Once in a while* means (sometimes, for a long time, seldom, forever).

   _____

4. In which of these words is the letter *s* pronounced like *z*: miss, pass, was, this?

   _____

5. *Pretty good* means (very good, rather good, awfully good, not at all good).

   _____

6. The word *tough* is pronounced to rhyme with (cough, love, enough, ought).

   _____

7. The opposite of *rough* is (shiny, lean, smooth, easy).

   _____

8. Potatoes grow in the ground, but tomatoes grow on (trees, bushes, vines, fences).

   _____

9. What is the corresponding noun form of the verb *explain*?

   _____

10. What is the corresponding adjective form of the noun *curiosity*?

    _____

11. Which one of the following verbs is a regular verb: see, take, swim, come, count?

    _____

12. To shave, a person needs a (knife, fork, map, razor, string).

    _____

13. We pronounce the contraction *she'll* to rhyme with (shell, will, pale, heel).

    _____

14. Which of these words is a synonym for *student*: child, orphan, companion, pupil?

    _____

15. Which of these has the lowest army rank: corporal, sergeant, lieutenant, captain?

    _____

16. What is the plural form of *mouse*?

    _____

17. What is the plural form of *sheep*?

    _____

Select the correct form. Write your answers in the blanks.

1. There (was, were) several students absent from class this morning.   _were_

2. Angela (slept, was sleeping) when I telephoned her.   _____

3. We (are going, go) to school by bus every morning.   _____

4. He (is, has been) in the hospital for several weeks.   _____

5. She is a very old friend of (me, my, mine).   _____

6. He wants (that we wait, us to wait) for him after the lesson.   _____

7. Isn't that Carlos who (waits, is waiting) in line?   _____

8. She said that she (can, could) speak French.   _____

9. The police refuse to let (someone, anyone) visit the prisoner.   _____

10. She works much harder (as, than) the other students.   _____

11. She is (a, an) honest woman.   _____

12. He is also (a, an) very honest person.   _____

13. He wanted to know where (I lived, did I live).   _____

14. When I got there, they (had, were having) dinner.   _____

15. He (said, told) that he would call me later.   _____

16. She didn't think that she (can, could) go with us.   _____

17. I thought that I (may, might) not be able to get there in time to see him.   _____

18. Adela sent (her, to her) some beautiful flowers.   _____

19. Hurry! The bus (comes, is coming) around the corner.   _____

20. They (have, are having) their music lesson now.   _____

21. They always (have, are having) their music lesson on Tuesday at this time.   _____

22. They (spent, have spent) two months in Mexico last winter.   _____

23. The teacher explained (us, to us) the correct meaning of the word.   _____

24. They (are, have been) very good friends for many years.   _____

80 Review: irregular verbs 2

Study and memorize the forms of the following irregular verbs.

begin	began	begun	sing	sang	sung
drink	drank	drunk	sink	sank	sunk
ring	rang	rung	spring	sprang	sprung
shrink	shrank	shrunk	swim	swam	swum

The following verbs have the same form for the present tense, the past tense, and the past participle. Study and memorize them.

bet	cut	let	shut
burst	hit	put	split
cost	hurt	set	spread

Write the correct form of the verb in the sentences below.

1. The meeting had already (begin) when we arrived.   _begun_

2. We (sing) all the latest popular songs last night.   _____

3. The telephone (ring) just as I was leaving home.   _____

4. We will (set) the table for dinner later.   _____

5. Felipe (put) on his coat and left the room.   _____

6. It has (begin) to rain very hard.   _____

7. Has the school bell (ring) yet?   _____

8. Paolo (hurt) himself playing soccer yesterday.   _____

9. Mr. Wong has (drink) his medicine already.   _____

10. The teacher (let) us go home early yesterday.   _____

11. The ship had already (sink) when help arrived.   _____

12. Pina's dress (shrink) when she washed it.   _____

13. The cat (spring) upon the mouse and killed it instantly.   _____

14. Joan has (put) every cent she has into that business.   _____

15. We went to the beach yesterday and (swim) in the ocean for several hours.   _____

16. Have you ever (cut) yourself badly with a knife?   _____

17. The boy threw a stone at his companion and (hit) him in the eye.   _____

18. The news of the explosion last night (spread) quickly.   _____

19. It has (cost) her a great deal of money to educate her five children.   _____

Supposed to

Supposed to, used with the simple form of the main verb, expresses anticipation, expectation, or obligation. It can be used in the past and present tenses.

Julia *is supposed to* get here before the weekend. (present)
We *were supposed to* mail you the package last week, but we just mailed it today. (past)

Write the correct form of *supposed to* in the sentences below. Include the main verb in your answer.

1. We (spend) two hours on our homework every night. <u>are supposed to spend</u>

2. He (leave) for Chicago last night, but he was delayed. _____

3. I (arrive) at school every day at nine o'clock. _____

4. Maria (be) here now. _____

5. We (go) to Florida next week. _____

6. Everyone (bring) a friend to the meeting tomorrow. _____

7. She (telephone) me yesterday, but apparently she forgot. _____

8. We (write) a composition for tomorrow's class. _____

9. The maid (clean) this room every morning. _____

10. The train (arrive) two hours ago. _____

11. Patrick (be) in Paris next month. _____

12. The plane (leave) last night at midnight, but bad weather delayed it. _____

13. They (deliver) the merchandise yesterday. _____

14. She (call) me long distance from New York last night. _____

15. This building (be) open to the public every day. _____

16. June (leave) for Chicago next Wednesday. _____

17. She (stay) there for about two weeks and then go on to California. _____

18. They (publish) the book last October. _____

(82) Used to

Used to describes an action that was a habit in the past or which occurred often in the past but that does not happen at the present time. It can also describe a state in the past.

I *used to* smoke a pack a day. (Now I only smoke a cigarette after each meal).

We *used to* live in Paris. (We moved and now we live in California).

In the blanks at the right, write the phrase *used to* followed by the verb in parentheses.

1. I (play) tennis well when I was a girl.   <u>used to play</u>
2. They (live) across the street from us.   _____
3. She and I (be) good friends.   _____
4. We (walk) to school together every day.   _____
5. He (work) for my father.   _____
6. She (be) one of the smartest girls in town.   _____
7. They (visit) us every summer.   _____
8. He (go) to Europe quite often.   _____
9. She (study) in our group.   _____
10. He (be) a teacher before he went into business.   _____

Substitute a verb phrase with *used to* for the italicized verbs. Write your answers in the blanks at the right.

11. He *spent* too much time studying.   <u>used to spend</u>
12. She *visited* us.   _____
13. He *played* the violin well.   _____
14. She *sent* her mother flowers.   _____
15. He *wrote* articles for the newspapers.   _____
16. I *caught* cold when I went out in the rain.   _____
17. She *helped* me with my lessons.   _____
18. We *danced* until dawn.   _____
19. She *took* Grace to school.   _____
20. I *walked* two miles to school.   _____

(83) Short answers

Short answers are the most common form of answering direct questions. (They are also considered more polite than a simple yes or no answer.) A short answer consists of the subject of the sentence and an auxiliary verb or part of *to be*. If there is no auxiliary verb, the verb *to do* is used.

Can you play tennis?	Yes, I can.	No, I can't.
Do you know my friend?	Yes, I do.	No, I don't.
Is she at home?	Yes, she is.	No, she isn't.
Did Henry call you?	Yes, he did.	No, he didn't.

Note that pronouns are used to replace the noun when the short answer is used.

Write affirmative and negative short answers for the questions below. Answer *you* questions with *I*, and answer *you and X* questions with *we*.

1. Did you do your homework last night?   Yes, I did.   No, I didn't.

2. Is the sun shining?

3. Did it rain hard last night?

4. Is Alice a good teacher?

5. Have you and Will ever been to Mexico?

6. Can Mercedes play tennis well?

7. Does it often rain during April?

8. Is Roger supposed to be here now?

9. Have you and Nora had your dinner yet?

10. Will you be in class tomorrow?

11. Are you going to the movies tonight?

12. Does Christine speak English well?

13. Were you late for your lesson?

14. Was Adela always such a good student?

15. Can Ricardo speak French well?

(84) Tag questions 1

Tag questions invite confirmation of a statement. They contain an auxiliary verb and a pronoun. Affirmative tag questions are used after negative statements; negative tag questions are used after affirmative statements.

You live in the city, don't you?
They had a long trip, didn't they?
You will be at the dinner, won't you?
Maria can speak Spanish, can't she?

In *there is/are* statements, treat *there* like a subject.

Add the correct tag questions to the following sentences.

1. Mario left for Chicago last night, _____?   didn't he
2. She is a very good lawyer, _____?
3. There are many students absent today, _____?
4. You wrote those letters, _____?
5. The traffic will be very heavy, _____?
6. Ana can help us, _____?
7. It was a good movie, _____?
8. He has been your teacher for a long time, _____?
9. He is a very nice fellow, _____?
10. That dog is yours, _____?
11. The bus stops on this corner, _____?
12. You gave me my change, _____?
13. I paid you, _____?
14. Angela is an excellent teacher, _____?
15. She has studied English for many years, _____?
16. Your father is an engineer, _____?
17. You will be in class tomorrow, _____?
18. It was raining at the time, _____?
19. He is supposed to leave tomorrow, _____?
20. You have had your lunch, _____?

84

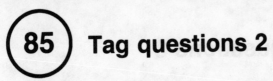

85 Tag questions 2

Remember that affirmative tag questions are used after negative statements.

You don't live in the city, do you?
They didn't have a long trip, did they?
You won't be at the dinner, will you?
Maria can't speak Spanish, can she?

Add the correct tag questions to the following sentences.

1. The plane didn't arrive on time, _____?   did it

2. The bus doesn't stop on this corner, _____?   _____

3. He is not a very dependable person, _____?   _____

4. Norma can't go with us, _____?   _____

5. You won't be back before noon, _____?   _____

6. It wasn't raining at the time, _____?   _____

7. You haven't had your dinner yet, _____?   _____

8. His wife didn't come with him, _____?   _____

9. You can't speak French, _____?   _____

10. You don't know how to swim, _____?   _____

11. He doesn't like to go to the beach, _____?   _____

12. She won't be able to go with us, _____?   _____

13. You haven't ever been to Europe, _____?   _____

14. It hasn't begun to rain, _____?   _____

15. Your roof doesn't leak, _____?   _____

16. You weren't driving fast at the time, _____?   _____

17. Marcella wasn't hurt badly in the accident,
    _____?   _____

18. The mail hasn't been delivered yet, _____?   _____

19. It hasn't rained hard in a long time, _____?   _____

20. You won't mention this to anyone, _____?   _____

Add the correct tag questions to the following sentences.

1. She always goes to New York by plane, _____?   <u>doesn't she</u>
2. Today isn't Wednesday, _____?   _____
3. His father is a rather well-known lawyer, _____?   _____
4. You saw that movie, _____?   _____
5. He won't be back until Wednesday, _____?   _____
6. It rains a lot during the month of April, _____?   _____
7. They have a very pretty home, _____?   _____
8. She is a surgeon, _____?   _____
9. You'll be in class tomorrow, _____?   _____
10. Your watch has stopped, _____?   _____
11. I paid you the money I owed you, _____?   _____
12. Bill hasn't been here today, _____?   _____
13. He didn't telephone you, _____?   _____
14. She dances very well, _____?   _____
15. They have already left for Chicago, _____?   _____
16. You spoke to Sue about that matter, _____?   _____
17. She can meet us after the lesson, _____?   _____
18. He promised to be here at noon, _____?   _____
19. You haven't had your lunch yet, _____?   _____
20. The car skidded, _____?   _____
21. But it was the driver's fault, _____?   _____
22. You see him at church on Sundays, _____?   _____
23. It has been a beautiful day, _____?   _____
24. He never mentioned it again, _____?   _____
25. She doesn't like to go to the beach, _____?   _____

87 Gerunds 1

A gerund is a form of verb which is used as a noun and ends in *ing*. **Certain verbs, like** *enjoy, mind, stop, consider, appreciate,* **and** *finish,* **can be followed by gerunds but not by infinitives.**

Gerund Form	Infinitive Form
I like *walking*.	I like *to walk*.
I tried *calling* you.	I tried *to call* you.
She enjoys *swimming*.	
They have finished *painting*.	

Supply the gerund form of the verb in the following sentences.

1. We appreciate (hear) from you.   hearing
2. The man denied (take) the money.
3. We cannot risk (invest) so much money.
4. The driver could not avoid (hit) the curb.
5. We are considering (move) to Miami.
6. They have already finished (eat).
7. We both enjoy (dance) very much.
8. Do you mind (come) back later?
9. He admitted (hide) the money.
10. She says she doesn't mind (wait) for us.
11. Steve and Tom have stopped (speak) to each other.
12. We enjoy (listen) to music.
13. He is going to stop (study) English.
14. We will enjoy (use) your cottage at the beach while you are away.
15. They have finally finished (paint) our apartment.
16. Would you mind (open) the window?
17. She denied (change) the address on the package.
18. We are considering (buy) a new car.
19. We would appreciate (receive) your answer immediately.
20. He finally admitted (make) the mistake.
21. I don't mind (ride) the subway.

(88) Gerunds 2

The following verbs may be followed by both gerunds and infinitives:

start	begin	continue	like	neglect
hate	try	love	prefer	intend

Complete the following sentences, once with the gerund and then with the infinitive.

1. She loves (work) for herself.   ____working____   ____to work____

2. He intends (leave) tomorrow.   _____   _____

3. She will try (study) in the library.   _____   _____

4. They will start (work) there next week.   _____   _____

5. She hates (do) secretarial work.   _____   _____

6. She will continue (work) in that same office until June.   _____   _____

7. He prefers (dance) with his wife.   _____   _____

8. I neglected (mention) it to Bill.   _____   _____

9. He likes (teach) English to foreign students.   _____   _____

10. They will begin (build) their new home soon.   _____   _____

11. He prefers (watch) television.   _____   _____

12. She intends (stay) right where she is.   _____   _____

13. He loves (criticize) others.   _____   _____

14. We tried (find) an apartment near the park.   _____   _____

15. They have finally started (speak) to each other.   _____   _____

16. Rose loves (do) that kind of work.   _____   _____

17. They continue (send) us a bill for the work.   _____   _____

Gerunds may be used after most prepositions in the same way as nouns.

I am fond of *hiking*.
You use this lever for *turning* on the heat.

Gerunds are used after the expressions *to be worth,* *no use,* **and** *do you mind*.

Your ideas *are* certainly *worth considering*.
It's *no use worrying* about it. It doesn't affect us.
Do you mind closing the window? I'm cold.

Supply the correct preposition and the gerund form of the verb in the following sentences.

1. We are thinking (move) to Miami.   of moving
2. She got tired (wait) for her.   _____
3. We are both very fond (dance).   _____
4. He insisted (go) with us.   _____
5. There is no chance (see) him today.   _____
6. We are excited (go) to Europe.   _____
7. It is a question (find) a good teacher.   _____
8. We all need more lessons (speak).   _____
9. We are looking forward (see) you again.   _____
10. She has had no instruction (teach).   _____
11. He takes great pleasure (help) others.   _____
12. She insisted (help) me.   _____
13. He has no intention (leave) the class.   _____
14. We are all interested (learn) English.   _____
15. Are you fond (swim)?   _____
16. We were finally successful (locate) him.   _____
17. We get tired (study) the same thing.   _____
18. We are thinking (buy) a new car.   _____
19. Is there any chance (see) Professor Frank today? _____
20. We had no difficulty (find) where they lived.   _____
21. She has a talent (manage) children.   _____

90 Review: irregular verbs 3

Write the correct form of the verb in the sentences below.

1. It has (begin) to rain very hard. _____begun_____
2. That dog has (bit) several people. _____
3. The teacher (let) us go home early yesterday. _____
4. All the birds have (fly) south for the winter. _____
5. At our club meeting last night, we (choose) Rolando as our new president. _____
6. Tom has (wear) that same hat for several years. _____
7. While skating in the park yesterday, Henry (fall) and hurt himself. _____
8. I have (give) them all the help I can. _____
9. I caught my coat on a nail and (tear) it. _____
10. I was born in Pennsylvania but (grow) up in New York. _____
11. The boy ran and (hide) behind a tree. _____
12. I have (know) Suzanne for many years. _____
13. We have (drive) to Florida several times. _____
14. We have already (sing) every old song we know. _____
15. I stayed home last night and (write) some letters. _____
16. During that storm last week, the wind (blow) down several trees in our block. _____
17. We have (eat) in that restaurant several times. _____
18. The police have not yet (find) out who stole the money. _____
19. Our guide (lead) us through one government building after another yesterday. _____
20. The dog has (lie) in that same spot all morning. _____
21. I hope that you have not (throw) away those magazines I left here. _____
22. The news of the accident yesterday (spread) quickly. _____
23. The lake (freeze) over last week. _____
24. They have not (speak) to each other in weeks. _____

(91) Idiomatic expressions

Select the correct answer and write it in the space provided.

1. To *look for* something is to (appreciate it, search for it, overlook it, look it up).   <u>search for it</u>

2. If someone goes somewhere for *good*, he or she goes there (for health reasons, to look for work, frequently, permanently).   _____

3. To *get on* a train is to (leave, board, inspect, walk through) it.   _____

4. To *call up* someone is to (wave to, criticize, respect, telephone) him or her.   _____

5. To *call on* someone is to (abuse, look down upon, visit, telephone) him or her.   _____

6. To *call for* someone is to (look up to, come for, name, send for) him or her.   _____

7. *I'd sooner study* means that I (dislike, hope, intend, prefer) to study.   _____

8. To *talk over* something is to (overlook, forget, repeat, discuss) it.   _____

9. To *look over* something is to (forget it, put it aside, examine it, postpone it).   _____

10. To be *about to do* something is to be (worried about doing, at the point of doing, opposed to doing) it.   _____

11. To *throw something away* is to (break, preserve, discard, need) it.   _____

12. *As yet* means (not at all, up to the present, suddenly, almost).   _____

13. To be *used to* something means to be (tired of, happy about, accustomed to, worried about) it.   _____

14. To *make believe* is to (pretend, discuss, withdraw, argue).   _____

15. To be *mixed up* is to be (annoyed, amused, confused, disappointed).   _____

16. To learn something *by heart* is to learn it (quickly, slowly, carelessly, by memory).   _____

17. If someone says to you, "Look out!", this means (look out the window, be careful, sit down and rest).   _____

92 Words used as nouns and verbs

Many words are used as both nouns and verbs, with no change in their form.

Verb	*Noun*
They *work* here every day.	Their *work* is excellent.
We *need* peace in the world.	There is a *need* for world peace.

A few of the many English words besides those in this exercise that may be used as nouns and verbs without a change in form are the following: *study, cry, help, drink, taste, wish, finish, tie, talk, kiss, smile, shout, play, surprise, start, walk, crowd, rest, fall, present, move, ride, watch, block, mistake, scream, curse, fire, fool, mark, result, call, offer, part, escape, play, time, fish, guide, mind,* and *point.*

Write *noun* if the italicized word of the sentence is used as a noun; write *verb* if the italicized word is used as a verb.

1. We *look* very elegant in our new clothes.   <u>verb</u>

   We saw the *look* of surprise on his face.   _____

2. It is a *question* of finding the right person for the job.   _____

   The police are going to *question* everyone about the robbery.   _____

3. There is no *need* to discuss the matter further.   _____

   We *need* some new tires for our car.   _____

4. All children *love* candy.   _____

   His *love* for her will never die.   _____

5. The *sound* of the shot was heard by everyone.   _____

   Both men *sound* angry to me.   _____

6. Martha's *face* looked pale and drawn.   _____

   All the buildings in our block *face* the park.   _____

7. She *plans* to go to Europe in June.   _____

   Their *plans* to go to Europe in June fell through.   _____

8. Did you *notice* the new dress Joyce was wearing?   _____

   Each teacher received a *notice* of the change in examination dates.   _____

9. Why did you *promise* to help him?   _____

   Ned's *promise* to help you means nothing at all.   _____

Many words have different, though similar or related, forms as nouns and verbs. Study and memorize the differences as you write the corresponding noun forms of the verbs listed.

1. to decide decision	23. to appear _____
2. to excite excitement	24. to believe _____
3. to weigh _____	25. to breathe _____
4. to oblige _____	26. to confuse _____
5. to recognize _____	27. to inspect _____
6. to insist _____	28. to admire _____
7. to repeat _____	29. to relieve _____
8. to locate _____	30. to choose _____
9. to arrive _____	31. to embarrass _____
10. to analyze _____	32. to destroy _____
11. to tempt _____	33. to complete _____
12. to argue _____	34. to satisfy _____
13. to adjust _____	35. to enjoy _____
14. to react _____	36. to hesitate _____
15. to expect _____	37. to paralyze _____
16. to prove _____	38. to identify _____
17. to describe _____	39. to protect _____
18. to arrange _____	40. to obey _____
19. to treat _____	41. to discover _____
20. to consider _____	42. to complain _____
21. to explain _____	43. to criticize _____
22. to annoy _____	44. to refuse _____

94 Corresponding noun and verb forms 2

Write the corresponding verb forms of the nouns listed.

1. imagination <u>to imagine</u>
2. existence <u>to exist</u>
3. growth _____
4. interference _____
5. burial _____
6. explosion _____
7. interruption _____
8. disturbance _____
9. apology _____
10. admission _____
11. repetition _____
12. proof _____
13. collection _____
14. relief _____
15. impression _____
16. marriage _____
17. denial _____
18. intention _____
19. choice _____
20. approval _____
21. advice _____
22. death _____
23. suspicion _____
24. agreement _____

25. amusement _____
26. excitement _____
27. robbery _____
28. success _____
29. punishment _____
30. decision _____
31. observation _____
32. reservation _____
33. adoption _____
34. deception _____
35. remainder _____
36. loss _____
37. failure _____
38. warning _____
39. entrance _____
40. beginning _____
41. withdrawal _____
42. paralysis _____
43. belief _____
44. conclusion _____
45. refusal _____
46. destruction _____
47. criticism _____
48. complaint _____

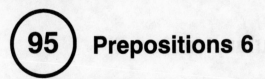

95 Prepositions 6

Write the correct prepositions in the blanks.

1. She is not interested _____ learning English.   _____in_____

2. He is worried _____ his wife's health.   _____

3. It is a question _____ getting permission from the
   authorities.   _____

4. She insisted _____ helping me with the work.   _____

5. For tomorrow's lesson, we will study from page ten
   _____ page fifteen.   _____

6. He poured the wine _____ the glass.   _____

7. The button fell _____ the shirt.   _____

8. She said that, _____ the circumstances, she could
   do nothing for us.   _____

9. He didn't mention anything to me _____ it.   _____

10. We have been waiting for him _____ twenty min-
    utes.   _____

11. Paris is famous _____ its many art galleries.   _____

12. I didn't interfere _____ his plans.   _____

13. Don't lean _____ that fence; it's just been painted.   _____

14. I mistook Jane _____ her sister.   _____

15. I want to ask a favor _____ you.   _____

16. He was absent _____ class yesterday.   _____

17. Don't drink _____ that glass.   _____

18. Her English is improving little _____ little.   _____

19. Who will take care _____ your dog while you are
    away?   _____

20. She should go _____ a diet.   _____

21. His face is very familiar _____ me.   _____

22. We'll have to postpone our trip _____ next month.   _____

23. The game was called off because _____ rain.   _____

24. Whom are they waiting _____?   _____

25. Take the dog out _____ a walk.   _____

Select the correct answer and write it in the space provided.

1. To *talk over* something is to (repeat, discuss, enjoy, forget) it.   discuss

2. The opposite of *temporary* is (soon, early, complicated, permanent).   _____

3. The word *sewed* is pronounced to rhyme with (rude, stewed, flowed, could).   _____

4. The word *scene* is pronounced to rhyme with (cent, tin, men, mean).   _____

5. Which of these words may be used as both a noun and a verb without any change in form: explode, agree, grow, sound, enter?   _____

6. Which of these is an irregular verb: talk, want, count, sing, paint?   _____

7. We pronounce the contraction *there's* to rhyme with (hers, fears, hairs, liars).   _____

8. My *niece* is my (second cousin, enemy, rival, brother's daughter).   _____

9. What is the corresponding noun form of the verb *choose*?   _____

10. What is the corresponding noun form of the verb *advise*?   _____

11. Which letter in the word *often* is not pronounced?   _____

12. Which letter in the word *autumn* is silent?   _____

13. Which of these do we use to sweep the floor: mop, dust rag, broom, soap?   _____

14. Which of these do you need in order to row a boat: sails, anchor, oars, portholes?   _____

15. To ride on a bus or streetcar, you must pay a (fee, lawyer, fare, debt).   _____

16. To get *used to* something is to get (sick of, annoyed at, accustomed to, tired of) it.   _____

17. A common synonym for *trousers* is (vest, pants, cuffs, sleeves).   _____

18. To whom do you take your watch when you want it repaired: tailor, jeweler, druggist, mechanic?   _____

Select the correct form. Write your answers in the blanks.

1. He insisted (to go, on going) with us. <u>on going</u>
2. They are thinking (to move, of moving) to Oakland. _____
3. We (have lived, lived) in this same apartment since June. _____
4. She is not interested (to learn, in learning) English. _____
5. Do you mind (to wait, waiting) a few minutes? _____
6. We would appreciate (to hear, hearing) from you as soon as possible. _____
7. They have finally finished (to paint, painting) our apartment. _____
8. Listen! The train (comes, is coming). _____
9. The baby (cries, is crying) frequently during the day. _____
10. When I got up this morning, it (rained, was raining) hard. _____
11. I am used to (study, studying) with Ms. Levine, and I don't want to change to another teacher. _____
12. The train (supposed, is supposed) to arrive at midnight. _____
13. He asked (that I go, me to go) with him. _____
14. She is an old friend of (us, our, ours). _____
15. The ship had already (sank, sunk) when help arrived. _____
16. He asked me what time it (is, was). _____
17. She said that she (can, could) not speak English well. _____
18. He wants to know what time (will you, you will) return. _____
19. I couldn't find my book (somewhere, anywhere). _____
20. She (works, has worked) in that office for many years. _____
21. He (studied, has studied) English for two years when he was in high school. _____
22. When we arrived, they (watched, were watching) television. _____

98 Questions in indirect speech

Questions in indirect speech are expressed as statements.

Direct: Tamara asked, "Where *does* Sean *live?*"
Indirect: Tamara asked where Sean *lived*.

When the direct question does not contain a question word, the indirect question requires the introduction of *if* or *whether*.

Direct: Tamara asked, "Does Sean live here?"
Indirect: Tamara asked *if* Sean lived here.
            Tamara asked *whether* Sean lived here.

Choose the correct form to complete the sentences below.

1. She asked me what time (was it, it was).   _____it was_____
2. Can you tell me what time (is it, it is).   _____
3. He wanted to know how old (I was, was I).   _____
4. She asked me when (would I, I would) return.   _____
5. Ask him what time (is it, it is).   _____
6. Tell her how old (are you, you are).   _____
7. Ask him why (was he, he was) late.   _____
8. I don't know where (does she live, she lives).   _____
9. He didn't tell me where (did she live, she lived). _____
10. The teacher asked me where (was I, I was) going.   _____
11. I don't know how far (is it, it is) from here to Seville. _____
12. She asked me how much (did I pay, I paid) for my car. _____
13. Ask Marc where (is he, he is) going.   _____
14. Sheila asked me how (did I like, I liked) my new class. _____
15. I don't know where (did Adam put, Adam put) all those old magazines. _____
16. No one seems to know where (did she go, she went). _____
17. Can you tell me how much (does this cost, this costs)? _____
18. I forget where (did I put, I put) it.   _____
19. He asked us in which room (we had, did we have) our English lesson. _____
20. I wonder what time (is it, it is).   _____

(99) Should, ought to

Should and *ought to* **mean the same thing. They both express obligation. The contracted form** *shouldn't* **is normally used.**

You *should spend* more time with your family.
You *ought to spend* more time with your family.
She *shouldn't (should not) smoke* so much.
She *ought not to smoke* so much.

Should **and** *ought* **are less strong in meaning than** *must*. *Must* **has almost the force of a command.** *Should* **and** *ought* **suggest that one has the obligation to do a certain thing.**

Substitute *ought to* **for** *should* **in the sentences below. Write the complete verb.**

1. She *should attend* class more regularly.   ought to attend
2. I *should go* to bed earlier every night. _____
3. He *should choose* his friends more carefully. _____
4. She *should not talk* back to her parents. _____
5. You *should not write* your compositions in pencil. _____
6. She *should be* more careful of her health. _____
7. They *should try* to arrive at school on time. _____
8. We *should get* more physical exercise. _____
9. She *should have* more respect for her parents. _____
10. She *should not speak* to him in that way. _____
11. Children *should obey* their parents. _____
12. Rod *should not read* so much. _____
13. I *should write* to my friends more often. _____
14. He *should try* to put on some weight. _____
15. They *should take* their studies more seriously. _____
16. We *should go* home by bus instead of by taxi. _____
17. This letter *should be sent* at once. _____
18. They *should arrive* at five o'clock. _____
19. These letters *should be written* by Regina. _____
20. He *should not spend* so much money. _____

(100) *Should, ought to:* past form 1

Form the past of sentences with *should* **and** *ought to* **by using** *have* **and the past participle of the main verb.**

We *should be* more careful.
We *should have been* more careful.
He *ought to finish* his work quickly.
He *ought to have finished* his work quickly.

Note that the past form of *should* **and** *ought to* **has a negative feeling, since it suggests that something that should have been done was not done.**

Change these sentences to the past form. Write the correct form of the verb in the blanks at the right.

1. Al *should study* more before his examinations.   should have studied

2. You *should go* with me to visit them.   _____

3. They *should arrive* at five o'clock.   _____

4. You *should go* by plane.   _____

5. She *should telephone* you more often.   _____

6. This letter *should be sent* at once.   _____

7. This package *should be delivered* immediately.   _____

8. She *should be* more careful in handling such things.   _____

9. You *should tell* me all about it.   _____

10. He *should go* to see a doctor at once.   _____

11. This letter *should be written* in ink.   _____

12. He *should write* to us more often.   _____

13. You *should telephone* the police.   _____

14. She *should write* to her parents more often.   _____

15. He *should spend* more time on his homework.   _____

16. They *should not waste* so much time.   _____

17. She *should be* more careful of her health.   _____

18. They *should not tell* anyone about it.   _____

19. She *should ask* permission first.   _____

20. He *should not talk* so freely with everyone.   _____

(101) *Should, ought to:* past form 2

Change the following sentences with *ought to* to the past tense. Remember that the simple form of the verb is changed to the perfect form.

1. She *ought to study* much harder.   <u>ought to have studied</u>

2. You *ought to go* with me to visit them.   _____

3. He *ought to travel* by plane.   _____

4. We *ought to save* more money.   _____

5. She *ought to be* more careful of her health.   _____

6. He *ought to sign* these letters at once.   _____

7. This letter *ought to be sent* by air mail.   _____

8. She *ought not to talk* so much.   _____

9. This package *ought to be delivered* right away.   _____

10. These letters *ought to be typed*.   _____

11. He *ought to see* a doctor at once.   _____

12. They *ought not to mention* it to anyone.   _____

13. We *ought not to waste* so much valuable time.   _____

14. You *ought to explain* it to her more carefully.   _____

15. We *ought to telephone* him at once.   _____

16. She *ought not to work* so hard.   _____

17. This material *ought to be prepared* right away.   _____

18. We *ought to telephone* the police.   _____

19. She *ought to get* more rest.   _____

20. You *ought to go* to bed earlier every night.   _____

21. She *ought to write* to her parents more often.   _____

22. These chairs *ought to be put* in the other room.   _____

(102) Conditional sentences, future possible 1

A conditional sentence has two clauses: the dependent clause introduced by *if* and the main clause.

If you study, you will pass your exam.
If you lend me five dollars, I will pay you back tomorrow.

In future possible conditional sentences, the dependent clause is in the present tense, and the main clause is in the future tense. The modals *can* and *may* may also be used in the main clause.

Write the correct form of the verb in the dependent clause of the conditional sentences below.

1. If Beatrice (study) hard, she will surely graduate.   studies

2. If he (work) hard, he will pass his exam.   _____

3. If she (hurry), she will be able to go with us.   _____

4. If it (rain), we will not go to the beach.   _____

5. If Randy (come), he can help us.   _____

6. If you (attend) class regularly, you will learn English quickly.   _____

7. If the weather (be) nice tomorrow, we will go to the beach.   _____

8. If he (telephone) me, I will let you know.   _____

9. If I (see) her, I will give her your message.   _____

10. If it (not rain), we will go on a picnic tomorrow.   _____

11. If I (have) time, I will call you tomorrow.   _____

12. If they (leave) early, they can get there on time.   _____

13. If she (get) back before four, I will call you.   _____

14. If Colette (call), I will tell her about our plans.   _____

15. If he (not come), I don't know what we will do.   _____

16. If we (decide) to go swimming, we will give you a ring.   _____

17. If the weather (get) any colder, we will have to buy overcoats.   _____

18. If the dog (bite) him, he will have to go to the hospital.   _____

19. If you (have) time tomorrow, we can go to the ball game.   _____

Write the correct form of the verb in parentheses in order to complete the future possible conditional sentences.

1. If Sue studies hard, she (pass) her examination.   __will pass__

2. If I have time tomorrow, I (visit) you.   _____

3. If he doesn't hurry, we (miss) our train.   _____

4. If the weather is good next week, we probably (go) hunting.   _____

5. If it doesn't rain tomorrow, we (go) to the beach.   _____

6. If you attend class regularly, you (learn) English quickly.   _____

7. If they leave early enough, they (be) able to get tickets.   _____

8. If Ann calls, I (tell) her about our change in plans.   _____

9. If we decide to go to the beach, I (let) you know.   _____

10. If it snows tonight, we (have) to stay at home all day tomorrow.   _____

11. If the weather continues to be so cold, I (have) to buy some warmer clothing.   _____

12. If I get a good grade on my examination, my parents (be) pleased.   _____

13. If I have time, I (give) you a ring tomorrow.   _____

14. If I have a car next summer, I (drive) to the beach every day.   _____

15. If we have enough money, we (take) a trip abroad next summer.   _____

16. If he works hard, he (earn) a lot of money in that job.   _____

17. If they get married now, they (have) to live with his parents.   _____

18. If Stella comes before I leave, I (explain) everything to her.   _____

19. If you go to bed earlier, you (be) less tired.   _____

20. If you practice every day, you (play) the piano well.   _____

Conditional sentences, present unreal 1

In present unreal conditional sentences, the dependent clause is in the past tense, and the main clause takes *would*, *should*, *could*, or *might*. In the negative form, the contracted forms (*didn't*, *wouldn't*, *shouldn't*, etc.) are generally used. This kind of conditional sentence is used to talk about a situation which is purely hypothetical.

If Joseph *studied* hard, he *would pass* his exam.
If it *snowed* in the middle of the summer, all the flowers *would die*.
If you *listened* more, you *would learn* what the problems are.

Write the correct form of the verb in order to complete the present unreal conditional sentences below. Use contracted forms for negative sentences.

1. If Stan (spend) more time on his lessons, he would get better marks. _____ spent

2. If I (have) more time, I would go to the beach every day. _____

3. If I (own) an automobile, I would take a trip to California. _____

4. If she (work) harder, she would get a better position. _____

5. If I (know) his telephone number, I would call him up. _____

6. If I (speak) French well, I would take a trip to France. _____

7. If she (go) to bed earlier, she would be less tired. _____

8. If he (pay) more attention in class, he would pass the course. _____

9. If I (know) how to drive, I would buy a car. _____

10. If we (study) together, we could prepare our homework more easily. _____

11. If she (like) languages, it would be easier for her to learn. _____

12. If they (have) more conversation practice, they would speak better. _____

13. If we (have) more time, we would make more progress. _____

14. If I (not have) to work tomorrow, I would go to the beach with you. _____

15. If he (not waste) so much time in class, he would make more progress. _____

16. If I (have) more money, I would spend it on travel. _____

Write the correct form of the verb in order to complete the present unreal conditional sentences below.

1. If Marcia studied harder, she (pass) her examinations easily.   _would pass_

2. If I knew how to play the piano, I (play) for my friends every night.   _____

3. If I didn't have to work today, I (go) swimming in our pool.   _____

4. If Tom had more practice in conversation, he (speak) English much better.   _____

5. If she knew how to drive well, she (have) fewer accidents.   _____

6. If I liked languages better, I (study) French as well as English.   _____

7. If Randy had the time, he (go) to Mexico with us.   _____

8. If she spent more time on her homework, she (get) better grades.   _____

9. If we studied together, we (make) more progress.   _____

10. If I had an automobile, I (take) a trip to Miami.   _____

11. If it didn't cost so much, I (go) to Europe by plane.   _____

12. If I didn't live so far away, I (walk) to school every day.   _____

13. If I had the money, I (buy) some new clothes.   _____

14. If I knew her better, I (ask) her to go with us.   _____

15. If I had the money, I (give) it to you gladly.   _____

16. If I had a good book to read, I (stay) at home tonight and read.   _____

17. If we left right away, we (be) there by two o'clock.   _____

18. If I took the noon train, I (get) there by two o'clock.   _____

(106) Conditional sentences, present unreal 3

Dependent clauses of present unreal conditional sentences use the past tense form of all verbs except *to be*. *To be* takes the special form *were* in all persons in these clauses.

> If he *were* smart, he wouldn't say a word.
> If I *were* in your place, I would not argue with the police officer.

Write the correct form of the verb in order to complete the present unreal conditional sentences below.

1. If I (be) in your position, I would not go with him.   _____were_____

2. If today (be) Saturday, I would not have to work.   _____

3. If the weather (be) warmer, we could go to the beach.   _____

4. If he (be) a friend of mine, I would ask him about it.   _____

5. If I (be) not so busy today, I would go fishing with you.   _____

6. If I (be) a millionaire, I would spend every winter in Miami.   _____

7. If Alan (be) here now, we could ask him about it.   _____

8. If Sue (be) more intelligent, she would never say such a thing.   _____

9. If I (be) not so tired tonight, I would go to the movies with you.   _____

10. If today (be) a holiday, we could all go on a picnic.   _____

11. If I were you, I (explain) everything to him.   _____

12. If Patricia were only here now, she (know) how to handle this matter.   _____

13. If today were a holiday, we (go) to the beach.   _____

14. If I were not so busy, I (go) with you.   _____

15. If you were a millionaire, you (travel) a lot.   _____

16. If she were more ambitious, she (not be) content with such a low-paying job.   _____

17. If I were in your position, I (continue) to study English for several years more.   _____

18. If she were my boss, I (ask) her for a raise.   _____

107 Conditional sentences, past unreal 1

In past unreal conditional sentences, the dependent clause is in the past perfect tense, and the main clause uses *would have, should have, could have,* or *might have.* The contracted forms (*I'd, wouldn't have,* etc.) are generally used.

If you *had studied,* you *would have passed* the exam.
If you *had studied, you'd have passed* the exam.

If I *had known,* I *wouldn't have said* anything.

Write the correct form of the verb in order to complete the past unreal conditional sentences below.

1. If he (study) more, he would have passed his examinations.   <u>had studied</u>

2. If I (know) you were waiting for me, I would have hurried to get here.   _____

3. If you (telephone) me, I would have waited for you.   _____

4. If the weather yesterday (be) nice, we would have gone to the beach.   _____

5. If yesterday (be) a holiday, the stores would all have been closed.   _____

6. If you (go) with us, you would have seen a good show.   _____

7. If she (tell) me the truth, I would have been less angry.   _____

8. If I (receive) an invitation, I would have gone with you to the party.   _____

9. If he (had) enough money, he would have bought a new car.   _____

10. If I (think) about it in time, I would have asked Giselle to go with us.   _____

11. If I (see) him, I would have given him your message.   _____

12. If it (not rain) so hard, we would have been able to make the trip.   _____

13. If she (leave) in time, she would have caught the train.   _____

14. If I (take) a taxi, I would not have missed him.   _____

15. If you (telephone) me, I would have been glad to go with you.   _____

16. If I (know) about this yesterday, I could have brought the money with me.   _____

Write the correct form of the verb in order to complete the past unreal conditional sentences below. Use contractions where appropriate.

1. If Saul had studied harder, he (pass) his examinations. `would have passed`

2. If I had had your telephone number, I (call) you. _____

3. If yesterday had been a holiday, we (go) to the beach. _____

4. If I had known about this last night, I (act) differently. _____

5. If he had attended class more regularly, he (get) a better grade. _____

6. If they had left earlier, they (catch) the train. _____

7. If I had been in your place, I (refuse) to give him the money. _____

8. If I had seen her, I (give) her your message. _____

9. If they had come on time, I (talk) with them. _____

10. If she had had more experience, she (get) the job. _____

11. If she had paid more attention in class, she (do) better on her examination. _____

12. If they had invited me, I (go) with them. _____

13. If I had had the money, I (buy) that car. _____

14. If she had acted differently, we (take) her along. _____

15. If I had been in your position, I (go) with them. _____

16. If you had gone with us, you (meet) her. _____

17. If I had had a car last summer, I (drive) to California. _____

18. If it had not rained, we (go) on a picnic yesterday. _____

19. If you had come earlier, you (have) a fine dinner. _____

20. If she had told me the truth, I (be) less angry. _____

21. If I had known it was going to rain, I (take) my umbrella. _____

22. If we had hurried, we (get) there in time. _____

109 Wish

Wish suggests a situation that is unreal. After _wish_, use a past tense clause to suggest present action and a past perfect tense clause to suggest past action.

I _wish_ I _knew_ what to do in this situation. (present)
I _wish_ I _had known_ what to do in that situation. (past)

Write the correct form of the verb in parentheses.

1. I wish I (know) how to swim.   _knew_

2. I wish I (go) with you to the opera last night.   _____

3. Vanessa wishes she (speak) Dutch.   _____

4. I wish I (have) an automobile.   _____

5. I wish you (telephone) me yesterday about this.   _____

6. I wish I (study) last night.   _____

7. Harry wishes he (be) in his native country now.   _____

8. I wish I (be) in Florida during this cold spell.   _____

9. I wish today (be) Sunday.   _____

10. I wish I (know) that you were going to the beach yesterday.   _____

11. I wish I (start) to study English long ago.   _____

12. I wish I (study) English with Michelle last year.   _____

13. I wish I (know) English perfectly.   _____

14. Kathy wishes she (have) today off.   _____

15. Peter wishes he (be) an engineer instead of a doctor.   _____

16. I wish I (have) today off. I would go swimming.   _____

17. I wish I (have) yesterday off. I would have gone swimming.   _____

18. I wish today (be) Saturday. I would not have to work, and I could go to the beach.   _____

19. I wish yesterday (be) Saturday. I would not have had to work, and I could have gone to the beach.   _____

20. I wish the weather (be) warm so that we could go to the park.   _____

(110) Present tense with future clauses

When a dependent clause introduced by *if* describes a future possibility, it uses the present tense. When dependent clauses introduced by *as long as*, *as soon as*, *before*, *unless*, *until*, *when*, and *while* describe a future condition, they also use the present tense.

I'll see him *when* he *comes*.
I'll see him *as soon as* he *comes*.
I'll wait for him *until* he *arrives*.
While I'm at the supermarket, I'll pick up a pasta salad.

Write the correct form of the verbs in parentheses.

1. I will see him as soon as he (get) here. _____gets_____

2. I will give it to her when she (arrive). _____

3. Before I (leave), I will explain everything to him. _____

4. We will leave as soon as Anita (get) here. _____

5. Do not leave until I (let) you know. _____

6. I won't go unless you (go), too. _____

7. Wait right here until I (telephone) you. _____

8. I'll let you know as soon as I (get) back. _____

9. Don't call unless you (need) me badly. _____

10. We will have to wait here until the doctor (arrive). _____

11. Keep an eye on my bag while I (get) my ticket. _____

12. When the weather (get) warmer, you can go swimming. _____

13. Give him my message as soon as you (see) him. _____

14. Don't leave until Olga (get) back. _____

15. Wait right here while I (telephone). _____

16. I must wait here until the mail (arrive). _____

17. Call me as soon as you (hear) from them. _____

18. Wait here until Ted (come). _____

19. We can tell her when she (return) from her trip. _____

20. The program won't begin until the president (arrive). _____

110

Homophones are words that have the same pronunciation but which differ in meaning. Write the corresponding homophone for each of the words listed.

1. their _____there_____
2. weight _____wait_____
3. threw _____
4. knew _____
5. waist _____
6. way _____
7. weak _____
8. wood _____
9. knight _____
10. know _____
11. cell _____
12. cellar _____
13. cent _____
14. scene _____
15. forth _____
16. die _____
17. flour _____
18. road _____
19. right _____
20. red _____
21. sail _____
22. sees _____
23. berth _____
24. heal _____
25. hear _____

26. seem _____
27. some _____
28. hole _____
29. higher _____
30. him _____
31. meet _____
32. made _____
33. mail _____
34. in _____
35. clothes _____
36. our _____
37. break _____
38. knot _____
39. pear _____
40. plane _____
41. piece _____
42. buy _____
43. role _____
44. guessed _____
45. steal _____
46. so _____
47. son _____
48. principle _____
49. pail _____
50. dear _____

Many words form their opposites by taking a prefix. Write the opposites of the words listed by adding the necessary prefixes.

1. happy _____unhappy_____
2. legal _____illegal_____
3. able _____
4. believable _____
5. regular _____
6. honest _____
7. (to) appear _____
8. (to) obey _____
9. (to) like _____
10. attractive _____
11. legible _____
12. (to) pronounce _____
13. (to) connect _____
14. (to) continue _____
15. (to) understand _____
16. (to) tie _____
17. (to) wrap _____
18. (to) button _____
19. advantage _____
20. mature _____
21. capable _____
22. organized _____
23. (to) dress _____
24. (to) fold _____

25. fortunate _____
26. fair _____
27. (to) agree _____
28. (to) approve _____
29. polite _____
30. discreet _____
31. correct _____
32. sincere _____
33. (to) cover _____
34. furnished _____
35. healthy _____
36. opened _____
37. armed _____
38. patient _____
39. accurate _____
40. (to) infect _____
41. (to) inherit _____
42. convenient _____
43. real _____
44. kind _____
45. satisfied _____
46. agreeable _____
47. pleasant _____
48. dependent _____

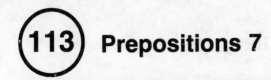

(113) Prepositions 7

Write the correct prepositions or particles in the blanks.

1. The boys in the class like to play tricks _____Tom.   _on_

2. She never pays any attention _____ what the teacher says.   _____

3. I think that he has fallen _____ love with Annie.   _____

4. The senator insisted that he had had nothing to do _____ the scandal.   _____

5. I see Jack once _____ a while in the school cafeteria.   _____

6. I know several of Frost's poems _____ heart.   _____

7. It took me several weeks to get rid _____ my cold.   _____

8. I want to pick _____ a present to give to Sue for her birthday.   _____

9. I feel sorry _____ anyone who is as poor as he is.   _____

10. Let's go _____ a movie. I don't feel like studying.   _____

11. We are looking forward _____ her visit.   _____

12. Peter insisted _____ helping me with my homework.   _____

13. Because of his dark hair and eyes, everyone always takes Sam _____ my brother.   _____

14. I refuse to put up _____ his actions any longer.   _____

15. During our telephone conversation, Pam became angry and hung up _____ me.   _____

16. The teacher always stands _____ front of the class.   _____

17. New York City is the largest city _____ the United States.   _____

18. My book is different _____ yours.   _____

19. Sally has been a teacher in this school _____ 1982.   _____

20. He has tried several times to borrow money _____ me.   _____

21. When are you going _____ vacation?   _____

Select the correct answer and write it in the space provided.

1. To *drop someone a line* is to (telephone, write, visit, save) him or her. <u>write</u>

2. The opposite of *sharp* is (broad, cute, dull, frequent). _____

3. Someone who is *punctual* always (arrives late, arrives on time, comes empty-handed, needs money). _____

4. What is the corresponding noun form of the verb *to widen*? _____

5. What is the corresponding noun form of the verb *to paralyze*? _____

6. What is the corresponding adjective form of the noun *truth*? _____

7. What is the corresponding adjective form of the noun *silence*? _____

8. Someone who is *hard of hearing* is (difficult to hear, difficult to locate, partially deaf, soft-spoken). _____

9. Which of these is a past participle: grew, draw, went, taken, saw? _____

10. Which of these verbs has the same form in the past tense as in the present tense: bring, sing, bend, break, let? _____

11. In which of the following words is the final letter *s* pronounced like *z*: takes, puts, bakes, comes, laughs? _____

12. A common synonym for *seldom* is (often, usually, frequently, rarely). _____

13. We pronounce the contraction *I'd* to rhyme with (lid, lied, led, lad). _____

14. Which one of these words is not spelled correctly (whisper, testimoney, fastened, tremble, February)? _____

15. We pronounce the word *touch* to rhyme with (couch, push, much, cough, rush). _____

16. If someone *gives himself up*, he (faints, falls down, gains courage, surrenders). _____

17. *In vain* means (rapidly, often, without effective result, continuously). _____

(115) General review 7

Select the correct form. Write your answers in the blanks.

1. He (said, told) me that his last name was Ortega. _____told_____
2. He asked me where (was I, I was) going. _____
3. Ronald said that he (will, would) be here before noon. _____
4. You ought (to do, to have done) this work yesterday. _____
5. If I (was, were) you, I would not mention it to him. _____
6. Call me as soon as Alice (arrives, will arrive). _____
7. If I (saw, had seen) Rose yesterday, I would have given her your message. _____
8. She wants to know where (do you live, you live). _____
9. We are old friends of (them, theirs, their). _____
10. This merchandise was supposed (to deliver, to have been delivered) yesterday. _____
11. Listen! I think the telephone (rings, is ringing). _____
12. Do you mind (to come, coming) back a little later? _____
13. He insisted (on waiting, to wait) for me after the lesson. _____
14. We had difficulty (in locating, to locate) him. _____
15. The train (supposed, is supposed) to arrive at two o'clock. _____
16. How long (do you study, have you studied) English? _____
17. We have been friends (during, for) many years. _____
18. Joan speaks Spanish (good, well). _____
19. He is (a, an) very honest man. _____
20. This is (a, an) easy exercise. _____
21. They (live, have lived) in that house for many years. _____
22. Ana always (comes, is coming) to school by bus. _____
23. When you telephoned, I (slept, was sleeping). _____
24. You (should telephone, should have telephoned) me last night. _____

Abbreviated clauses with *too*

We avoid repeating earlier words and phrases in English by using an appropriate auxiliary verb and *too* in short affirmative clauses.

Henry went to the movies, and I went to the movies.
Henry went to the movies, and I *did, too.*

I like New York, and Alice likes New York.
I like New York, and Alice *does, too.*

Rewrite the words in italics by using the correct auxiliary and *too*.

1. She studied English, and *I studied English.*   <u>I did, too</u>

2. She is going to New York, and *he is going to New York.*   _____

3. He knows Mr. Lee well, and *I know Mr. Lee well.*   _____

4. He used to live in Washington, and *his brother used to live in Washington.*   _____

5. I speak Spanish, and *she speaks Spanish.*   _____

6. She will be at the meeting, and *I will be at the meeting.*   _____

7. I had to work last night, and *Ed had to work last night.*   _____

8. I have seen that picture, and *she has seen that picture.*   _____

9. She saw the accident, and *I saw the accident.*   _____

10. He was absent from the lesson, and *his sister was absent from the lesson.*   _____

11. We enjoyed the concert, and *they enjoyed the concert.*   _____

12. He is supposed to work tomorrow, and *I am supposed to work tomorrow.*   _____

13. She can speak French, and *he can speak French.*   _____

14. Tony has gone to the movies, and *Ann has gone to the movies.*   _____

15. He is making good progress, and *she is making good progress.*   _____

16. Sean likes to play tennis, and *I like to play tennis.*   _____

17. He studies hard, and *his sister studies hard.*   _____

18. You will be late, and *I will be late.*   _____

19. He walks slowly, and *you walk slowly.*   _____

20. She may go, and *I may go.*   _____

Abbreviated clauses with *so*

We can also avoid repeating earlier words and phrases by using an appropriate auxiliary verb and *so*. Note in the examples that when we use *so*, the auxiliary precedes the subject.

Henry went to the movies, and I went to the movies.
Henry went to the movies, and *so did I*.

I like New York, and Alice likes New York.
I like New York, and *so does Alice*.

Rewrite the words in italics by using the correct auxiliary and *so*.

1. She studied English, and *I studied English.*   so did I

2. You will be late, and *she will be late.*   _____

3. They have seen that movie, and *I have seen that movie.*   _____

4. He knows her well, and *I know her well.*   _____

5. He can swim well, and *she can swim well.*   _____

6. He wanted to go there, and *I wanted to go there.*   _____

7. Penny will be absent from class, and *Gloria will be absent from class.*   _____

8. I saw the accident, and *my wife saw the accident.*   _____

9. She has many friends, and *her husband has many friends.*   _____

10. Tom was arrested, and *his accomplice was arrested.*   _____

11. He arrived late, and *I arrived late.*   _____

12. She likes to watch television, and *her husband likes to watch television.*   _____

13. They enjoyed the show, and *we enjoyed the show.*   _____

14. The meat was salty, and *the vegetables were salty.*   _____

15. I had to get up early, and *my wife had to get up early.*   _____

16. We'll be here tomorrow, and *Josie will be here tomorrow.*   _____

17. He would like to see the movie, and *I would like to see that movie.*   _____

18. Your watch is fast, and *my watch is fast.*   _____

19. She is studying French, and *her husband is studying French.*   _____

20. He promised to come, and *his sister promised to come.*   _____

117

We use *either* and *neither* to avoid repetition in negative sentences.

He doesn't like jazz, and she doesn't like jazz.
He doesn't like jazz, and she *doesn't, either.*
He doesn't like jazz, and *neither does she.*

Susan didn't go to the concert, and I didn't go to the concert.
Susan didn't go to the concert, and I *didn't, either.*
Susan didn't go to the concert, and *neither did I.*

Rewrite the words in italics by using the correct auxiliary and *either*.

1. She didn't like the movie, and *I didn't like the movie.* <u>I didn't, either</u>

2. We won't be there, and *Louise won't be there.* _____

3. He doesn't study much, and *she doesn't study much.* _____

4. Edna is not going to the party, and *I am not going to the party.* _____

5. I don't like the climate there, and *my wife doesn't like the climate there.* _____

6. Debbie won't be able to go, and *I won't be able to go.* _____

7. I didn't see the accident, and *Dick didn't see the accident.* _____

8. You won't like that picture, and *your wife won't like that picture.* _____

9. I haven't seen that movie, and *Molly hasn't seen that movie.* _____

10. He didn't arrive on time, and *we didn't arrive on time.* _____

11. She doesn't have many friends, and *he doesn't have many friends.* _____

12. Angie can't go, and *I can't go.* _____

13. Ralph didn't see me, and *the teacher didn't see me.* _____

14. I'm not sorry about it, and *Grace isn't sorry about it.* _____

15. You can't blame me for that mistake, and *George can't blame me for that mistake.* _____

16. My watch doesn't run well, and *your watch doesn't run well.* _____

17. I didn't remember his name, and *Henry didn't remember his name.* _____

Rewrite the words in italics by using the correct auxiliary and *neither.*

1. She didn't like the concert, and *I didn't like the concert.* <u>neither did I</u>

2. He didn't hear me, and *the teacher didn't hear me.* _____

3. I can't speak Spanish, and *my wife can't speak Spanish.* _____

4. He hasn't read the book, and *I haven't read the book.* _____

5. They didn't enjoy the novel, and *we didn't enjoy the novel.* _____

6. I couldn't hear him well, and *my companion couldn't hear him well.* _____

7. We don't have a television set, and *they don't have a television set.* _____

8. Cecile can't go, and *Gail can't go.* _____

9. She hasn't said anything about it, and *I haven't said anything about it.* _____

10. I won't be at the meeting, and *George won't be at the meeting.* _____

11. I didn't hear anyone in the room, and *my wife didn't hear anyone in the room.* _____

12. He hasn't prepared his homework, and *I haven't prepared my homework.* _____

13. Your answer isn't correct, and *my answer isn't correct.* _____

14. He doesn't eat lunch there, and *his friends don't eat lunch there.* _____

15. Gertrude isn't going to the party, and *I'm not going to the party.* _____

16. He didn't have any money with him, and *I didn't have any money with me.* _____

17. Pete can't go with us, and *Rodney can't go with us.* _____

18. You won't enjoy that show, and *your wife won't enjoy that show.* _____

(120) Abbreviated clauses with auxiliary verbs

In sentences where we have two conflicting ideas, we avoid repetition of words and phrases by using *but* and an appropriate auxiliary.

They can't speak French. We can speak French.
They can't speak French, *but* we *can.*

I like to ski. Harvey and Lisa don't like to ski.
I like to ski, *but* Harvey and Lisa *don't.*

Use the correct auxiliary to complete the sentences below. Where there are negatives, use contractions.

1. He won't be able to go, but I _____ .   <u>will</u>

2. She will arrive on time, but we _____ .   _____

3. I liked the movie, but my wife _____ .   _____

4. Robin is going to the party, but I _____ .   _____

5. She knows him well, but I _____ .   _____

6. She doesn't know her lesson well, but I _____ .   _____

7. I prepared my lesson, but she _____ .   _____

8. He arrived on time, but his wife_____ .   _____

9. She won't lend you any money, but I _____ .   _____

10. Henry has seen that movie, but I _____ .   _____

11. I have never been to Europe, but my wife _____ .   _____

12. Alex can speak English, but his sons _____ .   _____

13. Grace came home for lunch, but Helen _____ .   _____

14. She plays the piano well, but her sister _____ .   _____

15. My wife doesn't want to go to the concert, but I
_____ .   _____

16. She enjoys living in the north, but her husband
_____ .   _____

17. Murray isn't going to the beach, but I _____ .   _____

18. At first, I didn't like living in New York, but now I
_____ .   _____

19. She says she knows him well, but I don't think she
_____ .   _____

20. They don't have class tomorrow, but we _____ .   _____

Write the noun form which corresponds to each of the adjectives listed.

1. curious _____curiosity_____
2. innocent _____innocence_____
3. proud _____
4. sick _____
5. different _____
6. simple _____
7. foolish _____
8. young _____
9. sad _____
10. important _____
11. difficult _____
12. angry _____
13. deep _____
14. strong _____
15. high _____
16. nervous _____
17. dead _____
18. beautiful _____
19. convenient _____
20. ugly _____
21. gentle _____
22. bitter _____
23. possible _____
24. wide _____
25. sarcastic _____

26. ignorant _____
27. emphatic _____
28. strange _____
29. happy _____
30. free _____
31. weak _____
32. ill _____
33. sympathetic _____
34. dangerous _____
35. dignified _____
36. absent _____
37. kind _____
38. religious _____
39. true _____
40. silent _____
41. intelligent _____
42. generous _____
43. jealous _____
44. cruel _____
45. confident _____
46. wealthy _____
47. healthy _____
48. anxious _____
49. mysterious _____
50. noisy _____

Write the adjective form which corresponds to each of the nouns listed.

1. success   successful
2. enthusiasm   enthusiastic
3. advantage _____
4. sarcasm _____
5. anger _____
6. fortune _____
7. humor _____
8. dignity _____
9. mercy _____
10. patience _____
11. energy _____
12. dirt _____
13. absence _____
14. necessity _____
15. beauty _____
16. disgrace _____
17. rain _____
18. wave _____
19. affection _____
20. mystery _____
21. suspicion _____
22. style _____
23. pride _____
24. sentiment _____

25. religion _____
26. ignorance _____
27. noise _____
28. truth _____
29. ambition _____
30. power _____
31. silence _____
32. importance _____
33. depth _____
34. height _____
35. width _____
36. length _____
37. strength _____
38. cruelty _____
39. intelligence _____
40. presence _____
41. generosity _____
42. bitterness _____
43. death _____
44. freedom _____
45. simplicity _____
46. confusion _____
47. indifference _____
48. regularity _____

(123) Perfect form of infinitives

The perfect form of the infinitive is used to describe an action that happened before the time of the main verb of the sentence. Form the perfect form of the infinitive with *have* and the past participle of the principal verb.

I am glad *to have met* you.
We were sorry not *to have gone* to the play while it was in town.
You are smart *to have bought* your winter clothes during the sale.

Write the infinitives in the perfect form. Note how the idea of the action taking place before the time of the main verb is evident.

1. I am sorry *to tell* you this.   <u>to have told</u>
2. He is thought *to be* the best person for the job.   _____
3. You are lucky *to have* so many good friends.   _____
4. I am sorry *to miss* such an important meeting.   _____
5. It is a pleasure *to work* for him.   _____
6. I am glad *to meet* you.   _____
7. I am happy to *know* you.   _____
8. It is an honor *to know* such a distinguished woman.   _____
9. You are wise *to do* that right away.   _____
10. I am glad *to see* you again.   _____
11. He is lucky *to have* you as a friend.   _____
12. She is said *to be* the strongest person in the government.   _____
13. The train is supposed *to arrive* at five o'clock.   _____
14. You ought *to do* this right away.   _____
15. You are very wise *to save* your money.   _____
16. She is lucky *to know* about this beforehand.   _____
17. I am sorry not *to be* able to talk with her.   _____
18. She seems *to like* him a lot.   _____
19. They ought *to deliver* this immediately.   _____
20. You were wrong *to show* him so little respect.   _____

(124) *Must have, may have*

Must have **shows a strong probability that something happened in the past. It is followed by the past participle.**

> By the looks of the street, it *must have rained* while we were in the movie theater.
>
> They *must have gone* to bed. All the lights in the house are out.

May have **expresses a possibility that something happened in the past. It is also followed by the past participle.**

> They *may have gone* home already. I don't see them here.

A. **In these sentences, write the past perfect form of** *must*.

1. I cannot find my book. I (leave) it at home.   must have left

2. You (come) here by taxi.   _____

3. He speaks English so well that he (live) in England for many years.   _____

4. Gail (leave) home during the morning because she was not there when I telephoned at noon.   _____

5. I imagine, from things they have told me, that they (be) very wealthy at one time.   _____

6. Paula (study) very hard before her examination.   _____

7. She (be) a very smart woman when she was younger.   _____

8. You (work) very fast in order to have finished that work so quickly.   _____

B. **In these sentences, write the past perfect form of** *may*.

1. I haven't any idea where Joy is. She (go) to the movies with Tim.   may have gone

2. The bad weather (delay) them.   _____

3. You (lost) your keys on the bus.   _____

4. It's strange Joe is not here for his appointment, but he (forget) all about it.   _____

5. One of the strangers (steal) the money.   _____

6. Al (take) your book by mistake.   _____

7. They (telephone) while we were out.   _____

8. They (be) wealthy at one time, but I doubt it.   _____

Write the correct form of the verb in the conditional sentences below.

1. If I had known about this yesterday, I (help) him. _would have helped_
2. If I (be) you, I would not mention it to him. _____
3. I would have gone if I (have) the time. _____
4. If I see her, I (give) her your message. _____
5. If he had been driving fast, everyone (kill). _____
6. If I could help you, I (do) so gladly. _____
7. If the weather were warm today, we (go) to the beach. _____
8. If the weather had been warm yesterday, we (go) to the beach. _____
9. If I (see) Rose, I will tell her the good news. _____
10. If we decide to go, we (let) you know. _____
11. I would have bought the car if I (have) the money. _____
12. He will pass his examinations if he (study) hard. _____
13. He would pass his examinations if he (study) hard. _____
14. He would have passed his examinations if he (study) hard. _____
15. If I took the noon train, I (arrive) in New Orleans at nine. _____
16. I would certainly have given her the message if I (see) her. _____
17. If it were not raining, I (work) in my garden. _____
18. If I (have) your telephone number, I would have called you. _____
19. Joan would have gone with us if she (not be) ill. _____
20. If Ana had been with us, the accident (not happen). _____
21. Perhaps the man would not have died if there (be) a doctor present. _____
22. If I were a millionaire, I (spend) all my winters in Florida. _____

126 Review: negative form 5

Change the following sentences to the negative form.

1. She speaks English well.   does not speak
2. We went to the movies last night.   _____
3. She ought to tell him about it.   _____
4. He should have told her about it.   _____
5. He has lived there for many years.   _____
6. They were supposed to arrive yesterday.   _____
7. She can speak Spanish perfectly.   _____
8. She will return at five o'clock.   _____
9. He had to work late last night.   _____
10. He has three brothers.   _____
11. She is the best student in our class.   _____
12. You may smoke here.   _____
13. There were many students absent from class today.   _____
14. They were driving very fast at the time.   _____
15. I would like to have that kind of job.   _____
16. They go to the beach on Sunday.   _____
17. She knows him well.   _____
18. They got married in June.   _____
19. We should lend him more money.   _____
20. We arrived at the theater on time.   _____
21. She listens to her mother.   _____
22. They will go without us.   _____
23. He smokes a lot.   _____
24. He has been studying English a long time.   _____

Answer Key

Exercise 1

2. his	6. its	10. her	14. their	8. your
3. our	7. Her	11. our	15. their	19. her
4. their	8. your	12. his	16. her	20. his
5. her	9. my	13. my	17. its	21. his

Exercise 2

2. us	6. it	10. it	14. it	18. her
3. them	7. them	11. her	15. them	19. him
4. them	8. it	12. it	16. him/her	20. it
5. you	9. them	13. them	17. us	21. them

Exercise 3

2. myself	6. myself	10. themselves	14. himself
3. himself	7. itself	11. himself/herself	15. yourself
4. ourselves	8. herself	12. myself	16. himself
5. themselves	9. ourselves	13. himself	17. myself

Exercise 4

2. theirs	6. his	10. mine	14. yours	18. yours
3. mine	7. yours	11. theirs	15. yours	19. theirs
4. his	8. yours	12. ours	16. hers	20. hers
5. ours	9. hers	13. mine	17. his	21. his

Exercise 5

2. ties	11. oxen	20. tails	29. cars	38. cousins
3. classes	12. pencils	21. women	30. covers	39. pens
4. teachers	13. cafeterias	22. brothers	31. buses	40. sisters
5. beaches	14. students	23. notebooks	32. feet	41. matches
6. windows	15. wishes	24. hands	33. dishes	42. coats
7. doors	16. headaches	25. mice	34. men	43. cats
8. dresses	17. boxes	26. hats	35. kisses	44. noses
9. watches	18. schools	27. geese	36. faces	
10. books	19. children	28. losses	37. churches	

Exercise 6

2. dishes	9. classes	16. keys	23. leaves	30. lunches
3. children	10. buses	17. churches	24. dresses	31. feet
4. cities	11. streets	18. heroes	25. sisters	32. pillows
5. books	12. exercises	19. women	26. matches	33. companies
6. knives	13. wishes	20. armies	27. letters	34. ladies
7. boxes	14. copies	21. halves	28. hats	35. mice
8. potatoes	15. pens	22. brothers	29. men	36. wives

Exercise 7

2. likes
3. plays
4. goes
5. carries
6. teaches
7. shows
8. does
9. watches
10. tries
11. speaks
12. notices
13. says
14. passes
15. washes
16. catches
17. brings
18. leaves
19. sits
20. knows
21. thinks
22. sees
23. laughs
24. matches
25. dances
26. cries
27. pays
28. sings
29. wishes
30. pushes
31. pulls
32. dresses
33. misses
34. uses
35. passes
36. cashes
37. fixes
38. replies

Exercise 8

3. She must go
4. She is
5. She has
6. She will see
7. She may study
8. She has seen
9. She is studying
10. She will be
11. She can go
12. She should study
13. She plays
14. She carries
15. She goes
16. She ought to go
17. She can wait
18. She waits
19. She is waiting
20. She will wait
21. She has waited
22. She likes
23. She must see
24. She has been
25. She will take
26. She is working
27. She may work
28. She works
29. She wants
30. She does
31. She wishes
32. She can meet
33. She tries
34. She is leaving
35. She uses
36. She washes
37. She is going
38. She will know
39. She must try
40. She has tried
41. She will try
42. She ought to see

Exercise 9

2. has
3. study
4. studies
5. are
6. are
7. explain
8. are
9. watch
10. listens
11. play
12. is
13. lives
14. goes
15. come
16. does
17. makes
18. are
19. want
20. have
21. has
22. is
23. goes
24. stays

Exercise 10

2. These are
3. We are
4. They like
5. Those books belong
6. They were
7. The boys do
8. They are writing
9. The children are
10. These pencils belong
11. The tomatoes are
12. The dishes are
13. The classes have started
14. The women are waiting
15. These books are
16. We are going to study
17. They are making
18. The buses are
19. The men have left
20. They will leave
21. They can speak
22. The boys must study
23. They were
24. The leaves are falling

Exercise 11

2. low	12. backward	22. pull	32. high	42. bad
3. depart	13. rude	23. narrow	33. over	43. winter
4. outside	14. thin	24. tight	34. west	44. little/small
5. domestic	15. after	25. dirty	35. south	45. lose
6. asleep	16. behind	26. present	36. early	46. forget
7. cowardly	17. cheap	27. ugly	37. sell	47. past
8. soft	18. wet	28. sad	38. short	48. worst
9. dull	19. true	29. difficult	39. seldom	
10. rough	20. parent	30. wide	40. sour	
11. lend	21. full	31. find	41. effect	

Exercise 12

2. with	7. from	12. at	17. at	22. to
3. in	8. of	13. for	18. about	23. for
4. by	9. in	14. in	19. for	24. by
5. to	10. around	15. for	20. in	
6. to	11. in	16. by	21. to	

Exercise 13

2. lately	7. at the point of doing	12. difficulty
3. laugh	8. talked	13. explanation
4. know	9. w	14. sneeze
5. telephone	10. h	15. the third
6. visit	11. excellent	16. at eight at the latest

Exercise 14

2. is running	8. either	14. wrote	20. an
3. have lived	9. anyone	15. makes	21. has
4. were	10. has worked	16. me to go	22. are there
5. me	11. comes	17. to learn	
6. are having	12. on	18. he lives	
7. many	13. get	19. These	

Exercise 15

2. forced	9. married	16. cried	23. spelled	30. supposed
3. studied	10. managed	17. seemed	24. faced	31. referred
4. indicated	11. carried	18. enjoyed	25. worried	32. insisted
5. needed	12. played	19. appeared	26. depended	33. noticed
6. learned	13. guided	20. helped	27. decreased	34. admitted
7. practiced	14. planned	21. traveled	28. remained	
8. used	15. hoped	22. pleased	29. pointed	

Exercise 16

3. 2	10. 1	17. 1	24. 2	31. 1	38. 1
4. 1	11. 2	18. 2	25. 1	32. 1	39. 1
5. 2	12. 1	19. 1	26. 1	33. 2	40. 1
6. 1	13. 1	20. 1	27. 2	34. 1	
7. 1	14. 1	21. 1	28. 1	35. 1	
8. 1	15. 2	22. 2	29. 1	36. 1	
9. 2	16. 1	23. 1	30. 2	37. 2	

Exercise 17

2. bought	6. caught	10. taught	14. kept	18. kept
3. lost	7. brought	11. thought	15. knelt	19. bought
4. left	8. swept	12. felt	16. left	20. felt
5. meant	9. dealt	13. crept	17. meant	

Exercise 18

2. found	5. sat	8. found	11. fought	14. shone
3. met	6. struck	9. led	12. held	15. fed
4. held	7. read	10. hung	13. dug	16. stood

Exercise 19

2. must not tell	7. should not spend	13. has not gone	19. cannot meet
3. may not return	8. will not be	14. will not telephone	20. must not write
4. is not	9. cannot speak	15. were not	21. may not smoke
5. were not	10. are not going	16. am not	
6. is not studying	11. are not	17. is not	
	12. is not	18. were not	

Exercise 20

2. do not live	7. did not eat	12. did not come	17. did not find
3. do not know	8. did not sit	13. did not have	18. do not sit
4. did not get	9. does not read	14. did not drink	19. did not learn
5. do not want	10. does not speak	15. did not watch	20. did not hold
6. did not stop	11. does not smoke	16. did not hang	21. did not dig

Exercise 21

2. does not speak	8. will not be	14. may not smoke	19. will not tell
3. is not raining	9. did not come	15. should not spend	20. did not call
4. is not	10. does not feel	16. do not go	21. is not wearing
5. were not	11. was not	17. do not like	22. did not leave
6. did not meet	12. are not going	18. is not	23. do not understand
7. did not win	13. cannot speak		24. does not speak

Exercise 22

2. Can she speak
3. Is she
4. May he sit
5. Were they
6. Is she
7. Can he go
8. Should he mention
9. Will they be
10. Is she studying
11. Has Mr. Darbari gone
12. Will she telephone
13. Is he
14. Were there
15. Should he study
16. Are they
17. Were they
18. Is it raining
19. Are they going
20. Will she be

Exercise 23

2. Did they leave
3. Does she study
4. Did he buy
5. Does she drive
6. Did Daniela answer
7. Did he sit
8. Does he speak
9. Do they go
10. Did they meet
11. Did the child cut
12. Did she give
13. Do they live
14. Do you drink
15. Does the bus stop
16. Did the train arrive
17. Does he write
18. Did they bring
19. Did he lose
20. Did they catch
21. Does Valentina smoke

Exercise 24

2. Will he be
3. Is Harriet
4. Does he work
5. Did the boys spend
6. Does Paula play
7. Does his sister sing
8. Is the telephone ringing
9. Does it look
10. Do we have
11. Is the sun shining
12. Is the weather becoming
13. Did it rain
14. Can Loretta speak
15. Must he see
16. Will Antonia tell
17. Does the man speak
18. Could Beatrice understand
19. Did the train leave
20. Will it arrive
21. Does he have
22. Does she feel
23. Does he want
24. Did they spend

Exercise 25

3. ____
4. the
5. ____
6. The
7. ____
8. The
9. ____
10. ____
11. ____
12. The

Exercise 26

2. is ringing
3. writes
4. is writing
5. smokes
6. smokes
7. is smoking
8. rains
9. is beginning
10. is knocking
11. stops
12. is stopping
13. get
14. are building
15. have
16. are having
17. is waving
18. comes
19. is sleeping
20. sleeps
21. speaks

131

Exercise 27

2. were sitting
3. was shining
4. was walking
5. were having
6. was studying
7. was playing
8. were driving
9. was writing
10. was getting
11. was preparing
12. was having
13. was raining
14. was shining
15. was talking
16. were watching
17. was having
18. were sleeping
19. was suffering

Exercise 28

2. was sleeping
3. was blowing
4. rained
5. was raining
6. was playing
7. played
8. were having
9. read
10. was reading
11. wrote
12. was writing
13. was shining
14. was ringing
15. drove
16. was driving
17. played
18. was playing
19. saw
20. was leaving
21. waited
22. were waiting

Exercise 29

2. on
3. at
4. from
5. to
6. at
7. with
8. by
9. over
10. on
11. to
12. with
13. on
14. in
15. for
16. in
17. at
18. for
19. for
20. for
21. about
22. of
23. with
24. about
25. from

Exercise 30

2. literate
3. February
4. worst
5. best
6. did
7. will
8. have
9. danger
10. high
11. missed
12. l
13. giraffe
14. telephone
15. cancel
16. occasionally
17. take
18. pull
19. empty

Exercise 31

2. I lived
3. were
4. an
5. an
6. These
7. ran
8. could
9. smoke
10. is playing
11. for
12. saw
13. were eating
14. comes
15. her
16. is crossing
17. was raining
18. has worked
19. either
20. us to wait
21. were
22. seen

Exercise 32

2. has to go
3. has to leave
4. have to be
5. have to learn
6. have to have
7. has to work
8. has to go
9. have to wait
10. have to go
11. has to spend
12. have to go
13. has to be
14. have to leave
15. have to write
16. has to write
17. have to remain
18. have to get
19. has to remain
20. has to visit

Exercise 33

A.
2. had to leave
3. had to work
4. had to get up
5. had to walk
6. had to learn
7. had to have

B.
2. will have to return
3. will have to do
4. will have to be
5. will have to buy
6. will have to wait
7. will have to make

C.
2. has had to learn
3. have had to go
4. have had to return
5. have had to take
6. has had to cook
7. have had to buy

Exercise 34

2. didn't have to leave
3. don't have to study
4. don't have to write
5. didn't have to wait
6. doesn't have to spend
7. don't have to return
8. doesn't have to be
9. don't have to leave
10. didn't have to walk
11. won't have to send
12. don't have to wait
13. didn't have to pay
14. didn't have to go
15. don't have to cash
16. won't have to invite
17. doesn't have to take
18. didn't have to join
19. doesn't have to leave
20. don't have to write
21. didn't have to write

Exercise 35

2. Did he have to stay
3. Do the students have to learn
4. Will they have to write
5. Did she have to wait
6. Do you have to return
7. Did she have to go
8. Does she have to take
9. Did we have to invite
10. Does he have to leave
11. Will we have to write
12. Do they have to arrive
13. Does Tom have to get up
14. Does Sue have to help
15. Did she have to prepare
16. Does she have to work
17. Did they have to stay
18. Does he have to go
19. Do I have to sign
20. Did we have to send
21. Do we have to save

Exercise 36

2. said
3. said
4. said
5. told
6. told
7. said
8. said
9. tell
10. said
11. said
12. told
13. told
14. told

Exercise 37

2. lived
3. began
4. has studied
5. studied
6. began
7. lasted
8. were
9. have lived
10. had
11. have had
12. have been
13. became
14. has been

Exercise 38

2. one pound
3. one mile
4. seven ante meridiem
5. six post meridiem
6. six tenths
7. one half
8. one fourth/quarter
9. six percent
10. number five
11. sixty-eight degrees
12. alternating current
13. direct current
14. et cetera
15. one gallon
16. television
17. cash on delivery
18. quart
19. pint
20. yard
21. inch
22. and
23. Incorporated
24. two years
25. four feet
26. Ninety-sixth Street
27. Avenue
28. Boulevard
29. Road
30. Building
31. February
32. August
33. December
34. square feet
35. first
36. third
37. seventh
38. Thursday
39. Wednesday
40. National Broadcasting Company
41. New York
42. California
43. Illinois
44. Washington
45. Connecticut
46. Ohio
47. Michigan
48. Tennessee

Exercise 39

2. have been living
3. have been trying
4. has been driving
5. has been feeling
6. has been sitting
7. has been working
8. have been talking
9. has been speaking
10. has been working
11. has been teaching
12. have been going
13. have been waiting
14. has been raining
15. have been whistling
16. has been studying
17. has been wearing
18. have been working
19. have been planning

Exercise 40

2. since
3. for
4. ago
5. for
6. for
7. since
8. since
9. for
10. since
11. ago
12. since
13. for
14. since
15. ago
16. since
17. for
18. since
19. ago
20. for

Exercise 41

2. had stolen
3. had taken
4. had had
5. had found
6. had seen
7. had left
8. had played
9. had left
10. had lived
11. had looked
12. had taken
13. had had
14. had received
15. had done
16. had put
17. had left
18. had broken

134

Exercise 42

2. did not leave
3. is not
4. did not want
5. has not studied
6. did not tell
7. will not return
8. is not having
9. have not left
10. cannot speak
11. must not tell
12. are not going
13. is not
14. was not
15. has not worked
16. have not been living
17. does not have to work
18. did not have to go
19. did not come
20. are not making
21. did not tell
22. does not prepare
23. were not playing
24. has not finished

Exercise 43

2. Did he give
3. Is she
4. Are we going
5. Will they return
6. Did he leave
7. Can Marcia swim
8. Is she going to study
9. Has he read
10. Has she been studying
11. Is she
12. Do we have to have
13. Did Robert have to leave
14. Will he return
15. Were they having
16. Did they build
17. Will they deliver
18. Was she
19. Is it
20. Is the wind blowing
21. Were there
22. Did the child cut
23. Did the boy run
24. Is the doorbell ringing

Exercise 44

2. of
3. about
4. up
5. at
6. about
7. on
8. at
9. about
10. for
11. since
12. over/above
13. below
14. in
15. on
16. out
17. with
18. in
19. from
20. in
21. in
22. from
23. in
24. to

Exercise 45

2. prefer to
3. entrance
4. agreement
5. explode
6. put
7. been
8. home
9. lacks
10. alone
11. in addition to
12. advice
13. seldom
14. recently
15. joking
16. w
17. t

Exercise 46

2. Washington, D.C.
3. five
4. one syllable
5. wild
6. vowel
7. first
8. regular
9. November
10. rises
11. two
12. sixteen
13. Thursday
14. north
15. have/has
16. winter
17. fifty-two
18. irregular
19. taken
20. twenty-six
21. longer
22. Civil War

Exercise 47

2. had seen
3. was reading
4. yours
5. had to
6. don't have to
7. were
8. were taking
9. needed
10. leave
11. is coming
12. are having
13. to us
14. me to go
15. me
16. blows
17. anyone
18. went
19. have been
20. said
21. are singing
22. an

Exercise 48

2. You're	6. We're	10. I'll	14. don't	18. won't
3. She's	7. They're	11. You'll	15. doesn't	19. aren't
4. It's	8. There's	12. She'll	16. didn't	20. haven't
5. She's	9. You're	13. We'll	17. won't	

Exercise 49

2. for	5. for	8. to	11. to	14. to
3. for	6. for	9. for	12. for	15. to
4. to	7. to	10. to	13. to	16. to

Exercise 50

2. gave Antonia	8. brought me	14. told Sharon	20. send us
3. sent him	9. bought her	15. gave each of us	21. lent us
4. show Rudy	10. brought us	16. lent his brother	22. bring me
5. paid the landlord	11. write you	17. hand me	
6. sold his friend	12. gave her father	18. sent each of them	
7. took her	13. sent Ms. Pappas	19. gave Mike	

Exercise 51

2. flown	5. broken	8. did	11. ate	14. chose
3. driven	6. fell	9. drew	12. froze	15. bitten
4. broke	7. fallen	10. gone	13. gave	16. done

Exercise 52

2. is going to teach	8. are going to go	14. are going to spend
3. are going to be	9. is going to rain	15. is going to ask
4. is going to meet	10. are going to eat	16. are going to be
5. are going to stay	11. is going to have	17. are going to go
6. is going to go	12. are going to go	18. are going to fly
7. is going to take	13. is going to get married	19. is going to study

Exercise 53

2. was going to go	6. was going to see	10. were going to eat
3. was going to study	7. were going to buy	11. was going to send
4. were going to go	8. were going to visit	12. was going to lend
5. was going to call	9. was going to be	13. was going to let

Exercise 54

2. was	6. lived	10. could	14. had lost	18. might
3. could	7. was	11. would	15. meant	19. was
4. would	8. liked	12. might	16. was	20. was
5. was	9. lived	13. was	17. would	

Exercise 55

3. s	10. s	17. z	24. z	31. z	38. z
4. s	11. z	18. s	25. z	32. z	39. s
5. z	12. s	19. z	26. s	33. z	40. z
6. z	13. s	20. z	27. z	34. s	41. z
7. s	14. z	21. s	28. z	35. s	42. z
8. z	15. s	22. z	29. s	36. z	43. s
9. z	16. z	23. s	30. s	37. s	44. z

Exercise 56

3. t	10. t	17. d	24. d	31. d	38. t
4. t	11. d	18. d	25. d	32. d	39. d
5. d	12. t	19. t	26. t	33. t	40. t
6. t	13. d	20. d	27. d	34. d	41. d
7. t	14. t	21. d	28. d	35. t	42. d
8. d	15. d	22. d	29. t	36. d	
9. t	16. t	23. t	30. t	37. t	

Exercise 57

2. get home	6. gets on	10. get over	14. get drunk
3. got in	7. gets off	11. got into	15. get married
4. gets ready	8. get very tired	12. get to	16. get nervous
5. gets into	9. got excited	13. get home	

Exercise 58

3. d	12. g	21. p	30. c	39. k	48. h
4. t	13. b	22. b	31. b	40. k	49. c
5. s	14. t	23. l	32. g	41. c	50. b
6. b	15. l	24. s	33. b	42. l	
7. k	16. l	25. w	34. w	43. h	
8. w,t	17. l	26. w	35. w	44. t	
9. h	18. k	27. t	36. t	45. c	
10. t	19. k	28. t	37. w	46. l	
11. k	20. d	29. n	38. b	47. d	

Exercise 59

2. thin	8. dangerous	14. vines	20. 1492
3. get on	9. w	15. dozen	21. been
4. green	10. three	16. four	22. seen
5. an adjective	11. visit	17. thirty-six	
6. twelfth	12. west	18. Ms.	
7. tight	13. east	19. nine	

Exercise 60

2. in/at	7. at	12. over	17. of	22. by
3. from	8. from	13. of	18. on	23. by
4. of	9. in	14. of	19. about	24. about
5. in	10. on	15. by	20. on	
6. after	11. off	16. out	21. in	

Exercise 61

2. on vines	6. camel	10. h	14. the second
3. breeze	7. apple pie	11. k	15. recently
4. recover from	8. bed	12. pointed	16. guarantee
5. success	9. asked	13. coach	17. gone

Exercise 62

2. had had	8. to wait	14. is beginning	20. told
3. has saved	9. said	15. Not	21. could
4. were going	10. was	16. my name was	22. were having
5. went	11. would	17. much	
6. whom	12. between	18. hers	
7. which	13. sits	19. mine	

Exercise 63

2. Many newspaper articles are written by her.
3. The room is cleaned by the maid every day.
4. Their quarrels are heard by everyone.
5. The mail is delivered by the letter carrier.
6. All the letters are written by the secretary.
7. Her speeches are enjoyed by everyone.
8. The magazine is sold by them everywhere.
9. Our exercises are corrected by her at home.
10. Dinner is prepared by Joe every night.
11. The mail is delivered by them at ten o'clock.
12. Urgent information is brought by a messenger.
13. The papers are signed by them in ink.
14. Presents were brought by her from Hong Kong.
15. Our compositions are corrected by the teacher.
16. The books are printed by them in Boston.
17. The grass is cut by him once a week.
18. The letters are sent by them by air mail.
19. The contracts are prepared by the lawyer.
20. The money is provided by the foundation.

Exercise 64

2. The money was taken by someone.
3. The mail had been delivered by the letter carrier.
4. The letters have been signed by him.
5. Many books have been written by her.
6. The bills were paid by Marianne by check.
7. The work will be finished by them tomorrow.
8. The work had been finished by him in time.
9. The party has been planned by them.
10. Corn was grown by Native Americans in Mexico.
11. Several buildings have been designed by him.
12. The contract had been signed by him previously.
13. The plate was broken by her while she was washing it.
14. The accident was seen by Julia on her way home from work.
15. The tickets had been bought by them.
16. The child has been found by them at last.
17. The trees were planted by Sonia.
18. The dinner was prepared by them.
19. It will be sent by her immediately.
20. The key was used by him to open the door.

Exercise 65

2. It may be kept by the museum for two weeks.
3. The bill can be paid later.
4. It has to be delivered tomorrow.
5. Those things can't be put there.
6. It must be sent at once.
7. It should be delivered today.
8. It ought to be written now.
9. These exercises must be studied by Kevin.
10. It may be brought later.
11. This room can be used by Linda.
12. It has to be done soon.
13. He may be held by the police for several days.

Exercise 66

2. will not be delivered
3. must not be signed
4. was not shot
5. is not taught
6. was not wrapped
7. was not struck
8. has not been delivered
9. was not followed
10. were not heard
11. cannot be used
12. was not printed
13. were not sent
14. will not be delivered
15. cannot be sent
16. was not taken
17. were not disappointed
18. will not be prepared
19. has not been finished
20. had not been decorated

Exercise 67

2. Was the thief captured
3. Will the lecture be attended
4. Has the dinner been served
5. Are we invited
6. Will the work be done
7. Was the city destroyed
8. Must these letters be signed
9. Was America discovered
10. Has the house been struck
11. Was the tree blown
12. Were they arrested
13. Will the book be published
14. Must this work be finished
15. Is the mail delivered
16. Are the letters written
17. Was the car destroyed
18. Will their engagement be announced
19. Will they be married
20. Was the meeting held
21. Was it attended
22. Can all these books be borrowed

Exercise 68

2. ———
3. a
4. ———
5. ———
6. The
7. ———
8. The
9. the
10. an
11. ———
12. The
13. ———
14. The
15. The
16. a
17. a
18. ———
19. a
20. a
21. ———
22. The
23. the
24. ———
25. The

Exercise 69

2. torn
3. lain
4. known
5. shook
6. spoke
7. grown
8. threw
9. hid
10. worn
11. wrote
12. took
13. ridden
14. grew
15. seen
16. tore
17. spoken
18. knew
19. known
20. wore

Exercise 70

2. weak
3. no one
4. dead
5. true
6. rude
7. careless
8. start/begin
9. forget
10. right
11. late
12. always
13. fast
14. cause
15. rough
16. tighten
17. retail
18. cowardly
19. buy
20. noisy
21. wet
22. loose
23. backward
24. simple
25. full
26. sour
27. short
28. useful
29. decrease
30. lead
31. child
32. back
33. lower
34. comedy
35. different
36. west
37. fall
38. arrive
39. found
40. wild
41. absence
42. permanent
43. defeat
44. public
45. friend
46. borrow
47. add
48. innocent
49. rare
50. summer

Exercise 71

2. more intelligent than
3. earlier than
4. more interesting than
5. wider than
6. easier than
7. more beautifully than
8. faster than
9. sooner than
10. more clearly than
11. more often than
12. better than
13. colder than
14. busier than
15. harder than
16. more carefully than
17. more often than
18. earlier than
19. sweeter than
20. higher than

140

Exercise 72

2. as expensive as
3. as old as
4. as well as
5. as fast as
6. as soon as
7. as well as
8. as fast as
9. as soon as
10. as cold as
11. as quickly as
12. as easily as
13. as tired as
14. as hard as
15. as good as
16. as often as
17. as rapidly as
18. as carefully as
19. as beautifully as
20. as rich as
21. as often as
22. as soon as

Exercise 73

2. somewhere
3. anyone
4. any
5. some
6. anyone
7. anything
8. some
9. somewhere
10. any
11. anything
12. someone
13. anyone
14. some
15. anyone
16. any
17. anyone
18. somewhere

Exercise 74

2. 3   1st
3. 5   3rd
4. 4   2nd
5. 4   2nd
6. 4   3rd
7. 4   2nd
8. 3   1st
9. 3   1st
10. 3   1st
11. 3   2nd
12. 2   2nd
13. 5   4th
14. 3   1st
15. 2   2nd
16. 4   3rd
17. 3   2nd
18. 3   2nd
19. 2   2nd
20. 3   2nd
21. 3   2nd
22. 5   3rd
23. 2   1st

Exercise 75

2. had taken
3. gets up
4. saw
5. have not seen
6. has been
7. lived
8. were (you) doing
9. is knocking
10. took
11. is sleeping
12. rises
13. have not been
14. had seen
15. had not seen
16. were living
17. had discovered
18. is beginning
19. is crossing
20. arrive
21. were running
22. has taught/been teaching
23. will come
24. would come
25. will see

Exercise 76

2. twelve
3. northeastern
4. Mississippi
5. third
6. third
7. adverb
8. July 4
9. irregular
10. north
11. Alaska
12. Rhode Island
13. past participle
14. lay
15. sat
16. gone
17. autumn (fall)
18. one syllable
19. worst
20. third
21. February
22. George Washington

Exercise 77

2. to	7. from	12. in	17. on	22. at
3. on	8. from	13. by	18. at	23. in
4. off	9. against	14. on	19. at	
5. for	10. on	15. for	20. on	
6. around	11. to	16. of	21. for	

Exercise 78

2. because of	6. enough	10. curious	14. pupil
3. sometimes	7. smooth	11. count	15. corporal
4. was	8. vines	12. razor	16. mice
5. rather good	9. explanation	13. heel	17. sheep

Exercise 79

2. was sleeping	8. could	14. were having	20. are having
3. go	9. anyone	15. said	21. have
4. has been	10. than	16. could	22. spent
5. mine	11. an	17. might	23. to us
6. us to wait	12. a	18. her	24. have been
7. is waiting	13. I lived	19. is coming	

Exercise 80

2. sang	6. begun	10. let	14. put	18. spread
3. rang	7. rung	11. sunk	15. swam	19. cost
4. set	8. hurt	12. shrank	16. cut	
5. put	9. drunk	13. sprang	17. hit	

Exercise 81

2. was supposed to leave	11. is supposed to be
3. am supposed to arrive	12. was supposed to leave
4. is supposed to be	13. were supposed to deliver
5. are supposed to go	14. was supposed to call
6. is supposed to bring	15. is supposed to be
7. was supposed to telephone	16. is supposed to leave
8. are supposed to write	17. is supposed to stay
9. is supposed to clean	18. were supposed to publish
10. was supposed to arrive	

Exercise 82

2. used to live	8. used to go	15. used to write
3. used to be	9. used to study	16. used to catch
4. used to walk	10. used to be	17. used to help
5. used to work	12. used to visit	18. used to dance
6. used to be	13. used to play	19. used to take
7. used to visit	14. used to send	20. used to walk

Exercise 83

2. Yes, it is.	No, it isn't.	9. Yes, we have.	No, we haven't.
3. Yes, it did.	No, it didn't.	10. Yes, I will.	No, I won't.
4. Yes, she is.	No, she isn't.	11. Yes, I am.	No, I'm not.
5. Yes, we have.	No, we haven't.	12. Yes, she does.	No, she doesn't.
6. Yes, she can.	No, she can't.	13. Yes, I was.	No, I wasn't.
7. Yes, it does.	No, it doesn't.	14. Yes, she was.	No, she wasn't.
8. Yes, he is.	No, he isn't.	15. Yes, he can.	No, he can't.

Exercise 84

2. isn't she	7. wasn't it	12. didn't you	17. won't you
3. aren't there	8. hasn't he	13. didn't I	18. wasn't it
4. didn't you	9. isn't he	14. isn't she	19. isn't he
5. won't it	10. isn't it	15. hasn't she	20. haven't you
6. can't she	11. doesn't it	16. isn't he	

Exercise 85

2. does it	7. have you	12. will she	17. was she
3. is he	8. did she	13. have you	18. has it
4. can she	9. can you	14. has it	19. has it
5. will you	10. do you	15. does it	20. will you
6. was it	11. does he	16. were you	

Exercise 86

2. is it	8. isn't she	14. doesn't she	20. didn't it
3. isn't he	9. won't you	15. haven't they	21. wasn't it
4. didn't you	10. hasn't it	16. didn't you	22. don't you
5. will he	11. didn't I	17. can't she	23. hasn't it
6. doesn't it	12. has he	18. didn't he	24. did he
7. don't they	13. did he	19. have you	25. does she

Exercise 87

2. taking	7. dancing	12. listening	17. changing
3. investing	8. coming	13. studying	18. buying
4. hitting	9. hiding	14. using	19. receiving
5. moving	10. waiting	15. painting	20. making
6. eating	11. speaking	16. opening	21. riding

Exercise 88

2. leaving	to leave	10. building	to build
3. studying	to study	11. watching	to watch
4. working	to work	12. staying	to stay
5. doing	to do	13. criticizing	to criticize
6. working	to work	14. finding	to find
7. dancing	to dance	15. speaking	to speak
8. mentioning	to mention	16. doing	to do
9. teaching	to teach	17. sending	to send

Exercise 89

2. of waiting
3. of dancing
4. on going
5. of seeing
6. about going
7. of finding
8. on speaking
9. to seeing
10. in teaching
11. in helping
12. on helping
13. of leaving
14. in learning
15. of swimming
16. in locating
17. of studying
18. of buying
19. of seeing
20. in finding
21. for managing

Exercise 90

2. bitten
3. let
4. flown
5. chose
6. worn
7. fell
8. given
9. tore
10. grew
11. hid
12. known
13. driven
14. sung
15. wrote
16. blew
17. eaten
18. found
19. led
20. lain
21. thrown
22. spread
23. froze
24. spoken

Exercise 91

2. permanently
3. board
4. telephone
5. visit
6. come for
7. prefer
8. discuss
9. examine it
10. at the point of doing
11. discard
12. up to the present
13. accustomed to
14. pretend
15. confused
16. by memory
17. be careful

Exercise 92

2. noun
   verb
3. noun
   verb
4. verb
   noun
5. noun
   verb
6. noun
   verb
7. verb
   noun
8. verb
   noun
9. verb
   noun

Exercise 93

3. weight
4. obligation
5. recognition
6. insistence
7. repetition
8. location
9. arrival
10. analysis
11. temptation
12. argument
13. adjustment
14. reaction
15. expectation
16. proof
17. description
18. arrangement
19. treatment
20. consideration
21. explanation
22. annoyance
23. appearance
24. belief
25. breath
26. confusion
27. inspection
28. admiration
29. relief
30. choice
31. embarrassment
32. destruction
33. completion
34. satisfaction
35. enjoyment
36. hesitation
37. paralysis
38. identification
39. protection
40. obedience
41. discovery
42. complaint
43. criticism
44. refusal

Exercise 94

3. to grow	15. to impress	27. to rob	39. to enter
4. to interfere	16. to marry	28. to succeed	40. to begin
5. to bury	17. to deny	29. to punish	41. to withdraw
6. to explode	18. to intend	30. to decide	42. to paralyze
7. to interrupt	19. to choose	31. to observe	43. to believe
8. to disturb	20. to approve	32. to reserve	44. to conclude
9. to apologize	21. to advise	33. to adopt	45. to refuse
10. to admit	22. to die	34. to deceive	46. to destroy
11. to repeat	23. to suspect	35. to remain	47. to criticize
12. to prove	24. to agree	36. to lose	48. to complain
13. to collect	25. to amuse	37. to fail	
14. to relieve	26. to excite	38. to warn	

Exercise 95

2. about	7. off	12. with	17. from	22. until
3. of	8. under	13. on	18. by	23. of
4. on	9. about	14. for	19. of	24. for
5. to	10. for	15. of	20. on	25. for
6. into	11. for	16. from	21. to	

Exercise 96

2. permanent	7. hairs	12. n	17. pants
3. flowed	8. brother's daughter	13. broom	18. jeweler
4. mean	9. choice	14. oars	
5. sound	10. advice	15. fare	
6. sing	11. t	16. accustomed to	

Exercise 97

2. of moving	8. is coming	14. ours	20. has worked
3. have lived	9. cries	15. sunk	21. studied
4. in learning	10. was raining	16. was	22. were watching
5. waiting	11. studying	17. could	
6. hearing	12. is supposed	18. you will	
7. painting	13. me to go	19. anywhere	

Exercise 98

2. it is	6. you are	10. I was	14. I liked	18. I put
3. I was	7. he was	11. it is	15. Adam put	19. we had
4. I would	8. she lives	12. I paid	16. she went	20. it is
5. it is	9. she lived	13. he is	17. this costs	

Exercise 99

2. ought to go
3. ought to choose
4. ought not to talk
5. ought not to write
6. ought to be
7. ought to try
8. ought to get
9. ought to have
10. ought not to speak
11. ought to obey
12. ought not to read
13. ought to write
14. ought to try
15. ought to take
16. ought to go
17. ought to be sent
18. ought to arrive
19. ought to be written
20. ought not to spend

Exercise 100

2. should have gone
3. should have arrived
4. should have gone
5. should have telephoned
6. should have been sent
7. should have been delivered
8. should have been
9. should have told
10. should have gone
11. should have been written
12. should have written
13. should have telephoned
14. should have written
15. should have spent
16. should not have wasted
17. should have been
18. should not have told
19. should have asked
20. should not have talked

Exercise 101

2. ought to have gone
3. ought to have traveled
4. ought to have saved
5. ought to have been
6. ought to have signed
7. ought to have been sent
8. ought not to have talked
9. ought to have been delivered
10. ought to have been typed
11. ought to have seen
12. ought not to mention
13. ought not to have wasted
14. ought to have explained
15. ought to have telephoned
16. ought not to have worked
17. ought to have been prepared
18. ought to have telephoned
19. ought to have gotten
20. ought to have gone
21. ought to have written
22. ought to have been put

Exercise 102

2. works
3. hurries
4. rains
5. comes
6. attend
7. is
8. telephones
9. see
10. does not
11. have
12. leave
13. gets
14. calls
15. does not
16. decide
17. gets
18. bites
19. have

Exercise 103

2. will visit
3. will miss
4. will go
5. will go
6. will learn
7. will be
8. will tell
9. will let
10. will have
11. will have
12. will be
13. will give
14. will drive
15. will take
16. will earn
17. will have
18. will explain
19. will be
20. will play

Exercise 104

2. had	5. knew	8. paid	11. liked	14. didn't have
3. owned	6. spoke	9. knew	12. had	15. didn't waste
4. worked	7. went	10. studied	13. had	16. had

Exercise 105

2. would play	7. would go	12. would walk	17. would be
3. would go	8. would get	13. would buy	18. would get
4. would speak	9. would make	14. would ask	
5. would have	10. would take	15. would give	
6. would study	11. would go	16. would stay	

Exercise 106

2. were	7. were	12. would know	17. would continue
3. were	8. were	13. would go	18. would ask
4. were	9. were	14. would go	
5. were	10. were	15. would travel	
6. were	11. would explain	16. would not be	

Exercise 107

2. had known	6. had gone	10. had thought	14. had taken
3. had telephoned	7. had told	11. had seen	15. had telephoned
4. had been	8. had received	12. had not rained	16. had known
5. had been	9. had had	13. had left	

Exercise 108

2. would have called	9. would have talked	16. would have met
3. would have gone	10. would have gotten	17. would have driven
4. would have acted	11. would have done	18. would have gone
5. would have gotten	12. would have gone	19. would have had
6. would have caught	13. would have bought	20. would have been
7. would have refused	14. would have taken	21. would have taken
8. would have given	15. would have gone	22. would have gotten

Exercise 109

2. had gone	6. had studied	10. had known	14. had	18. were
3. spoke	7. were	11. had started	15. were	19. had been
4. had	8. were	12. had studied	16. had	20. were
5. had telephoned	9. were	13. knew	17. had had	

Exercise 110

2. arrives	6. go	10. arrives	14. gets	18. comes
3. leave	7. telephone	11. get	15. telephone	19. returns
4. gets	8. get	12. gets	16. arrives	20. arrives
5. let	9. need	13. see	17. hear	

Exercise 111

3. through	13. sent	23. birth	33. male	43. roll
4. new	14. seen	24. heel	34. inn	44. guest
5. waste	15. fourth	25. here	35. close	45. steel
6. weigh	16. dye	26. seam	36. hour	46. sow
7. week	17. flower	27. sum	37. brake	47. sun
8. would	18. rode	28. whole	38. not	48. principal
9. night	19. write	29. hire	39. pare	49. pale
10. no	20. read	30. hymn	40. plain	50. deer
11. sell	21. sale	31. meat	41. peace	
12. seller	22. seas	32. maid	42. by	

Exercise 112

3. unable	15. misunderstand	27. disagree	39. inaccurate
4. unbelievable	16. untie	28. disapprove	40. disinfect
5. irregular	17. unwrap	29. impolite	41. disinherit
6. dishonest	18. unbutton	30. indiscreet	42. inconvenient
7. disappear	19. disadvantage	31. incorrect	43. unreal
8. disobey	20. immature	32. insincere	44. unkind
9. dislike	21. incapable	33. uncover	45. dissatisfied
10. unattractive	22. unorganized	34. unfurnished	46. disagreeable
11. illegible	23. undress	35. unhealthy	47. unpleasant
12. mispronounce	24. unfold	36. unopened	48. independent
13. disconnect	25. unfortunate	37. unarmed	
14. discontinue	26. unfair	38. impatient	

Exercise 113

2. to	6. by	10. to	14. with	18. from
3. in	7. of	11. to	15. on	19. since
4. with	8. up	12. on	16. in	20. from
5. in	9. for	13. for	17. in	21. on

Exercise 114

2. dull	6. true	10. let	14. testimony
3. arrives on time	7. silent	11. comes	15. much
4. width	8. partially deaf	12. rarely	16. surrenders
5. paralysis	9. taken	13. lied	17. without effective result

Exercise 115

2. I was	10. to have been delivered	18. well
3. would	11. is ringing	19. a
4. to have done	12. coming	20. an
5. were	13. on waiting	21. have lived
6. arrives	14. in locating	22. comes
7. had seen	15. is supposed	23. was sleeping
8. you live	16. have you studied	24. should have telephoned
9. theirs	17. for	

Exercise 116

2. he is, too
3. I do, too
4. his brother did, too
5. she does, too
6. I will, too
7. Ed did, too
8. she has, too
9. I did, too
10. his sister was, too
11. they did, too
12. I am, too
13. he can, too
14. Ann has, too
15. she is, too
16. I do, too
17. his sister does, too
18. I will, too
19. you do, too
20. I may, too

Exercise 117

2. so will she
3. so have I
4. so do I
5. so can she
6. so did I
7. so will Gloria
8. so did my wife
9. so does her husband
10. so was his accomplice
11. so did I
12. so does her husband
13. so did we
14. so were the vegetables
15. so did my wife
16. so will Josie
17. so would I
18. so is my watch/mine
19. so is her husband
20. so did his sister

Exercise 118

2. Louise won't, either
3. she doesn't, either
4. I am/I'm not, either
5. my wife doesn't, either
6. I won't, either
7. Dick didn't, either
8. your wife won't, either
9. Molly hasn't, either
10. we didn't, either
11. he doesn't, either
12. I can't, either
13. the teacher didn't, either
14. Grace isn't, either
15. George can't, either
16. your watch/yours doesn't, either
17. Henry didn't, either

Exercise 119

2. neither did the teacher
3. neither can my wife
4. neither have I
5. neither did we
6. neither could my companion
7. neither do they
8. neither can Gail
9. neither have I
10. neither will George
11. neither did my wife
12. neither have I
13. neither is my answer/mine
14. neither do his friends
15. neither am I
16. neither did I
17. neither can Rodney
18. neither will your wife

Exercise 120

2. won't
3. didn't
4. am/I'm not
5. don't
6. do
7. didn't
8. didn't
9. will
10. haven't
11. has
12. can't
13. didn't
14. doesn't
15. do
16. doesn't
17. am
18. do
19. does
20. do

Exercise 121

3. pride
4. sickness
5. difference
6. simplicity
7. foolishness
8. youth
9. sadness
10. importance
11. difficulty
12. anger
13. depth
14. strength
15. height
16. nervousness
17. death
18. beauty
19. convenience
20. ugliness
21. gentleness
22. bitterness
23. possibility
24. width
25. sarcasm
26. ignorance
27. emphasis
28. strangeness
29. happiness
30. freedom
31. weakness
32. illness
33. sympathy
34. danger
35. dignity
36. absence
37. kindness
38. religion
39. truth
40. silence
41. intelligence
42. generosity
43. jealousy
44. cruelty
45. confidence
46. wealth
47. health
48. anxiety
49. mystery
50. noise

Exercise 122

3. advantageous
4. sarcastic
5. angry
6. fortunate
7. humorous
8. dignified
9. merciful
10. patient
11. energetic
12. dirty
13. absent
14. necessary
15. beautiful
16. disgraceful
17. rainy
18. wavy
19. affectionate
20. mysterious
21. suspicious
22. stylish
23. proud
24. sentimental
25. religious
26. ignorant
27. noisy
28. true
29. ambitious
30. powerful
31. silent
32. important
33. deep
34. high
35. wide
36. long
37. strong
38. cruel
39. intelligent
40. present
41. generous
42. bitter
43. dead
44. free
45. simple
46. confused
47. indifferent
48. regular

Exercise 123

2. to have been
3. to have had
4. to have missed
5. to have worked
6. to have met
7. to have known
8. to have known
9. to have done
10. to have seen
11. to have had
12. to have been
13. to have arrived
14. to have done
15. to have saved
16. to have known
17. to have been
18. to have liked
19. to have delivered
20. to have shown

Exercise 124

A. 2. must have come
3. must have lived
4. must have left
5. must have been
6. must have studied
7. must have been
8. must have worked

B. 2. may have delayed
3. may have lost
4. may have forgotten
5. may have stolen
6. may have taken
7. may have telephoned
8. may have been

Exercise 125

2. were
3. had had
4. will give
5. would have been killed
6. would do
7. would go
8. would have gone
9. see
10. will let
11. had had
12. studies
13. studied
14. had studied
15. would arrive
16. had seen
17. would work
18. had had
19. had not been
20. would not have happened
21. had been
22. would spend

Exercise 126

2. did not go
3. ought not to tell
4. should not have told
5. has not lived
6. were not supposed to arrive
7. cannot speak
8. will not return
9. did not have to work
10. does not have
11. is not
12. may not smoke
13. were not
14. were not driving
15. would not like
16. do not go
17. does not know
18. did not get married
19. should not lend
20. did not arrive
21. does not listen
22. will not go
23. does not smoke
24. has not been studying